Published by Intera Press
5 Cherry Hill Drive, Suite 120
Danvers, MA 01923

Quantity sales: For information on bulk purchases, please contact McDougall Interactive.

First Edition   June 2013
Editor   Kate Victory Hannisian, Blue Pencil Consulting
Book Design   Cliff Schinkel Design
Proofreader   Dee Netzel
Printing   King Printing

ISBN: 978-0-61579-122-7

Web Marketing On All Cylinders

Kick-Start Your Online Presence

John McDougall

INTERA
PRESS

Table of Contents

Chapter 4 - Search Engine Optimization (SEO) Implementation............69

Chapter 6 - Public Relations in the Digital Age......................129

Chapter 7 - Remarkable Social Media Marketing and Optimization....147

Chapter 10 - Highly Profitable Paid Search Marketing...........................261

Chapter 11 - Actionable Analytics and Reporting................................279

Foreword

Most people don't appreciate the phenomenal impact Google has had on our lives. It's much more than a search engine. Google has changed human behavior.

Think back to the days before Google caught the wave of public attention. In 2002, the Internet was a bombed-out shell of unrealized promises. Billions of investment dollars had evaporated in dubious ventures like Webvan and Pets.com. Search engines were so overrun with spammers that they were all but useless. Office parks that had been rented to house hundreds of dot-com workers stood vacant. Some people were questioning whether the commercial web would ever be all that important.

Then Google came along. Do you remember the first time you used it? I sure do. It was magical. Here was a search engine that seemed to know what I was thinking, and it was love at first sight.

Google is much better today. It now anticipates what I want to know before I finish typing. It includes recommendations from my friends in its results. It suggests who to include on mailing lists. It reminds me when I forget an attachment. It finds the faces of friends in my photos. It translates documents from Russian to English. It even houses my 40-gigabyte music collection and delivers songs to me whenever I want and wherever I am.

But Google's impact has been far greater than that. It has changed the way people relate to information. For thousands of years we sought knowledge by browsing, a tedious and often unsatisfying process. In less than a decade, Google changed us from browsers to searchers. We tossed out our *Readers' Guide to Periodical Literature* and the *Encyclopaedia Britannica* in favor of the much more fulfilling process of discovering through search. This is just the beginning. As computer power becomes embedded into everything from bathroom mirrors to teeth, we will take for granted that the answer to nearly any question is just a few clicks away.

In November 1991, Bill Gates stood before an audience at the giant Comdex trade show and outlined a vision he called "information at your fingertips." I don't think the Microsoft chairman had any idea at the time what his vision would look like—or that Microsoft would be only a bit player in realizing it—but twenty years later, anyone with a smartphone knows just what he meant, because of Google.

Comdex is gone. So are most of the big tech trade shows. Gone also are the tech magazines that used to stuff more than 1,000 pages of printed content into IT managers' mailboxes each week. Google made them irrelevant. The advertising model that supported them was done in by the vastly greater efficiencies of search. Why browse the aisles at a trade show or the pages of a magazine when the recommendations of your peers are free and easy to find online?

I think Google's most important contribution to our culture, however, was something many people don't think about. It democratized information. We are just at the very earliest stages of understanding the enormous power of that change. But consider the implications.

For 500 years, information was a precious resource controlled by a privileged elite. Those who owned the means of production–the publishers, broadcasters, and professional journalists–were the people who controlled information. Power was defined by circulation lists, Nielsen ratings, and FCC licenses. Citizens were at the mercy of what big media permitted them to know.

Google changed all that. It doesn't care about your brand, your subscriber list, the size of your publisher's Rolodex or your mailing budget. It only cares about the quality of what you say. Thanks to Google, interior design blogger Holly Becker can amass an audience of one million monthly viewers and write Amazon's top-selling book on the subject. Computer security expert Bruce Schneier can build a newsletter subscriber list of 150,000 fans all by himself. Jody DeVere can grow AskPatty.com, a business that teaches auto dealers how to sell to women, into a significant industry force. There are thousands of others just like them. Google made social media possible, and we are forever in its debt for that.

I've had the pleasure of working with John McDougall and his team at McDougall Interactive for three years, and I've learned a lot from them about how search engines work. I opened this book thinking that there was little they could tell me about search that I didn't already know, and even less about my own specialty of social media marketing.

Wow, was I wrong.

This book is packed with advice, tips, and action items that anyone from a sole practitioner to a corporate marketer can put into practice right away. What really surprised me was how much it taught me about social media, an area in which some people call me an expert. The recommendations in this book may seem overwhelming at first, but John frequently reminds his readers that success in building social authority is a marathon. Spend 15 minutes each day applying one lesson from these pages and you'll be amazed at how far you'll have come a year from now.

When technology comes along that changes the way people think and act, the unanticipated changes are profound. We're just beginning to understand the implications of what happens when barriers that have stood for half a millennium collapse in a few years. For businesses, one thing is for sure: your relationship with your constituents has changed forever. This book will help you understand what that means and give you a running start on your competition. Get out your old-fashioned pen, because you're about to start taking a lot of notes.

Paul Gillin
Author
The New Influencers
Secrets of Social Media Marketing
Social Marketing to the Business Customer
Attack of the Customers
May 2013

Acknowledgments

Without my father's constant guidance, tremendous support, and bringing me into the world of advertising, this book would not be possible. All of my family has been amazing as well, and for that I am very lucky.

The support of my team at McDougall Interactive in exploring the depths of web marketing has been an indispensable part of my learning. I want to thank John Maher for his constant dedication to growing our business for a decade and help writing the analytics chapter; Bob Rustici for writing the Paid Search chapter; Julian Flynn for adding some sections in the social media chapter and being a great resource to run ideas by; James Hall for his amazing technical SEO knowledge; Jon Cahill for his creativity, leadership and help keeping all our projects and the book design process on track: Christa Terry for her spunk and help with the blogging chapter; Steve Boudreault for writing the book's sub-title, Steve Swartz for help on the PR chapter; Brian-Logan Reid for his fresh ideas and deep HubSpot Knowledge; Anthony Schwartzman for his ideas on scalable and mobile web design/development; and Jimmy Craig and Justin Parker (who run FatAwesome in addition to working with us) for being the wackiest viral content creators and people I have ever met and for making me scream on film while riding a tricycle around the office.

I also want to thank Paul Gillin for his support and partnership on our seminar series (www.searchsocialseminar.com).

Kevin Browne deserves a special thanks for breaking my writer's block and getting the book back on track by adding his bits of spice to it.

A huge thanks to HubSpot for their endless knowledge and content, and to Meghan Anderson in particular for her contribution to the HubSpot chapter. I also want to thank Mark Greco for bringing us into HubSpot.

I am constantly inspired by great minds in the industry like Eric Enge, Aaron Wall, Rand Fishkin, Jim Boykin, Eric Ward, Bruce Clay, Bryan Eisenberg, Avinash Kaushik, Tim Ash, Danny Sullivan, Matt Cutts, and Robert Cialdini. There are way too many to name here, but the back and forth on blogs and in conversations with these people is how we learn in this space that has no definitive manual and rewrites itself daily.

Without the help of my editor, Kate Victory Hannisian of Blue Pencil Consulting, I am not sure how I would have kept so much information organized and polished.

Thanks to Dee Netzel for proofreading, and to Cliff Schinkel for the interior book layout.

Without the stream of hundreds of clients over almost two decades, we would not have had the opportunity to excel and learn so much.

I thank God for creativity and for being able to be part of such a great mystery.

Dedication

In memory of my amazing mother Elizabeth,
whose love, creativity and personality
helped to make my dreams possible.

Introduction

What's your pulse rate standing still? Sixty? Sixty-five?

That's probably what a doctor would tell you.

I humbly disagree. If you are attempting to harness the power of the web, your pulse rate sitting comfortably should always be over 100, thinking about all of the ways you could be better dominating your niche online.

This is one of the most fierce competitions on earth, and to grab your piece of what you know should rightfully be yours, you need to play to win.

The more educated you are in the rules of the game, the more strategically you can think. This is key, because many people who are great at individual web marketing tactics can't always see how they all combine with each other and align with your business goals. Only YOU can do that once you put on the magic new strategy glasses you will get from this book.

Considering web companies like Google, Apple, and Amazon are now some of the world's top brands, understanding how to harness the power of Internet marketing can make or break your business.

Buckle up. It's time to dig deep to get your arms firmly around this online rocket ship.

What's your pulse rate now?

The Death of the Webmaster and the Arrival of Strong Internet Marketing Teams

Wow, have things come a long way since just yesterday. That really is the way online marketers think and dominate. What used to work last Friday may not and probably does not work as well today.

The two keys for businesses are simple. First, always be abreast of the latest trends, because they come and go and you have to ride their waves for their short life spans and then shift to the next ones! There really is no time to debate. In the time it takes you to get on board, others have already killed or diminished the usefulness of that tactic! A client gave me a book called *It's Not the Big That Eat the Small...It's the Fast That Eat the Slow*. In the online marketing world, that has to be part of your mantra.

Second, become familiar with those few strategies and techniques that *always* deliver results. Even online, there are several constants, and one of the strongest of them is the delivery of great content.

The web craves it.

Always will.

And if your business figures out the way to deliver killer content to the masses, you will be rewarded with the most amazing feeling of success and a fistful of high-quality leads that you can then convert for high return on your investment!

One of the biggest misconceptions about Internet marketing (and business websites in general) is that "geeks" can do it all. Sorry, the so-called webmasters and IT department-driven websites are long gone.

Having run an Internet marketing company for almost 20 years, I have learned that the most successful web projects are done by teams of highly specialized people who have very different talents. As a business owner looking to get online, rebuild your website, drive more leads, or participate in social media, make sure you don't fall into the trap of thinking that one person (who many used to call a "webmaster") can handle every single aspect of the Internet marketing process. "Webmaster" is a term that needs to be retired. Period. In fact, one entire marketing agency may not have the highly specialized skills to be effective in each channel!

Today, it's clear that print advertising is in trouble, TV ads can be skipped over, and the Yellow Pages are now used to hold swinging doors open. Internet marketing is no longer a sideline to traditional advertising and as such can't always be done well on a shoestring by people who don't focus on it full-time.

Right now, do a Google search on "mobile advertising" or pick up your smartphone and Google "Italian Restaurants" and look at the search results. This is the new world order. It is personalized, local, and social. This is where your business has to be.

In fact, every day, millions of savvy people are clamoring to secure market share in the ranks of the search engines by populating websites with massive volumes of engaging content, widgets, videos, and social interactivity. Drop the notion that you are simply going to create a better website and adopt the idea that you need to be constantly competing in the game online and on mobile in a way that will make you more money. And to be competitive, you need your team to be constantly devouring articles and blogs about where marketing is headed next. That's what I hope this book will get you to understand...that being ahead of the curve is everything.

What has always amazed me is that some companies really get it, while others hem and haw, and endlessly complain about the effort involved and wish it really was just a matter of paying to flick a magic optimization switch. In April 2012, Google Penguin (a search algorithm update) took that switch and blew it up by getting *much* smarter at stopping the easy stuff from helping your site rank higher. People tend to forget that Google's main mission is to highly rank only the highest-quality sites, not the most optimized, and that a winning lead generation strategy is about content more than technique. Here at McDougall Interactive, we have a saying: "We're not here to make pigs fly." What it means is that it is best to optimize quality sites. In other words, the trick is not to fool Google with keywords, but to show Google what a great website you actually have. Google's recent Panda and Penguin algorithm updates have deepened the need for authentic, engaging content versus just lots of fluff pages and backlinks (a tactic that once worked reasonably well). And if you are not working SEO with social media, you are getting creamed by competitors who are. Not on Google+? Well, your competitors are and photos of their faces show up in the search engines while you have a boring text listing with no authority! (For more on the concept of authority building using Google+ Author Rank, see the social media chapter, Chapter 7.)

What remains consistent is that for every one successful company that closes tens of thousands or millions of dollars in business generated from online marketing, there are a dozen or more companies doing the bare minimum with their websites while complaining that they are not getting enough return for their efforts. A successful website is not made by the subcontractors or employees a company hires, but by a highly synchronized, combined effort that gracefully combines SEO with social marketing. Internet marketing needs to be treated like any other serious business. People hear stories of websites working magically and bringing in millions with relative ease. In the early days of the web, before the search engine algorithms became complex, this was true for some of the early adopters. Unfortunately, the complexity grows by the day, and website owners need to think about their websites' strategy as they would any business model. This means you need to write a business plan for your website and ensure that the goals and tactics are mapped out as clearly as they are for your offline activities. Without this type of thinking, and with only a lonely webmaster as your Internet marketing army, the battle is already lost.

What This Book Is About

When I started doing Internet marketing in 1995, there were not many books on the subject. Since then, there has been a surge of books on search engine optimization (SEO) and social media. What always strikes me is how dense and complex they are, given that many website owners and marketing directors have more on their plates than their websites. They need practical information that's clearly implementable.

This book will give you a strategic overview of—and practical tips for handling—the issues I have seen hundreds of site owners and marketing directors grapple with. In doing so, we do need to cover some fairly technical details or you won't really understand the way it all fits together. With SEO for example, you need to know a bit about URLs and things like 301 redirects or it would be hard to see why we are recommending certain strategies like hiring an SEO company *before* your website design project begins. So please don't skip over this level of basic technical info if you want to see the bigger picture of how the strategies truly work and fit together. Our blog (www.mcdougallinteractive.com/blog) provides more details and offers insights as new options become available and old techniques evolve. If you understand the big picture, you will save yourself from numerous heartaches, because in this industry, doing it right the first time can make or break your business and your budget.

If your website is poorly designed, or worse, looks good on the surface but has significant flaws that block conversions, your offline marketing dollars are being wasted. People almost invariably check out a company's website when they are thinking about buying from or using the services of a company. So please read the conversion optimization chapter *before* you do a website redesign.

Additionally, the rise of social media has proven without question that web users are discovering detailed information about individual people and brands by looking at search results and mentions of companies on blogs, forums, review sites, Facebook, and Twitter. If you don't keep track of what people are saying about you online and fail to join the conversation, you will look suspect to the even moderately web-savvy consumer. If you fail to track what people do when they get to your website and then update it with no knowledge of how your changes are affecting visitors, search results, and your social media presence, you are missing out on the power of the web. By formulating a solid plan to develop a quality site with engaging content that drives more traffic, encourages longer visits, and increases conversions, you can often transform your business more radically than you could with traditional media, at a fraction of the cost.

While Internet marketers may have a laugh at things like Newspaperdeathwatch.com, the effects of emerging changes in media now appear to be more serious than amusing. We are in the midst of a radical upheaval in the way marketing works. A handful of major brands have even gone so far as to drop *all* traditional advertising after seeing the power of the web. Many others are shifting budgets in ways we have never seen. Some companies are rethinking their actual products and services in response to new online marketing methods.

The CEO of Razorfish, one of the most respected and followed online marketing companies in the world, recently gave a presentation on why CEOs are terrified of Internet marketing.

It all came down to one thing. They don't get it. And what they don't understand terrifies them.

A monster in the dark is much scarier than the actual monster. You can shed light on this monster and how online marketing can help you grow your business, but it will take a relatively deep understanding of this world before you can get more comfortable in it or change your company's foundation to keep up with it.

Two of the biggest forces are Google and Facebook, and the monthly visitor counts are staggering. Google sites surpassed *one billion* unique monthly visitors and Facebook has more than one billion users. Compare that to the eyeballs you get from traditional advertising and it's no wonder the stakes have been raised for your web marketing projects.

Now that Facebook and sites like Pinterest and Twitter are a serious threat to Google's supremacy, the shift to include user-generated media is in full force. One of Google's biggest challenges currently is to index the masses of user-generated content and provide search results that take your peers' comments and suggestions into account. Since Google and Facebook aren't exactly working in friendly cooperation, Google has created a rival social platform called Google+. Results from Google+ show right up in the main search results and some speculate that activity there and on other social platforms helps you in the "organic" search engine rankings. While we have little proof that there is currently more than a negligible impact on SEO from social signals, activity in social channels will get you more backlinks when people share and buzz about your content, and that will definitely help your ranks. Even the SEO super-gurus' opinions on this issue vary widely, ranging from those who say that by the end of 2013, social signals will be equal to backlinks, to others who say it will be many years away, if ever, before social makes a significant direct impact on organic SEO rankings. Either way, social media and SEO are now truly joined at the hip and you can't just do one or the other.

If you can tap into active web searchers and social media users and gain their trust by branding your company as a thought leader, you can grow your business in a way no traditional advertising agency can. However, this requires a new way of thinking that is more focused on providing useful content and having a two-way conversation than on broadcasting an advertising message, and it requires a system for drawing more people to your site who turn into customers. That's what this book is all about.

Chapter 1

Modern Advertising and the Influence of the Web

Remember the old days when there were three major television networks and one or two daily newspapers per city? Do you have any idea how easy it must have been to get reach and frequency during those times?

Poof. Gone.

We're not going to spend a ton of time rehashing "Mad Men" here. But just bear in mind that what used to be available in terms of tactics for hitting the target has changed dramatically.

And that's a very good thing!

That said, it is very important to understand that there are just two main methods of increasing website profits:

1. Increase targeted traffic

2. Increase conversions on your site (the rate at which visitors turn into leads and sales)

These are the two most important keys to successful marketing online and always will be.

Driving targeted traffic to your pages and getting those people to do something on those pages is the core of success and it should drive each and every action you take from now on.

Now, to be fair, "action" online does not necessarily mean generating sales. It could mean getting people to opt in to receive email newsletters to learn more about you and your business, getting people to take a poll, or getting people through to your social channels. You want to make people do something while they are visiting your site—otherwise they are simply window shopping. You need to get them to move towards an action on every page you create.

Building a pretty site or driving traffic is not enough to generate leads and sales. You need to bring all of the top tactics together, from Google and email marketing to Facebook and banner ads, in a way that is aligned with your core business goals, matches your marketing and branding efforts, and is not just the "geek stuff." Again, successful Internet marketing is less about "geek" stuff and far more about understanding how people shop online and tapping into that mentality.

A Paradigm Shift Is Occurring This Second

"The marketing funnel is a broken metaphor that overlooks the complexity social media introduces into the buying process. As consumers' trust in traditional media diminishes, marketers need a new approach. We propose a new metric, engagement, that includes four components: involvement, interaction, intimacy, and influence. Each of these is built from data collected from online and offline data sources. Using engagement, you get a more holistic appreciation of your customers' actions, recognizing that value comes not just from transactions but also from actions people take to influence others. Once engagement takes hold of marketing, marketing messages will become conversations, and dollars will shift from media buying to customer understanding."

— Forrester Research

Quick translation: We buy online very differently than we buy offline.

With such a radical shift in the marketing foundations and many print publications going under, TV moving toward on-demand programming and convergence with online media, the Internet simply has to be the center of your marketing activities. (If you're not convinced of that by this point, hand your offline keys to your competitors right now…because they are doing these things.)

With the rise of Internet TV and various set-top boxes that allow you to access the Internet, the line between TV and the web is gone. As these two media blend, the opportunities for your content to be shared will expand again, as in the early days of the Internet. Is your content ready for prime time in a world where people are no longer willing to watch "cute" and "market-y" commercials? Online video is exploding and TVs are in nearly every home—when these converge, the heart of the marketing world will skip a beat. Video is a great tool and should be a considerable part of your marketing, but the content has to be engaging, entertaining, or informative to stand out in a sea of professional and user-generated content. Are your YouTube videos in a specific channel? Are you reaching out to build your subscriber base? Are you treating YouTube less like a place to put a single video with a great keyword and more like a place that brings you consistent business?

Businesses rarely fully use YouTube as the social network force that it is.

Mobile phones are quickly allowing TV and video access that lets content flow from anywhere, at any time. The days of fixed timeslots and ads being put in front of captive couch potatoes are numbered. People still watch a ton of TV, of course, but be prepared for a deeper convergence and for this blending of web and TV to happen quickly.

With increased competition, to get the full benefit of Internet marketing you can't just dabble in it. And if you cannot spend the time on it yourself, you need to hire a resource that can.

More important than using all the new bells and whistles is your ability to engage visitors, track their behavior, and make 100 percent sure they are eventually converting into sales. Can your traditional account executive or marketing director do this? Does he or she even really know how to use Google Analytics or how to decide what makes good landing page content based on conversion testing? The shift to a 50/50 split of traditional and online marketing spend is happening so fast that old-school marketers are struggling to explain and deal with these processes. Their clients are suffering because they are often misinformed by traditional strategists who simply don't know what they are talking about and don't push the right mix of spending.

A Strategic Marketing Mix

Make sure your web activities are a big part of your overall marketing strategy. All advertising will increase traffic to your website and if your site is weak, does not rank well, or does not integrate well with your other campaigns, you will lose conversions from offline media. Regardless of what it cost you to build and get your site live, if it is not "working" then visitors are moving on ("bouncing") in about 30 seconds. That can and must end right now. The book *Blink* talks about our immediate perceptions of everything within seconds. We walk into a restaurant and know instantly if we belong there. We enter a car dealership and our instincts tell us if we are in the right place in seconds. We are hardwired to listen to our internal dialogue...and you need to know that people are doing that on your site every single day, no matter which advertising and marketing channels you use to get them there.

Your website should be the center of all marketing activities: PR, direct mail, ads, radio, TV, etc. If your marketing director tells you to simply amp up your print budget or even just your paid search budget without utilizing the techniques we discuss in this book, it's time for a second opinion. You need to let smarts drive your limited marketing dollars. Run a tiny Pay per Click campaign for $5 a day and test it against a control page. Are you converting better on one versus the other? Great. Make that the "king of the hill" and then beat that page. Every single day is an opportunity for your website to smarten itself based on what people do when they visit it.

Before we go into detail on Internet marketing strategy, let's take stock of the radical change in approach that the Internet has made possible.

A New Approach

Traditionally, advertising has been centered on ringing a Pavlovian bell and assuming customers will respond like a conditioned dog, doing whatever is asked of them. And to be honest, in the old days, that used to be the case. Of course, in the old days, there were also just those three television networks and more people actually read newspapers.

Now that customers have control over media and can get just the information they want whenever they want it, the control marketers used to have is gone. You simply cannot assume that the old methods of mass marketing are still working. Savvy marketers have discovered that going with the flow of customer control and helping the customer along in their search for information is what works best. By sharing information that you know the customer wants to see before making a purchase and offering social proof of why your product or service is the best (e.g., blog comments and reviews by other customers), your brand has an opportunity to do honest marketing that wins in the long term.

Sharing versus the Cutesy Ad

Now that content is easily available on a moment-by-moment basis (e.g., content on Twitter), there is a new opportunity to forge deeper relationships with customers.

One of the smartest ways that some of the biggest brands in the world (Coca Cola and Home Depot, for example) are using social media now is to immediately respond to anything negative that is said about their brands. They "make good" on their relationships with customers and let everyone read how far they are willing to go to make things right, even when someone buys the wrong screwdriver. As a smaller brand than Coca Cola, your tactics on Twitter and Facebook need to be somewhat different, but you should always be learning from what the leaders are doing. Where you once had 30 seconds to catch a customer's eye, you now might see customers spending many hours on your website watching your You-Tube videos and reading your blog. You may even have them following your every move on Twitter or subscribing to your news channel. Before the modern Internet, the vehicles of expensive TV ads and print production did not provide this ongoing flow of information and, perhaps more importantly, instant interaction. Now, at the click of a button you chat with live customer support people, you can download ebooks that were uploaded moments ago, and you can tune into podcasts that were recorded this morning. This is a big change and it's only coming faster.

Watch as your feedback on a company's products and services flows into their R&D process, resulting in products that better fit your needs. Johnson & Johnson, for example, became an early adopter of social media when they made a space online for women to share their needs with regard to feminine hygiene products and responded to those concerns.

Now, if sites do not have review sections or places to comment, they often do not get the Google, Bing, and Yahoo visibility they crave. Once again, social integration is paramount online. You must be involved in involving your customers in you. That is why truly static sites are now being left in the dust after Google's recent Panda and Penguin search algorithm updates.

While the old marketing models are being undermined, new models are emerging. Post a comment on the Facebook page belonging to Red Bull and you can "speak" to over *one million people.* Join a group on LinkedIn about your niche that is "Very Active" and has several thousand participants, and not only is your discussion featured on that home page, but it also appears in the email boxes of each and every one of those people as every new comment on that discussion comes in.

Wow. That is an immense wow.

The new age of marketing is one of sharing around a digital campfire where everyone gets a chance to tell their story and/or react to someone else's.

The number of interactions taking place at any given moment on the Internet between people in different parts of the world is staggering. The ability to not only reach more customers in more countries but to also get to know them and invite them to share your products is unprecedented. Local listings online are also so much more accessible now that with your smartphone, you essentially have a Yellow Pages on steroids with a GPS that will take you directly to a company with top reviews, 24/7. Perhaps that explains why several years ago, Google saw local search becoming as big as it is and suddenly decided to add 49.5 million Google Places listings out there for the taking. (Have you claimed yours?)

Given these radical changes, I have recently seen a major shift in my own sales process. It used to be that I was like a crazy preacher, rambling on and on about the glorious advantages of Internet marketing. Now when I go to business meetings, many of my prospective clients hand me lists of things they have been hearing about—like Facebook, Twitter, Pinterest, Tumblr, Flickr, and organic search—and beg for both an explanation and a roadmap. Thus, there is a temptation for many marketers to jump on a particular bandwagon like Facebook or Twitter because it is hot, without really understanding how a particular platform ties in with the company's own long-term strategy. If you can stick with me through some relatively technical details that are in reality only scratching the surface of the things

Internet marketers do, you will start to see how important and cost-effective it is to develop a holistic strategy. Again, none of this matters one lick if your website is not bringing in traffic and getting those visitors to take action.

Engagement is the new metric, since customers want to interact with brands to see if they really have something to offer that fits their needs. They will no longer fall for weak PR spins or fluffy campaigns, and the shift will move from simply acquiring new customers to making good customers happy enough to be brand loyalists and even cheerleaders.

Some of the top techniques you will learn in this book may be enough to quickly get you up to speed and ahead of much of your local competition online, while you develop deeper strategies either in-house or with a specialized team.

How Much Does Internet Marketing Cost and How Long Does It Take?

Marketers are in a state of confusion regarding Internet marketing pricing. And that is totally understandable as it seems everyone who is out of work is now a glorified social media expert.

Some search marketing companies will say they can "guarantee results" for $399 a month, while others charge thousands or tens of thousands of dollars per month for organic SEO. Generally, you get what you pay for. While you may be tempted to save money, be aware that search marketing and effective website building is a long process when done right. It takes more time and effort to do it right, but the results are radically different and pay for themselves in increased sales.

You also must understand that the more competitive keywords like "golf" are almost impossible to rank highly for. In the new paradigm, your focus needs to be on long tail keywords (the ones that use more words get much less traffic but are much easier to rank highly for and convert better since they are so specific), like "best selling golf clubs for women." Only the top spots on a Google keyword page matter and you simply cannot compete for the toughest keywords and win every time.

However, if your keyword selections include lots of long tail words or phrases, you can add up the volume of those clicks and see an incredible surge in search. Again, this is just a matter of playing the game to win, not just to play.

Over the years, many business people have told me that Internet marketing just doesn't work for them. When I inquire as to what they have done, it becomes clear that they have not really done significant organic or paid search, they have neglected content development or useful social media marketing, or that their website is so bad that it is driving people away. Add these together and it becomes a problem that must and can be solved. In addition, when asked how they are tracking the results of their efforts, they often have no real answer. Real Internet marketing is more often than not multifaceted, time-intensive, and most importantly, trackable.

Expect the cost of real Internet marketing, at a local level, to start at $2,000–$3,000 per month for a very basic level of quality local service. Once you get up into $5,000 and $10,000+ a month and are doing integrated marketing using SEO, social media, PR, content marketing, advanced link building, paid search, and conversion optimization, things kick into high gear. That is when you are marketing on all cylinders and the tactics play off of and enhance each other. It is as if there is some magical threshold that gets crossed and the amount of leads and sales negates the spending, making everyone—including customers— happier. For top providers and larger competitive campaigns, companies can expect to pay thousands or even tens of thousands of dollars per month, but if they do it right they will end up with the equivalent of a V12 Bentley that leaves competitors in the dust. Even out-sourcing to India can mean spending thousands per month for Internet marketing, so you need to be aware that it has become a highly evolved and very detailed process.

For your money, you should receive a certain amount of hours each month dedicated to SEO, paid search, analytics, content adjustments, content development, content sharing, conversion enhancements, social media, link building, and PR. If you don't have enough hours devoted to each, you won't beat the competition. And as you already know, time is money. The real question is, where is yours spent best?

The people who generate lots of great content (by paying or doing it themselves) will usually get the best results, especially if they find a quality partner to work with. While you can get initial results in a matter of two to three months with local organic search and in a matter of days with paid search, be aware that the tougher SEO terms that drive the most traffic can take six months to a year to even gain traction. That's yet another reason why my position is that you should be competing for the most competitive keywords on a long-term basis, but that your short-term organic traffic will come from long tail keywords.

Search marketers hate to tell you this because they don't want to scare you away, but you just can't expect top organic ranks for highly profitable and competitive terms in a few months. Google tracks how quickly you get backlinks and add content, and the best results take time to build. In the long term, the reward is often lasting rankings that have an incredible ROI.

For example, I had the number one rank in Google for the term *saxophones* for many years for a client, and he eventually stopped paying our monthly bill after the government cut school music funding. Two years later he was still ranking in the top three. Four years later, he was still in the top ten for that term, and we did not charge him a penny for anything other than basic web edits during that time. The ROI on that rank alone over time is incredible compared to paid ads that disappear when you stop paying. In fact, a company just called this same client and offered to buy his business! We were called in to examine if the high search engine rankings could be brought back and we explained how a good Google ranking history will go a long way when we try to get things back on track. (Hint: history is one of the biggest and most compelling authority factors used by Google.)

So if you focus on doing things correctly and with the right mindset, eventually leads will pour in, maybe even buyout offers. Expect overnight success and you will be disappointed.

When it comes to social media, you're right if you think it's somewhat easy to set up a Facebook page or a blog. But without lots of great content on those venues and a smart strategy that truly connects them all, they will go nowhere fast.

So you will either need to pay someone to write content or be prepared to write consistently yourself. In a nutshell, the more blog entries, Facebook posts, and tweets you write, the more leads you get.

Don't Assume Bigger Is Better When Hiring

We built a site for a client in 2001 and quoted a price for search marketing. At the time, the client said he was going with a larger firm for SEO because the price was three times our quote and he was hoping the bigger the firm the better the results. We still made the website updates and, after a short time, we got a call from his search marketing "experts" asking us how to add meta tags to the shopping cart pages. Apparently they just handed the project to an intern because they were growing too fast. We called the VP and told him that they were ripping off our client if they didn't know that:

a) the dynamic shopping cart pages wouldn't rank well (ten years ago) and

b) adding meta tags is Web Design 101.

We continue to see and hear stories like this even today. And that is tragic.

In the end, we did answer their questions and they ended up giving our client 10 new, free static html pages along with optimization on each. Our client then kept us in the loop on future correspondence with this company, but we were horrified by this very popular, branded marketing company's practices. Not to mention, one of their packages cost $130,000!

Another client came to me because his traditional ad agency ruined his existing SEO and charged him for it. I was actually hired by the ad agency to get the search engine rankings back so he would stop the pending lawsuit. We got him his rankings back, but the ad agency kept the client's $8,500 since the person they had outsourced the work to had flown back to Romania and spent it all. This sizable agency, which even had a private plane, later stopped offering Internet marketing, hid their head in the sand by pretending traditional marketing would stay dominant forever, and eventually went out of business.

The point here? You need to trust who you work with so that the fees you pay don't end up going to a trip to Romania. Look for real offices and real people. Don't be lured by a big agency and assume the best. Be cautious with your money, given that everyone seems to claim expertise in web marketing (but not everyone has it).

Tips for Outsourcing Your Internet Marketing

If you decide to get outside help with your Internet marketing, here are a few ideas to consider before deciding which outsourcer is best for you:

- Ask for references, ask to see their work, and ask to read reviews.

- Ask for a list of deliverables and approximately how long each takes.

- Ask about any other services the company offers and how strong their focus is in the areas you are interested in.

- Make sure you know what is outsourced and what is done in-house.

- Ask which people on their team do what parts of the job so you can be sure they actually have qualified people focusing on key tasks.

- Big or small, agency or webmaster, it is the hands-on experience that matters.

What You Can Do Yourself

If you have a lot of time on your hands you can definitely learn a bit about do-it-yourself Internet marketing or you can focus on building content. A huge part of getting a keyword to end up on page one of Google search results is creating 100% original content for your website and for blogs (your own and other peoples'). Having people writing and creating content in-house can be a huge asset to you and your marketing team that can help promote your website and make it rank higher.

Another task that you can do in-house is appoint a community manager who responds to questions on your Facebook page and other social media platforms. Having a non-agency person with deep knowledge of your business available to engage with your customers can dramatically enhance an outside agency's other strategies and tactics.

Don't waste a big salary on a senior marketing executive who has only outdated skills. Senior strategists are great, especially when they "get it," but dinosaurs are not useful unless they can write prolifically.

If you have interns or other non-experts work on your technical Internet marketing tasks, be aware they may get you banned from the search engines or social sites if they don't understand the rules or if they do things that border on using "black hat" tactics. Again, the "easiest" thing to do yourself for search engine optimization or social media (and something that very few Internet marketing companies do well) is create lots of engaging content.

Parts of the Same Engine

Think of your internal team and your marketing agency as parts of the same engine. You have to work in unison. Pointing fingers and just expecting the agency to go from zero to sixty on watered-down gas just doesn't work. The days of easy web profits are gone and your humble help is needed, given the myriad tasks that Internet campaigns require. By making all cylinders align at the same time, you will get to your destination much more quickly. Before you step on the gas pedal, though, you'll want to have a strategy so you know where you want to go, so turn now to Chapter 2, on creating an Internet marketing strategy.

Chapter 2

Internet Marketing Strategy Roadmap

Your Internet marketing strategy is the roadmap that integrates all the actions your company will take to achieve a set long-term goal. Before digging into the specifics of strategy planning, let's look at a successful strategy put in place by one of our local clients, Montserrat College of Art.

When we initially began working with Montserrat College of Art, they had almost no visibility on the search engines outside of branded organic search terms, almost no social media presence, a blog that was not on their main website, no paid search, and mostly local public relations. More importantly, the college was not filling all its classes and was only attracting students from the surrounding region. Our goal was to not only increase their visibility online and in the media, but to help them sign up more non-scholarship students and to reach more funders in the art world. We also wanted to position them as the thought leaders in the elite art community.

Before moving forward, we met with the president, the marketing director, and a dozen other key people to make sure we truly understood their brand, business, and marketing needs. We quickly realized that the brand message was unclear and suggested some brand strategy research by a partner with an advertising background. We interviewed faculty, staff, students, and parents. We then created a mission statement, a tagline ("Where Creativity Works"), and a scrapline ("See What You Can Do with an Art Degree"), which we presented to the board.

Strategy

In order to achieve the best success, we decided to use an approach that combined a variety of tactics that would work well together.

SEO

We started with SEO because, given the overwhelming number of searches for topics related to art, we felt that nationally and locally focused search engine optimization was an essential activity. SEO is one of the most tried and true high-ROI activities in all of web marketing and can't be overlooked just because something newer comes along. First, we focused on the college's website to ensure that it had clean URLs and search engine-friendly site architecture. Next, we attacked keywords ranging from "art colleges" and "art schools" to phrases related to specific academic majors and careers like "animation colleges" and "graphic design careers." At the same time, we optimized large volumes of individual course areas with local geo-targeting (e.g., Beverly, MA, Massachusetts, etc.). We also optimized the long tail keywords in blog posts.

Social Media

The college's brand was being harmed by unauthorized social media accounts and the Facebook page was not set up properly or being actively maintained. After closing down the unauthorized accounts, fixing the Facebook page and designating specific people to share content on it, social engagement increased significantly. The YouTube channel was resurrected and video activity increased along with video optimization. Twitter was suggested but a decision was made to hold off on that channel. Long-term, Twitter could be significant way to share information, create ties to journalists, and be seen as a thought leader, and retweets help SEO (even if mostly indirectly).

Content

By generating content like infographics, podcasts, and videos, we increased social sharing, which further improved organic SEO results and thought leadership. An editorial calendar for blog content was created to encourage consistent activity that focused on long tail keyword searches.

Blogging

Initially, we redesigned the college's blog and transitioned it to an on-site URL at montserrat.edu/blog to take advantage of the SEO boost and to grow the overall size of the website. The eventual goal was to release a series of blogs (some on the URL and some off) to create a variety of activity on various topics to attract links and social media attention.

Graphic Design

We created a new look for just the home page while a budget was being created for a complete site redesign. We added three calls to action (visit the campus, see what you can do with an art degree, and apply now) to catch people at various stages of the buying cycle while we were working on segmenting content by personas.

Public Relations

Starting with the college's annual art auction, we provided information, materials, and access to all local (North Shore) media outlets, consisting of daily and weekly newspapers. Only two weeks into the initiative, when the auction was held, we had generated so much coverage that at least 150 people walked in who only knew about the event through publicity generated by McDougall Interactive. By consistently pushing out and sharing news releases ranging from local events, thought leader segments like the Encaustic conference, and more unusual exhibitors like Guerrilla Girls, we sought to gain traction in a wider variety of art communities nationally. This attention resulted in increased social and media buzz, connections to influencers, backlinks, and corresponding search rankings.

Then we focused PR efforts on exhibits in the college's gallery and had the college's news repeatedly covered in the *Boston Globe* (the region's largest daily newspaper), as well as in all local dailies and weeklies. During this phase of our PR efforts, we suggested that the college use the phrase "*See What You Can Do with an Art Degree*," positioning the school as an important avenue for young people to understand and join the "creative economy."

Finally, by connecting to art magazines and their blogs, we were able to secure high-quality press coverage such as the front cover of *ArtScope* as well as highly relevant and quality backlinks such as those from *ArtScope*'s blog.

Conversion Optimization

The online applications and continuing education areas were optimized for improved usability and trust after usertesting.com videos revealed consistent negative feedback. New calls to action on the home page were tested with Google Website Optimizer.

Paid Search and Facebook Ads

Google AdWords and Facebook Ads were successfully used in small, cost-effective doses to drive traffic to summer workshops.

The Results

For the first time in its 40-year history, Montserrat had a waiting list of applicants and we generated leads from states such as Colorado, where the college has never had enrollment come from before.

There was a strong increase in visits to Montserrat's website and search engine results page penetration for targeted keywords. Through SEO, we had a 1,454% increase in top 50 results of Google organic search engine results pages. Rankings in the first six months included #1 in Google for the keyphrase "Art Colleges," beating the Rhode Island School of Design and the rest of the national, larger schools. We feel this was a phenomenal success. Paying for an equivalent amount of traffic using Google AdWords would have cost over $1 million!

We used Google Analytics to track all of the sources driving traffic to the application pages and summer workshop pages, and we've tracked major increases in goal conversions. With shared management and a limited budget, we increased the college's Facebook engagement to over 1,000 "likes" with a large increase in engagement and page visits.

Below are just a few of the media highlights:

- WGBH-TV, Boston and national

- Cover and feature articles in *ArtScope, Art New England,* and *Art News*

- *Boston Business Journal*

- The Associated Press

- *Boston Globe* (frequently for exhibitions) major front page coverage of "For the Record"

Considering that Montserrat College of Art has just 400 students and is a small local college, this level of search engine ranking and amount of publicity is a phenomenal start to their long-term successful web strategy.

When we began working with the college, prospects, recruits, students, faculty, staff, and the general public were—as they continue to be—judging colleges by the quality of their websites and by their presence in search and social media. Our comprehensive approach is what made the difference between being tactical and being strategic, and it created the strongest impression.

Only by combining these various tactics with a focus that ties into business goals outlined at the start of a project through intensive interviews can you get the best visibility online that will impact your organization's bottom line in the right ways.

Ways to Improve

The president of the college, who is a PhD from the Massachusetts Institute of Technology as well as a very creative person, always pushed us to think more strategically and asked questions such as:

- Why are these results good? (When we bragged in our monthly reports.)

- Who are they reaching and why?

- What is our 3–5 year strategy?

Great strategy is neither created nor executed in isolation, so monthly meetings (at the very least) need to be set with various team members on the client and agency (or subcontractor) side, to make sure you're not drilling down into one tactic without knowing why or how it connects to the larger strategy.

How Is This Approach Different than Just SEO, Paid Search, or Social Media as a Strategy?

I can't tell you how many jobs we get where the client requests we only implement one tactic due to limited budgets. We also have plenty of situations where we are doing SEO and someone else does paid search and social media. In addition, it is amazing how few people share their traditional marketing plans with us in detail.

How can you expect an Internet marketing company hired to implement one or two tactics to truly think strategically and help you with your strategy if you don't share with them your overall marketing plan and connect them to your other marketing team members?

If you are doing it all in-house, two of the most important questions will be: 1) how does this connect to our overall marketing plan, and 2) do we have the internal resources to do each of these tactics at optimal levels, given the fast-moving changes in the marketing world?

We have had many advertising agencies approach us to help them with their Internet marketing strategies. We are often hired behind the scenes to implement some of the web tactics that traditional agencies don't understand. Eventually, as marketing dollars shift from 25% being spent on the web to 50% or more being spent on the web, traditional and web specialty agencies will be forced to better understand each part of the puzzle. Until then, we all must work together transparently to make the most efficient and effective strategy.

Tactics for Internet Marketing

Before you can develop and implement a strategy, you need to have a birds-eye view of the many tactics that web marketers use. Below is a "short" list.

SEO Essentials for Web Design: Consult an expert before designing or fail

SEO Implementation: Adjusting your website to make it rank better

Link Building: Without links from other websites and social engagement, your SEO will fail

Public Relations: The Internet has revitalized and socialized public relations

Social Media Marketing: Engaging and interacting with your customers

Content Marketing: The backbone of your campaigns

Blogging for Business: The heart of strong SEO and social campaigns

Paid Search: Quick to set up, "expensive" but can be very profitable

Actionable Analytics and Reporting: Examine visitor behavior, track ROI

Conversion Rate Optimization: Increase leads through trust and calls to action

Email Marketing/Lead Nurturing: Follow up and stay top of mind with your customers

Local Search/Mobile: Local/Mobile is skyrocketing, so go for a ride

Affiliate Marketing/Adsense Basics: Pay commissions only for sales, run ads

Internet Marketing Tools: Tools are simply not optional; they're essential (see Chapter 16 for a list)

Traditional marketing agencies always develop a very detailed strategic plan based on market research before they begin writing copy or doing any creative work.

Online marketing companies, on the other hand, are typically not trained in strategic marketing and hence the web is full of sites that have weak "brochure-ware content" that does not position the company well or engage the user. The days of such pseudo-engagement are long gone and TV advertising is suffering because people want control of their experiences and to be able to comment on the products and services they use. With such radical paradigm shifts happening in the marketing word, you had better devise a solid strategic Internet marketing plan or you won't be able to leverage the best practices of the many unique Internet-specific tactics available.

In order to make an impact long-term, you need to assess how much engaging content you have and how you will develop it, how many people currently link to you or "vote" for you online, and how you might use a number of social media sites. Only then can you chart a course of action for long-term success online. In the search engine optimization chapter (Chapter 4), you will learn about the specific tools for assessing the preliminary status of your website before you begin.

The Top Seven Must-Have Internet Marketing Tactics

1. Original content

2. SEO (search engine optimization)

3. Pay per click (PPC) – (paid search)

4. Social media marketing (buzz and user-generated content)

5. Tracking/analytics

6. Conversion enhancements

7. Link building

For each of those seven considerations, define your mix of activity and then set budgets for each. All too often, an agency or webmaster will be a one-trick pony. They will list all these services in general, but mostly focus on one or another. Make sure you are paying for or specifically doing each of the above.

After three to six months, re-assess which tactics are creating the most and best leads and focus on the ones generating visitors who convert and *buy from you*. Then keep using those successful tactics, but also look deeply into why the unsuccessful tactics are failing. Keep in mind that SEO can take a year or more to have its greatest effects, so re-analyze leads and ROI per channel every three to six months.

Symbiosis Is the Key for Kicking Results into High Gear

Failing to understand the relationships among these techniques will mean that your marketing campaigns lack cohesiveness. Once you see how all of these pieces fit together, you will be much less likely to fall into the trap of using only one or two tactics in isolation. More importantly, you will come to the realization that what works for your business may not be what works for a company in an unrelated industry. There are no absolutes here, so patience and willingness to work with as many techniques as possible will ultimately enable you to hit your online sweet spot.

Consider that:

1. Without content, search engine optimization and social media will fail.

2. SEO has a very high ROI and is rising in popularity while pay per click (PPC) is losing some of its early dominance. Learning how these fit together is essential (each certainly has a critical role).

3. Paid ads can help you determine the most profitable, high-converting terms to work extra hard to rank for organically. Why optimize heavily for search terms you don't convert well on? (Make sure you are bidding on lots of longer tail keywords and watch to see which of those is most profitable. Then use those in your content and watch your free organic traffic soar.)

4. Social media marketing can make a huge impact on your reputation and can therefore make or break your brand. It provides a benefit to SEO partly because people "like" you, talk about you, and share or, most importantly, link to your amazing content.

5. Website analytics help you determine what keywords are driving traffic and sales. You can use this knowledge to improve your website. In order for there to be synergies between tactics, you need tracking across channels, multiple site visits, and long stretches of time.

6. Conversion enhancements increase the value of each click by making more sales from the same amount of visitors. By optimizing conversions, even your traditional marketing dollars will go further because any site visitor from any channel will yield greater profits.

7. Without links, search engine optimization will fail. Content should be the heart of your link campaigns and the "bait" to get people to link to you. You need great links from places that the search engines adore and you need them to be built every month to show consistency. Nothing says "red flag" like starting a link building program and then stopping. A good brand will have lots of mentions, links, and social shares that grow year-round.

We work with many marketing directors, CEOs, and site owners who get excited about one particular facet of Internet marketing (often the one that is the trend of the moment). One example is YouTube. Companies start adding corporate videos that are essentially infomercials and wonder why they get no views or people clicking away immediately. When we do a YouTube campaign, we think about what information users are *not* getting via existing site pages or from the company in any other way. We then develop informative or humorous videos that relate to the concepts that we know people are searching for. We also use related keywords in the content and descriptions around the same phrases. We then add the video to YouTube and the company's blog so that users can also click to see it at ourclientswebsite.com/blog/keyword. Having the content on the blog means the user also gets to comment, providing a social element. YouTube should be gathering subscribers for you. That's because subscribers are your mailing list and are yet another signal to Google that you are for real.

Google loves YouTube and you would be wise to integrate with it. People can now link to this new blog post with the embedded video, which also positively influences your search engine ranks. Your YouTube descriptions/annotations should also link to this page. This blog post should interlink with your main website pages that have more product details and calls to action. You need to see that everything online should be working together. That is where you get the most play. Synergy...it's a beautiful thing.

It may sound complicated, but in fact it's quite basic. These interlinking structures are part of proper website architecture and programming based on marketing principles, not programming logic alone. Track your efforts for effectiveness through analytics and compare the cost to the equivalent clicks in a paid search spend. The content of your videos needs to fit in the grand scheme of your content architecture. And so on. Your website, your content, your social feeds, your ads, and the relationships you form through customer interaction all work together. This is very different than mumbling, "Hey, webmaster, did you add our video to our home page?" Strategy plus integration *rocks* because it means you are working smarter not harder.

Content and Customer Engagement Are at the Core

While only the people who work at places like Google and Bing know the algorithms (the weights given to all of the factors about your site), one thing is certain: those algorithms change considerably and often (hundreds of ranking factors get updated 500 to 600 times a year!), so don't just follow trends. Do things that will be good for your site and visitors long-term. Add unique value to the web. That is what will make your marketing safer and less susceptible to the whims of search sites like Google.

Google is said to track how many people click your links from the results pages and how long people stay on your site. Throw in all of the other weighting factors and you can see why engaging and then converting people on your site has become so valuable.

So if people leave quickly once they get to your site (known as a high bounce rate) because you're not offering them anything of value, it may affect how Google values you, and ultimately affect your organic rankings. Why? Because it is the job of a search engine to send searchers to the most *relevant* web page.

Some people call it pogo-sticking when a user clicks to a site from the Google search results page and then hits the "back" button. Google likely looks at this behavior when deciding whether or not to rank you well. Ideally, users should not only stay a long time on your site and not hit the "back" button, but they should also take some form of conversion action like filling out a form or buying from your shopping cart. The smartest website owners have come to the conclusion that keeping new visitors on their pages is incredibly valuable, possibly even for rankings. That's why you see so many videos, polls, and even engaging games on home pages these days. These are potentially strong signals to Google that you are worth ranking highly to give their users a good experience. Long-term, you need a site that looks great, engages visitors, and has valuable content that people will naturally want to share with others. Whether you get traffic from pay per click or the free results, repeat visitors who are satisfied visitors can make a big difference. The best way to build a bigger and better site is to start by knowing your current situation and developing an integrated strategy around your objectives.

Building a Holistic Strategy That Is Trackable

In 1995 when I was selling websites and studying SEO at McDougall Associates Advertising, I witnessed the Internet gold rush in its infancy. I have seen my share of trends and am amazed at how currently some companies are scurrying to get high ROI from web marketing but can't see the forest for the trees. As I've mentioned, Facebook and Twitter and other social media platforms can be great tools and are clearly a major part of the wave of the future, but they are only one part of the bigger picture.

Facebook and Google are the big monsters online in terms of traffic, we all know that. And the media pumps up everything related to Facebook and Twitter and now Pinterest to the point where some marketers think they can drive all their traffic solely through these mediums. One banker, during a new business pitch I gave, showed me a long list of Internet marketing activities he was researching and said, "I think we should just start with Facebook and do only that." In some industries like travel and entertainment, where people often rely on social connections to help them search out vacations, movies, events, or restaurants, you may drive even more traffic using Facebook and Twitter than through Google. This is generally not the case in other industries. Our monthly review of sources of traffic in the analytics for our clients shows clearly that organic traffic and sometimes email marketing are the largest drivers of high-ROI traffic. Social media generally provides earlier-stage leads, though it has many other benefits besides immediate sales. A recent webinar from HubSpot about the state of inbound marketing included these statistics based on over 1,000 surveyed customers:

Lead to customer-close, percentage by channel

SEO 15%

Direct Traffic 15%

Referrals 9%

Paid Search 7%

Social Media 4%

Traditional "Outbound" Marketing 2%

Forrester Research has surveyed marketers about what forms of advertising they think will increase in effectiveness moving forward. Social media is at the top and traditional media is at the bottom. If you look at Forrester's predictions through 2016, the spend on search marketing will still be more than six times the spend on social media. So just because social and mobile are hot, don't forget where the bulk of the actual spend is going when determining how much to spend in each category. You need to focus on the buyers!

It's worth mentioning here that results will almost always differ by industry.

Don't Put All Your Clicks in One Basket

We have seen numerous things in clients' analytics reports that greatly surprise us. Email marketing, for example, drives over 20,000 visitors a month for one of our new clients. It had the highest ROI and was by far the largest traffic driver. Facebook, just one of the referrers, drove only a handful of visits. Twitter, despite the client's 1,400 followers, didn't do much in terms of immediate sales. While you clearly can drive a lot of traffic through Facebook and various social sites, you can't put all your clicks in that one basket and ignore other channels that are tried and true. If in your industry people click the organic results and take action from searches more than social inquiries, it is critical that you widen your net significantly to include these tactics.

While these percentages will shift over time and 2012 data may not be compiled until mid-2013, check out the breakdown of ROI per channel below.

Return for every $1 spent per marketing channel in 2011

Email Marketing	$40.56
Internet Search Advertising	$22.24
Internet Display Advertising	$19.72
Mobile	$10.51
Catalogs	$7.30

Source: Direct Marketing Association

The Direct Marketing Association says that email marketing returned $40.56 for every dollar spent on it in 2011, is projected to bring in $39.40 for every dollar spent in 2012, and $35.02 for every dollar spent in 2016. Those are stunning numbers even with a bit of a decline due to people's frustration with spam. This is why so many of the most successful affiliate marketers work so hard to acquire the name and email address of someone showing interest.

Email marketing builds trust over time and can easily be one of the strongest weapons you use.

Internet search advertising (paid search) came in second at $22.24, Internet display advertising at $19.72, mobile at $10.51, and catalogs at $7.30. Social media has some staggering case studies but is still in its infancy in terms of tracking. The key is to try a variey of channels to figure out what works best for your business.

Don't Take the Easy Way Out by Doing Only Paid Search

If you think paid search is the easiest (e.g., Google AdWords pay-per-click campaigns), you will need to check the prices of each click and know your conversion rate and profit margin to see if you can make money on buying ads. Paid search is only fully trackable when you've set up Analytics goal tracking (on all types of conversion, including using a tool like Mongoose Metrics to track phone leads), and is usually only profitable when you are adept at frequently adjusting ads, prices, copy, and landing pages. In the case of some clients that resell overstocks or closeout items and have constantly changing inventories, pay-per-click programs can be so complex to manage daily that they require a full-time person in-house and a $20,000/month spend. For other clients, buying local terms like "Salem Massachusetts roofing contractors" can provide great leads for as low as a few hundred dollars a month, supplementing gobs of "free" organic listings while being fairly easy to manage.

Incredibly, only a few years ago, you could set up a paid search campaign and drive cheap traffic to any web page you wanted. Now the quality score (a Google AdWords rating that requires such things as quality content) of your destination page may mean that your ad never even runs...no matter how much you spend per click.

Also remember that those long tail keywords are far less expensive to buy. Less traffic, but far less expensive. With that said, we have examples of over $1,000,000 in revenue from a single $180 click! "Mesothelioma Lawyers" and related terms can go for over $200 a click, but considering some of these lawsuits bring in tens of millions of dollars, there are numerous firms willing to pay these prices 24/7/365.

New options for paying to promote Facebook posts and for Twitter ads are sprouting up and are worth testing. Keep a budget for a variety of paid options.

Connect Traditional Campaigns to Web Campaigns

Make sure your TV, radio and print campaigns feed the funnel and do so in a trackable way. For example, make a specific offer in offline ads that goes to a web page that you can only get to from those ads and look for an overall spike in traffic and sales during an offline spend. The online dating sites are especially good at this and they watch their media buys in each different market and ramp up or down based on media-directed signups.

Online and offline integration destroys the former weakness of not being able to prove advertising works. Magazines, for example, may not provide the power they used to in terms of the printed component alone, but they now provide huge benefits in the form of the content footprint they offer you with a high-quality, highly visible link to your site. Media sites are by nature content-rich, and Google tracks how connected you are to these mediums and how often you are in the news. By doing public relations and being part of various media listings, you can boost your organic search ranks by proving to Google that you are a "player" or a thought leader. The corresponding bump in organic ranks has a trackable value, giving concrete added ROI to a traditional media spend that non-digital ad agencies may not fully understand.

Track It or You Are Shooting in the Dark

Once you've created an integrated campaign with amazing content, go check your ranks in Google and you will see Google is proud of you! By handing the search engine's killer content, you enable it to send people to more relevant pages. This means you deserve to be on the search engine's first results pages and you are not a spammer, temporarily flying on a false wave of gimmicky ranking techniques. With your quality content being published regularly on social media sites, your visibility is expanding outside of search. Add a healthy dose of paid ads that have a low cost and high conversion rates, and your brand starts to be seen consistently across many channels, making customers trust and buy from you more readily. But to make absolutely sure that your hard work is paying off, track it all through a program like Google Analytics and/or HubSpot, so that you know which programs are working best and can improve or ditch whatever strategies aren't working for you. (More on this in the chapter on analytics.)

Google, Facebook, Twitter, Pinterest, and others are racing to see who can control the promised land of online brand advertising. With such volatility and uncertainly in the fate of the online race, it makes a lot of sense to carefully diversify. After all, each tactic has its own strengths and weaknesses. Internet marketing should be handled similar to investing. If you put all your efforts in one area and that area fails, you fail.

Internet Marketing Strategy Worksheet

Before developing a site or starting any individual web marketing tactics, it is essential that you have a documented plan of action. The worksheet below can help you organize your strategy and will serve as a map that the whole team should be referencing.

The act of writing down the following items and answering the questions can often inspire new ideas and solidify your strategic brainstorming. Only after you have measurable goals in place can you can proceed to the individual tactics. To aid you in the process, we have developed a more complete online worksheet that will help you uncover essential information on which to build your campaigns, keep them tied together, and keep them in line with your brand.

Before beginning a project, complete the worksheets in our Internet marketing planning software at www.plansprout.com so you have a record of where you are currently and where you hope to go.

Having a basic document like this to reference as you go and to serve as a place to store new ideas can be a huge asset, given there are so many moving parts to an Internet marketing strategy.

◇◇◇

INTERNET MARKETING STRATEGY WORKSHEET

Company name: _____

Site URLs: _____

Web Marketing On All Cylinders - John McDougall

Company description and plans for growth: _____

Team members and roles: _____

Worksheet Sections

Strategy

SEO Essentials for Web Design

SEO Implementation

Link Building

Public Relations

Social Media Marketing

Content

Blogging for Business

Paid Search/Display Ads

Actionable Analytics and Reporting

Conversion Rate Optimization

Email Marketing/Lead Nurturing

Local Search/Mobile

Internet Marketing Tools

12-MONTH STRATEGY SUMMARY

While you may want to create a more detailed plan later, for the purposes of this book I will keep the strategy template brief to help you get started quickly. Having a shorter plan can also help you share it with senior executives to get buy-in before you create a comprehensive Internet marketing strategy Roadmap.

Keep your answers to a few lines each at first. Emphasize the need for investment in online marketing and share the major issues that must be addressed.

Keep the benchmarking and tactical worksheets separate from the main plan at first to keep your executive team focused on high-level strategy, not tactics.

After you have completed the benchmarking and tactical worksheets, you will likely need to rethink your initial strategy answers. That's because this process is likely to bring you new insights to help you restructure your plan and make better use of synergies between tactics.

---

1. Situation Analysis

Summarize the current situation and the most important issues to address:

Consider the following areas when determining your current situation:

a. Your customers (demographics, personas, segmenting, and targeting) – Use the personas worksheet in the conversion section of this Roadmap as a good starting point for creating a clearer picture of who your customers are.

b. Your market – Describe your market and what is happening in it. What customer needs can you satisfy?

c. Competitors – Review what your competitors are doing, using the benchmarking worksheet below. I strongly recommend a subscription to HubSpot, as this will track many of these things for you and allow you to compare your results to those of your competitors. At the very least, use the free HubSpot tool at marketing.grader.com on your site and competitors' sites.

d. Influencers – Where are your customers most likely to look for you and who is influencing them now? What media do they consume? Are they more active in search or social media channels or both?

e. Your capabilities – What can you realistically do in-house and what should you outsource to experts in specific categories?

SWOT Analysis

SWOT is an acronym for Strengths, Weaknesses, Opportunities, and Threats. It is usually used to examine the business as a whole for viability as an enterprise, but it can also be used to improve your web marketing. At the very least, writing down a few quick thoughts on each aspect of the SWOT analysis can generate ideas and identify problems to get you on the right track.

Web Marketing On All Cylinders - John McDougall

S (Strengths): What do you have online that others don't?

W (Weaknesses): What are your weakest points in your Internet marketing strategy?

O (Opportunities): What opportunities can you capitalize on that could put your site ahead of competitors?

T (Threats): What does a competitor's Internet marketing have that you don't?

2. Set Objectives

Summarize your overall vision for your marketing plan here:

Goal Planning

Write down your goals in a paragraph or two and how you intend to get there. Be specific and make sure these goals are measurable, actionable, realistic, and can be done in a reasonable timeframe (so-called "SMART" goals). Don't add so many goals that you will get confused. Here are examples of possible goals:

- Sign up *x* number of subscribers in the first quarter

- Sell *x* amount of product this year

- Generate *x* number of form submissions or phone calls per month

- Increase brand awareness and reputation by *x* amount of views and positive first-page Google listings (good links to your site(s) and social profiles) per month

- Improve customer service by doing *x*

- Track increases in positive sentiment by measuring the conversations (and their tone) about your brand on the web

Set goals that align with the broader goals of your business, and set deadlines for each goal.

List your short-, medium-, and long-term goals

Short-term:

Medium-term:

Long-term:

It is also a good idea to have goals based on each stage of the REAN framework, which was first coined by Xavier Blanc in 2006. REAN helps you to plan ahead for and analyze the various marketing activities necessary for building and nurturing customer relationships. REAN stands for:

R - Reach: activities needed to increase attention paid to your brand, product, or service

E - Engage: activities to engage the prospects you just won

A - Activate: getting your customers to take the actions you want them to take

N - Nurture: activities needed to nurture the customers you just won

For example, if you are solely focused on closing deals and not nurturing customers, you are missing part of the complete cycle of building a strong Internet marketing presence.

Make sure that you have ways to track the path to and completion of your goals using various analytical reporting methods. You will learn more about this in the analytics section below.

Reach Goals:

Engage Goals:

Activate Goals:

Nurture Goals:

3. Strategy Documentation

Your strategy will start to answer how, in terms of approach and not in terms of tactics, you will achieve your goals. Make sure your strategy aligns to your main off-line marketing strategy and business plan.

Key items to keep in mind when documenting your strategy:

- Positioning: Your unique value proposition

- Target audience/personas

- Brand recognition

- Content and customer engagement

- Customer acquisition

- Increasing conversions

- Your web properties and overall online real estate/properties

- Customer retention and growth

Online Branding and Unique Value Proposition

In today's marketing world, a brand name, unique value proposition, and image are as important as the strategy itself. Make sure your interactive agency and your branding agency are working in sync so that the brand gets properly extended online. If people don't understand in the blink of an eye why they should buy from you, your traffic-driving efforts will be wasted.

Your unique value proposition:

Your target audience and/or list of personas:

How will you increase brand recognition?

How will you engage people and with what content?

How will you acquire new customers?

How will you persuade customers to buy from you?

What website(s) (your domains, subdomains, etc.) and/or social profiles are most important to your success?

How will you nurture and retain customers?

4. Tactics

Tactics are what fuel your marketing engine. Here is where you will outline the specific marketing tactics you will use, as well as how and when things will get done. I like to break up the list of activities by quarters of each year.

After completing the tactical worksheet below, come back to this section and outline your vision of what tactics you will focus on. Try to avoid repeating the strategic reasons for each tactic that you may have listed above.

5. Measuring Success

Since the analytics section below goes into more detail on creating key performance indicators, keep it simple here and just answer the following questions:

1. How much is a sale worth to you? (Include the lifetime value of a customer.)

2. What does it cost you now to get sales?

3. What are your hot products or services that make you the most money and that will bring quick/obvious wins when judging return on investment?

4. What tools will you use to track success, and which team member is responsible for this critical activity?

6. Internal Processes

Without an organized process, the attention to detail will fail and so will your Internet marketing campaigns, so make sure you have a well-oiled marketing machine.

What is your budget?

Who will be assigned to each task and what companies will you hire to help in the campaigns?

What is your timeline for your most important tasks?

BENCHMARKING

It is critical at the start of any campaign to get a sense of how you are doing in each of the major tactical areas such as SEO, social media, and paid search. If you can't do it all, at least make note of major successes and things you are not doing. This list should help illustrate how much goes into a deep Internet marketing strategy.

Traffic

Are you doing enough to bring visitors to your website?

Leads

How do you do when it comes to converting traffic into leads and leads into customers?

Analytics

Do you know which marketing activities are working? List how you are determining ROI.

Visitors, Leads, and Sales

Number of unique visitors to website per month:

Number of total sales contacts across all channels:

Which traffic sources convert into leads?

Which lead sources convert best into actual customers?

Number of website leads per month:

Number of website sales per month:

Search Engines

Number of indexed pages in Google:

Number of top 50 ranks in Google:

Number of keywords driving traffic:

Number of leads and sales directly from organic search engine traffic:

What keywords most often drive leads and sales?

Number of leads and sales directly from pay-per-click traffic:

Backlinks in total from root domains/unique websites:

Average number of links being built per month:

Social Media

Facebook fans/likes/number of monthly referrals to website:

Leads and sales generated from Facebook:

Twitter followers/monthly retweets/number of monthly referrals to website:

Leads and sales generated from Twitter:

LinkedIn connections/number of monthly referrals to website:

Leads and sales generated from LinkedIn:

Pinterest followers/likes/number of monthly referrals to website:

Leads and sales generated from Pinterest:

Videos and views on YouTube and subscribers/likes/number of monthly referrals to website:

Leads and sales generated from YouTube:

Number of people in Google+ circles, Plus 1s, and number of monthly referrals to website:

Leads and sales generated from Google+:

Number of Google+/Yelp reviews (list how many positive and negative)

Blog

Number of blog visitors per month:

Number of blog posts per month:

Number of blog subscribers:

Average number of monthly blog comments:

Number of leads and sales from the blog:

Names of and Google Author Rank of key authors:

Email Marketing and Lead Nurturing

Number of email "newsletters" sent per month:

Number of email subscribers:

Number of lead nurturing campaigns:

Conversion Optimization

Conversion rate from site:

Conversion rate from blog:

How often do you build and launch new calls to action to drive traffic to your landing pages?

Have you defined characteristics of an ideal lead, and if so what are they?

Public Relations

Number of press releases done per month:

Are you getting trackable leads and sales from PR?

Content

Number of downloadable ebooks/white papers posted on website:

Number of videos:

Number of infographics:

Number of podcasts:

Number of slidehows:

Do you have comprehensive image galleries?

Connecting with the Sales Team

Is your CRM system (such as Salesforce) connected with your website (i.e., when someone fills out a form, do the leads go straight into and get tagged in Salesforce as having originated from the website)?

Does your web analytics program notify you/your sales team when a sales prospect that is in your CRM database is visiting the website?

Does your website analytics program track the traffic source/marketing campaign for each lead, including if a lead was generated originally by a salesperson or a cold call?

Do you have a lead quality/quantity goal between marketing and sales?

Does your sales team use social media like Twitter, LinkedIn, and/or Facebook to connect with leads or journalists?

Now that you have a better picture of how well you are doing currently, it is time to work on your website goals and ensuring it gets the very critical SEO architecture it needs as a foundational element in your overall strategy.

SEO ESSENTIALS FOR WEB DESIGN

Don't even think about building a website without talking to an Internet marketing expert first, because programming issues can sometimes ruin your chances for high rankings with Google.

What is your main goal for the website?

How will you judge success?

What are the top 3 pages people should view?

What are the top 3–5 actions you want users to take?

List any technical roadblocks that need to be corrected before the site can excel in the search engines and be more shareable. (For example, poor URL structure and categorization, excessive/sloppy code, slow download times, un-indexable content, etc.)

Competitive Analysis

If you will be building a new site, do a competitive analysis of the content of three sites that rank well in the search engines. Start by running sitemaps for each competitor and categorize their content by type, amount, and frequency. Then you can start to plan the size, URLs, and type of site you will need to build in order to compete.

You should also look at what type of social media activity those competitors have and what content on their site is linked to most often. If they have a social community or a cool resource section that is driving lots of engagement and links, this should be a consideration for your site *before you redesign*, otherwise your content strategy, link/social potential, and usability will suffer.

ON-PAGE SEO IMPLEMENTATION

SEO is driven by keywords, content, links, and, even if mostly indirectly, by social media. SEO takes longer but also lasts longer than paid ads, usually converts better, and has very high ROI. This section is specifically referring to adding and editing keywords and content on your site.

What is your main goal for SEO?

How will you judge the success of SEO?

List the keywords you feel will drive visitors to your site. Then perform extensive keyword research. List your top 5 keywords:

Do you have content that is more than one page for each of these keyword categories such as product or services pages, blog posts, case studies, white papers, etc.? List any new content you would consider creating for SEO.

Perform on-page optimization referring to the chapter on SEO.

LINK BUILDING

Links are the roadways of the web and may be more than half of the reason you rank high organically. When you marry your on-page SEO with your off-page SEO/links, that's when the magic happens.

The days of faking it with links are gone. It is now very similar to true public relations where a handful of great stories with links to your site can make a huge difference.

What is your main goal for link building (refers and/or SEO ranks)?

How will you judge the success of link building?

What content do you have (in-depth blog posts, contests, widgets, infographics, viral videos, interactive games, or repositories of statistics and information) that could provide a real reason for someone else to link to your site?

Perform competitive backlink analysis on your competitors; analyze what pages on their sites get linked to the most, where they get links, and what links many of your competitors have in common. Then go ask those sites to link to you. What 3 to 5 sites of competitors that rank really well could you use in this analysis?

What blogs and magazines are well-known in your niche? Wordtracker's Link Builder tool and Radian6 can help find such sites.

Example of a basic backlink analysis and the essentials to document before starting a campaign:

yoursite.com (domain):

Domain Authority   45/100

This is how powerful your site is based on its links as determined by SEOMoz.

Total External Links   4,463

This is how many times you are linked to.

Total Linking Root Domains   101

This is exactly how many unique sites link to you versus counting multiple links from each site.

Niche or Industry Directories

List any very high-quality industry/niche directories you are listed in or want to be listed in. Examples of niche directories include the knot.com for wedding-related businesses and findlaw.com for lawyers. Make sure not to do directory submissions just for the SEO benefit or you could cause serious ranking problems.

PUBLIC RELATIONS

Public relations now includes the use of social media for outreach and connecting with bloggers. You still need a "newsworthy" story and it helps to be part of (or relevant to) a current trend. If you send out a newsworthy press release, you can generate direct sales and reach the end user, news outlets, and the blogosphere all at once. Links from magazine sites, bloggers, and news sites play a part in organic rankings and increase conversions by showing that you are a trusted company.

What is your main goal for your public relations campaign?

How will you judge the success of your public relations efforts?

What makes you so unique that media outlets and others will want to write about you?

What major events coming up for your company this year can you publicize?

What trend is your story part of?

Who gets more publicity than you and which journalists cover them?

Make a spreadsheet of competitors' news stories and include the websites/blogs and social profiles of the journalists and bloggers who wrote them. Regularly reach out to these bloggers and journalists with significant stories and high-value content. Use social media platforms such as Twitter as part of your way to reach them.

SOCIAL MEDIA MARKETING

Social media marketing can generate a two-way conversation and leverage users to promote for you. Make sure to do it in a way that gets people to also link to your site (they will link to you if you create cool/engaging content). Social media can make or break a business reputation these days, so there is no more hiding your head in the sand.

What is your main goal with social media?

How will you judge the success of social media?

What social media monitoring tool will you use?

Who will be your community manager to react in real time to visitor questions?

Who will create original content for social media?

What team members and employees will contribute?

Are there any major restrictions or compliance issues regarding what your company can say or do on social media?

Who will define the keywords used to develop posts/status updates and content for social media?

CONTENT DEVELOPMENT AND MARKETING

Content is now the heart of Internet marketing, partially due to the extreme measures Google has taken to rule out fake tactics. You must now build the Author Rank and social status of your team, not just blindly fling average content at the wall.

What is your main goal with content marketing?

How will you judge the success of content marketing?

Do you have an editorial calendar with amount and frequency of content mapped to seasonal activities (as applicable)?

Who are the main content developers in each category such as video, blogs, white papers, ebooks, webinars, seminars, podcasts, and presentations?

Do you have social "share" buttons on all your content?

BLOGGING FOR BUSINESS

Since content has become 100 percent essential to web marketing, blogs have become the backbone of many social media and SEO activities.

Blogs allow you to share with your customers easily and regularly. The fresh new content fuels organic rankings, generates backlinks, and starts conversations.

What is your main goal with blogging?

How will you judge the success of blogging?

Do you have a spreadsheet of pre-researched long and short tail blog post topics mapped to the keywords that align with your business goals?

How many times a week will you blog? (Blog AT LEAST once per week.)

Who are the bloggers?

Are you using Google+ Author Rank (Google's way of determining the quality and authority of your writers)?

Do you have a blog comment system installed on your blog that allows users to sign in with their Twitter and Facebook accounts?

PAID SEARCH/DISPLAY ADS

Paid search is a great way to get fast traffic and sales. In some campaigns we have seen most of the sales come from paid search, while other times it does not convert well, so you simply have to test it. Paid search includes Google AdWords, Facebook, Twitter, and LinkedIn advertising, banner ads, and more.

What is your main goal with paid search?

How will you judge the success of paid search?

Do you have a Google AdWords account?

Do you know what Google Quality Score is or how to increase your conversion rate in order to get more leads? If you don't, you need to or you will pay double the fees or more and miss out on lost sales. Google Quality Score is Google's way of making sure your ads go to relevant and high-quality pages. When you have a quality score of 7 or better and a conversion rate of at least 2% to 5%, your success will increase significantly.

Do you pay for promoted posts and ads on Facebook?

What is your paid search budget for Google AdWords, Bing/Yahoo, Facebook, Twitter, and LinkedIn ads?

If you are not doing paid search and something bad happens to your Google organic rankings and non-paid social media, you could be in a heap of trouble. Google and Facebook make most of their money from ads. Embrace paid search because it is not going away anytime soon and offers a stable traffic- and sales-driving element.

ACTIONABLE ANALYTICS AND REPORTING

Tracking visitors' activity, their bounce and exit rates, their time on site, and leads/sales is central to a successful Internet marketing campaign.

What is your main goal for analytics?

How will you judge the success of using analytics?

In order to have a reasonably complete sense of what is generating sales and leads, you must have multiple forms of tracking in place. Document if you have confirmed tracking set up for each of the following and which ones need to be addressed.

- Tracking of unique phone number(s) on your site

- Form submissionsShopping cart salesLive chat

- Email address clicks

- Printable/PDF application downloads

- Printable coupon/specials downloads

- Third-party applications (i.e., mortgage applications off your main URL)

- Offline conversion tracking

- Attribution tracking/conversion assists (consider using HubSpot)

List the tracking options you will use here:

Sales don't always happen on someone's first visit to your site. Sales tend to develop over time and multiple touch points. "Conversion assists" reporting shows you all of the tactics and pages that have been influential to buyers in the past.

Analytics can help you make better decisions as to what tactics to keep using or to stop using and to optimize the content that most commonly leads to a decision and speeds up future sales cycles. If you don't have this type of tracking, you are flying blind. I have gotten fired by a client more than once only because we were not able to prove the sales we really generated. I say this with great confidence as industry experts now agree that things like social media are often undervalued because people don't have a way to see whether they suc-ceed over time by eventually driving sales through SEO or direct URL type-in. Without this tracking, making real strategic decisions is more like being a drunk throwing darts in a dark bar. HubSpot is amazing in many ways but the conversions assists feature alone is worth the price of the software. It far exceeds what you can do out of the box with Google Analytics.

Measurements that help you see how you are doing against your objectives are called KPIs or Key Performance Indicators.

What are your top three KPIs?

Examples include:

1. Conversion rate

2. Share of search for a particular term against a competitor

3. Number of days and visits from initial visit to "purchase"

4. Average order value

5. Visitor loyalty and visitor recency

Knowing just how much you can track will get you excited and help you impress your boss or peers. No strategy is complete unless it is driven by measurable objectives. If you have Google Analytics installed and don't yet use it, you're about to enter a whole new world.

CONVERSION RATE OPTIMIZATION

For every $92 spent driving traffic only $1 is spent converting it! Enough said. Get on it before the word spreads and you will be way ahead of many competitors.

What is your main goal for conversion rate optimization?

How will you judge the success of doing conversion rate optimization?

It all comes down to trust. That is why social media works and is here to stay. People want to see that others believe in you. So be sure your website and social media content include industry awards, testimonials, case studies, mentions of big clients, news stories, shopping cart security trust badges, and affiliations.

What are some of the "trust factors" you can add to your site?

CONVERSION TRINITY

Your conversion rate hinges on the following three main factors, called the conversion trinity.

1. Relevance: Does your content closely match what the visitor is expecting to see? (If they search using a particular keyword, for example, they expect to see that in an ad and then on the page they click to.)

2. Value: How clear is your unique value proposition and how quickly and consistently is it imparted to visitors?

What is your unique value proposition?

3. Call to Action: How obvious is your main call to action?

If we do nothing else, we need to properly address these three critical factors in alignment with your business goals.

Call-Outs/Calls to Action

Make sure to have a call to action for each of these marketing stages:

Top of the funnel

Stage 1: Roughly 80% of web traffic is in this "research and surfing" stage

Call to action ideas: Guides and ebooks

Question to answer: What do I need?

List your top of the funnel call to action:

Middle of the funnel

Stage 2: Roughly 15% of web traffic is in this "compare and contrast" stage

Call to action ideas: Case studies, webinars, comparison charts/guides

Question to answer: Why do I need it from you?

List your middle of the funnel call to action:

Bottom of the funnel

Stage 3: Roughly 5% of web traffic is in this "buy it now" stage

Call to action ideas: Free consultation forms, audits, "buy now" buttons

Question to answer: Why should I act/buy now?

List your bottom of the funnel call to action:

If you have only a bottom of the funnel call to action, the good news is you are about to be pleasantly surprised (after you add at least a top of the funnel call to action like a free ebook/white paper), because not all of your problems revolve around merely driving traffic. This is one of those "light bulb" moments when your heart rate should be increasing!

If you at least cover these three main factors, your company will have a head start on a conversion strategy.

EMAIL MARKETING/LEAD NURTURING

Email marketing has among the highest ROI on the web, yet I am amazed how few clients do it consistently. I have had numerous clients with email lists of 200,000 or more names that drove more traffic than SEO, paid search, social media, and other tactics combined. Start your email list and you might just build an empire. Your list is everything.

Lead nurturing is often accomplished by emailing leads at scheduled intervals with automated software like HubSpot, Eloqua, or Marketo.

What is your main goal with email marketing and lead nurturing?

How will you judge the success of email marketing and lead nurturing?

How many email addresses do you have that you can market to?

What content will you send (such as daily or weekly deals or a compilation of your best blog posts each month)?

What software will you use? Options include MailChimp, Vertical Response, Constant Contact, or something more high-end like Blue Sky Factory.

Or will you go for a whole different level and use an integrated tool like HubSpot? An integrated tool is much smarter because it ties into your website and Salesforce at the same time to make email marketing more like a symphony than a solo instrument.

What information does the sales team send for follow-ups?

Make sure your activities map out to the processes you have in place, not just what the IT or marketing departments dream up.

LOCAL SEARCH/MOBILE

At the top of any search that Google deems to have local intent you will see the Google+ Local listings. These push down the organic results because they take up so much room and can ruin your traffic if your company does not appear in them.

What is your main goal with local/mobile marketing?

How will you judge the success of local/mobile marketing?

Make sure to claim and completely fill out/optimize your Google+ Local profile by adding text with a reasonable amount of keywords, images, and video. Add a physical address and a local phone number for a business that has a bricks-and-mortar location offline. Encourage citations of your name, address, and phone number online. Get reviews and ratings as well as links from directories, guest blog posts, and quality sites to your local listings page.

Is your Google+ Local listing complete?

Do you have good reviews on Yelp?

Is your website mobile-friendly? Responsive design takes some extra time to do, but it is well worth it when you rebuild your website.

Do you have a mobile version of your shopping cart or an app such as a coupon of the day feature or mortgage rates tool?

Do you have lots of Flash animations or videos? If so, get them converted to a different format or HTML5. (The reason is that mobile devices tend not to play well with Flash.)

Google, Facebook, and many other sites are hyper-focused on mobile and local, yet so many people leave these tactics up to chance. Remember that they don't get corrected on their own.

AFFILIATE MARKETING

While I have chosen not to include an entire chapter on this, it is a great strategy for many retailers.

Affiliate marketing is a pay-for-performance model where you pay others a commission when they sell your product via links or banner ads on their sites. They essentially do all the marketing work for you and you only need to pay them if they are successful in making the sales.

What is your main goal with affiliate marketing?

How will you judge the success of affiliate marketing?

Do you have a product that others could market for you that you are willing to pay a commission on?

If you do, then using a program like Commission Junction or Linkshare could be worth looking into. It is not uncommon to get 10,000 affiliates placing banner ads on their sites if you have a good product that matches their visitor bases. With some of these programs, you can reap big rewards. Some vendors charge $5,000 to $10,000 a month to run an affiliate program for a client.

INTERNET MARKETING TOOLS/SOFTWARE

Tools are an essential part of Internet marketing. Below are some of our favorites. Some are free, some are low-cost, and others are higher in cost but are well worth the expense for many companies.

Google Analytics is essential for tracking visitor behavior and sales. (Free)

SEOMoz PRO is the top SEO software for SEO management, with dozens of tools and valuable SEO resources. ($99 to $500 per month)

Radian6 is a ShareSocial media monitoring, engaging, and sharing tool that is the industry leader. (About $600 per month per URL)

Usertesting.com tests go for about $39 each and allow you to assess the usability of your website. For the money, you get a 15-minute video of people speaking into a microphone as they try to do tasks you assign them on your website (such as to try to find and buy a certain product). The text summaries and videos show you what is wrong with your site and sometimes show you what people like about it.

Google Webmaster Tools Essentials is a very useful tool that you can use to analyze your website's performance and fix errors. (Free)

Google Website Optimizer is a free website testing and optimization tool which is now integrated into Google Analytics and is called Content Experiments. Testing alternate versions of headlines, images, and various other elements is the only scientific way to know you are using content that converts.

Click Tale lets you watch users click paths and how much they scroll, etc. on your website. It is a lot of additional/essential analytic info that Google Analytics does not have. ($99 to $990 per month)

HubSpot is one of the most amazing all-in-one tools I have ever seen in my life. It offers a variety of functions ranging from SEO recommendations and social media management to lead nurturing. ($200 to $1,000 per month)

Marketing.grader.com is a free tool that measures and analyzes all of your marketing efforts and gives you actionable advice on how to improve.

Mongoose Metrics is the authority for exposing what happens before, during, and after phone calls from your website down to the keyword level. (Priced from $100 per month)

HootSuite lets you publish updates, track activity, and analyze results across multiple social networks including Twitter and Facebook. (Free, $9.99 per month, and enterprise-level pricing upon request)

WordPress is a free and open source blogging tool and a content management system (CMS) based on PHP and MySQL. It is simply the best. So many people use it that the add-ons/plug-ins, like **Yoast's SEO** plug-in, make it a must-have.

Bitly.com offers URL shortening/redirection service with real-time link tracking. Essential for Twitter, etc. (Free URL shortening, enterprise pricing starts at $995 per month)

Basecamp is project management software used to increase productivity and collaboration. It is a great way to make sure all your marketing information gets backed up from your team's computers. ($20 to $150 per month)

What tools do you use now?

What new tools would you consider?

What is your monthly budget for tools?

If you are not aware of the many tool costs that you could incur, look into this more deeply before planning next year's Internet marketing budget.

If you're not into tools, you're just not with it. With Internet marketing, there is way too much to do and track to handle it all manually. No Internet marketing strategy would be complete without the creation and maintenance of a healthy toolbox.

NEXT STEPS

Always keep an active list of tasks and next steps that have been discussed and let the list build over time. Since so many of the tasks we undertake have multiple steps and roadblocks in the way, it is important to maintain a list of immediate goals and goals that can wait. Set deadlines for each task and assign each task to just one person so there is ownership. Map each task and micro-task in a tool like Basecamp, Evernote, or getdonedone.com. You will never succeed with Internet marketing if you don't step up your organizational skills. (High-test coffee, ginseng tea, and punching bags are also in many web marketers' toolboxes.) Make sure you are mentally prepared and even psyched up for the journey, because it's not uncommon for the fruits of your hard work to result in mind-blowing profits.

Just be absolutely certain you are working on *all* cylinders, not just one or two.

Compare your results to other companies' using tools like marketing.grader.com. If you are beating your competitors, congratulations! If you aren't, it's time to get busy.

Chapter 3

SEO Essentials for Website Design

One of the most important purposes of this book is to help you understand that your website absolutely must be planned out in minute detail, before you design and build it, from a content, SEO, PR, conversion, and social media perspective.

If you don't create keyword-rich URLs and file names, properly categorize your content in a way that Google understands, have a place for calls to action, or use social media integration and resource areas like a blog and a newsroom, you will find that adding these things will be a lot harder to address after the website is built. Your website simply won't rank well if you don't take these essential steps and it just isn't efficient to try and add them later when the website structure is already built. I have seen dozens and dozens of sites over the years that look like Frankenstein because the novice web person or even supposedly high-end agency that built the site didn't understand the essentials of SEO-friendly web design or conversion optimization. Then when they tried to correct the issues after the fact, they ended up making an absolute mess.

Building a truly efficient website is like building a skyscraper. You just can't do it without architects, and your typical web designers, programmers, and ad agencies generally don't have many of these technical SEO and advanced internet marketing skills, no matter how good they are at other forms of marketing.

Domain Name Strategy

SEO-friendly website design begins with your domain name, or URL. This is at the foundation of all websites. No website design strategy would be complete without some understanding of domain names and hosting, so here are the basics. Whether you are building a new site or working on an existing one, domain name issues can radically affect your results. Domain names are like real estate, but better. The amazing thing about domain names is that in 1995 you could lease/own names for $35 that are now worth millions. How many houses can you say that about? Business.com sold for $7.5 million ten years ago and then sold along with the entire business for $360 million!

You must remember that the name you select can affect your rankings and the eventual value of not only your site but your business. Sometimes keywords in a name can help if added in a subtle way because Google picks up on the fact that your relevant keywords are in the name and uses them to position you higher. Exact match domains (EMDs) were very popular among black hats, however, who used them obsessively to game the results, so in 2012 Google lessened the positive impact they have. Now they still help but are one very small factor. If your site is weak, an EMD will do almost nothing to help it. Keywords in the domain name can also hurt if you use too many or use multiple hyphens and end up with spammy sounding names like www.securities-lawyer-stocks-bonds-chicago-illinois.com.

The equity you create in your domain name builds up award points as you market the domain name because Google is watching (over stretches of time) how people link to and mention your domain and brand name online. The search engines look at the history of your URL and so there is more to a name than meets the untrained eye. That is why you don't simply toss an old name without using a 301 redirect (this tells Google you own the old domain and its pages with all their links and brand mentions) to send the "award points" to the new name that you have selected. I have discovered dozens of times that our clients changed their names and never did a 301 redirect and when we looked at the domain authority and Google Page Rank of the old domain found that it still had some value. In some cases we got really lucky and a single 301 redirect from a carelessly dis- carded domain name skyrocketed the new sites' rankings due to the imparted trust and authority. Do you see now why/how domain names can build up so much value?

You will find that most domain names—and I mean most—are already taken unless you go to an aftermarket site like Buydomains.com, where basic names start around $2,000–$4,000.

There are now many options for domain registration, including standard sites for names that are actively available and aftermarket sites where you can buy pre-owned domains in an auction-style format. I prefer the smaller domain name registrars and have issues with some of the top sites, primarily that while the top sites have good deals, they try to sell you everything under the sun. The hosting that comes with a domain name registrar like Alldo- mains.com or Godadddy.com is not always the best or most flexible choice.

Standard sites	Aftermarket domain sites
Register.com	Buydomains.com
Network Solutions	Afternic.com
eNom.com	Sedo.com
Namecheap.com	Flippa.com (You can buy whole sites and domains with content)

When possible, consider a domain name that includes keywords that people search for, but do not pick a name based solely on this.

Most of the top sites online have short names like eBay, Amazon, Google, Twitter, and Facebook, so when a good, keyword-rich name is not available, simply match your name to your brand. Err on the side of what users will like and share more.

Don't buy dozens of domains thinking that will help your rankings. It will only help if you have real sites on each domain with unique content or if each domain gets a lot of type-in/direct traffic (meaning people type in the exact URL instead of searching for a name or term). Multiple domains also require advanced search marketing contracts for *each* site versus getting lots of links to, upkeep on, and marketing for just one site, so be aware of the issues and effort that come with having multiple sites before going that route. Microsites for a niche part of your business can be great for conversions, but be sure you are ready to truly manage and promote that site or it will just be a distraction and dilute your marketing efforts and dollars. If you buy many domains and don't put a unique site on each but want them to forward to your main domain, use an IP funnel (a way to point multiple domains without being penalized) to direct all the names down to one domain and then point that with a 301 redirect to the main domain. This will ensure Google does not think you are trying to make a big network of bogus sites just to inflate your rankings. (See the glossary at the back of the book for more information on the various technical terms.)

Good domains are worth money because of their potential for branding, the amount of potential type-in traffic they can bring you, the hard-earned links they have pointing at them, and their keyword-rich content, which helps your ranking, so care for them like the valuable pieces of real estate they are.

Hosting Basics

Once you have your domain name in place, you will need to point it to the server (website host) where your files are stored. Make sure you have a good hosting company or your search rankings will suffer. Google keeps ratcheting up the part of the algorithm that penalizes you for a slow-loading site. This is partially because so many people are on mobile, which is at times as slow as dial-up Internet service in the 1990s. Google also checks to see what other sites are in your same IP block or "neighborhood," and if you sit next to a porn or gambling site, you get negative points. Use tools to check how clean your "neighborhood" is, and check on the speed of your server. Pingdom is a nice tool for site speed/uptime analysis, and *W3 Total Cache is a nice WordPress plug-in for reducing load times.* Don't assume the cheapest hosting is the best! (Cheap is no good if your website is down—and customers can't reach you—because your hosting company's servers keep crashing.)

Key Hosting Considerations

- Cheap hosting may not allow some things, like 301 redirects, which are essential.

- Cheap hosting may mean that you have a virtual IP address, which may make it look to Google like you are part of the network of sites in your IP range. If you aren't sure who is hosted near you on the server, check it out. It is best to have no porn, spam, or gambling sites near you.

- Load time and up time (how fast your site loads and how consistently it is live) are important to Google.

- If you want to rank well in the USA, host in the USA. Consider a second site in a country where your main site does not rank well, possibly using a country-specific domain.

Domain-Branded Email Addresses

Configuring email is often part of buying a domain and getting hosting. Make sure you always use a domain-branded email like "firstname@mywebsite.com," not a generic address like "susy@gmail.com." It instills more confidence in your site and brand when you have proper email addresses.

Content Architecture Is the Cornerstone of a Quality Website

There are plenty of popular websites that look bad or aren't visually entertaining, but very few cool-looking sites with poor content ever get recognized by visitors or the search engines. No website design project is well thought out if you are merely focused on design and expect to do your search engine work and content development later down the road.

Website content—including white papers, articles, FAQs, and tips—plays a psychological role in converting visitors into customers. Overall, website size matters to Google as well. If you go to Google.com and search on the term "site:bankrate.com" you will see a site with over 500,000 pages indexed. Do the same search on any local competitor that offers mortgages and you will likely see no more than 200 pages indexed. When vying for top ranks, you can't expect Google to treat you with the same respect they give to sites with large volumes of content unless you have lots of great content of your own! Your site is only as good as its content, and if your content is poor, no amount of magic SEO dust will help you get to the number one spot in the search engine rankings.

Google says that 20% or more of all searches per day every day are brand new...meaning they have never been searched for before! So your opportunities are vast. Each page of your site should be optimized for a couple of keywords and include some of the related keywords you can find via Google Suggest.

There is no better use of your time before putting up your website than taking the time to map out content, phrases per page, deciding where your calls to action will appear on every page, and determining where your critical social icons will go. Do this before you think about the pretty face of your site via design elements like color, fonts, and images.

A blog is a great way to add regular content to get and then keep the attention of the search engines, so think about how a blog button or call to action will be placed in the design before you build your site. Some people even like to feed the latest blog and social content right into a box on the bottom of the home page to get a credibility and thought leader status boost. User-generated content such as blog comments, forum posts, user reviews, and testimonials are all great ways to keep things fresh.

Part of the new rules is that the search engines want to see a combination of valuable new content that includes social commentary like blog comments. Fresh content and social interactions like retweets, shares, and likes that lead to actual links combine to push your marketing beyond the tipping point and can launch you into high gear; static content cannot.

Blogging was the beginning of the social media movement. Blogging allowed people to comment on posts. This changed the landscape of the web forever.

Leverage that. Create blog posts that are engaging, elicit comments and shares time after time, and you will build yourself a search engine magnet.

Make absolutely sure your website architecture is built to the above formula or the usability will suffer and people will hit the "back" button to return to the search results, which could contribute to your rankings going down. Avoid that vicious loop with proper planning and the web gets fun.

Here's a great way to test how your site plays to the crowd: run a usability test with a handful of people who are not a part of your company. This can result in incredible insights, yet few companies perform this simple step. If you want to run a simple usability test, just write down ten tasks that you think should be easy enough to do on your site and ask someone who has never used your site to perform them (such as find and fill out an application form) and comment on how easy or difficult completing those tasks was for them.

Check out usertesting.com for an inexpensive way to run tests. Steve Krug, author of the famous usability book, *Don't Make Me Think*, told me that he recommends people do tests on their site before, during, and after development, not just after it's built. If you can't do live tests in person, use usertesting.com throughout the process and, ideally, at each major iteration.

Design with Search Engines in Mind

We have worked with dozens of companies that say their web designers "know SEO" only to have to give them the bad news that we have to make significant changes to their sites just to get them properly indexed in Google, much less ranking well. Below is a short list of some top issues to consider when designing a web site that's optimized for search engines. Some of these tips may be repeated elsewhere in the book, but they are too important not to share with the programmer *and* the designer. You should always have:

- SEO-friendly programming such as clean URLs (i.e., site.com/keywords-separated-with-hyphens. html) and clean CSS-driven code that loads fast (or you may have to redo it later).

- Important content placed not too far down in the file structure. If you have content at yoursite. com/folder/foldername/another-folder/wow-this-is-too-far-down/name-of-yourpage.html it will be seen as less important. (Bet your programmer didn't tell you that one!)

- Home page HTML text that uses your main general keyphrases and related keywords.

- Headlines that clearly express what the page is about with keywords woven in.

- Scraplines (mini statements similar to a tagline but not connected to your logo) that express benefits and your unique value proposition.

- Calls to action—clearly visible actions you want people to take. Don't design your site before you've mapped these out for each stage of the buying cycle.

- Persona development and content targeted to demographic/persona segments. Make sure you are clear on the types of customers who will come to the site and build content into the design that lets them go down "aisles" made just for them.

- Credibility factors—awards, affiliations, testimonials, etc.

- Scan- and skim-friendly elements like bulleted and numbered lists.

- Useable navigation. If you have to use drop-down menus, use mega drop-down menus; Jacob Nielsen, the godfather of usability, says they are far superior to old-school drop-downs because they often contain images, icons, and/or well-thought-out bars of color to categorize the options. For more information, see useit.com/alertbox/mega-dropdown-menus.html.

- The ability to add more content into the navigation later by having enough high-level concepts in the initial design.

- A reasonable amount of text, even on the home page (ideally 300 to 500+ words when possible, and some SEOs prefer considerably more). If you have to go light on home page text, try to have *at least* one small paragraph with a heading above it, both of which use your main keyword.

Web Marketing On All Cylinders - John McDougall

- Use H1 and H2 tags on your pages to aid the search engines in finding out quickly what each page is about. The <h1> to <h6> tags are used to define HTML headings. <h1> defines the most important heading. <h6> defines the least important heading.

- Text links to other pages (interlinking) using keywords, not simply "read more" or "click here." It is incredibly powerful from an SEO and conversion perspective if you link to subpages on your site from within your own copy. Links that are in the context of paragraphs as opposed to in footers, navigation, and sidebars, etc., are loved by the search engines.

- Implement tracking and reporting (such as Google Analytics and Clicktale.com), even on a site you are about to redo, so you have data on what customers have been doing and what content they like. If a page that is visited often on your site is hard to get to, add better calls to action on it in the new site design. Highlight that page and stop burying it!

Did your web designer ever suggest things like this? If not, it is because they don't focus on these skills and you need more team members. Using analytics as a foundation for understanding what customers are doing on your website is essential, so make sure your analyst is thoroughly trained. The conversion rate and the trackable customer experience truly prove a great design, not what the boss or the designers say based on their opinions.

Here are key things to avoid in SEO-friendly website design:

- Headings and text in graphics: Google can't read these. At the very least, use alt tags on your images, to explain to search engines and disabled visitors what it says, if you are stuck with graphical headings. Make sure you are using great keywords as you describe your images in your alt tags.

- HTML frames: They cause the search engines to index only portions of your content (such as the right column of a page only with no logo or left navigation column).

- All Flash sites: Flash sites do not index nearly as well as HTML sites and are bad for mobile users largely due to Apple not supporting it. Use HTML5 and JQuery instead.

- Dynamic content: Dynamic URLs have long names (and use lots of numbers and special characters like "?" and "%"), which are difficult for the search engines to crawl. That said, today dynamic URLs are easier for search engines to index than back in the 1990s, but the cleaner the URL the better.

- Image maps for navigation: Use text-based navigation, even if just in the sitemap to ensure that crawlers can find your inner pages.

- JavaScript for navigation: This is generally bad. Disable JavaScript in your web browser and then look at your website. If you can't see the site navigation then web crawlers won't see it either. A sitemap or text links in the footer can help offset this, but it is better to use crawl-able navigation.

- The Robots.txt file: This is a file containing instructions for search engine crawlers telling them where they can and can't go. If the web designer accidently blocks the root folder of the website in this file it prevents the crawlers from crawling the entire website. If your Robots.txt file says "Disallow: /" then you are blocking your entire website.

- Duplicate, shallow, or poorly written content: These were the focus of Google's Farmer/Panda algorithm update. Avoid copying even small amounts of other people's content or making multiple versions of your own.

- Doorway or splash pages that load before the main site: Your first page should be rich with text and part of your main site structure.

- Pages you want Google to index that require registration, cookies, or passwords: These can turn the search engine crawlers away.

Too many graphics, too much code, or lots of multimedia above your text: Make sure your important keywords don't get skimmed over because the search engine's spider bailed out before seeing them because the page loaded too slowly.

Avoid Deceptive Tactics

Do not do anything deceptive while optimizing to trick the search engines (e.g., coloring text and background the same to hide lists of keywords) or your site may be seen as SPAM. You need to be aware that once your site has been "red flagged" it can take significant time to recover. Google has even said that some sites will never recover after they get busted for spam or overaggressive link building, so be aware there are tactics that can completely ruin your domain name. Why put yourself into that situation when the likelihood that you will be caught increases daily?

As a rule of thumb, if the pages you create or the changes you make help the user, you should be okay. If pages or changes are designed only to help your search engine ranking, it may be perceived as spam.

Potentially Dangerous, Spammy, or Unethical Practices (Black Hat)

Below is a short list of SEO techniques you must avoid. New ones crop up weekly because "black hats" (unethical SEOs) are making *huge* money, like $100,000 a month or more, and it pays for them to use even criminally deceptive tactics to game Google. However, the search engines are getting smarter all the time, so make sure your website designer doesn't dabble in unsavory SEO tactics and do things that will hurt you.

- Cloaking: Showing the search engine a different page than what you show the user.

- Hidden or invisible text: White text on a white background or in comment sections of the code, etc., will not be visible to the end user of the site.

- Multiple instances of the same tag: Overuse of html tags just for ranking purposes.

- Mirrored/duplicate sites: Submitting identical pages with different URLs.

- Keyphrases in your keywords' meta tags that do not directly relate to the content of your page.

- Automated submission services: Companies that bombard the search engines with submission requests.

- Overuse of keywords: Stuffing way too many instances of a keyphrase or keyword in your text.

- Meta refresh tags: Using meta refresh code to send people automatically to a new page.

- Link farms: Sites that exist only for linking.

Search-Friendly Web Programming and Development

While programmers (who much prefer to be called developers) are often very smart and talented people, don't assume they know anything at all about search engine optimization or marketing in general. I have had senior programmers work for me who, even after a year of being asked to build search engine-friendly sites, still would occasionally do things that made it so Google couldn't even see the content. Most programmers still need regular and detailed guidance from SEO experts, and that's fine. You just need to go into this stage with eyes wide open.

Programmers often require significant rounds of explanation to make the correct adjustments. It's critical to conduct regular site reviews to make sure optimization not only happens but does not get deleted. If you can find a developer who works well with SEOs, has some understanding of SEO, and is humble and eager enough to take advice, do anything you can to keep that person around.

We also frequently uncover code issues that are not always easy to detect immediately. These include hidden frames, iframes, and invisible text generated by previous unethical SEO techniques. For example, we have seen such things as 1-pixel gif links littered throughout a client's website code, linking to their old SEO company's gambling sites. Have someone look at your code for possible fraud if you're not entirely comfortable with your programmer.

Search-Friendly Site Architecture

One of the first things we do when a client says they want to build a website is keyword research. Making the site's file names and categories coincide with keyphrases and concepts ensures that users can easily find your key topics and that the search engines see groups of content in each area. Doing development before you work out these concepts is a poor strategic move.

Tip: One of the best ways to help yourself here is to go to the free Google External Keyword tool and type in your main keyword.

Let's say it's "golf clubs" because you run a golf equipment business.

This Google Keyword tool was created to show you the incredible list of variations on your main keyword that are being searched for on a monthly basis in the US and all around the world. This is where you start to become smarter than any of your competitors...because while everyone is attempting to compete for "golf clubs," you've read this book and you know that it is far smarter to go after many different variations of that keyword than to try to rank just for that one highly competitive keyword. For a client, we ranked #3 in Google years ago for "golf clubs," and it took us years and a wide array of tactics to hit that point. Along the way, the huge variety of long tail terms is where the traffic and sales came from.

Your goal is to walk away from this stage with one or two great keywords for each one of the website pages that you are about to build. Then you can make what we call a "phrases per page map" of the main site pages you are creating. For your blog, you will create a spreadsheet of pre-researched terms to use in titles and URLs before you do any writing.

Let's compare a typical sitemap concept to a search engine-friendly sitemap. Here's what a typical sitemap looks like:

- Home

- About

- Products (all products simply listed on this page)

- Services (all services simply listed on this page)

- Contact

Notice that with a search engine-friendly sitemap concept, there's another level of detail:

- Home

- About

- Widget Products

   1. Red Widgets (Separate pages with URLs named accordingly)
   2. Blue Widgets
   3. Green Widgets

- Widget Services

   1. Widget Service A
   2. Widget Service B
   3. Widget Service C

- Contact

A site has to be more about themes than just targeted keyword phrases. Like the chapters in a book, a silo (categorization of content in folders/multiple URLs) represents a group of themed content on your site. Much like in a dissertation, you need a title, abstract, table of contents, and content mapped out to reinforce the overall theme, including references and footnotes.

A silo might look something like this:

widgets.com/red/fuzzy-red.html
widgets.com/red/sorta-red.html
widgets.com/red/really-red.html
widgets.com/red/wicked-red.html
widgets.com/red/ultra-red.html

In addition to the silo folder names, make sure that each of the subpages (such as "ultra-red.hmtl") links back up to the main "/red/red.html" page, which further tells Google it is the main red page that is the "parent" of the silo.

Silos are great and highly recommended, in addition to keeping URLs fairly simple. Do your silo folders but don't go overboard. In a search for "discount nike golf shoes," the following URLs show up as the first ten sites in ranking order, illustrating how Google prefers the sites with a cleaner architecture and content closer to the root URL (fewer subfolders and less gobbledygook in the domains):

site1.com.com/nike-golfclub1.html
site2.com.com/nikegolfshoes.php
site3.com/nike-golf-shoes-c138m61

site4.com/nike-golf-shoes

site5.com/sale/nike/c_b-16.aspx2006-2012

site6.com (just the homepage)

site7.com/shop/Product_Type-Shoes

site8.com /Nike-Womens-Summer-Lite-Golf/dp/B0041MY76G

site9.com/customer/category/product.jsp/SUBCATEGORY_ID/16743/refScid/155

site10.com/nike-lunar-control-white-golf-shoes.html

While there are a fair amount of cases where the number one search result has a long URL with many numbers and special characters, why not make it easier on Google with simpler, keyword-rich URLs and do as many things right as you can? SEO is won by lots of small things adding up to excellence.

For non-e-commerce sites, consider URLs that work like this:

/investment-consulting.htm (A page right off the root URL)

/investment-advisory-services (A folder right off the root URL)

/services/investment (A folder [part of what makes a silo] right of the root URL first and a page inside that. The index page for this folder gets indexed and does not display the name of the page itself but does at least get the folder name included.)

/services/investment-consulting.html (A folder right off the root URL with a page that gets listed using keywords instead of just an index page right after the folder. I prefer this.)

All of these should index and rank well. Go too many folders deep in terms of site structure and the content gets less important in the eyes of Google.

Avoid this type of thing: (Unintelligible URLs)

serv5463543/folder4/personal/wealthmgt/invsmntconsulting/Pages/home.aspx

We'll cover much more about this in Chapter 4, but make sure if you skip over that level of technical detail that you share at least this essential information with your designers and developers. By doing this from the start you will be integrating the design and development phase fully with the marketing phase and saving yourself endless heartache and wasted money.

Site Technical Issues

Once you have your content organized into key phrase groupings, you will be faced with a large number of technical issues that will either make or break how well your site will rank.

Search-Friendly Content Management Systems (CMS)

Timeliness of information is critical to any website. Information can be published instantly and updated immediately, but surprisingly, a fair number of companies still rely on a designated "webmaster" to make all edits and updates. That is a huge miss.

A simple, powerful content management system allows your marketing team, with limited technical know-how, to update the main elements of a website such as text and photos. Unfortunately, many CMS systems use a database that produces URLs that the search engines can't crawl. If the search engines can't see your pages as *unique pages*, you are in big trouble if your goal is to rank highly in the search engines. Even when the search engines can see many CMS pages, most page names will have special characters such as ?ID=Etc. This is bad. Make sure that if you are building a CMS, that the URLs will be clean and keyword-rich, like Yoursite.com/jobs/mechanical-design-jobs.aspx.

Always remember that if free traffic from the search engines is the goal, then your sole focus is to make the search engines love you and all of your updates.

Here is another one to give your web design/development company:

Also make sure that the CMS allows you control over title and meta tags separately from each other. We have seen horrible content management systems that even force the heading, URL, and title tags to all be the exact same. That means you lose the ability to tweak the title tag, which is very important and not very visible to the user, with a bit more keyword specificity than the heading tag.

Here is how a page with good silo-ing/URL architecture, a proper title tag, and a keyword-rich heading might look:

URL: financialadvisors.com/services/investment-consultants.htm

Title tag: Investment consultants MA | Your brand name (appears in code and often in search result pages and at the top of the browser. Go for keywords first and brand second.)

Headline on the page: Award-winning investment consultants

If you can change each of these elements separately, you can experiment with variations. Sometimes you might want the headline to include "Investment Consultants MA" and other times, perhaps if your focus is more on international business, you might only want to use the title tag as a way to boost local ranking but not be so intensely local at the visible content level. Make sure your CMS allows these options.

Search-Friendly Shopping Carts

You've heard the old saying that in retail, there are three things that are critical for success: Location, location, location! The same is true of e-commerce. If you're selling products or services via the web, your customers have to find you quickly and easily.

Shopping carts, like content management systems, benefit from keyphrases in the URLs and proper site architecture.

The following SEO benefits should be built in:

- Keywords in the URL

- Categories pages with keywords in URLs

- Subcategories pages with keywords in URLs

- Product detail pages with keywords in URLs

- CSS-based navigation so that keywords are in the links to pages

More helpful tips:

- Use an HTML and XML sitemap to increase crawl-ability

- Add manufacturer/brand pages with original content

- Create blog posts and resources to support and link to the product pages using keywords

Make sure you don't simply take the manufacturer's descriptions as your category and product description text. This is your opportunity to get your keywords out there via your uniquely written text. Don't forget that if the search engines find that your copy is an exact match of what the manufacturer or another reseller has published, that is not good.

Nothing is worse than going through all the effort to have your category and product pages get indexed and then to be totally discounted, due to a lack of original content. If you can't spend the effort to write original content (and you can), you will need to focus on paid search, since your SEO won't likely work.

Sorry for the bad news, but Google has put the nail in the coffin of people who use duplicate content. If your site doesn't add unique value, it won't have secure rankings no matter how well-designed or well-coded it is. (The SEO chapter goes into more detail on this and gives specific suggestions for e-commerce and duplicate content issues.

What Is Great Web Design?

The best sites look clean and professional but ultimately support the users getting to the information *they* want.

One example of this concept in action is bhphoto.com. Instead of adding individual products to the home page, they made categories of products with images such as flat-screen TVs and cell phones next to the headings. They did this because they know the likelihood of users being interested in the handful of featured products you select for the home page is far less than them simply wanting to navigate immediately off the home page to the topic they are interested in. So design is about getting into your customer's head and getting them where they want to go, as quickly as possible. If your sales push is in their way, it may actually hurt you.

Websites can no longer be designed in isolation from all the factors we've covered in this chapter. Integrate SEO, conversion, and social concepts before you start designing and you won't have to redo things significantly later. Always be ready to adjust/test on a monthly basis, so the design and content grow with what your users are looking for. A website is never "finished" but is a growing, changing organism that needs to be consistently fed, tested, and nurtured in order for it to produce consistent results.

By letting users tell you what to change based on which pages they hate the most (where you see high bounce rates) versus which pages they interact with the most (time on site and sales are highest here) your website design and development get smarter day after day.

Chapter 4

Search Engine Optimization (SEO) Implementation

What Is Search Engine Optimization? Search engine optimization, also known as SEO, is a set of techniques and tactics designed to increase the amount of visitors to a website by obtaining a high-ranking placement in the search engine results page (SERP) of search engines like Google, Bing, Yahoo, and others (see Figure 1). Tactics include using keywords in web page content, link building, social media optimization, and writing content that engages customers and helps search engines "value" your site. Some people engage in "black hat" SEO, using unethical tactics to get their sites to rank high in the search engine results, even at the risk of getting those sites banned or penalized.

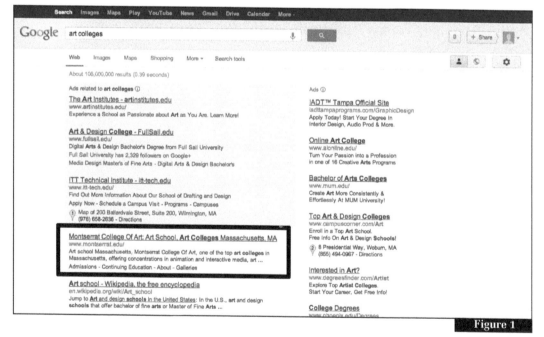

Figure 1

What Is the Value of SEO?

The majority of web traffic is driven by search engines. While social media and other marketing techniques online and offline can generate visits to your website, search engines are the main way people find the sites they want to visit and how they navigate the web. This makes SEO simply indispensable for business success. If people can't find you or don't find what they are looking for once they are at your site, they won't buy from you.

High ROI for the Long Term

SEO has great long-term return on investment (ROI) since the adjustments to your website and corresponding natural/organic "free" ranks are typically cheaper than paid ads and can last for years. The moment you stop a paid ad campaign online, it is back down to zero traffic as there is no residual effect from paid banner or text link ads.

24 hours a day, 7 days a week, 365 days every year. That's how hard your SEO efforts can work for you.

It's really like having an incredible sales force out there driving visitors, leads, and sales continuously while you sleep.

Active Searchers versus Forcing People to View Your Ads

When people go to the search engines, they are looking for you (or what you have), instead of you pushing yourself on them through paid ads.

Credibility

The organic ranks are like the articles in a magazine, whereas the paid ads are more like the print advertisements. So, just as in public relations, you are considered more of an authority if you have high organic ranks, versus paid listings only.

How Profitable Is It?

The ROI is different for every industry. Lawyers can make a million-dollar profit from a single click, where many of our e-commerce clients are working on tight margins and have to add up many pennies/dollars to track success.

Here are some ideas to get you thinking about ROI. Based on leaked AOL data from 2006, the number one position on a given Google page gets about 42% of the traffic and the number two position gets about 12%. A number one spot is said to be worth 8.5 times what a number five spot is worth (with 4.92% of the traffic).

A newer Slingshot SEO study revealed the following click-through rates for each position in the search engine results pages:

Number 1: 18.2%

Number 2: 10.05%

Number 3: 7.2%

Number 4: 4.8%

Number 5: 3.1%

While this is not an exact science and expert opinions vary on the specifics because the search engines won't reveal facts, you can use this type of data to extrapolate what you will get for each keyword in terms of ROI.

Let's just say you rank number one for "cheap golf clubs" and you get 2,000 visitors per month from that. With a 2% conversion rate, you can close about 40 deals.

If you make $35 gross on average per order, that number one rank is worth $1,400 per month ($16,800 gross profit per year) from that one keyword. If you figure that 50% of your customers will buy more than once, you can add another $35 x 20 or $700 from those customers. Not to mention these new customers are now on your email list and may be encouraged to buy from you year after year. Unlike the paid ads, these ranks may continue to stay reasonably well-placed for a time, even if you stop doing aggressive SEO. So calculating the value of search must be looked at over the long term.

In addition, if you are not factoring in the number of people who call or come to your store versus use an online shopping cart or submit a form, you may be leaving out ROI from offline conversions. And if you are not tracking (in your website analytics) when people come from other sources, if they originally found you from SEO, you are not giving full credit to organic search. When all things are factored in, the marketing world agrees that SEO is a tremendously strong channel and capable of generating millions of dollars in revenue.

If you had to buy the same "cheap golf clubs" keyword in Google, it could cost several dollars or even $10 or more per click. Some terms, like "mesothelioma lawyers," are as high as $220 per click! Let's say "cheap golf clubs" was a reasonable $3 per click. If you get 2,000 clicks through organic search, that's a savings of $6,000 per month ($3 x 2,000 clicks) because you didn't pay for ads. So make sure to add in the value of costs averted.

Forrester Research says that even by 2016, the foundational spending of online marketing will still be weighted toward SEO and paid search. Social media and other strategies are picking up speed—partly due to the fact that social media now helps your organic ranks, even if mostly indirectly. However, it is a fact that the highest percent of the money spent on online advertising goes to search engine marketing. Interestingly, Google watches to see if around 20% of your traffic comes from referral sources like social media sites and from quality links, so, once again, the interconnectedness is a key element in a successful strategy.

Google Rankings Can Make or Break a Business

- Matt Cutts of Google is quoted on Search Engine Land as saying: "Google has had sight of 30 trillion URLs." He adds, "Google crawls 20 billion pages a day" and "100 billion searches are conducted per month" on Google.

- According to a press release from Google itself, the percentage of local searches is about 20%. That equates to roughly 2.187 billion local searches per month.

- Each month, over 800 million unique users visit YouTube (which Google owns) and watch over 4 billion hours of video. Considering YouTube is the second-largest search engine in the world after Google, it is essential that you get on board.

- Despite mixed reviews, Google+ is now growing at the same pace as Facebook when it was similarly sized. Google+ and Author Rank can increase your search rankings, so their social media and trust monitoring can't be ignored.

Since Google dominates about 70% of search traffic, you must perform well in Google to get any serious business from search.

Yes, the 35% of searches that Google doesn't control is still a huge amount of searches and can't be ignored. But you should shoot to rank well in Google and then expect to generally do well in the other engines.

Google Doesn't Hate SEO

The goal of SEO is to make websites more relevant with more defined content and terminology, more crawlable by the search engines' "robots," and faster. Google likes that. If you go overboard buying links, doing comment spam links or keyword stuffing, then you get into trouble. So it is not that SEO is bad, it is the spammers that give it a negative connotation at times.

SEO Is Not for Dabblers

SEO is not rocket science, but it is complex and is growing more difficult every day. While

Web Marketing On All Cylinders - John McDougall

it may be tempting to dabble in it on your own or with an intern or low-end SEO company, keep in mind there are people fiercely battling against you who have computer science degrees and no morals. Look up "black hat SEO" and be prepared to see just what people are willing to do to get their pages seen and clicked. These people stay up all night generating thousands of backlinks and paying people overseas to write thousands of pages of content and then optimizing that content with every method imaginable.

This is precisely why social media has become such a profound influence in the eyes of the search engines. They want to see real people sharing your content, not just the content itself!

SEO Today

In 2012 there were explosive changes in the way the search engines "ranked" sites and it is more critical than ever for you to have a road map of where you are headed long before you step into SEO.

Google's algorithm has hundreds of factors, some of which we will explore later. Keep in mind that this book is not a complete SEO manual but an overview of what we consider essential.

Looking at SEO and Internet marketing from a 30,000-foot view, you need to understand the following key factors:

5 Key Factors That Drive Search Engine Rankings

1. Content

2. Links

3. Social media citations and influence (even if just an indirect factor, largely from links generated or for separate social search results)

4. The quality of your authors (content writers) and potentially in the future, their Author Rank, which may be influenced by things such as Twitter authority

5. Referrals/engagement vs. high bounce rates (even if an indirect relationship to rankings)

In this chapter we will break down each of these in terms of how to understand what you need to do to succeed from a high level. For much deeper descriptions of what to do, read the content marketing, link building, social media, and analytics chapters.

10 Essential Steps to Truly Embrace the SEO Process

1. Initial site and target audience analysis

2. Initial snapshot of website status and comparison to competitors. This includes:

   - Competitive content analysis
   - Link building
   - Social media citations and influence (as these at the very least illustrate how much people value any given piece of content)
   - The quality and authority of your authors' referrals/engagement vs. high bounce rates

3. Measure success (only possible if you know where you started)

4. Keyphrase research

5. URL architecture and phrases per page map

6. "On-page" optimization basics

7. Mid-level technical SEO

8. Review the hundreds of factors in the total algorithm

9. Understand the top reasons SEO campaigns fail

10. Build links using analytics and social media marketing (see advanced details in the corresponding chapters)

Let's go through these ten steps one by one.

Initial Site and Target Audience Analysis

Document who you will be targeting, so that your key-phrase research and content will appeal to and be specific to multiple personas. Provide as much data and reasoning as possible to support your choices.

What sites are meeting your target audience's specific needs in search results? What can you do to make your site superior so it will steal traffic from competitors?

The more you think like a writer, the more you will engage customers and win, according to the new rules of Google. The acronym (AUDIENCE) is a nice guide if you answer the following questions.

Web Marketing On All Cylinders - John McDougall

Analysis - Who is the website's audience?

Understanding - How knowledgeable is the audience on the subject?

Demographics - What is their age, gender, educational background, etc.?

Interest - Why are they coming to your site?

Environment - Where will the site be viewed? (On a desktop computer or a mobile device?)

Needs - What are the audience's needs associated with your topic?

Customization - What specific needs/interests should you address relating to your specific audience?

Expectations - What does the audience expect to learn from your site? Visitors should have many of their questions answered by your site. This not only helps drive them to your site via questions they ask the search engines, but will also help them feel that you are worth contacting or buying from.

Share of Voice

Share of voice is a traditional marketing term, used to describe a brand's or product's share of the available market or inventory. Public relations people used to measure it based on the number of column inches taken up in publications where they placed their clients and then calculated what that share would have cost if they had had to pay for ads instead of being mentioned for free in articles or TV interviews.

In the Internet search world, you must understand where your competitors rank for the keyword groups that matter.

Identifying where you and your competitors show up across images, videos, social, local, and mobile also helps you determine how much work you have ahead of you and decide where to invest your time.

Is any company dominating the rankings in your niche? Which keywords are they strong for and where are they weak?

If you want to take this to a deeper level, you can run ranking reports on hundreds of the main keywords in your space and then also run the same reports on your competitors to get a glimpse of how well you do compared to them. HubSpot and Brightedge can help automate this and new tools are appearing all the time.

Besides the most famous Compete.com, a very interesting tool for estimating search traffic for you and your competitors is SEMrush. It gives you click volume and click value estimates side by side. While it is not 100% accurate, it is fascinating to see what it thinks your site's and your competitors' sites' organic traffic is worth based on the AdWords cost-per-click estimates. SEMrush can also help you spot valuable up-and-coming keywords where you might not yet get much traffic because you rank on the second or third page of the search results, and it can help you see what terms a competitor might be about to do well on.

Knowing where you fit into the mix of who is getting traffic and why your competitors are doing well is a very significant part of SEO.

Initial Snapshot of Website Status

You need to determine the existing status of a website in the search engines before your Internet marketing campaign commences so you can determine what level of effort is needed. Knowing where you are right now also lets you look back later at how far you have come. The following are some of the key things to research for your snapshot:

Content

The amount and quality of your content is hugely influential on your rank in the search engines. Text is a primary part of the algorithm and cannot be ignored. Text is an indication to the engines whether you are an authority or not. The better the content, the easier it will be to get people to link to you and connect with you in social channels, making content perhaps the most critical aspect of internet marketing.

Number of Indexed Pages

Go to Google and do a search, but instead of using a keyphrase, type in: "site:yoursite.com" as a search. The results will show you how many pages Google knows you have on your website. It will look something like this: *Results 1–10 of about 138 from yoursite.com."*

You should also check the size of your site in Yahoo! and MSN as they often index your content differently than Google. Many times the numbers will vary because one site can't see your content as well as another based on such factors as too much dynamic content or a poor site structure, etc.

The point is that you want a "snapshot" of where you are in the eyes of the search engines and you want to see that ranking climbing weekly, if not daily. Record these details as benchmarks in your strategy document (the one you prepared back in Chapter 2) so you can look back later and see how far you have come.

Competitive Content Analysis

You need to compare yourself to top-ranked sites or you won't realize what you are up against. While your direct competitors need to be researched, you also have to look at the people ranking highly for the terms you want to rank for. For example, a local business that wants to rank for a term like "Amesbury MA Apartments" can't just look at the other apartment complexes in the area when doing competitive research.

The sites that come up in a search for "Amesbury MA Apartments" are mostly large directory sites. So ranking high for this term is not as easy as it might initially seem. The good news is that one of these sites, amesburybritish.com, is only 17 pages and it "only" has 104 backlinks. In other words, this is one site that Google might bump down in favor of your site if you can establish more pages and backlinks, among other things. Reviewing the top-ranked sites is essential because they are truly standing in your way, whether or not they appear to be direct local competitors. Remember, the top three spots on that Google page produce up to 70% of all the clicks, so you have your work cut out for you with this particular keyword.

> "Amesbury MA Apartments" Search results from Google
>
> www.realestate.yahoo.com/Massachusetts/Amesbury/apartments-for-rent
>
> www.rent.com/rentals/massachusetts/...and.../amesbury/results
>
> www.apartmentratings.com/rate/MA-Amesbury.html
>
> www.local.yahoo.com/MA/Amesbury/Real+Estate/Apartments
>
> www.move.com/apartments/amesbury_massachusetts
>
> www.amesburybritish.com
>
> www.mynewplace.com/.../amesbury-apartments-for-rent-massachusetts
>
> www.rentometer.com/us/massachusetts/amesbury/index.html
>
> www.forrent.com/search-apartments.../MA/.../Amesbury.php
>
> www.rentals.com/Massachusetts/Boston/Amesbury/ - Cached - Similar

There is much to gain by doing competitive research. Here are some more elements to check. (Since this book is not intended to be an exhaustive technical manual, please check our blog at mcdougallinteractive.com/blog as we often post how to's on some of these more complex tactics.)

- Competitor ranking analysis on the same terms you used in your initial ranking report

- Competitor PR (PageRank) analysis

- Competitor site SEO levels analysis (Are they heavily optimized?)

- Competitor site social media content sharing analysis

- Competitor keywords in their site, title, and meta tags

- Competitor keywords that they are using in paid search campaigns

- Competitor paid ad copy

- Competitor content and content architecture/URLs

Using Google AdWords Keyword Tool to "Spy" on Competitors' Keywords

The Google AdWords Suggestion Tool is great for checking out what keywords to use, but try this as well: instead of adding a keyword to access keyword data, use the second option, which allows you to add a website page or domain URL to extract related keywords from the page or site. Use it on your own site or a competitor's to get useful information on where they rank and for which keywords and how much the competition is "working" each term. Then download the results into an Excel spreadsheet for analysis.

It's almost always startling to uncover how your competitors are using keywords to draw visitors. There's no reason why you can't benefit from their hard work, "borrow" those keywords, and then outrank them!

Make sure to do keyword research based on what your audience wants, not solely on what content the site already has. Here are ways to determine what your audience is interested in:

- Conduct surveys of your audience by putting surveys on your site.

- Conduct focus groups and/or use social media listening software to determine what content would be valuable to your audience and then build your SEO efforts around that.

Use the content analysis technique in the content development chapter (Chapter 8) to really get a great sense of what categories of content your competitors have and how much and how often they add to it.

Link Popularity

The more popular your site (largely judged by backlinks), the higher your search engine ranking. I'll go into this in more detail later, but for now you need to be aware that this is part of the optimization process.

Even links from a local chamber of commerce site or a partner you work with in your industry are worth pursuing to some degree. Just remember that the best "in pointing" links will come from those sites that are most relevant to your business niche and right behind that are those sites that Google just loves in general (like .edu and .gov sites). But before you start link building, you need to know your existing link profile.

The point is that the more authority or highly trusted links you have pointing not just to your home page but to all of the pages on your site, the far better your long-term SEO results.

Google doesn't provide the best information on this, possibly because the heart of their secret algorithm is built around this concept, so we use a number of tools such as opensite-explorer.org (from SEOMoz) and majesticseo.com.

Look at how many unique websites link to you (root domains in SEOMoz) versus how many total links. Since one site can link to you thousands of times from the footer at the bottom of the site, don't get over-excited about numerous links from one site. It isn't a bad thing if a site keeps mentioning and linking to you from relevant content, but don't fake it by trying to get many links from one domain.

If your competitors have many more high-quality links with high domain authority than you, then you need to get links comparable to theirs.

While some experts go so far as to say social links may out-do traditional links in a couple years, it may also take ten years for that to happen if at all. However, no SEO plan is complete without a strategy for link building and social links/brand citations/PR. Read all three of those chapters (Chapters 5, 6, and 7) for a complete picture of link building, post-Penguin (the Google search algorithm update).

Social Media Interaction

Social media marketing at the very least has an indirect impact on search engine rankings, and search engines are grappling with how to use social indicators to determine quality sites. Future search engine algorithms might put a premium on how your content spreads over the web on Google+, Pinterest, Twitter, Facebook, and many of the other social media platforms.

Currently likes, follows, shares, comments, and retweets all help spread your content and make people more likely to link to it, so using social as a part of link building is essential.

Social Media Citations

One key element to review when doing competitive analysis is how much social media activity you are doing/getting as compared to competitors that rank well.

Review Facebook, Twitter, LinkedIn, Google+, YouTube, Pinterest, and more. Tools like Sprout Social, HootSuite, or the $600-a-month Radian6 can help streamline your efforts.

Check out the following types of data for both your site and those of competitors, by hand or with one of the above-mentioned tools:

- Number of fans/followers

- Posting frequency and perceived quality

- Types of content (images, video, blog posts, cartoons, surveys, etc.)

- How much original content versus content grabbed off the web to share?

- How engaged are fans?

- Video views, channel views, and subscribers on YouTube

- Author Rank status of competitors' Authors (search for Authors' names in Google and get a feel for where they are posting)

If you don't have as much social media activity as your competitors it hurts your overall content sharing and engagement levels.

Can you correlate your competition's social media activity with their search rank performance? If your competitors do lots of social media and rank well, then you should ramp up your own social media activity, especially in relation to particular keywords you are targeting. While you may not be able to prove social media optimization is playing a part in their ranks, if they do it and you don't, you are losing potential ranking points.

Author Rank and the Reputation of Your Authors

The search engine algorithms are moving away from valuing your website and towards valuing your authors (meaning the people who write your web and blog pages). Not only do

Web Marketing On All Cylinders - John McDougall

you need content but you need authors who have high value. See the social media chapter (Chapter 7) for more details, but be aware this is an important new factor.

Mike Arnesen, Senior SEO Analyst of SEOMoz, says that some of the factors used in calculating Author Rank (Google's method of rating authors) are:

- PageRank of the author's content

- Number of comments on each post

- Google+ shares of author's content

- Number of Google+ circles the author is in

- Social media followers (e.g., Twitter, Facebook, and StumbleUpon)

- Connections with other high Author Rank authors

Here are a few tips for improving your own and your other authors' Author Rank and potentially your SEO as Google figures out how to use these signals directly:

- Connect with other quality bloggers and influencers

- Use Twitter, Facebook, LinkedIn, and Google+ to network

- Create great content and share it

- Start using Google+ more

- Get in the circles of quality bloggers and influencers

- Guest blog post on high-authority sites

- Leave helpful comments on high-authority sites

Measuring Success

Referrals/Engagement versus High Bounce Rates

Google is said to like to see at least 20% of your traffic coming from referrals or links that people click to get to your site. If your links and social activity are not driving real traffic that engages with your site in a meaningful way, then from Google's perspective, you must have gamed it and are a spammer. Making sure your content is not just for SEO but keeps people clicking and engaging is now a critical part of SEO. The days of building weak pages just for the search engines have come and gone.

The only way to be sure you are increasing engagement is through analytics. At the very least, look for pages or whole categories of content on your site that have weak engagement and either delete them or make them better. Then monitor the results in analytics at least monthly to make sure all of your content is of good quality and gets visited and engaged with.

Google Analytics Preliminary Snapshot of Visitor Behavior

Make sure you have your website analytics set up properly so as the months go by, data is being stored that you can analyze. Make sure you have a program at least as powerful as Google Analytics. Sign up for a Google Analytics account, get the code snippet, and have your web person place it in the bottom of the code on every page of your website. If this is not set up from day one of your Internet marketing campaign, you won't have as strong a comparison later of your unique visitor count and user behavior as it grows and changes. After Google Analytics is set up, test it and make sure it is collecting data before moving ahead.

You also need to benchmark how many sales you are getting before and after promotional campaigns commence. Make notes of your conversion rate and your overall monthly unique visitors from the very beginning of any campaign.

See the analytics and conversion chapters to learn more about how important these factors are in themselves and how they tie to SEO.

Ranking Reports

Ranking reports tell you where you rank for each keyphrase without having to check by hand. If you use a tool like Ranking Manager or Advanced Web Rankings, add your keywords and the report checks your ranks in the various search engines.

These are useful but can also be misleading since not every person will get the same results for the same website. That's because the search engines display different rankings to different IP addresses (essentially users) and display different ranks at their different data centers. Plus, search engine rankings can vary throughout the day. Many search results are personalized and vary by user based upon a number of factors such as what they last searched for or if they are logged into Google.

So use ranking reports as a good general indication and then dig into your analytics program (and Google Webmaster Tools) for more specific details on who is actually finding your site (by what non-branded keywords and referrers) and what they are doing while they are there.

While reviewing your ranking report, do not be overly concerned by a mix of small increases and decreases in rankings. Google and the other search engines are constantly updating their algorithms, and the thousands or millions of sites that are competing for the same keywords are also being updated, ensuring that your rankings will almost always be in a state of flux.

What we generally look for are large increases or decreases in rankings (up or down by more than a few positions in a month), increases or decreases over time (up or down for several months in a row), and groups of related keywords that all move up or down at the same time.

Your Results in the Top 50

Be sure to run a pre-optimization ranking report so you can later see how you progress. Taking a "snapshot" of where you stand before all of your SEO efforts and then comparing that to where you get to on a week over week basis is a powerful indicator of the effectiveness of your efforts. It is also completely addictive and fun (especially for us SEO folks).

It is important to note from day one the number of rankings you have in the top 50 so you can monitor overall movement. While showing up in the top 10 results is the best, looking at search engine results five pages deep (5 pages x 10 sites per page) gives you an understanding of your rankings across the board, whether they are good or just so-so.

By knowing that you have keywords "in striking distance" of ranking, you can identify quick wins for pushing good keywords into the top 10. And it may be the case that very simple on-page or off-page SEO could do the trick.

Speaking of keywords, let's dig into how to select them before we look at how specifically to use them to optimize because it is paramount you use the right ones.

Keyphrase Research

Keyphrases are what people type into a search engine when they are looking for something on the web. Remember that a keyphrase can be simple, like "golf clubs," or it can be very descriptive, like "left-handed golf clubs for women." The more descriptive long tail keywords get far less traffic but are far easier for you to "rank" for.

In the early days of the Internet, keywords were often just one word and were therefore called "key words." Over time, linguistic patterns for search terms have changed and now people search via phrases and even sentences. Utilizing high-, medium-, and low-traffic keywords is essential, so be sure to research each. Adopting more of a "long tail keyword" stance for your SEO is one of the smartest things you can ever do. It means you are jumping into a winnable war.

Keyphrase Examples

High traffic level/general keywords: "Shoes" or "Shoe Store"

Medium/niche keywords: "Leather Shoes" or "Gucci Shoes"

Long tail keywords: "Gucci Brown Leather High Heel Shoes"

Local keywords: "Shoe Store Hamilton Massachusetts"

Long Tail or Longer Keyphrases Are the Absolute Key to Initial Success

Can you see how much more likely it is for someone searching for a long tail keyword to be a buyer rather than a browser? That's a critical piece of the SEO puzzle that you must appreciate if you are to dominate in your niche.

Long tail keywords also contain short or medium tail terms (e.g., "Gucci brown leather high heel shoes" contains "high heel shoes" and the split-up version of "Gucci shoes" and "leather shoes") and allow the possibility of ranking for each subset. In addition, the kinds of people who type in three- to five-word phrase keywords often convert really well. Think about it—if you type in "Gucci brown leather high heel shoes," you are looking for something quite specific. You're not writing a term paper about leather shoes in general. You are looking to buy brown leather, high-heeled Gucci shoes, and you're ready to do your cost comparisons.

So make sure you include a variety of terms, knowing that the long-term goal is to get traffic from each level of keywords. Ultimately you want to have a radical increase in website visitors coming from the search engines, but until you develop deep content, do link building, and implement a strategy of social media marketing, you will likely only rank for long tail or local terms. Once you establish long tail/local ranking, if you feel you are not getting enough clicks or leads, the harsh reality is that the high level/really competitive terms are what you need to rank for next and that will come only via a fully integrated and in-depth SEO campaign.

If you add up hundreds or thousands of long tail keywords, and rank in the top one to five results, you can generate an enormous amount of traffic that is often much more than many people would get from ranking between 1 and 5 for a handful of their top terms.

Rather than only fighting like mad for the most general keywords, assemble a basket of keywords that (if you add all of their monthly search volumes together) represents HUGE traffic numbers. This is a war that can be and needs to be won.

Variety Is the Spice of Life

Deepening your keywords means more opportunities to develop and optimize quality content.

Real-World Example: A Health Club

I recently met with a prospective small business client, the owner of a local health club. The client wants to rank better for health and fitness clubs in his area and drive more overall leads. While *health clubs Peabody MA* and *fitness clubs Peabody Massachusetts* are good terms, it is important to make sure to target the services offered and questions potential customers will have as well. We noticed the client does not rank for the following terms:

Peabody MA Spinning Class *Peabody MA Pilates*
Peabody MA Yoga   *Peabody MA Martial Arts*
Peabody MA Karate   *Peabody MA Swimming Pool*
Peabody MA Spa

The client also does not rank well for blog/long tail keyphrases like:

How to learn Pilates for women

What burns more calories treadmill or elliptical

Spinning bikes vs. stationary bikes

The list goes on and on...there are so many potential services and FAQs the client could be ranking for to drive incoming visitors. He was focused on high-level terms only, but the very specific offerings should also be optimized with a page for each service. This same concept can be applied to any company. *Lawyers Peabody MA* might be a good local term, but *real estate lawyers* also needs to be addressed and have a unique page. Long-term, think about how you will add new content and terms on targeted pages, blog posts, and/or multimedia files like videos and podcasts, so you are always expanding your keyphrase sets and media that will rank in universal searches.

The Stages of the Buying Process

Understanding the stages of the online buying process is a powerful way to start attracting the *right* traffic through SEO. Be sure you include content that is optimized for keywords that relate to these various stages, not just your general company or inter-office marketing concept.

Marketing on the web is often different than offline marketing in the sense that people use the web to get things done. They research by looking at reviews, FAQs, how to's, etc., and then they evaluate and compare before making a purchase.

The speed of this research and ability to click from you to a competitor so quickly is why you need to supply more information to support your customer's buying process than at any other time in history.

Stages of the Buying Process

Stage 1: Identifying the problem or growth opportunity

Stage 2: Initiating interest in finding a solution

Stage 3: Getting educated on the solution landscape

Stage 4: Validating choices

Stage 5: Rationalizing the decision

Stage 6: Deciding to buy or not to buy

People may use searches such as:

Research-Based/Informational: "Best Running Shoes for Plantar Fasciitis," "New Hampshire Wedding Ideas," "Mortgage Rate Trends," "Salt Water Fishing"

Transactional Searches: "Buy golf clubs," "Cheap Mexican Restaurants," "Free trial of photo editing software" (intent to potentially buy later)

Navigational Searches: Are performed with the intent of "surfing" directly to a specific website. Gender-Based: "Best Golf Clubs for Women," "Men's Health"

Product Specific: "Shimano Stradic GTM 3000," "Leo's Quantum Jazz Tap Shoes"

Income-Based: "Luxury Resorts," "High-End Spa"

It is important to understand the intent of the user so that you provide them with a page that matches what they are looking for. If you don't have pages for each of these stages of the buying process, you will not only have fewer "hooks in the water," but you will also lose the fish to the boat next to you.

One of the coolest parts about SEO is looking at the buying stages in the way that you shop online. At first you have a certain level of interest, but that grows as does the way you search. You begin to narrow your focus to less generic keywords and more towards price and color and spec considerations.

You want to create content and calls to action that map to each stage of the buying cycle to get a larger share of total search impressions. While the best keywords in some ways are the ones that create more customers not just visitors, if you can help move that potential customer closer to a purchase, why not have information for them at each stage? After all, with SEO you don't pay by the click, you just have to create content and get people to share it.

Using a thesaurus or a lexical database such as wordnetweb.princeton.edu/perl/webwn can help you think up various ways people may be searching for or thinking about your products and services. Looking at your competitors' sites can help you see offerings they have as alternatives to your site. If your competitors are using FAQs, case studies, how to's, and reviews to create venues for keywords, you simply can't expect Google to rank you for your main keywords when others have adjusted for a more thorough keyphrase set.

One of the best ways to "peer" in to see what your competition is doing in terms of their SEO efforts is to head to the free Google External Keyword Tool (https://adwords.google.com/o/KeywordTool) and then type in the websites of all of your competitors. Google provides an option to type in a URL and add it to the keyword tool instead of just researching by keywords.

I can *guarantee* you that your eyes will be widened when you see what Google shows them using for keywords and how they are fishing at each of these stages.

Keyword research is the heart of search marketing and must be done very thoroughly. In fact, you should do keyword research at least every six months to ensure you are using new terms that reflect the latest trends and/or products. Add new content regularly to update for a variety of terms that may not have been addressed in the first round of search engine optimization.

Here's an incentive to keep your keywords and your content as fresh as you can. Upwards of 20% or more of all search terms on any given day have never been searched for before!

Comprehensive Keyphrase Analysis Shortlist

- Allow for many rounds of revisions, since this is the heart of search marketing.

- Use multiple sources for gathering possible terms—competitors' websites, all of your team members' ideas, multiple keyword suggestion tools.

- Be clear about what you want to rank for and why.

- Test keywords in Google AdWords to see the number of impressions and how well you convert.

- Target terms you convert well for in organic search, since organic ranks take so much effort.

- Define personas for your target customers and the stages of the buying process to aid in your research.

- Look at your Google Analytics and Google Webmaster Tools to see which keywords are pulling in the most traffic. Use those keywords in your research to drill down to uncover better and smarter keywords.

Tools We Use in Our Research

https://adwords.google.com/o/KeywordTool (URL must be typed in exactly as shown)
http://www.google.com/insights/search
http://www.google.com/trends (Google Trends Keyword Demand Prediction)
www.wordtracker.com
www.keyworddiscovery.com
www.keywordspy.com (Ethical Competitive Spying)
http://wordnetweb.princeton.edu/perl/webwn (Lexical Database)
www.semrush.com

Tips for Using the Google Keyword Tool

Keep your keyword matching options in mind when you use Google's Keyword Tool. You can set the tool to show you how many people searched using exactly and only the keyword you want to know about, or any search containing that keyword and variations. If you want the most accurate measure of any keyword, head to the Google External Keyword Tool and make sure you set the setting for "Exact" match. Then you will see precisely how many times each keyword is searched for month over month.

"Broad match" means searches that come close to a particular word or phrase. You may want to have a look at those search volumes as well, because you will also get people typing in your keyword with a variety of modifiers. Don't get discouraged when using exact match if you see lower search volumes than you hoped for, as you are looking at only one exact way of searching at a time.

You just can't preplan for every way people will search. So don't be afraid to include some keywords that get low or no search volume if your common sense tells you they are worth experimenting with. When we look at analytics, we have often seen traffic driven by keywords that the keyword tools said were useless. Focus on keywords that get real search volume, but do some experimenting based on your own intuition as well.

Do several rounds of brainstorming and many hours of research across multiple tools to accumulate a set of high-, medium- and low-level terms you can target when you get to the on-page adjustments phase (actually changing the text on your website's pages). Make sure you make a map of the content on your site to see if you have landing pages to support the inclusion of your most desired keywords.

Search Engine Optimization Basics

Once you select your keywords, it's time to apply and optimize them. The page text is critical to the search engines. Search engines value very highly the titles and headings, or emphasized text. Items at the top left (i.e., things that come first) are often given more weight. So make sure you have just one or two main keywords for each page and plenty of text, headings, bullet points, photos, etc., to adjust.

There are over 200 items you can address for search engine rankings and these change over time, but I've boiled it down to nine key items to address:

Top 9 Essential Elements to Optimize

1. **The <title> tag:** This defines a title in the browser toolbar, provides a title when a page is added to a visitor's "favorites," and often displays a title in the search engine results pages. It is required in all HTML/XHTML documents. The title tag is the most important tag on the page and is the first element a search engine encounters. Write title tags that are not overwhelmingly long, as search engines display only the first 65–75 characters of a title tag in the search results. Beware, if they look overly SEOed, you might not engage people enough to click, even if you do rank. If title tags only have your company name or are too long, your rankings will suffer significantly. Make sure your keywords are listed here at least once, ideally at the beginning. We like to add the brand name toward the end. Don't overuse keywords in the title tag—or anywhere else for that matter.

2. **Heading and subheadings:** The page heading and subheadings are the next most critical elements on the page. Add keywords, ideally at the beginning of the headings, because in general, search engines value anything that comes first. Headings are not only an essential place to add keywords, but they also help the user feel grounded by making it obvious what a page's topic is. Don't use graphics for these tags, as the

search engines can only fully read text. To check if a heading that looks like text is text or an image, left-click and drag over it to highlight it. If you can't highlight it, then it's likely an image. You can also right-click on it and if there is an option to "save image as," then you know it's an image header that the search engines won't care about. If you are stuck with graphical headers, use alt tags (text that pops up when you mouse over an image) on each graphic, but realize that alt tags only give you a small fraction of the benefit gained from text-based heading.

3. **Body copy:** In addition to the title and page headings, your page should have some text that describes what the page is about. This is often displayed in the listing in the search engine results pages, so use keywords in the top section of your text. The first paragraph of your page is the most critical section to optimize. Don't be too worried about specific keyword density. You can add the keyword in the heading and a few times on the page. That is often enough if your links and social media activity are strong. Do what is natural, but obviously you must use the exact keywords you have chosen and in the exact order they were defined in the keyword research. Using related keywords such as those suggested by Google Instant will also help.

4. **Bold and italics:** Keyphrases that are made to be bold or italicized also help the search engines understand the page's key topics. This technique also helps the user scan and skim the page more easily.

5. **Bullet points and lists:** These also help the user see clearly what the page is about (making it scan- and skim-friendly).

6. **Hyperlinks:** Use keywords when linking to another page on your own site. Link to the green widget page by saying something like "Check out our Sale on Green Widgets," not "Click here." Don't use the keyword you are targeting as a link on that page; instead, have other pages link up to the page that wants to rank for a given keyword, using that keyword.

7. **Silos—themes and sub-themes—interlinking:** Make sure your site has a main theme and sub theme. If you are about widgets, make sure you have mostly widget-related information. To strengthen a sub-theme silo, like the red widget section, have other website pages in and outside the silo link up to the main landing page for all types of red widgets using the keyphrase "red widgets" in the anchor text. That funnels energy to the primary page of the silo and will help it rank better than its subpages. You will likely prefer people to land on a general page about red widgets than for them to land on a page about fuzzy red widget shipping procedures. Do not link out from the page you are optimizing for an exact keyword using that keyword, as it sends a signal that the page you are pointing at is also about that term. That dilutes the message to Google in terms of what page to rank.

8. **Alt tags and photos:** Make sure your images are named with keywords, not randomly named. Also add alt tags to each image to describe what it is in a logical way, using keywords when possible. This way you will make your site more accessible to the disabled, while at the same time adding in more keywords.

9. **Meta tags:** Meta tags were once the godfather of all SEO. Now they don't do much to affect your rankings. To see your meta tags, you can right-click on your website and select "View Source" or select the menu item "View" in the top of the browser bar, and then select "Source" or "Page Source," etc. The *meta description tag* is valuable because the users can often see it in the search results—versus the keyword tag that is hidden and just for the search engines. If Google knows the user is involved, it is more likely a ranking factor. We still use the title and description tags but see almost no value in the meta keyword tag.

Meta tags look like this:

<title>Abortion Facts and Pro Life Information from Priests for Life</title>

<meta name="description" content="Priests for Life is a movement of clergy and laity of all denominations working to end abortion and euthanasia.">

<meta name="keywords" content="Abortion facts, Abortion information, Pro Life, Abortion videos, Abortion pictures">

Format of the Meta Description Tag

The meta description tag is a snippet of HTML code that goes inside the <Head> </Head> section of a web page. It's usually placed after the title tag and before the meta keywords tag, although the order is not important.

The proper syntax for this HTML tag is:

<META NAME="Description" CONTENT="Your description goes here.">

What Is the Meta Keywords Tag?

The meta keywords tag is a just a list of keywords or phrases that relate to your page. Back in 1995, if you put a few more instances of your keywords in than the next site, you likely had a better rank. Because people abused this beyond belief, meta keywords no longer hold much or any weight. Google basically ignores it.

Now that you understand the simpler concepts, it's time to dig deeper into site architecture and more complex issues.

URL Architecture and Phrases per Page Map

Make an exact map of the terms you will be targeting and list the pages where the terms will go, as well as a list of suggested file names such as:

Widgets – widgets.html
Red Widgets – red-widgets.html
Blue Widgets – blue-widgets.html
Green Widgets – green-widgets.html

An easy way to get this started is to run a sitemap report of all your page names and import it into Excel. If you can, use a tool to show the existing title tags, such as www.audit-mypc.com/free-sitemap-generator.asp as this helps you understand what each page is about, especially if the webmaster made an attempt to describe each page in either the page names or title tags.

If your site map looks like this:

mckenzie-law-firm.com

home.html — McKenzie Law Firm (bad title)
about — McKenzie Law Firm (bad title)
pi.html — McKenzie Law Firm (bad title)
re.html — McKenzie Law Firm (bad title)
fm.html — McKenzie Law Firm (bad title)
contact — McKenzie Law Firm (bad title)

Note: "about.html" is referring to an inner page with a full URL like "mckenzie-law-firm.com/about.html" and the title is what is listed in the meta title tag such as "McKenzie Law Firm." I have left out the first part of the URL to make it easier to look at.

…change it to something like the following:

home.html — California Lawyer – McKenzie Law Firm
about.html — Law Firm In California Specializing in Real Estate Law
real-estate-law.html — Real Estate Law California – McKenzie Law Firm
family-law.html — Family Law California – McKenzie Law Firm
personal-injury-law.html — Personal Injury Law California – McKenzie Law Firm
contact.html — Beverly Hills CA Lawyer – McKenzie Law Firm

If you see areas where you have no content but you've made a list of keywords that you have researched that you would like to rank for, then write new content and develop new pages. If you become a source of those keywords to the big three engines, they start coming back to feed more and more.

Please also refer back to the chapter on SEO-friendly web design (Chapter 3) for more details on silos.

SEO Copywriting/Text Optimization

Edit your existing text to add keywords. Mark up Word documents in red indicating possible places where you can add keywords or modify the copy. After you find the keywords you want to use and have mapped out what pages they will live on, you will need to write copy for those pages or add keywords into the existing copy.

The first step is to select primary and secondary keywords. The secondary keywords are easy to find. Just go to Google and turn on Google Instant and type in your main keyword per page. The keywords that drop down are the LSI keywords (formerly known as latent semantic indexing—to keep it simple we will just call these related keywords) that Google *expects* to see surrounding your main keyword on every page.

So as you prepare your pages, you should think a bit like a football coach, with a "play" for each page. At the top of each "play" is your main keyword, below that are your secondary keywords that need to be on the page supporting the main keyword.

You will also use the keywords in the meta and title tags of the page as follows:

Terms selected:

1. Search Engine Optimization Massachusetts

2. Interactive Marketing Services

<title>Search Engine Optimization Massachusetts | McDougall Interactive Marketing **</title>**

<meta name="description" content="Award winning interactive marketing firm offering, Search Engine Optimization, PPC and social media marketing services, located in Massachusetts">

<meta name="keywords" content="search engine optimization, interactive marketing

firm, search engine optimization services, sem, seo, smo, social media optimization services, link building company, massachusetts, ma">

*While the meta keyword tag is basically useless, I left it in so you understand how it works. It also doesn't hurt to use it and there may be a tiny search engine or two that cares about it.

Then write the first paragraph of your page text, which should be a summary of the overall content on the page and should include both primary and secondary keywords. Here's an example of how ours looks:

<H1> Search Engine Optimization and Marketing Services **</H1>** (Large heading…)

(Text) Search engine optimization can increase your bottom line. While paid search (the little ads to the top and right of the "main" search results) can offer quick placement, search engine optimization is more long-lasting with a higher ROI.

At McDougall Interactive Marketing, we are not only experts in web marketing; we are pioneers in the field.

<H3> Our Interactive Marketing services include the following: **<H3>** (Smaller – sub heading…)

- Search engine optimization

- Keyword research

- On-page optimization

- Link building

- Google Analytics

- Social media strategies for backlinks

Check out our SEO pricing and our recent blog post on landing page design.

Notice how I have given heavier weight to the primary keyword by using it in headings, first in text and also more frequently (at least a few times on the page without overdoing it). I left the word "Massachusetts" out of the heading after we started ranking #1 for that term, since it looks a bit better and luckily the rank did not change. If it did I might have added that back in. So sometimes you need to experiment and test results and then modify based on how Google reacts. I also used the related search engine optimization "pricing" keyword I found at the bottom of Google where it says: "Searches related to search engine optimization." And then I used the word "optimization" separate from "search engine optimization" to mix things up and not look overly spammy.

Note that I offer visitors a free blog post with valuable content. This helps brand us as experts and works as a means of imparting credibility. Supplying relevant content will also tremendously increase the amount of time people spend on your site.

Since search engines run on keywords, copy edits are truly essential to any search marketing campaign. While it is sometimes a pain to have keywords that are a challenge to add into your text, adding them is *not* optional. (A clever writer can fit those keywords in smoothly.)

Conversion-Optimizing Titles and Descriptions

Making your page titles and descriptions persuasive is good for increasing click-through rates. Novice SEOs just stick keyphrases all over the place, but experts do it in a way that is as subtle as possible and helps conversions by being relevant and showing unique value. This is part of the reason why, when you are coming up with your primary keyword list, that your list has lots of "buyer keywords" and will lead not just to traffic (even targeted traffic) but to *conversions*.

What to Check in a Technical Analysis

Since this book is not intended to be an exhaustive resource, I won't go into a lot of the finer details on things that we examine in a technical analysis, but the list below can get you started on your own research into some of the more mid-level SEO techniques.

- **Report Card:** Check your URL on marketing.grader.com for a whole variety of factors from SEO to social media.

- **Internal and External Link Check:** Check the status of both external links and internal links on an entire website: internetmarketingninjas.com/seo-tools/google-sitemap-generator.

- **Site Architecture Analysis:** Solve issues with site structure that can lead to anything from duplicate content problems to the inability to get pages indexed. Examples of items to check: Click depth because pages that are the least amount of clicks from the home page rank better, presence of splash pages, use of frames, excessive inline code, lack of sitemap, server folder names, and technologies used, as well as URL format/filename considerations.

- **Site Navigation Analysis:** Review the technical methods used for navigation and improve using keywords and categories of information from a conceptual and architectural viewpoint. CSS for navigation, for example, strengthens the internal linking of your site versus image-oriented rollover buttons or JavaScript drop-down menus. (Consider additional/alternative internal linking if drop-downs are used.) When using CSS navigation, remember the anchor text being read from the navigation may be viewed as the most important link to the inner pages (because it is likely the first link/instance of that keyword seen on the page). Choose navigation names carefully.

- **Interlinking Analysis:** Use Wikipedia-style linking with lots of *anchor text* from within paragraphs to link to important pages. Pages with the most internal and external links to them tend to rank best. Remember that Google *loves* to see links happening not just from navigation bars and footers, but, much more importantly, from the actual content on your pages.

- **Usability Analysis:** Try usertesting.com to help address any significant methods you use that make getting information from your site difficult. Usability is now a ranking factor, so make sure your site is engaging and easy to use. Track this through analytics, but user-test frequently.

- **Search Engine Spider Simulator:** For a simulation of how the search engine robots see your site, try SEO-browser.com. This tool "spiders" your home page like a search engine crawler. Excessive code, lack of text or keywords, or other problems that may hinder the search engines' ability to index your website can often be found here.

- **ADA Compliance Check:** The Americans with Disabilities Act (ADA) requires stores, restaurants, and other businesses to provide access to people with mental and physical disabilities. SEO and making your website accessible to the disabled are very similar, so checking for ADA compliance issues is a healthy part of any SEO strategy. Check out JAWS, the screen reading software, and ada.gov for more info.

- **Website's Age:** With age comes wisdom and Google prefers to date older men, so to speak. Older sites are easier to rank due to their built-up trust factors. This can be checked at Whois.net.

- **Clean IP Check:** Check your server's IP block for other websites that may cause your site to be blacklisted, banned, or otherwise negatively impacted. Porn and gambling sites on your server won't do you any favors in the eyes of the search engines.

- **Title Tag Report:** Listing of your site's page titles (e.g., www.auditmypc.com/free-site-map-generator.asp).

- **Cache Checker Report:** Shows pages indexed/not indexed by Google. Check to see when the last time your home page was cached, or stored, in Google's index. If the cached page is old, it can be an indication that Google is not visiting your site often or that there are deeper issues with indexing.

- **Domain Name Factors:** Check for multiple domain names pointing to your website. We generally recommend using only one domain name for your main presence on the web. Having more than one domain name pointing to the same web content is considered "duplicate content" by the search engines, and can create major problems with search engine indexing, as the search engines attempt to sort out your multiple domain names and decide which one is the "primary" domain. If multiple domains are necessary (for example, if your company changed domain names at some point in the past, and you have a lot of links or traffic going to the old domain), then Google recommends setting up a 301 (permanently moved) redirect, which redirects users (and links) from the old domain to the new one. If you want multiple domains for SEO purposes, each site has to have original content and not just forward to the main site.

- **Canonical Issues:** Even if both the www and non-www versions of your site are getting indexed, you should 301 redirect the less authoritative version to the more important version. The version that should be redirected is the one that does not rank as well and has fewer inbound links. That helps Google know which URL you prefer to be canonical. Always use the preferred format for your internal links to be consistent. As smart as Google is, you can confuse it.

- **Duplicate Content Check:** Try copyscape.com to check for content that you might have put on your site intentionally or inadvertently that has been taken from somewhere else. Also check to make sure your site does not contain two versions of the same content.

- **Custom 404 Error Page Check:** A "404" is a "file not found" error message, meaning that the server cannot find the requested page. A custom 404 error page should be set up on the site in order to inform the user that an error has occurred, and to offer helpful advice for how to find the content that they were looking for. Not having a custom 404 page can result in users dropping off the site, and not returning, in the event that they encounter an invalid link. Check to see if it exists, then create one if it doesn't. Also, check the HTTP headers to ensure that a 404 message is passed from the server in the header information. This 404 message tells the search engines that the page requested does not exist, which helps to un-index old pages that may still be coming up in the search engine results.

- **Robots.txt:** The robots.txt file is located in the root directory of your server. Search engine crawlers access this file, which tells them what files and directories to access or ignore. Google prefers to see this file on your server. If one does not exist, we recommend creating one.

- **Meta Robots:** Index/noindex tells the engines whether the page should be crawled and kept in the index. If you opt to use "noindex," the page will be excluded from the engines. Follow/nofollow tells the engines whether links on the page should be crawled. If you use "nofollow," the engines will disregard the links on the page both for discovery and ranking purposes.

- **Spam Check:** Check your home page code for undesirable methods of "tricking" the search engines into giving you better results, including white-on-white text, hidden links, excessive or hidden keywords, etc.

- **Page Load Time/File Size:** Check various factors that affect how fast your site loads, including file size, number of objects, number of images, CSS files, and scripts. Page loading speed is one of those factors that Google weighs heavily, so it is very important that your pages load as quickly as possible for the best end-user experience. This will also prevent a higher-than-necessary bounce rate from the loading page. Consider using a tool like Pingdom to check load times.

- **XML Sitemaps:** Generally, if you have enough people linking to your site, you won't need to submit your site to the search engines because they will find you through those links. However, if you find that some pages don't get indexed, it can't hurt to do some limited, non-automated submissions, or supply an XML sitemap so the search engines can crawl all your pages.

- **Google PageRank:** An indication of what Google believes the "importance" of your page is. The main way to increase PageRank is to get links to your site and inner pages. Don't put too much emphasis on this, but keep it in mind.

- **Alexa Traffic Rank:** Alexa rates every web page based on the number of visitors to it and how long they stay. The lower the ranking, the better. We don't put a ton of stock in Alexa, since much of the data only comes from people who have installed the Alexa toolbar, but it is interesting to check out. They have one really cool feature called Clickstream. It is the farthest-right tab when looking at a site through Alexa. It shows you what sites a person visits before and after the site being reviewed. You can look at what sites people leave your site to visit and what sites people visit just before going to your competitors.

Hundreds of Ranking Factors—Direct and Indirect—Here's What's Essential

A simple list of a number of ranking factors is below. This list is incomplete and changes all the time, but it is intended to help you appreciate the hard work it will take to have a comprehensive SEO strategy. If you search for SEO ranking factors you will find several numbered lists going into the hundreds. David Mihm has one list of a hundred or more ranking factors just for local search.

It is a good thing advertising budgets are headed to SEO and away from traditional advertising because there is much to do with a large team of experts. You can make great progress doing the basics, even on your own to some degree, but to get into the higher levels of competitive SEO takes more extreme measures and integration with other channels.

The items on this list are not in order of importance (quality links and reams of quality content are still king at the moment). Instead, I've listed some of the newer factors at the top to show that they are now connected to the long list of factors. Note that numbers 1–7 are not believed to be significant direct ranking factors at this time, so do not go out and buy Twitter followers and social shares, etc. Instead, use the signals that you build authentically to make people aware of your site and to get them to link to you. We are waiting to see if these factors may start to be more directly factored into search algorithms in the future.

Eric Enge, who co-authored *The Art of SEO* with Rand Fishkin of SEOMoz, recently emailed me the following on this subject:

"Tests performed by Searchmetrics explicitly show that Google does not use Facebook Shares or Facebook Likes to discover a page.

Google Plus +1s and shares, and tweets are used to:

1. Discover new content, and

2. Identify content as newsworthy and give it a short-term boost based on Query Deserves Freshness (QDF)."

Scott Willoughby of SEOMoz describes QDF like this:

"When the [search] engines recognize that the 'best' results for a certain search may change drastically from day to day, or moment to moment, they may mark the search QDF, which will help promote new, related content from trusted sources to the top of the search engine results page, even if that content doesn't yet have any links."

So while the idea of social as a signal is a super-hot topic, do your research before you invest in it solely as a direct ranking factor. The following two links provide great reading on this subject:

stonetemple.com/graph-search-social-search-with-bings-stefan-weitz

pointblankseo.com/links-vs-tweets

Without further ado, here are the direct and indirect ranking factors:

1. Facebook Shares and Likes (Not used a ton for web ranking except in velocity.)

2. Twitter Followers (Possibly an authority metric that factors in ratio of following to followers.)

3. Tweets and Retweets (Not used a ton for web ranking except in velocity, but it is one of the more interesting authority signals to keep an eye on and test. Some limited direct signal in Google for regular and news results.)

4. Followers to Google+ Business Page

5. Google+1's (May start to be a factor moving forward. Currently affects social search rankings but not treated in regular search like a link. May be used to enhance other signals such as links.)

6. Number of People Who "Have You in Their Circles" (Google+)

7. Author Rank Rating (Likely a metric moving forward.)

8. External Links Global Link Popularity (PageRank) (+ Anchor-Text related issues)

9. Internal Links (+ Anchor-Text related issues)

10. Links from topically relevant pages/sites

    A variety of domains linking to you vs. links from a few sites
    Anchor text diversity
    Different IP addresses of linking sites
    Geographical diversity
    Different TLDs (Top-level domains)
    Topical diversity
    Different types of linking sites (Blogs, directories, etc.)
    Diversity of link placements

11. Page-Specific Trust/Rank

12. Use of External Links to Reputable Sites

13. Links from Hubs/Authorities

14. Reciprocal Links Ratio

15. Consistency of Links Being Built

16. Quantity and Quality of Nofollowed Links to the Page

17. Percent of Followed vs. Nofollowed Links

18. Trustworthiness of the Domain Based on Link Distance from Trusted Domains

19. Keywords in the Beginning of the Body Text

20. Keywords in Body Text

21. Keywords in the Title of a Page

22. Keyword Synonyms Relating to Theme of Page/Site

23. Keywords in the Beginning of Page Title

24. Keyword Use in Heading Tags

25. Keyword Use in Heading Alt Tags

26. Keyword Proximity (Higher on page, at beginning of title tag, etc.)

27. Keyword Density (Percentage of keywords used as compared to the amount of text.)

28. Keyword Use in the Domain Name and Subdomains

29. Keyword Use in Filenames/URLs

30. Keyword Use in Image Alt Tags

31. Keyword Use in Folders on Server

32. Overall Site Theme (For instance, how many pages/title tags, etc., on a particular topic?)

33. Keyword Use in <b>, <strong>, <I,> or <em> Tags

34. Keyword Use in List Items <li> on the Page

35. Keyword Use in the Page's Query Parameters

36. Keyword Use in the Meta Description Tag

37. Keyword Use in the Meta Keywords Tag

38. Keyword Use in Comment Tags in the HTML

39. Unique Content and How Much of It

40. Freshness of Content

41. Content Architecture of the Site (Is the content buried?)

42. Query Parameters in the URL vs. Static URL Format

43. Ratio of Code to Text

44. HTML Validation to W3C Standards

45. Use of Flash Elements

46. Use of Advertising on the Page

47. Use of Google AdSense (specifically) on the Page

48. Domain Age

49. Length of Domain Registration

50. Domain Registration History

51. Domain Registration Ownership Change

52. Domain Ownership (Who registered the domain and their history?)

53. Domain Registration with Google Local

54. Domain "Mentions" (Text citations of the domain name.)

Web Marketing On All Cylinders - John McDougall

55. Server/Hosting Uptime

56. Hosting Information (Are you hosted next to spam sites?)

57. Inclusion of Feeds from the Domain in Google Blog Search

58. Yahoo! Directory (Citations and link.)

59. DMOZ.org (Citations and link.)

60. Wikipedia (Citations and link.)

61. The Librarian's Internet Index - Lii.org (Citations and link.)

62. Alexa Rank

63. Compete.com Rank

64. Feeds from Google News

65. Being Regularly in the News

66. Use of XML Sitemap(s)

67. Google Webmaster Tools Registration

68. Use of the Domain in Google AdWords

69. Use of the Domain in Google Analytics

70. Country TLD of the Root Domain

71. Language of the Content Used on the Site

72. Links from Other Domains Targeted by Country

73. Geographic Location of the Host

74. Click-Through Rate from Search Results

75. Search Queries for the Brand

76. Load Time

77. Length of Visit on Site

78. Bounce Rate

79. Robots.txt File Content

80. Links to 404 and Other Error Pages

A Short List of Negative Ranking Factors

1. Cloaking (showing one page to Google and another one to users) with bad intent

2. Link buying from known link brokers/sellers

3. Lots of weak backlinks, including obsessive directory and forum submissions

4. Overuse of the same anchor text in links (internal and external)

5. Links from banned sites and site hosting malware

6. Linking to spammy pages

7. Duplicate content

8. Lots of content just for SEO that causes high bounce rates

9. Regular server downtime

10. Hidden text (white text on white background, etc.)

11. Overuse of the same anchor text

12. Redirects ending in 404 error

13. Keyword overuse/keyword stuffing

14. Past hackers' attacks records

If your site is full of engaging content, and has lots of trust like good links, then your ranking will likely not be hurt even if people try to link to you from bad sites. But if your site is weak and you add some crummy links back to it, you could be penalized. Google will basically ignore anyone who tries to destroy your ranks by negatively linking to you if you are already perceived as "good."

A big takeaway here is that the future of search engine rankings is likely to weigh heavily in favor of an analysis of a site's perceived value to visitors based on comments/engagement and potentially social signals, quality of site design/content/usability, and click-through rates/lack of bounces back to the search results pages. Anchor text in links, exact match domains, and spammy techniques are getting weaker by the day, so make sure that your Internet marketing strategy focuses on giving users what they want and having something remarkable and worth sharing on your site. Think like a public relations expert and always be looking for the "hook" or what makes you stand out from the crowd. Answer the questions that keep your customers up at night with optimized content and you will be in good shape.

Tips for Hiring an SEO Person or Agency

If you don't hire a very senior person to work for you in-house, hire someone who has content development and organizational skills who will work well with an agency. There's an incredible number of details to track and follow up on with SEO. Most people—especially programmers who say they do SEO—don't know what they are talking about unless they do it full-time.

The horror stories are everywhere.

Part-time SEOs (or ones that use black hat practices) can get your website banned by the major search engines. It is essential to take a long-term approach and do your SEO ethically and consistently. If you take a break from it, Google will notice and your rankings will drop, so plan on keeping a team engaged indefinitely. Check references, ask how the experience was, and see what the ROI was from their work. Do keep in mind, though, some SEOs can't do their jobs due to a client having a tiny website and being too stubborn to allow new content to be developed or significant changes to be made. If the references you check appear to fall in this category, find another reference from a client with a larger site that was more open to working with the SEOs to get the best from both sides.

It is very important that you are honest about your expectations.

A great SEO plan will take months or even years to implement and then show results. So budget your time and marketing dollars accordingly.

Wear a White Hat, Not a Black Hat

If you want lasting search engine results, you have no choice but to either pay for each click (a great deal in some cases and terribly overpriced in others) or create an amazing website that deserves solid rankings. As Google gets better at not only tracking the quality of your site and the amount and quality of topically relevant sites that link to you, it is also getting better at analyzing spam (things that black hats do to get better rankings, even if they are known to be "prohibited" by Google).

If no one ever clicks on your organic rankings, if no one ever visits, if no one ever bookmarks your site, or if no one follows the bogus links you have to your site, Google can simply overlook all the "fake" hard work you did. Do everything with the user in mind and be aware that many black hat gimmicks that sound too good to be true probably are, and may get you banned from the search engines.

Top Reasons SEO Campaigns Fail

Targeting the Wrong Keywords

If you don't include high-, medium-, and low-traffic keywords, your campaign will not be fully successful. The low-hanging fruit for any business is keyphrases that are three words or more. Yes, these will have far smaller amounts of traffic searching for them, but you need to get your keywords to the top of page one of the search results. You do that with long tail keywords that get some traffic (approximately 200+ searches a month) and have low competition.

Not Having a Complete Plan

You need to have all the steps in place, from exhaustive keyword research and site-friendly design analysis to optimization and tracking implementation. Don't forget that this war is waged on-page and off-page. Content, links, engagement, and social citations must work together.

Not Implementing SEO Suggestions/"Code"

Not putting new SEO "code" on your pages or making suggested edits is a far too common reason for poor results. Campaigns need all facets of SEO to be implemented for the full benefits to be obtained.

Not Tracking and Then Editing Based on Findings

If you don't analyze your results, you can't expect to make changes that will take the marketing campaign to the next level. When it comes to keywords, you have the ability to get smarter with your efforts on a daily, weekly, and, especially, on a monthly basis. Take full advantage of that and let visitor behavior (as seen through Google Analytics and Google Webmaster Tools) tell you what your best keywords are. Why guess when you don't have to?

Not Giving Continued Input to the SEO Agency

If you don't offer input on why you may not be converting on certain keyphrases, your SEO may not be able to discern what keyphrases would be better. Work together using your knowledge of your business and the SEO's research and implementation skills.

Giving Up Too Soon Without Making Adjustments

The companies that say "SEO failed" are usually the ones that expected to do it once and then not make further edits to the site. If you track what works and what doesn't, and make changes to pages that have lots of traffic but few conversions, you can make more out of the traffic you already have. All most people want is more traffic, which should lead to more conversions. But what about the traffic you already have? It can often be easier to make better use of existing customers than to bring in new traffic. This requires that you take a fresh approach to how you are "converting" people on each page. If your conversion rate is terrible, more traffic might not help much, and you can't blame SEO for that.

Keep in mind that some campaigns bring results in a matter of weeks or months, while others blossom over many months or a year later. Especially with new websites, be aware that rankings can take a while to mature, especially if you have just implemented a links campaign. Google wants to assign your site the right "overall value" to the rest of the web. They can only do that over a considerable amount of time.

Now it's time to learn more details on link building, which may just be more than half of the reason your site will rank well or not.

Chapter 5

Link Building Essentials

The web is a massive online popularity contest. When someone likes your site, they may link to you to tell others how interesting or cool you are. Think of this as a vote being cast for you in this contest.

Google became famous because it discovered a way to analyze a site's relevance in part by observing how many other sites linked to it and how highly it regarded those other sites. In other words, if the sites that link to you are "bad," then those links don't count for much. Conversely, if not only the sites but the actual "inner" site pages that link to you have lots of "good" links back to them and are of high quality, then you get a strong boost in your search engine ranking. PageRank is the name of this link analysis algorithm, named after Larry Page, one of Google's founders.

People pay for links from directories and public relations (PR) sites, beg for them via email, and even bribe for links with incentives. But one thing's for sure: links affect your search engine rankings at times more than even your actual website content.

Link building now works hand in hand with social media marketing so that not only are you getting "votes" from the authority sites that the search engines trust, you are also (and perhaps more importantly) getting links from real people who care about your brand enough to want to talk about it.

This is the one-two punch that you now must have working for your website on a daily basis. The chapters on social media, public relations, and content marketing will also make you a better link builder if you understand how they all fit together. This chapter is intended to help you understand where link building came from and what to avoid. It will also show you how it has evolved, its natural progression into something more akin to PR via content marketing and social sharing of content worth linking to.

Link building is about getting topically related and (ideally) authoritative websites to point back to your website pages using keywords (and your brand name so it appears more natural) in the actual text so that users can click from one page to another.

You obtain a link when another website creates a link that people can click on to get to your site, either by listing your URL directly ("http://yoursite.com"), creating some keywords called "anchor text" that link to you (<a href="http://yoursite.com">keyword phrase</a>) or by making a banner ad that sends people to your site when clicked. Links also can be used within your website—these are often referred to as internal links. These can be from navigation bars or set up as clickable links in your written content on your web pages.

Google would love it if we all just let links happen naturally, but that is not the way the Internet marketing community works. "Backlinks Gone Wild" might well be the name of a documentary on link building. People have gone absolutely crazy getting backlinks because they hold so much power.

Since getting a real link from the paragraphs of an important site is comparable to getting an article about your company in a national magazine, link building is one of the hardest parts of Internet marketing. Yet when businesses pay for SEO they expect thousands of links and are surprised when their SEOs come back with links from crummy sites. If you want really high-quality links, it will cost you thousands per month, not hundreds, and it *requires* your website to have a solid base of content, a newsworthy blog, or something truly worth linking to. Expecting impressive backlinks from your SEO efforts when you have a very average website is like expecting your company to be on the front page of *The New York Times* or on "The Today Show" when there is no real differentiating factor between you or your competitors, or no "hook" as they say in the PR world. If you want real links, work on your "hook" and your base of amazing content first. That is the number one best way to get links. Once you have impressive content, SEOs have options for sharing it with bloggers, journalists, and other website owners.

The SEO community at large, not just the "black hats" on the fringe, has been doing things like excessive directory submission and article marketing for many years. This is where you write weak articles that include your link and toss these on article submission sites like bigarticle.com. While this worked like a charm for years, much of this activity has been killed by Google Penguin (the search engine algorithm update that essentially targeted people who were being over-aggressive with link building). It still makes sense to have a high-quality article placed on a topically related website, but you no longer get much benefit from the run-of-the-mill article marketing. You must think bigger and be more creative, even though this can cost significantly more time and money.

Every night, Google spiders crawl the web and find more of these links pointing to your website pages. If it trusts the sources of these links, this helps you in terms of search engine ranking or passes along what we call "link juice."

Don't overlook the extreme importance of this part of search marketing, or underestimate the level of complexity involved in building solid links from topically related, quality sites.

Don't just get links for the search engine ranking benefit, or you will be missing the original purpose of a link, which was to share content and create a way for users to find your website. If search engines start placing more value on links only if people actually follow them, then the crummy links you get may be worth nothing at all.

Link building techniques include (but are not limited to):

- Directory submissions (Now largely devalued and poses significant risks when abused)

- Reciprocal linkage

- Press release creation and submission

- Article creation and submission (Now must be done only on high-quality sites)

- Links from authority and hub sites

- Content building and "link incentivizing" to help generate natural links

- Viral links or "link bait"

- Forum link building (Now largely devalued and poses significant risks when abused)

- Social media links (Mostly for the indirect benefit)

- Updating existing links with varied anchor text

- Fixing broken links you already have

- Recreating content people still want to link to

- Comments on other blogs (not your own) that are in your niche

- Guest blogging

The first thing to be aware of is that all links are not created equal. In reality, much of the low-level link building techniques like directory submissions, social bookmarking, and, to some degree, article and PR submissions (depending on how you do them), can provide a very small value compared to a link from a significant site with a URL ending in .edu, .org, .k12, .gov, or from high-quality topically related sites in general.

You also ideally want links that are within paragraphs of content, as opposed to appearing in a list of links. This is more likely when you have a relationship with a website owner or blog that you are asking to link to your site. Be sure to vary and control the anchor text (the text in the underlined link) to contain keywords instead of only your domain name. If you have gone too far and have too many of the same keyword anchor texts, you can start encouraging people to link to you a fair amount with your domain name as a counterbalance. You want the links to come from pages on the site that have many people linking to them (powerful subpages). The problem here is that getting links from the best sites that meet all those requirements is incredibly difficult.

At one point, we had a full-time link builder sending 2,000+ emails to website owners offering to pay them $50 a link or more, and we still only got a dozen links (or fewer) per month that way. We have completely stopped this tactic after seeing one of our peers get many of his clients' sites banned from Google. (Not to mention it was a ridiculous pain in the butt.) Buying links is not acceptable, and Google is now smart enough to catch most people at this. We stick to content-based link building now, and it is so much more fun and productive. When people link to amazing content that is about your best keywords, the proper anchor texts will come more naturally.

Many people still use various sketchy tactics and try to stay under the radar, but the risk of getting caught isn't worth it. That means you have to try 10 times harder than the people willing to risk getting caught (the ones who are buying links or using all kinds of black hat software to get tens of thousands of links). At times, I have even been jealous of some hackers I have seen getting people to the top of Google with crazy "link tactics," but in the end, we sleep better at night knowing the methods we use are ones that Google approves of. Let me say this again, in boldface type, so it's clear:

Content-based link building is the only link building left worth doing.

For those of you who know blogging and marketing expert Seth Godin, I am playing on his statement that **"Content marketing is the only marketing that's left."**

The old way of marketing is an interruption with your "cute" agency-level message, and that is similar to the old way of begging for links, in the sense that it no longer works. Begging for links is next to useless now unless you are really building a relationship with someone that makes sense. Today, link building focuses on building content that journalists, bloggers, and other people (like your prospects and customers) will find just too informative or cool to ignore.

Quality content can attract people who will then share your content with their networks of their own free will. You should be building up a cache of content that informs, inspires, or makes your target audience laugh. What is this content? Basically, it's anything really cool, informative, or sometimes just free—like a free trial software download that generates a ton of people clicking on your site. Widgets, calculators, and infographics are also examples of content that can generate links.

My cousin Lucas Brunelle has a website about crazy bike videos. Over a million people have viewed his videos on YouTube and roughly 15,000 people link to his site. He never did search engine marketing officially until I shared it with him and yet these numbers blew me away. He had great ranks in the search engines simply because people linked to him based on how unusual his content was. A search marketer's job is to replicate that natural or organic process in a healthy way that actually adds value.

We have built video games, infographics, cool articles, and more in order to get links for our clients. It has paid off much better than emailing a million people to request links or taking huge risks buying links.

While not all campaigns get the links you want, if you build good content your users still benefit.

For example, we designed and built a video game for Rock Bottom Golf years ago. While it didn't get the links we hoped for, it had people sharing their high scores on Facebook and engaging with the branded game like crazy.

Content Examples and Ideas for Link Building

- Lists (Top 10, Top 20, Top 100)

- How-to Guides

- Humor

- Controversy

- Reviews and Comparisons

- Interviews (with celebrities, experts, industry bigwigs)

- Free Tools and Software

- Awards

- Blogs with Deep Content (using text, images, video, and infographics, etc.)

- Niche News

- Breaking News

- Images

- Videos

- Webcasts

- Podcasts

- Polls and Surveys

- Video Games

- Widgets

- Infographics

- Webcams

6 Ways to Create Great Linkable Content

1. The key: Try not to solely think of it as link bait. In other words, don't create content solely as an attempt to attract eyeballs and links. Make sure your content helps people and is truly funny, educational, or useful to a large number of people. Provide value by answering questions or meeting needs that your customers lose sleep over. If you can make it have an emotional impact as well as a logical one, it has a better chance of truly resonating (and then being shared).

2. Provide social media widgets (i.e., "share" icons) on your content to make it easy for people to spread it around. Also add a comment feature (like Social by MailChimp) to encourage tweets and Facebook shares.

3. Create a title that really stands out, as it will be much more likely to get linked to that way.

4. Create a well-designed special area on your site (or even a second blog) just for cool or helpful content. People like to bookmark a chunk of funny or high-quality content more than just a one-off.

5. Add bulleted lists, images, video, and lots of variety. SEOMoz.com has an informative set of posts (some of my all-time favorites) on what makes a link-worthy blog post. The bottom line is that posts that are not just plain text do better and posts that have a wide variety of cool content and multimedia get more links.

6. Lastly, don't try to hit a home run every time or you will get nothing done. Go hit a bunch of singles, do it regularly, and promote all of your great content, because

you never know what will go viral. Share all your posts on platforms like Facebook, Google+, Pinterest, Twitter, StumbleUpon, and Tumblr so your posts have a better chance of going viral, or at least being widely shared.

What Does Link Bait Look Like?

Here are examples of videos, reviews, humor sites, and more that have helped people build links.

Viral Video for Business

www.willitblend.com
www.dollarshaveclub.com

Reviews

www.dpreview.com (has over 500,000 backlinks)

Funny Sites

www.collegehumor.com
www.funnyordie.com
www.madtv.com
www.chucknorrisfacts.com

Infographics

www.infographicsshowcase.com

SEOMoz generated 1 million-plus links from content as follows:

Web 2.0 Awards: 72K + 30K = 100K+ links

Beginner's Guide to SEO: 6.5K + 5.6K = 12K+ links

Page Strength: 4K + 3.5K = 7.5K + links

Search Ranking Factors: 14K + 9K = 23K+ links

SEO Blog: 19K + 34K = 53K+ links

Don't be afraid to try something new. If it fails, as Ben Franklin said, try again.

"I didn't fail the test, I just found 100 ways to do it wrong."

— Benjamin Franklin

Avoid Using Social Media for Link Building Only

Doing social media for the sole purpose of building backlinks is just plain bad strategy. Social media links are usually "nofollowed," meaning the developer has inserted a "tag" in the underlying code, so they pass along no "link juice." Social media linking is about connecting with people more than just "link building," though the possibility of social media playing a deeper role in search engine rankings is rising extremely fast.

If you want your rankings to go up, use social media to spread your cool content and build relationships.

Getting your cool content on the following sites can make it go viral, which can result in thousands of backlinks, some good and some bad, but lots of links just the same.

Some great places to spread content:

1. Facebook	2. YouTube
3. Twitter	4. Google+
5. LinkedIn	6. Reddit
7. Digg.com	8. StumbleUpon
9. Tumblr	10. Delicious
11. Pinterest	12. Instagram

Although many top SEOs firmly believe that social shares such as tweets, likes, and plusses will soon affect rankings, at the moment "regular" links are what we know have a significant direct impact. Since this could change, you must start building social connections now.

Web Marketing On All Cylinders - John McDougall

Back to the Basics

When you're out of great ideas and you want to do some basic link building to make for a more regular and varied link profile, there are plenty of things you can do. These techniques won't necessarily generate the top links, but they can generate a good number of basic links that can go a long way—especially at the beginning, when you're trying to establish an online presence.

Directory submissions are still one of the simplest ways to build links and hence are not worth much.

Most directories are useless now and pose significant ranking risk post-Google Penguin— not to mention they are laborious to submit to. Only certain paid directories are decent. Yahoo! at $299 a year is generally worth the expense. Better Business Bureau, Best of the Web, and business.com are other big directories to consider that could either pass along some link juice or at least drive some visitors to your site. Go for quality only and relevance to your business. DO NOT do loads of directory submissions just for a ranking benefit.

Another typical strategy is putting your brand name on what are called community web-sites (forums, social networks, review sites) and then interacting with these communities. If you can deeply connect with a legitimate forum and have engaging conversations with its members, then occasionally sharing your content/link is okay, but using this as a link-building strategy post-Penguin is very risky.

Reciprocal Links

Google largely devalues a link to your site if you link back to the site doing the linking, but if two-way links are the only ones you can get, then it is certainly better to have some recip-rocal links than no links at all. You may want to ask peers in your industry, fellow business owners, and your friends for links from their sites in exchange for one from yours.

Google knows that sometimes people do link to each other for practical purposes, like experts in a particular field who value each other's content and contributions. Top experts don't always cite another expert without a linkback, so there is something to be said for some reciprocal links having real value.

My advice? Don't waste a lot of time on this method, but don't ignore it entirely if the linking sites are topically related. In addition, you need a variety of links, so it could be a red flag if all your links are one-way and have the same anchor text.

What you are looking for is a natural-looking link profile that evolves over time, uses dozens of different anchor text links, and points to all of the pages on your site...not just your home page.

Press Release Creation and Submission

Online public relations (PR) can increase targeted traffic to your website.

Stop thinking about press releases as being only for NBC, CBS, and ABC. Think of them more as tools that can bring you hordes of visitors online.

When you create and submit press releases to sites like PRWeb.com, part of the goal is to get others to resubmit them to news sites and blogs that either re-release your submission or write their own take on it, thereby creating a viral snowball and increasing your website's search engine rankings and backlinks. See Chapter 6 for details on this important tactic.

The best way to create online press releases is to start with one of your premier keywords and use the keyword in the newsworthy press release. We've had numerous examples of our releases getting to Google page one in only hours using this technique.

With press release sites, it is very, very important to realize that there is a hierarchy to where you need to post first and why.

For instance, if you are going to take the free PR route, post to PRLog.com first as they will then syndicate your release out to others. Generally the free sites are almost a waste of time and the paid sites offer much more substance. They get your releases in front of more people than free sites and will certainly get you picked up for mass distribution if you write your release with enough of a hook. While news sites are generally "no followed" and don't pass "link juice" or "PageRank," when bloggers and other sites see the news and write about you, you get high-quality relevant backlinks that do pass "link juice." Not to mention, journalists can see the site and call to interview you, and the general public can take actions right from your release.

Top PR Sites

Marketwire.com (Starting around $300 per release)

Businesswire.com (Starting around $300)

PRnewswire.com (Starting around $300)

PRweb.com (Starting around $150)

Free Press Release Submission Sites

PRLog.com

PressExposure.com

Information-Online.com

Free-news-release.com

Article Writing and Submission

Did you know that you can write articles and give them away in order to receive a link from the site that accepts that article?

While article marketing post-Penguin is all but dead in terms of the value of the links it generates for you, it can still bring some instant traffic if done right.

Article directories that are meant just for the search engines are where you run into the most trouble. It is much better to make a handful of profiles on niche sites in your vertical market that you keep updated with high-quality content than to spin a bunch of weak articles from hundreds of sites unrelated to your business.

By writing articles, you not only have the opportunity to look like an expert in the eyes of the people you want to attract to your business, but also in the eyes of the all-important search engines (because topically-related content is linking to your site).

Especially since the April 2012 update of Google's Penguin search algorithm, we have seen Google become less trusting of article marketing sites that allow endless submissions. So if you do this at all, tread lightly. Article-based link building used to work as the base of your link building efforts. These days, it should only be a very small portion of your link profile.

Your articles should be informational so as to add value. A growing trend is that your article should be written both passionately and authoritatively.

The text of the article should be genuinely helpful and should not obviously promote your website.

Give great tips, information, and insights. Near the end of every article, most sites include an "about the author" section, where you can include a link back to your business website. These two or three sentences let you share a brief summary of your expertise. It is as important as the article itself in that it can include a call to action and contains a link to your website.

Guest Blog Posting for Backlinks or, as I Call It, Blogger Blitz!

Time to start thinking outside of that box. If you're going to hit big (and you are) then you need to start leveraging off the traffic that the heavy hitters are already getting. This is an awesome way to explode the growth of your site. You just need to know why and how much.

One of the best ways to show off just how much you know about your niche is to become an expert on some of the biggest blogs in your niche and for you to give 'em everything you've got.

Write with Old-School Passion and Add Real Value

The biggest, most popular blogs have many writers submitting guest posts, so if you want to get noticed right away for all the right reasons, you cannot be afraid to get in line.

Connecting with popular blogs by offering them amazing free content that only you could develop enables you to create some great, consistent backlinks.

About five years ago, we had a small business client who is a professional organizer. She paid us for on-page optimization only, for terms like *professional organizers Massachusetts*. We told her how important backlinks are and gave her some insight into the value of blogging. She became a columnist at an organizing blog that ranked well in Google. We were frankly amazed at how good her ranks got very quickly, knowing that we did nothing but on-page optimization. While you might not think that just a single post on one blog would help that much, Google apparently did and her site ended up being deeply regarded as an authority in her field. Plus, she got great traffic from a new audience. That is really what you are after with this strategy. You want to get people to fall in love with the way you think and see your writing across a multitude of related sites.

Creating strategic partnerships with bloggers means you can produce content and get it in front of an audience of prospective clients while also driving traffic to your website and showing Google that your site is valuable. The key to success when it comes to guest blogging is to write such great content that people are thirsting for more. If you can write content that gets people talking, high-profile blogs will be more willing to accept your blog posts for publication. Remember this:

Bloggers need your content as much as you need them. It's symbiotic...

But don't just approach random blogs! It's important to read a blog before asking to be a guest poster on it. The blogs you approach should regularly feature content in line with what you're offering and have an active readership. Your job is to make sure the content you're offering bloggers is similar to what they usually publish, in terms of length, subject matter, and style. Look at the volume of comments on all of the posts on the blog to get a sense of the social interaction, because you want tons of it.

The approach is fairly simple. Either send an email to a blogger with a sample post that is right for their blog and ask them to publish it, or ask them what content they would like you to write. If you send pre-written articles, the bloggers you approach already have the content in hand when deciding whether to work with you, but we have found some prefer to guide your writing. If you can get them to buy into the idea of a piece you write for them based on their input, they will feel more a part of it. Keep your emails short and let them be wowed by your content or Author Rank/social authority (such as your massive Twitter following or email subscriber count), rather than your sales pitches. You can find related blogs by searching for your keywords and "guest blog post" or on blog directories like technorati.com.

Broken Links Can Hurt Your Business Website

Improving your business website's broken links (often referred to as "404 links") can improve your search engine rankings in Google. Whether it's one of your pages linking to a 404 page on your site (a broken *internal* link) or your website linking to another site's 404 page (a broken *external* link) you could be missing out on great backlinks or may be viewed negatively by Google because of dead pages.

What Google Thinks About Broken Links

Google's main goal for their search engine is to bring users the highest-quality experience and results possible, so it makes sense that things that ruin the users' web experience (including broken links) will cause your website to be placed lower in search results compared to competitors who might be giving users a better experience. If your website has 404 links, Google will see it as less of a trustworthy resource, because users will not find what they wanted/searched for (which could be in those dead links).

"If someone is linking to a non-existent page on your site, it can be a bad experience for users (not to mention that you might not be getting credit for that link with search engines unless you're doing extra work). Some of the easiest links you'll ever get are when people tried to link to you and just messed up."

—Matt Cutts

If that quote from Matt Cutts (who is the head of Google Web Spam) doesn't convince you that you should pay attention to your broken links, there are even more clues that Google grades you on it if you look at their program Webmaster Tools. In Google's Webmaster Tools, you can preview your "Crawl Errors" under your "Site Health." This means that Google perceives 404 links as an error on your behalf, and **expects you to change them** (that's why they're offering the tool).

Two Possible Benefits to Fixing Your Broken Links

Google rewards sites that strive to provide a good user experience. Here are the two main ways that removing 404 pages from your website can benefit you:

1. The first benefit is what Matt Cutts outlined in the quote above. Redirecting your broken links to better pages or replacing the page with new content is probably the easiest way to build quality backlinks to your website. Right now your website could have valuable backlinks pointing to 404 pages, so you would not be getting that valuable *"link power."* That means many businesses are so focused on getting new backlinks to their website that they could possibly have many links that are not being utilized because the links are pointing to dead pages.

2. The second benefit is potentially higher rankings from being considered a more trust-worthy website (in Google's eyes). A site cannot be useful if there are dead links to possible helpful resources. Even if Google was not a factor, you would not want to have your visitors leaving your website unsatisfied because they ended up at a broken link. That will make them trust you less (and it looks like you aren't maintaining your site).

Three Resources for 404 Link Information

If you would like more information on broken links and how they can affect your website, try these resources:

1. Wikipedia's Definition of "404 Error"

2. Google Webmaster Tools Blog

3. Wikipedia's Definition of "Link Rot"

Rebuild Missing Content

Trustbait is when we find a resource page that many .edu's link to, but that has been deleted, causing links on the school's website to break. We then re-make the page and alert people that they should fix their broken links and point to our new version of the resource page instead.

Imagine you're the manager of a law school website and you get an email that says: "Dear Joe Smith, Did you know that your link to the top 50 law blunders of all time goes to a page that no longer exists? You might want to link to our version of that content instead using the following code (insert code for your link). Sincerely, Me." Notice that the email is directed to a specific person, not just "To Whom It May Concern." It's always a good idea to know who you're targeting.

Below are some steps you can take, if you want to try this yourself.

How to rebuild content that people still want to link to

Step 1. Find "resource" pages on powerful sites (especially those with URLs ending in .edu and .gov)

Example:
- Search Google for: site: .edu "art career resources"
- Click on results to find a page with a number of outgoing links (long link resource list pages are great for this).

Step 2. Run the URL through the Xenu Link Sleuth tool (http://home.snafu.de/tilman/xenulink.html)

Under "File | Check URL..." enter the URL of the link list/resources page. Also, add the first part of the URL (just through the root domain) to the "Do not check any URLs begin-ning with this" box, to eliminate internal links.

Look for links that come back with a status of "not found" (a 404 error).

Step 3. Put those URLs into www.opensiteexplorer.org to find out how many sites link to those URLs. Look for pages that have lots of links to them.

Step 4. When you find a site with lots of backlinks to it, put it into the "Wayback Machine" tool (www.archive.org), and click through the crawl dates until you find the content that USED to be on that page.

Step 5. Recreate/rewrite that content in your own original way—and even make it better—and put it on your website as a page people can link to.

Step 6. Export a list of the backlinks to the broken page from www.opensiteexplorer.org into Excel.

Step 7. Find a contact email address on each of those sites and email the person letting them know that their link to that content is broken, and give them the link to the new version of the content, asking them to change their link to the new URL. Keep track to see which ones make the change!

By re-creating great content that already had fans linking to it, you will more quickly convince people of high value to link to you and you will get a boost in your search engine rankings.

Authority Sites/Common Backlinks

The most valuable links pointing to your site will be those that come from URLs that not only have lots of quality links pointing to *them* but that also link to many of your competitors. Links from .edu and .gov sites are considered more valuable because they are more authoritative and trusted. Use software such as SEOMoz or Seo Book's Hub Finder to find out who links to the top-ranking sites and go after the same sites. Also make sure to get links that none of them have that only you can get. By having unique links in addition to the great links that top-ranked competitors have, you can put yourself in the top spots.

Typical Backlink Reports Using Tools like SEOMoz or Majestic SEO

1. Link monitoring and tracking (check your links monthly to make sure you are gaining more than you are losing)

2. A list of your backlinks with the anchor text so you can see if you have too many of the same keywords in the links

3. Common backlinks (as seen below in example)

Example: Link Building Competitive Analysis Report

This chart shows your site plus 10 other sites that rank well in the search engines and the links they all share in common. See the information below for greater clarification on how to read this report.

Common Links:

	1	2	3	4	5	6	7	8	9	10
en.wikipedia.org	*	*	*	*	*	*	*	*	*	*
univsource.com	*	*	*	*	*	*	*	*	*	*
utexas.edu	*	*		*	*	*	*	*	*	*
smargon.net	*	*	*	*	*	*	*	*		*
guide-to-us-colleges.com	*	*		*	*	*	*	*	*	*
realcollegelife.com	*	*		*	*	*	*		*	*
subleaser.com	*	*		*	*	*	*		*	
staff.bcc.edu	*	*	*	*		*				*
educationplanner.com	*			*	*	*			*	*
schooldirections.com	*		*	*	*	*				*

The theory is that if you see that a lot of sites ranking well and have links from the same common places, then those places must be good to get links from. Why? They may be part of what makes those sites rank well. Go after these links more aggressively than others with more confidence that the rewards will be great. **Note how all 10 of the sites have a link from en.wikipedia.org and univsource.com.** Lots of sites are also linking to 5 or more competitors, making them part of the overall network of powerful sites in that niche.

Summary

Link building is *by far* one of the hardest and least professionally implemented tactics. Develop more content and get more links, and you will surely make progress. Should you choose to ignore links and say it's just too hard, you will surely have very limited ranking results. Get links mostly for SEO value and not because you deserve them, and the links won't be powerful. A very small handful of high-quality links within real content (e.g., as few as five great links from powerful subpages) can do more than 10,000 low-quality links.

What does an ideal link look like? Having the first link in a paragraph that also cites reputable experts or documents would be a nice, natural link. By linking to other similar sites that are reputable, Google sees the link as more trusted. And if this link is on a page that has a ton of backlinks to it, it will be even more powerful.

Generally seek out in-content links versus links from long pages of links with a page name like "link-partners," but don't completely shy away from being listed on resource pages.

When it comes to great links, it's all about quality.

Link build slowly so it appears more natural, and get a variety of types of links including links using your brand name in the anchor text.

Get fresh links every single month or it looks unnatural.

The first link on a webpage is the one that Google uses most in terms of giving you a ranking benefit. Put your most important links first when you can and try to get sites that link to you, to add your links above links to other sites.

Just like with links coming into your site, remember that the most internally linked-to pages on your site (especially when using wiki-style linking right from within paragraphs using keywords) will make pages rank better.

Buying links is a bad idea. Even though you might not get caught, if you do it can cost you dearly by getting your site penalized.

Remember to link to each and every page on your site, not just to your home page. This is called deep linking and helps your "inner" page rank well.

Google Penguin and Links

Google's Penguin search algorithm update targeted such things as:

- Low-quality content on sites/pages that link to you

- Link farms/spam

- Anchor text overuse

- Fake blog networks

- Site-wide links

- Percentage of low-quality to high-quality links

Penguin-proof Your Site:

- Ask yourself: "Would I want this link if there was no such thing as Google?"

- Use varied anchor text so you don't overdo linking from the same keywords

Web Marketing On All Cylinders - John McDougall

- Use only high-quality guest blogging. Don't just target "guest blog sites." Use social media to find great guest blog posts where you can publish content with links to your site.

- Poor usability can hurt you.

- Focus on share-ability (connecting content to social).

- Use the Google bad link identification tool only in very extreme cases. Instead, concentrate on getting more high-quality relevant links and building a better ratio of good to bad links. Build links every single month.

- Relevancy is one of the most important things with linking now, so don't stray too far outside sites that should logically be good link connections for you topically.

- Don't focus only on Google and find other modes of generating traffic. If you get banned from Google, what will you do for traffic while you are trying to get back in or selecting a new URL?

Think Relationship Building More Than Link Building

Small business link building is really hard, because small websites often don't have a ton of great content or newsworthy activity. But if you can build an amazing blog and a repository of regularly updated content, you can start to engage in relationship building.

Here are four steps to building relationships with the eventual aim of getting links:

1. Set up Google Reader with RSS feeds of blogs and news sites on your topic.

2. Start following users and retweeting/commenting on their content via Google+ and Twitter, etc.

3. Create relationships by being a regular presence where people discuss your industry online.

4. Curate other people's content, link to it, and share it.

By freely sharing the content of others and letting them know you have interacted with their work, you will create friends. Those friends will sometimes feel obliged to give back to you. Two of the top persuasive tactics of Dr. Robert Cialdini, author of *Influence: The Power of Persuasion*, are likability and giving something for free. Cialdini says that we're more likely to be influenced by people we like. So be a nice guy or gal and share with others, and they might just give you a link without your asking or be more receptive when at some point you share something you ask them to link to. If we give something like a retweet away, then the chances of them feeling that they should return the favor are even greater. Cialdini believes that we innately feel a sense of responsibility to give back to those who give to us.

Remember that Google prefers links that are given based on merit and that stand the test of time. Do remarkable things and create relationships, and long-lasting links will follow.

Chapter 6

Public Relations in the Digital Age

With all the other marketing changes taking place around us, is it any surprise that public relations (PR) has gone digital? Consequently, you need to reevaluate the old methods of PR and incorporate new media strategies into your marketing plans. Your audience is online, and journalists no longer have the same level of "gate-keeping" power they once did now that businesses and individuals can also reach out to people directly. While connecting with journalists is still important, it is now only one part of the PR equation.

However, regardless of the online, print, or broadcast media channels available to you, the problem still can be stated as:

Doing business without public relations is like winking in the dark.

You know what you're doing, but no one else does!

After all, the primary job of PR is to attract attention, delivering high visibility with something advertising simply cannot match: *credibility.* When a third party such as a journalist, blogger, or even a chat-room member says nice things about your company and/ or product, your credibility soars. This is because someone else, not you, is saying the nice things. Let's face it, wouldn't you rather be advised to "check this out" than be told to "buy, buy, buy"? Sure you would. And if people say bad things about you, you need to be listening to the conversation and respond quickly. Social media and online sites make it so much easier for your customers and critics to complain, but also much easier for you to respond (on a real-time basis in some cases).

How PR Has Changed

Not so long ago, PR professionals measured their effectiveness by the number of press releases sent out, number of calls made to journalists, and other quantifiable tasks. For example, getting a major magazine or top network news show to run a feature story about your company is an achievement, yet the PR department always correlated the amount of print space or broadcast time to the amount of advertising dollars it would have taken to generate the same amount of coverage.

In some cases, this helped justify the PR budget. For example, our PR person generated a five-page feature article about a small New Jersey software company in *Wired* magazine which is valued the same as a $350,000 ad spend! But that kind of visibility is hard to come by on a regular basis. The new way of practicing PR in the digital age has changed the measuring stick.

Today, it's much more common to see marketing and PR specialists counting how many people actually opened an email newsletter containing a press release or how many people found a press release by searching Google, Bing, or Yahoo! News. You can even track how many people saw your pages mentioned in the release, filled out a form, downloaded a white paper, or signed up for one of your services. Southwest Airlines, for example, way back in 2005 sold $2.5 million dollars' worth of tickets from a series of SEO-optimized press releases. This is a major improvement in measurement of the effects of PR!

What's Changed: The Highlights

- Old PR is for journalists only.

- New PR is for the masses as well as journalists.

- In 2002, Google News took headlines from thousands of news and distribution sites and then in 2004 Yahoo! News created a whole new era of online PR.

- Now, press releases show up in the search results and can drive huge volumes of traffic.

- Over 50,000 press releases are issued each month, so journalists have little time to spare for your release.

- Blogger and social media connections are a big part of the new Rolodex for journalists and marketers.

- Content created by you and your agency plays a big part in getting media coverage.

- Press releases and blog/media site referrals can now be tracked to see which ones send you leads and conversions.

How the Media Has Changed

Having your press release reach the number one spot on Google and Yahoo! News or having your content featured on a top blog can be as good as or even better than a front-page article in print. While many offline news channels have been steadily declining, online news has been growing like wildfire.

Households that canceled cable service are an indicator of the shift to web TV, at least as an additional option. Month after month, hundreds of thousands of cable TV subscribers keep closing their accounts. Thanks to dozens of videocasting websites (such as Hulu, TV.com, Joost, and Fancast), full-length episodes of more than 90 percent of the shows carried by the major broadcast networks are legally accessible within a day of being broadcast, according to Forrester Research. (Only about 20 percent of what's on cable is similarly available.) It is uncertain just how far this disruption will go, given that cable is still fairly strong, but clearly online is an amazingly strong channel. Online video is really just in its infancy and as it gets better, so will its ability to draw eyeballs away from cable.

Given that top blogs now command traffic at rates as good as or better than traditional media, the online channels are a must to master.

Newspaper Advertising Revenue Drops Like a Rock

Advertising revenue for newspapers, adjusted for inflation, has dropped to 1950s levels. After rising for over 50 years, newspaper ad revenue dropped radically in 2003 and then for good in about 2005. Online classifieds and blogs put the nail in its coffin. Online communities that people can join became more interesting and were free. Craigslist, Monster.com, eBay, and other websites that replaced traditional classified ads stole huge ad dollars from newspapers. Paul Gillin, our partner for our seminar series, started Newspaper Death Watch to chronicle the demise of newspapers. *Newsweek* magazine published its last print edition in December 2012, and is launching an all-digital format in 2013. The venerable Encyclopaedia Britannica also announced in 2012 that it would cease print publication.

Suffice it to say the news business is in a big transition. The dust hasn't settled yet by any means, but from a PR perspective, companies need to understand that the old yardstick of counting column inches of coverage is not so relevant—you want your news online.

The top 15 most popular news sites from eBizMBA in October 2012

News Source	Estimated Unique Monthly Visitors
1. Yahoo! News	110,000,000
2. CNN	74,000,000
3. MSNBC	73,000,000
4. Google News	65,000,000
5. New York Times	59,500,000
6. HuffingtonPost	54,000,000
7. Fox News	32,000,000

8.	Washington Post	25,000,000
9.	LATimes	24,900,000
10.	Mail Online	24,800,000
11.	Reuters	24,000,000
12.	ABCNews	20,000,000
13.	USA Today	18,000,000
14.	BBC News	17,000,000
15.	Drudge Report	14,000,000

Newspaper losses open a door for those willing to adapt. Newspapers and other print media are gunning it with online editions. If you have a real content marketing plan and a trending story to tell, you can ride the new wave. Rather than spending so much in print ads and in traditional PR, website owners must nurture relationships with reporters, editors, and publishers through blogs and other social media. TV and print ad revenues have seen significant declines, though some niche magazines and local cable are doing reasonably well despite cutbacks. We live in a brave new world and an ever-shifting landscape.

Think Strategically for PR: What's the "Hook"?

Regardless of the medium—newspapers and magazines, broadcast and cable TV, radio, social networking platforms, or blogs—the key to getting your story picked up stays the same: every writer, reporter, and editor must feel that your information is relevant, timely, and useful to their audience(s). However, they won't feel that way unless you serve up your story with a "hook" that gets their attention.

With the barrage of press releases every media outlet faces daily, editors and reporters apply selective filters to separate the mundane from true "news." Getting your story through those filters is the primary responsibility of your PR professionals. The hook is what helps. Your company's story may not be urgent "breaking news," but if you can demonstrate in your press release that your information is relevant and useful to that media outlet's audience, or you have a timely comment on something in the news, you increase your chances for PR coverage.

A recent media phenomenon is the rise of hyperlocal news sites—websites that focus directly on a local community, providing readers with a wide range of relevant news and information each day. These aren't mom-and-pop websites—some of the biggest media players, including AOL and The New York Times Company, have launched hyperlocal news sites all across the country. The Patch.com sites are one example, set up for an increasing number of cities and towns in 23 states at this writing.

The best news about this explosion of hyperlocal and other online news sites is they all need content. If you want coverage, you need to deliver relevant, timely, and thoroughly edited content, and the "hook" or angle still counts.

With all the changes in technology and the media, it's hard to keep up with the many activities it takes to succeed. Write down your PR plan to make it more concrete and likely to succeed. Before creating a PR strategy, ask yourself these questions:

1. What's the hook?

    Without an angle that relates to the concerns or needs of a given media outlet's audience, your story is likely just fluff (and not likely to be picked up).

    What's different about you or your company?

    What are you the expert on?

    What makes you better than your competitors?

    What's your "Unique Selling Proposition" (USP)?

    What can you use (beyond your company or expertise) to help you stand out?

2. Do you want national or local coverage or both?

    This can help narrow or broaden your research in the media outlets to target.

3. Who's the audience (of the media outlet)?

    Your angle/story has to match the audience of the media it targets.

4. Which media outlets are most effective?

    Target online and offline outlets but pick media that match your own target audience well. Use competitive analysis to see which media outlets are covering your peers and competitors.

5. Who are the journalists who cover your topic area or "beat"?

    Develop a list of the top journalists and bloggers in your industry.

6. When should you send out your information to be timely?

    Release stories that match a season or a trend. For example, the owner of a gift store (whether online or bricks-and-mortar) might send out "Top 10 Mother's Day Gift Ideas" lists in March (or earlier for media outlets with longer lead times) in hopes of getting coverage in the weeks running up to Mother's Day.

7. How often should you send out press releases?

Old-school PR people tend to be concerned about sending releases too often. Still a valid concern, depending on the media outlet and what you're sending out—a steady stream of fluff does not build a company's reputation but gets the press releases tossed or deleted. However, since online sites drop your releases after about a month, you should submit a series of releases to keep your information reappearing online. But don't bug your local paper with a fluffy announcement every day—you will wear out your welcome *fast*.

8. Do you have a story that includes a customer rather than just a pitch?

Journalists prefer juicy stories that involve real people (including your customers) and tend to dislike straight sales pitches.

9. Is your story part of a larger trend?

If you can connect to a larger trend, you have a better chance of being taken more seriously and having your story picked up or being considered as a source for an interview. Use Google Trends/Insights/Suggest or Google News for research.

10. What is hot on Google News?

11. Is your reputation good or bad when you search for your company and product names on Google?

Crisis and reputation management is more important and complicated than ever. Be aware that there are tactics that allow you to fill up the first several pages of search engine results with pages that you promote. But nothing is better than responding to and diffusing rough situations and winning people over so they become brand cheerleaders.

Understanding PR's Many Moving Parts

Media Relations

While outreach to the media is still essential, it is just one component of PR. Reaching bloggers should now be a major part of your PR outreach. Use tools like Wordtracker's Link Builder and Technorati to find top blogs. Then don't just call them or email them, connect with them via social media. Some bloggers are journalists at "traditional" media outlets.

News Releases

Submitting press releases to online distribution services like PRWeb.com can cause your releases to be picked up "as is" and/or elaborated on by news sites and blogs. These syndications and news stories about you can be found in the search engines and generate links/traffic to your site. While some free sites for submissions are okay, you get what you pay for. Spend $150 to $300 on a local release of significance on top sites like businesswire.com, marketwire.com, and PRWeb.com to get the most out of it.

Company Blog

Use your company blog to share routine news and more personal versions of the news you have submitted to wire services. That way, long after sites like Google News have buried your release, it will still live via keyword search online that takes people to your blog post.

Newsroom

Create a news page on your site. Clearly list your contact information for journalists and key information about your company, and include something that gives your company some personality—perhaps an overview video or links to award pages or a calendar of speaking engagements. Include social media contact points like your Twitter handle. Also make sure there are links from the news page to biographies of key team members. Having images and video on your news page just might make the difference between getting a story or not.

What's the Hook?

We mentioned earlier in this chapter that every press release and story pitch needs a news hook. Without one, a story is doomed to obscurity. Here are some ideas for news content to get you started:

1. Awards and accomplishments

2. Promote or recap speaking engagements

3. Inspirational stories

4. Share tips and lessons

5. Highlight an event

6. Chime in on an industry trend or event in the news

7. Share what you have done with a charity

8. Announce new products and services

9. Research and data you just created

10. New website or significant upgrade to existing website

11. Offer free information: ebook, newsletter, or white paper

12. Celebrate an important company anniversary

13. Announce the opening of a new office or a relocation

14. Signing a large client

15. Hosting a seminar or webinar

16. Partnering with another business or organization

17. Hiring a new executive

18. Hosting a major contest, sweepstakes, or promotion

19. Reveal industry scams

20. Announce holiday sales and events

21. Make predictions for your industry

22. You're the first at something

23. Announcement that involves a large amount of money

24. "Man-bites-dog" type of weird or controversial stories

25. Publish great case studies the press can use in stories about your topic or industry

SEO-Optimized Online PR Is Winning the Race

When you optimize and send out a press release to online media distribution services, you can bypass journalists and editors—the goal is to get your info to the people directly via the search engines. The hope is that your release will get picked up as written and shuttled right into massive online channels. We have, for example, sent a press release for a law firm via Marketwire that got redistributed on dozens, if not hundreds, of news sites, including places like a local NBC station in Texas. Shortly after, our PR person got a call from a newspaper looking to interview our client. We have also had lawyers get cases directly from a potential customer seeing the release when searching Google and then calling to sign up as a client.

As usual, content is key here. When you create and submit press releases, part of the goal is to get others to resubmit them on news sites and blogs, thereby creating a viral effect and increasing your website's search engine rankings and backlinks.

One of the big challenges bloggers and journalists face is finding fresh, relevant news regularly. They are on deadlines and need stories fast. In the modern PR landscape, Google is their main research tool. We have had many clients get media coverage because of our having them ranked well in the search engines. So PR and SEO go hand in hand, and they are easily driven by keywords on a second-by-second basis using a free tool like Google Alerts. This means that everyone in every conceivable niche can now have access to the latest press releases the second they are released. That's just wild.

Offline PR also drives people to your website, but often they will simply hear about you and later search for you using Google. When a story about you or a press release about your company appears in a search on Google, Google News, and Yahoo! News, you win! The important thing is to make it easy for consumers and journalists to find you.

Most journalists use Google and many visit corporate website online newsrooms weekly for the companies on their beat. Now that Google is pushing universal search (where news, videos, Flickr streams, and more may all appear as part of the main search results), your press releases, news videos, and online content have a greater chance of being found by both consumers and journalists.

Another example of one of our client's press release successes is when Jiffy Lube got sued for $47 million for text spamming and they did a release about it. The release on PRWeb is the number one regular Google result for a search for "Jiffy Lube sued for spam" and their site comes up number four for the same search (and ranks for numerous "Jiffy Lube lawsuit"-related long tail terms). Their helpful perspective on the case in the release generates visitors and phone calls, straight from the search engines, even if it never gets any or significant media coverage. As a side note, my client's Jiffy Lube release has over a dozen retweets and many likes/shares.

The benefits of optimized online PR include:

- Traffic to your website

- Inbound links to your website that help your search rankings

- Pickups by industry publications and blogs

- Credibility that stems from your company being "in the news"

- Leads

- Getting sales and clients directly from releases

- Making more money!

Typical content to optimize:

- Press releases/news releases

- Online news rooms and media kits

- Blog posts

- Reports/white papers

- Webinars/demos

- Email newsletters

- Podcasts/interviews (where you structure an interview around keywords)

- Videos

Essentials of an Optimized Press Release

Here's how to optimize your press release so it does the most for you online.

- Determine keywords. Pick 2–3 keyphrases per release and don't overuse them.

- Write a headline that packs a punch and has a keyword (subtly) included in it, in 80 characters or less.

- Use keywords in your first paragraph. Pick both short tail and long tail keywords. If you only go after terms that get high traffic with high competition, you may be relegated to obscurity. Add terms like "Italian leather running sneaker trends" not just "running sneakers" and you have a better shot at getting some effective traffic (even if the volume is small).

- A strong summary paragraph in which the keyword from the headline is repeated.

- Use anchor text links in the first paragraph of your release. Anchor text links are links that you click on that have a keyword in the link text itself. Vary this as you don't want all your links coming from a few keywords. If you don't add links in the first paragraph or so, the links may not get used. Only add a few anchor text links per post.

- Make sure one link (the first link) also has a full address that includes "http://www." at the beginning for the sites that don't create a live link without that. Be sure the URL is not immediately preceded or followed by punctuation, including a period.

- Link not just to your home page but to pages deep within your site that are relevant to the press release. Keep in mind it is not the "no followed" news site (links that don't pass link juice) links that you are after. You want to reach the people who will see the story and write about it on their blogs and tweet about it, which gets you more SEO-friendly links.

- If you add a unique link to the press release it becomes even more trackable, as only people who saw the release clicked that link.

- Match the page title with an important keyword like the one in the headline and anchor text.

- Keep your press release short, about 300 to 500 words. Press releases need to get right to the point, with the most important information in the first sentence and paragraph.

- Add an interesting image and/or video. A link to a video saves money with the submission services and can still be effective. Journalists love images and video because they make a story more interesting to their readers. Make it easy for them to find your visual materials to support their content.

- Check your release for proper spelling and grammar. Don't depend on the computer; have a human check it too. Spellcheck doesn't know if you meant "to," "too," or "two."

- Add juicy quotes from key people in your company or from customers.

- Eliminate industry jargon (or explain it if you must use it) and avoid clichéd terms like "cutting edge" and "innovative."

- Add a call to action that is not overly salesy but offers a point of action. If you are selling tickets, then link to the sale page. If you have a free ebook, then provide the download link.

- Consider sending people to a specialized landing page that is specific to the press release.

- Optimize the "about your company section" with keywords and contact information. If people will need to contact your company after hours, provide a cell number that will be answered. Add social connection options.

- If you need to get started quickly, write a release about a new employee, a new service or product offering, or an upcoming event. This may not go viral but it will still generate those much-needed backlinks and give you a feel for the process. Google likes to see regular mentions of you coming from outside your site, so issue a press release at least monthly, more if possible.

How to Distribute the Press Release

Select one top PR wire service and don't go crazy submitting to dozens of free sites.

Top PR sites that cost more but get you more coverage:

Marketwire.com	Businesswire.com
PRWeb.com	Prnewswire.com

The cost to distribute a press release through one of the above services can range from $150 to $300 per release to as much as $600 to $1,000 or more for national releases with extra features. Spending just under $300 often does the trick.

A few free press release submission sites:

prleap.com	i-newswire.com	prfree.com

These free sites change constantly and are much weaker in terms of distribution reach and SEO potential than the paid sites.

Timing is everything. Make sure your best ideas launch when people will be searching for them or when the topic will be on people's minds. For example, the Golf Zone would run its promotion during the PGA Championship.

Track the Results of Your Online PR Submissions

You may never actually pitch anyone if all you do is submissions. Most of our clients use the online wire services and don't do full media outreach, so they need to know they can track this apart from full PR.

- Use Analytics to see what media and blog sites drove traffic and which converted to sales.

- Track pickups via the wire service tracking tools and Google alerts. Share these with your team and put together background info on how big the sites/blogs are that featured you.

Pitching Tips

Start an Excel document or journalist database of people to target. Bulldog Reporter, MEDI-Atlas, Batchbook, Highrise, and Salesforce are good tools to consider.

Identify media outlets—both online and off—in your targeted industries; for example, business and marketing. Add local, regional, national, and international channels to cover television, radio/talk radio, newspapers, magazines, online publications, newswires, and other services.

After submitting your release to the wire services, you can also share it with journalists via email, calls, Twitter, etc. Never—ever—send a press release as an attachment. It will never be opened. Make sure your headline (see "What's the Hook?" above) grabs attention in the message line. The text of the press release should be the body of the email message. Attachments should be limited to photographs and other visuals.

When pitching the media, keep the following in mind:

- Know your audience and target only the media people who make sense for your story.

- Be brief.

- Accept "no" if they turn you down after a couple tries.

- Read their publication/blog and point out exactly how your information helps their audience.

- Make sure your hook/angle is worthwhile for that audience.

- Create amazing content and use that as the hook if you don't have much of a news hook. In other words, you can create news.

Learn What the Media Is Looking For

There are a number of very useful services that can let you see what reporters and bloggers are looking for, every day. They were begun as a way for journalists to put out the word about stories they are writing and find expert sources to interview, but they also serve as an excellent way for potential sources (like you) to offer to help. In fact, one of the services is called "Help a Reporter Out" (known as HARO).

HARO is famous in the PR world and if you haven't seen it I recommend checking it out. HARO is an email newsletter that goes out three times a day, listing journalists working on stories for which they need experts to interview. If you subscribe to this free email newsletter, you can scan it for journalists who need help on your topic and respond quickly. It was started as a Facebook group in 2008 by Peter Shankman, and now is a mailing list with over 100,000 members. It is now owned by Vocus.

Another service, "Reporter Connection," works the same way, although this free email newsletter comes out once per day and was started by Bill and Steve Harrison of Bradley Communications. There's also ProfNet, a paid service offered by PR Newswire, which helps connect experts and journalists.

Social Media and PR

Sharing your press release brings you more buzz and traffic and opens up the potential for media coverage. Social networks like Twitter, LinkedIn, Facebook, and Google+ help journalists find subject matter experts quickly. So position yourself as just that and make your social connection points readily available on your website, blog, and marketing materials.

Authority through Social Proof and Google+ Author Rank

It makes sense that bloggers and journalists check out how many other news and blog sites have covered you previously. No one wants to take a chance and cover you for the first time if it is unclear you are sought after or interesting. They are also potentially more likely to share your story (when they are looking for an expert) if you have lots of Twitter followers, many "shares" of your content, and significant Google+ connections and Author Rank. So ask yourself the hard questions: "Am I worthy and, if I am, does my social connectivity make that obvious?" Check out Dan Schwabel and his personal branding blog. He has massive followers and subscribers, making him an obvious choice for interviews on the topic of personal branding. These connections can make journalists more intrigued by your story.

Additionally, monitoring social media platforms and participating in social communities are critical. If you give some information away and have a hot blog along with an on-site newsroom with regularly submitted releases, your visibility, links, and ranks will increase and create new viral exposure.

Join relevant LinkedIn, Facebook, and Yahoo! Groups where you can see what people are buzzing about, and offer your helpful tips and share your releases/stories as part of the conversation. But don't spam discussion groups with a barrage of press releases; make a helpful comment and give people a link to your release.

Twitter and PR

Twitter has become a strong player in the news world and is only getting stronger. Twitter updates have been a vehicle for stories in such places as Iran, when no other outlets were allowing stories through.

Tweet your story several times and vary the headline. Don't overdo it, but do it more than once.

Categorize it by adding a #hashtag that journalists and bloggers may be following.

Acknowledge retweets with a "thank you."

Build a Twitter influencer list. Search Twitter using a hashtag like #marketing or #restaurants, whatever is relevant to you. The reporters in that space are likely using those hashtags, making them easier to find.

Some cool Twitter tools are JournalistTweets.com (helps journalists connect with each other but you can find them with this tool), Muck Rack (journalists listed by publication/topic), and Twitter Grader (listed by how influential they are).

Use Localtweeps to find reporters in your area.

Facebook, LinkedIn, and Google+

Link to your story from your Facebook and Google+ pages to encourage "shares." Send out new messages that pull interesting facts from your press release.

Like and comment on journalists' Facebook posts.

Facebook groups can be a great way to get involved in discussions about niche topics, and you might be able to connect with journalists there or on LinkedIn if you have something worth sharing. But don't go right out and ask to be friends on Facebook or connect on LinkedIn with journalists if you haven't yet established a relationship. Twitter is different and less personal, so you can follow journalists and connect with them there easily. On Facebook and LinkedIn, you can get yourself in trouble if you get too personal too fast. Once you are reasonably connected, however, it's okay to reach out on LinkedIn.

Optimize your LinkedIn profile so you can be found by reporters looking for a source: use keywords in your title, summary, and throughout your past job descriptions.

Pin your release as a photo on Pinterest and use keywords in your filename, the board you pin it to, and description text.

Make a more personal, less formal, and summarized version of the story for your blog.

Share your press release on SlideShare if it contains or relates to lots of images, facts, statistics, and figures.

RSS and PR

RSS (most commonly expanded as Really Simple Syndication) is a way to publish frequently updated content such as blog entries, news headlines, audio, and video so users can get it delivered to them through a feed reader rather than having to visit your website to see when new stuff comes out. RSS feeds can be read using software called "RSS readers," "feed readers," or "aggregators."

PRESSfeed (press-feed.com) is a service specifically for PR and is one way to let people get feeds of your news content without having to visit your website. PRESSfeed's philosophy is that having a place on your website where journalists, bloggers, and consumers can find and share your social media content is a critical step in your social media and SEO strategy. Your newsroom should be partly a social media newsroom, and not a dull list of press releases.

Posting news on your website, tagging it, and distributing it in an RSS feed that lets others tag and share it on sites like Delicious (a social bookmarking site) spreads your content to key influencers who may be inspired to comment on it and share it.

If you haven't tried RSS to get the news for yourself, see how it works here: nytimes.com/services/xml/rss/index.html

Track the Results of Social Media and Releases

1. Use Google Analytics to see which media and blog sites drove traffic and which converted to sales. Focus on media that converts!

2. Track pickups via the wire service tracking tools (such as CustomScoop) and Google Alerts.

3. Set up Google Alerts on your brand/product names and the same for your competitors.

4. Use Facebook Insights to monitor the growth in number of fans and page views.

5. Use Google Reader to set up RSS feeds of searches in social news sites like Reddit, etc.

Web Marketing On All Cylinders - John McDougall

6. Track increases in the number of your Twitter followers.

7. To show how your PR campaigns are impacting SEO, check the number of PR-related back-links you have generated. Tools like Majestic SEO can show you the recent links you got. Scan through and see which media and bloggers link to you, to determine which of these links came as the result of your releases.

8. Track metrics like social shares and comments.

9. Use tools such as Topsy, Trackur, Sprout Social, or Radian6 to monitor and measure social media buzz.

Don't think you are not worthy of press coverage—get out there and ask! As Wayne Gretzky said: "You miss 100% of the shots you don't take!"

For More Info on Public Relations

www.Instututeforpr.org: Institute for Public Relations

www.prsa.org: Public Relations Society of America

www.iabc.com: International Association of Business Communicators

www.prnewswire.com/mediainsider: Media Insider

www.odwyerpr.com: O'Dwyer's PR Marketplace

www.infocomgroup.com: InfoCom Group Bulldog Reporter

www.prnewswire.com: PR Newswire

www.prweek.com: PRWeek

Now that you have the skills to make a highly search-optimized website with lots of backlinks and publicity, it's time to hone in on social media marketing and optimization.

Chapter 7

Remarkable Social Media Marketing and Optimization

A well-executed social media campaign can result in favorable branding, instant PR, and higher organic search engine results. Some companies are using social media to replace large numbers of customer service reps, while others have used it to make some of the highest-ROI ad campaigns in history—based on content and conversation versus broadcasting cute sales pitches.

The basic concept behind social media optimization is simple: implement changes to make a site/brand and its content more connected to online communities. By spreading around your great content and knowledge through articles, photos, videos, and free downloads, you show off your industry expertise. You then get linked to, which helps your SEO efforts, and you receive visits from people interested in what you have to say or share. Your social profiles then show up in searches on search engines and are more frequently included in relevant posts on blogs.

Social media marketing, especially as it ties in so perfectly with SEO, is one of the lowest-cost ways to create targeted traffic, exceptional relationships, more credibility, engagement, and links. That makes it hard to justify not getting involved in social media and putting some of your marketing budget into this new area. Given a lower cost per lead, big dollars are tumbling down from traditional ad spends and are headed this way.

By now, you're nodding your head. You understand that "pull" marketing to start conversations that could lead to conversions is *so* much smarter than trying to sell/push stuff on anyone ever again.

You understand that you have to give to get and you are reading this saying to yourself, "Yes, that's what I have to do."

Then you close the book for a moment and say to yourself…

"How do I do that?" or "I am terrified by what this means to my company."

And you *should* be scared and maybe even terrified, because your competitors are dreaming up things you just won't believe. Take the case of Vail Resorts. They are so dedicated to digital marketing that they shifted 80 percent of their marketing budget to digital production and social media strategy. They got their entire team together and decided that if new media is the way of the future, then they need to make a radical change. They discovered that their audience is more than just about skiing and leaving. They love to be social. So they made a site that lets users share photos, videos, and stories. They hired photographers and videographers to film people and have it uploaded to their personal portal set up for each visitor on the resort site. They put digital "receivers" in the ski tickets that marked what visitors did during the day and their journey was uploaded online to the portal. In other words, they changed their products and services radically to keep up with the new possibilities created by the wild, wild Internet. Are you ready for that kind of remarkable change?

You and your company are standing at the doorway of a revolution in online marketing. If this does not cause you to look twice at every other way to market, then you need to get yourself checked out. By a professional—LOL!

This is about you having the unique ability to create content and campaigns that are moving so steadily that they bury your competitors, who will never be able to catch up.

And that just plain rocks.

Writing blogs and using social networking sites such as Facebook, LinkedIn, Twitter, Pinterest, Google+, and YouTube is great, but you have to do it in a strategic fashion or you'll just create a mess. You also need to be prepared to spend some time, money, or both, because each tactic and channel has its own requirements for using it effectively.

11 Tips for a Strong Social Media Strategy

Since there are already many books that go into great depth on social media, we'll focus here on the gory details of creating and sharing great content in various channels. Before we dive in, there are a few things you should know about social media marketing from a 30,000-foot view.

1. Get on board. A huge percentage of the world's population is using Facebook and other social media and that number is growing. Google created Google+ because it had to compete or die. They take it that seriously and so should you. Almost every news show you see these days has mentions of things trending in Twitter. Social media is here to stay. Failing to pay attention to and quickly diffuse negative comments about your brand can crush your company, while being an active part of the positive conversations can make you shine.

2. Know your audience. Writing to the wrong crowd will be very ineffective, but knowing and defining the personas of the people you are targeting allows your content to move people more emotionally and deeply. If you can move people, you have a better chance of converting them into customers and retaining them.

3. Create clear objectives. Unless you know what you want to get out of social media, you will never be able to set up analytics tracking based on key performance indicators. It is much easier at the end of the year or quarter to report back success or failure when your objectives are in a clearly documented form that have been agreed upon by the whole team.

4. Make sure your various social channels have a similar look and feel.

5. Develop a social media policy and playbook so your team is all on the same page. Everyone should be working from a playbook that sorts out potential compliance issues and encourages brand message consistency.

6. Create a content marketing plan so your content has a greater impact and is timelier. For example, releasing a recipe guide to the Italian Christmas "feast of the seven fishes" on the Fourth of July won't have the best impact. Riding the wave of a trending topic can propel you to huge content success, while writing in-depth about old news can be a waste of time.

7. Hire an agency to help you with strategy at the very least and determine who—likely an individual or a team at your company—is extremely knowledgeable, tactful, and able to respond in real time to things that would be harder for the agency to handle.

8. To help you write content, hire people who are strong writers and who know (or can learn) your business. If you can't do it all yourself, having a flow of content from outside sources that is vetted by you will go a long way in creating a steadier steam of blog posts, ebooks, and perhaps eventually an actual printed book to solidify your reputation as a leader in your space.

9. Set up deep tracking systems using Google Analytics (and ideally HubSpot). Studies show much of social marketing is undervalued because people don't always buy immediately after a first warm-up touch from social connections. They bookmark you and/or remember you and are influenced more the next time they see you. In traditional marketing, we have always been aware it takes many impressions before someone trusts you. The number of impressions needed before someone buys from you is going up because people have more options than ever, so you need to get in front of people in a variety of ways to get the eventual sale. You need what is called

attribution tracking, which lets you see the influence of the first and every touch a customer has with your site over time, not just the last tactic that made the sale. Don't be too quick to throw tactics out until you get this type of tracking figured out. Attribution tracking is the most exciting thing about marketing in my lifetime. The old-school "Mad Men"-style died off because it didn't have this tracking capability. While tracking like this is possible to do, few have real control over it without a tool like HubSpot or a really tweaked Google Analytics.

10. Get to know the tools. Radian6 is about $600 a month but is a very powerful way to monitor the buzz around your brand and respond in real time. HootSuite is a great low-cost tool that is hugely popular that does some similar things but not nearly as much. Software can be a huge time-saver, so budget for software and training even if you have an outside agency helping you.

11. Know that social signals play a part in users coming to trust that you are someone they should do business with. They may also eventually send more powerful signals to the search engines than they do today. Start building your authority levels as these signals will only grow in terms of influence.

Where Is Social Marketing Going? Hope You're Sitting Down

To not realize that social marketing is a force to be incorporated into your business is to bury your head in the sand.

From YouTube to Pinterest (the fastest-growing website so far) to Twitter to, of course, Facebook and all of the other social sharing sites, you need to have boots on the ground (where it makes sense for your business) when it comes to social media.

But there is something that you must do before you do that.

You must start! As simple as that sounds, it is not simple for many (if not most) companies to get the ball rolling.

Start with content you know best...the stuff that rolls out of you at cocktail parties and school functions about what you do and how you do it. Get that down in written, video, and audio formats.

Guess what? It's not hard to do. It's hard to *start doing*...and therein lies the opportunity.

The most powerful online marketing companies will tell you that saying content is king is like saying money is valuable. But not all content is created equal and to get to the point where you are producing great content, you must begin the process so you can learn as you go and only get stronger.

The biggest mistake we see businesses making in social media is the creation of blah content. A few videos that don't get the heartbeat up. Some photos on Pinterest that are just okay. Tweets that are relatively tame. And Facebook updates that are surprisingly self-serving.

Social marketing is being led by companies willing to take the time to create strong content that really adds value for others and starts a conversation. It has to inform and excite and create a stir. But none of that happens until you push away from the dock.

Do not create content about your business that doesn't get people excited about the information that you are willing to give them! Please spend an extra week to map out blog posts, video content, and photos that are powerful and compelling.

Create video blogs where you let people into how car sticker prices really work. Tell us how to shave dollars off when we buy concert tickets online. Be willing to reveal to us how caterers cut corners and how to make sure you don't fall for it.

Interview your customers and have them talk about the issues they face...not about how great you are. (Use the video capability in your smartphone.) Have them tell their stories and let them reveal why you were such a great choice when you showed up...no matter how you showed up.

Start the flow of gripping content that gets the conversations going. That is when you can very slowly and carefully start introducing yourself as a solutions provider.

The number of useless YouTube videos out there is staggering. Many business owners wonder why their view counts are so low. They are low because the value of the video is so low! Push yourself to make sure your videos get attention.

Social marketing is the new frontier. It is a beautiful stage upon which all inbound marketing sits. It is extremely cost-effective, but only if you commit to producing truly powerful content.

Over and over and over again.

How Social Media Affects SEO Rankings and Conversions Simultaneously

"People buy from people they know, like, and trust" is an old saying, but it couldn't be timelier. Your authority, derived from being a thought leader with great content, is a huge asset to your overall web presence. By having lots of fans, blog subscribers, likes, shares, +1s, and followers, you are seen as a leader. When you rank high in the search engines results, you are seen as a leader. These things go hand in hand, and when you do both at once it creates a domino effect that helps your Internet marketing reach levels you never dreamed of.

Google can potentially monitor who comments on your blog from an authority perspective, so you want real people to comment, people who have weight in Google's eyes. When your golf club blog content gets a comment from the newest PGA champion retweeting it, Google (if not now, in the future) could use that directly as an authoritative signal. It's all about author authority, and the source of it is what really matters moving forward. This is why Google created Google+ Author Rank to indicate an author's value, not just a website's or a page's value. We will have more on this in the section on Google+, but first let's look at what the search engines are doing with social signals.

Personalized Search

Many people don't realize that search results are based on location and the recommendations of your connections. If you are signed in to your Google account, you will be given results based on what your Google connections have +1'd. If you are signed in to Facebook and conduct a search in Bing social results, you will be given relevant sites that your Facebook friends have "liked." People trust their friends and family and the search engines are now struggling with how to incorporate these signals.

Google believes in social so much it built is own social network (Google+) along the lines of Facebook, while Bing chooses to integrate data from sites like Facebook and Foursquare to enhance the user's experience. The things that used to be only in the minds of people (like their opinions of restaurants and travel tips) are now index-able and usable by others.

Social Signals

Danny Sullivan, one of the most famous search engine marketing experts, interviewed Bing and Google representatives in December 2010 on how Facebook and Twitter may impact a company's search engine rankings. He asked about the weighting of Twitter users and links shared in their tweets.

Bing: "We do look at the social authority of a user. We look at how many people you follow, how many follow you, and this can add a little weight to a listing in regular search results."

Google: "Yes, we do use [tweeted links and retweets] as a signal. It is used as a signal in our organic and news rankings. We also use it to enhance our news universal by marking how many people shared an article."

(See http://www.seoconsult.com/seoblog/social-media-optimisation/confirmed-twit-ter-facebook-influence-seo-rankings.html for more.)

Sullivan also asked, "Do you track links shared within Facebook, either through personal walls or fan pages?"

Bing: "Yes. We look at links shared that are marked as 'Everyone,' and links shared from Facebook fan pages."

Google: "We treat links shared on Facebook fan pages the same as we treat tweeted links. We have no personal wall data from Facebook."

So some social signals influence ranks directly in small ways, but make sure to build them for the right reasons, while keeping an eye on the future.

Consider this quote from Matt Cutts of Google in his keynote address at Pubcon 2010: "Don't look at us where we are today, but look at the direction we are moving and what we are focusing on, the big five are the mobile web, local search, social, blended results in the search engine results, and HTML5."

Even now in 2013, these still seem to be largely where Google is focused.

Here's another quote from Google's Matt Cutts: "By doing things that help build your own reputation, you are focusing on the right types of activity. Those are the signals we want to find and most value anyway."

Are you sold yet on where things are headed and how you can leverage social in a variety of ways?

Since most of the social sharing is done by power users, you can't get overly fixated on exactly how much these signals will do directly for your rankings, but know that taken as a whole it is a powerful and authoritative realm of signals you just can't ignore. Any answer to exactly how signals are passed is highly debatable due to the secrecy of the search engine algorithms, but I believe that social signals have both some limited direct and a strong indirect impact on organic search rankings. Sometimes it might be due to causation like retweets directly being used in the Google Algorithm as a limited signal, to give a temporary boost for certain types of queries, such as when a news item gets retweeted heavily. You could then say retweets caused your rankings to get better. Other things might be more cor-relation, like things Google can't see behind the Facebook wall and that are not used exactly in the algorithm, but that influence others to link to you and then lift your ranks indirectly. That would be a case of more Facebook activity correlating with better rankings but not directly causing it.

In addition, it may actually depend on the individual query as well. For example, if you have herpes and use herpes cream, you may not want to share that query as readily as one for an entertainment site that easily gets shared. So these factors are still evolving as scalable ranking factors.

Social media's ability to generate new inbound links by improving brand awareness and visibility is one of the most important factors because links are still at the heart of Google's search algorithm. It is also a good idea to share content that mentions you on other sites, such as press releases, YouTube Videos, SlideShare presentations, or guest blog posts.

At the July 2012 SMX Advanced conference, Matt Cutts of Google hinted that links were still the most important criteria, compared to social signals. Cutts said: "So, there's this perception that, yes, everything will go social, or links are completely obsolete, and I think it's premature to reach that conclusion. I don't doubt that in ten years things will be more social, and those will be more powerful signals, but I wouldn't write the epitaph for links quite yet."

Guest Blog Posting and Links from Blogs

Having other people's blogs post the articles you write, mention you, or link to you is a significant ranking factor because of the backlink energy. The more authoritative the blog, the more it counts. This is best done with a public relations mindset. Think big, not how much lame content you can pump out across thousands of low-quality guest blog posts. Google is catching on to that, but it is hard to imagine that getting mentioned on and sharing content on top blog/media sites isn't going to stay a ranking factor for a long time. News has shifted online and if you have a great hook or story, you can improve your rankings through *real* coverage in social outlets. The more bloggers who see that you have a quality blog with fans and followers, the more likely they will write about you and/or allow you to guest post for them.

Authority Reviewers on Social Sites

SEO and social media are tied at the hip, and that extends to local SEO as well. According to Marissa Mayer, Google's former VP of location and local services, reviews are the cornerstone of any local strategy and social is often local.

Yelp and Google+ Local pages are great for earning reviews about your business. It is important to get reviews from authoritative or influential individuals.

If your physical location is consistent on these sites and the reviews start to flow from the "elite," it will help your site rank locally.

What Is the Future of SEO and Social Ranking Signals?

The world is becoming more social and the search engines must integrate this more deeply over time.

Google+ Authorship, in my opinion, will continue to gain ground. So many "black hats" that got good at gaming links are now gaming social media by creating fake accounts and personas. This can be weeded out of the search engines to some degree when they factor in more deeply the authority of the people liking and sharing your content.

Given that becoming an author and publishing great content can only help your brand, what do you have to lose by adopting a strategy built around building a team of quality authors?

Maybe we should revise Seth Godin's saying: "Content marketing is the only marketing that's left" to say this: "Authority/content marketing is the only marketing left."

By creating content that grips, and then reaching out to those authority authors for the possibility of a comment or tweet you put yourself in place for the beautiful melding of social marketing and SEO.

Your new charge for the future of your company and its online presence is the creation of content that is at first compelling and then becomes remarkable over time. This does not happen overnight. It is something that you grow into.

Again, the key is to begin to put pen to paper to realize just how much you have to offer the outside world. Most business owners simply do not realize just how much their passionate followers want to know about how picture frames get made, or how cars can be leased for less or why and how chainless bikes work.

You do know these things.

And they want to absorb what you know.

When you start to create content that has real worth to the outside world, understand that Google takes notice.

In a very big way.

So it's time to push, and push hard.

To get you started, here are 13 ideas for developing content that can be used to leverage social media sites:

1. Engaging blog posts that incorporate photos and videos

2. Podcasting and transcribing the interview text

3. Expert interviews and "how to" videos (use transcribed text/video in blog posts)

4. Videos that have the potential to go "viral" or be shared

5. Ebooks

6. Infographics

7. SlideShare presentations

8. Top 10 lists, Top 13 lists, etc.

9. Product reviews

10. White papers

11. How to and FAQ articles

12. Widgets, such as an interactive vacation planner

13. Video slideshows based on industry statistics

This type of content marketing often kills two birds with one stone by 1) making you more of a trusted author and 2) generating links.

Each of these types of content has a channel it can be pushed to. Videos go on YouTube; podcasts can get you on iTunes; white papers can go on SlideShare; photos get posted on Flickr, Instagram, and Pinterest; and everything can be shared on Facebook, Twitter, Google+, and LinkedIn. Your blog grows its authority on Technorati. Your amazing content might even just become a sensation on Reddit, Digg, Tumblr, and StumbleUpon.

Before you get started in any of these channels, have these elements in place on your own website:

Web Marketing On All Cylinders - John McDougall

- Share buttons (like, recommend, tweet, bookmark, etc.)

- Connect buttons (like a Facebook page, follow on Twitter, follow on LinkedIn, etc.)

- A blog

Why Content Drives Social

I hope this next story opens your eyes to the true potential of your social marketing. After you devour this, let's make sure that you never look back.

Two different caterers in Boston each start a three-month social marketing blitz to attract more business. Their margins on landing new clients are very strong, so they are each willing to put in the effort.

Caterer #1 starts writing two blog posts a week about her business, her prices, and why she's got the lowest costs around. She puts the same type of content on YouTube by setting up a simple camera and talking about her prowess in the kitchen, why everyone who's ever hired her loves her, and why she's so determined to make your next occasion one you will never forget.

On Twitter, she tweets her newest dishes and the prices.

On Pinterest she does the same. Same too on Tumblr and Delicious.

Boy, oh boy. What Caterer #1 does not realize is that she is trying to *interrupt* people and get them to listen to her pitch.

Guess what, Caterer #1? No one cares. No one has the time for that interruption. We don't know you. We don't trust you. Good luck with your pitch, but leave us out of it!

Caterer #2 knows that if she kills it with content, she will attract potential clients to her.

That is a crucial difference.

So Caterer #2 creates blog posts about how anyone can create gluten-free tortellini, prepare lemonade sorbet, and roast a pig outside.

On YouTube, she does live demonstrations of recipes and shows people how to carve duck. She walks everyone through the way Baked Alaska rises. She takes the time to give of herself to show people seven different alternatives to salt and sugar.

Then she blogs about those YouTube videos. She heads to groups on Facebook and LinkedIn that are about "cooking," and she posts links to her relevant content.

Then she tweets about it.

Are you feeling it? Would you be more receptive to these no-sell or soft-sell messages from Caterer #2?

What Caterer #2 realizes is that given the time to really think it through, the best way that she will stand out from every other caterer in Boston is to give of herself until it hurts because if she does that...it will come back to her in multiples.

Take an extra week or an extra month before you release your content.

Take your ideas to a white board and look at them every night and invite people to tell you what they think. Is this content share-worthy or not?

Are you giving out amazing content that gets people jazzed about what you do? And by the way, no matter what you sell, you can make it sexy...or someone can show you how.

Stop trying to sell and start trying to make people crazy excited. Why on earth do you think Pinterest is the fastest-growing website in the world? Because people are sharing things they *love*.

Starting tomorrow morning, the creating of great content is a "must do" and not a "should do." It's not necessarily expensive to make...it just takes some real thought.

Content drives everything about social...and that is pure opportunity for you.

Social Media Competitive Analysis

Before you move a social muscle, check out what your competitors are doing on Facebook, Twitter, LinkedIn, Google+, YouTube, Pinterest, and more. Tools like Sprout Social, Hoot-Suite, or the $600-a-month Radian6 can help streamline your efforts.

Check out the following type of data by hand or with a tool:

- Number of fans/followers

- Posting frequency and quality

- Types of content (images, video, blog posts, cartoons, surveys, etc.)

Web Marketing On All Cylinders - John McDougall

- How much original content versus content grabbed off the web to share?

- How engaged are their fans?

- Numbers of video views, channel views, and subscribers on YouTube

- Author Rank status of competitors' Authors

Redo your analysis every now and then to keep tabs on what the Joneses are up to across Social Media Street.

Now that you have a benchmark for your own social status and your competitor's social status, you can start employing the individual tactics.

Now that you have a greater appreciation for how social media fits into the mix and affects other channels, it's time to discuss the many individual social tactics and sites you can use.

Sometimes it's hard for the average website owner or marketing director to appreciate just how much goes into each of the Internet marketing tactics. Just in social media alone, as can be seen from the list of 16 tactics below, it can be truly overwhelming to stay up to date in each specific area. Each of these sites and tactics changes on a regular basis as the sites evolve and expand with new options. It's easy to get overwhelmed, but this "short list" will help you cover some essential ground.

Top 16 Tactics for Social Media

1. Blogging

2. Facebook

3. Twitter

4. Google+

5. YouTube/Video

6. LinkedIn

7. Pinterest

8. Instagram

9. SlideShare/Presentations

10. Docstoc/White Papers

11. Flickr/Images

12. iTtunes/Podcasting

13. Social Bookmarking

14. StumbleUpon and Tumblr

15. Forums

16. Reviews and Recommendations

Add a variety of content to your content marketing plan, and as you will see in the pages that follow, you will have many opportunities to share it.

Create Powerful Blog Posts

Here's an overview of key blogging practices to get you started.

Use high search volume/popular keywords in the blog post title and in the content of the blog post itself, but also consider working the long tail since this can generate immediate success for easy-to-rank-for keywords and drive some immediate traffic to your site. HubSpot uses a long tail method of creating titles that contain keyphrases that get 200 searches a month and keyphrases that get 60 or less in terms of a competition score. This is long tail blogging and differs from short tail blogging, where you go after terms that are much harder to rank highly for. Infuse your blog posts with the LSI (related) keywords that Google loves to see surrounding your main keyword.

Then take the time to reach out to the authority influencers in your industry and ask for comments. We like a tool by Wordtracker called Link Builder. It helps you identify top blogs and news sites that go with a keyword. Reach out for interaction. Be bold and be willing to push your content to those people who can move mountains for you. Don't forget to call and email bloggers in your niche to offer them a guest post as well.

Facebook Marketing Tips for Business

Topping the 1 billion user mark means that Facebook now reaches one out of every seven people on the planet. In the United States, more than three-quarters of all Internet users are on this monster site, with the average active user having about 130 friends and connected to no less than 80 communities, groups, and events.

That is reach like you cannot get anywhere else.

So where will Facebook's next 1 billion users come from? China and mobile use might just be the elements that help Facebook grow out of the stock slump it experienced when people started to ask how it will properly monetize itself. No guarantees, but can you afford to miss the boat if it just keeps getting bigger?

Having surpassed Google to become the largest website in the world, Facebook is a must for your marketing messages.

17 Tips for Highly Profitable Facebook Marketing

1. **Determine your goals and strategy:** Getting more fans, assembling a list of prospects and customers, developing relationships, more brand exposure, more authority, and increasing revenues.

2. **Know your audience:** Defining personas can help you deliver stronger content because you are writing to targeted groups of people. The better you know your audience, the more effectively you can engage them.

3. **Keep a consistent look and feel:** Your brand, website, Facebook image, and your social media profiles should all have a similar look and feel from a design perspective.

4. **Create a custom welcome tab:** This helps people who are not yet fans and provides a call to action to get them to "like" your page.

5. **Know that size matters:** The number of "likes" does actually matter. This is your list of people to engage. Without a database of clients, what is your company, after all? Email lists and Facebook "likes" are an incredibly valuable tool. Don't buy "likes" or you will mess up your EdgeRank, which is Facebook's way of valuing your page.

6. **Keep an eye on EdgeRank:** Understand the constant changes in how the Facebook system works and adopt a realistic attitude that this is just one tactic. It is in Facebook's economic best interests to make sure that few brands' fans see all advertisers' posts. For a brand to reach beyond the fraction of core fans who see every post, an advertiser must pay to run campaigns such as promoted posts, which last longer in users' news feeds and are therefore seen by more people. Some people, like "Shark Tank" star and Dallas Mavericks owner Mark Cuban, are taking all their fans and leaving, accusing Facebook of driving away brands. Many are in an uproar while others are paying to play and getting great results. Whatever your take on this is, you need to be aware of the giant upheavals going on.

   One user comment on the Business Insider blog says: "When a service completely centered on letting people choose to follow friends and companies so that they can see their posts starts not doing that, then the service is broken and someone else will take their place." If Facebook were to blow up tomorrow, would you be prepared to make up for the traffic in another way?

7. **Budget for promoted posts and ads to get "likes":** You won't get enough likes just from having a Facebook icon on your site or possibly even from sharing cool content. Sometimes you just have to ante up some cash and drive people in your direction

with a shiny Like button waiting for them when they get there. If your ads are targeted to the right demographics and your page has real value, likes will follow.

8. **Use both profiles and company pages:** A Facebook Profile is your one and only personal persona while a Facebook Page is for business. Use both Profiles and company Pages to get double the exposure. (The CEO can have a personal profile, and the company has a Facebook Page.)

9. **Create a branded Timeline photo:** Your timeline cover image can't be overtly promotional. Facebook's rules specify that you can't have a call to action, prices, contact info, or reference to likes or shares in the cover photo. But you can include a message in your cover photograph and switch it up often to get more attention. You can have a product/service box right under the main image with a call to action such as "check out our latest training program at yoursite.com/training."

10. **Create custom Facebook apps:** Facebook apps from Facebook itself include Photos, Videos, Links, Events, and Notes. Any other app you install will be made by someone else. By now there are many thousands of Facebook apps. In fact, there's an app for almost anything. There are apps like Polldaddy to make polls happen right on your Facebook page. The YouTube Involver app provides a feed of your most recent or preferred video clips to show off. The Facebook Causes app allows non-profits and supporters to set up campaigns. It is well worth exploring apps to spruce up the user experience.

11. **Include a "subscribe" button on your Facebook Page:** With "subscribe," users can receive News Feed updates from a page without indicating that they like it. They can also add your page to interest lists to get a separate feed of posts on a particular topic.

12. **Keep people engaged:** Make sure you respond to people who comment or you will appear like an aloof cat and alienate people. Remember, social media is all about being *social* and engaging in conversations.

    Improve engagement with Facebook's cool features. Pin a post so it can stay at the top of your Facebook page. Highlighted posts stretch across the page and stay there, taking up lots of space. Schedule your posts on Facebook for greater engagement. Use "Promoted" posts to get more people to see your news.

13. **Create brand cheerleaders:** By creating relationships with fans and nurturing them, they will in turn create more relationships by marketing for you by sharing your posts or images on their own pages.

14. **Post tons of images as they get a lot of likes and shares:** Remember, the web is a visual medium.

15. **Experiment with length and timing:** Longer posts (450 characters) tend to have more shares. Try posting after work and on weekends as people tend to be more personally engaged with Facebook at those times.

16. **Get personal:** Use "I" and "me" in your posts as these tend to get more likes.

17. **Measure your results:** Facebook Insights lets you see what is working and what is not. Google Analytics can help you track what happens when people come from Facebook to your website. HubSpot has great conversion assist and attribution tracking to see what clicks first came from Facebook, didn't buy then, but bought months later even if they appeared to only come from another source.

The true power of Facebook lies in your ability to create content that increases engagement and can go viral, which leads to super fans who help you market your company for you! Please stop the eye-rolling. By viral, I don't mean like the video of the cats that fight inside the dryer. I mean the kind of content that people will post on their own walls to have their friends see it too, and which will prompt them to comment and take part in the conversation about your topic.

Social media and Internet marketing always come back to great content...let's be very clear about that. If you expect people to post on their walls about your lists of sizes of electrical tubing available, then you really have been working too hard. Perhaps you will find unique ways to shoot video about how your electrical conduit stands up to 1,200-degree heat so your family stays safe. Then you have content people will want to share on Facebook.

One potential bank client told us his great idea for Facebook was to add the bank's standard brochure text and images to separate tabs. That is hardly engaging. Video mortgage tips would be a far better way to go, or sharing news about the direction mortgage rates are heading, or offering tips about saving money for college. People want to make connections these days, so making yourself not only interesting but available for responses to comments is essential.

You have to realize the difference between content that engages and content that doesn't.

No one cares about you marketing your business...especially on Facebook. What they care about is written, or photographed or videotaped content that they are convinced their "friends" will appreciate.

That content naturally links back to your site and can occasionally close deals right inside Facebook through subtle offers such as "download this ebook or white paper." Use the 80/20 rule and make sure only 20% of your content is promotional. The other 80% should be entertaining, informational, or inspirational.

While you will surely hear about the amazing targeting on the Facebook ad platform, which can be used to promote your posts and/or website, you must make sure that just as with Google pay-per-click, you watch your costs like a hawk and create conversions either in terms of opt-ins or sales (or likes at the very least). Otherwise you are only adding to the valuation of this eighty-billion-dollar beast called Facebook (and nothing to your own).

Use Twitter to Build Trust, Buzz, and Engagement

Imagine that you have just 140 characters (not words) to reveal what you are doing right this second, and you get a small sense of why Twitter exploded onto the web scene just a few years ago and why so many people are on it all day long.

When Michael Jackson passed away, people ran to Twitter to find out how and why. When the conflicts in Iraq and Egypt blew up, word got out using Twitter when other communication channels were blocked.

The world changed the moment this microblogging site went live. As a marketer, you need to know how to handle it to get the best results from Twitter. And until the arrival of Pinterest, Twitter was the world's fastest-growing website.

As of the first quarter of 2013, Twitter was estimated to have some 500 million users (although estimates place the number of "active" users at about 200 million). With all those people, the chances for networking are endless.

And while Twitter has evolved greatly since its inception just several years ago, it is still an incredible way for you to build your brand awareness and visibility.

If you are late to the party, we strongly suggest that you go and set up your free account at Twitter now.

You can use your company name as your corporate Twitter handle but don't overlook the power of your personal Twitter account for sharing what you are passionate about in business. You will have to use a hyphen or a number at the end if someone else has already taken your exact business or personal name.

Fill out your profile as best as you can and upload a photo. Make sure your Twitter background image is consistent with your brand and the look and feel of your other social media profiles.

The next step is a very important one.

How do you want to brand yourself on Twitter? Are you the authority who knows everything? Are you more approachable? Who are you on Twitter, and is that compatible with and consistent across all of your social marketing communications?

With that in mind, decide who you want to follow, because on Twitter you follow to get followed back. That really is the plan of attack here. If you sell golf clubs, you want to follow avid golfers in the hope that they will see your "tweets" and then follow you back.

The amazing thing is that getting thousands of followers is not that hard, if you follow some simple steps, like sharing valuable information from your blog posts and links to industry information. A program like TweetAdder.com can be a great help in carefully managing some of the adding and un-following processes. Just be careful, as some people use this program too aggressively and it might be shutting down automation.

You have a unique opportunity on Twitter, which is to show your chops for your business niche. Always remember that the more you give, the more you get. So, telling people how square grooves are etched into the golf club is great content. Telling people how graphite shafts reduce the tendency to hook or slice is great content.

Have facts and figures. Do not just "fluff" your content.

The more real data you have, the more opportunities you have to drop it into the laps of those on Twitter who simply cannot get enough about that particular topic.

I once heard Jeffrey Hayzlett speak. He's considered a celebrity chief marketing officer, and ran Kodak's marketing. If I remember correctly, he had a billion-dollar advertising budget! He takes chances, isn't afraid to make mistakes, and says that no one dies when your marketing goes haywire. If you aren't a bit daring, you may not have big wins. He is awesome on Twitter and has the following stats:

Jeffrey Hayzlett

16,275 tweets

58,133 following

58,790 followers

Hayzlett tweets on anything from "becoming a modern marketing leader" to "it's the marketer's job to create tension" to "happy birthday from the smart asses in your new hood!"

By listening to online conversations and using them, Kodak turned a Twitter suggestion about a product enhancement into the next iteration of the product, which outsold the competition 10 to 1. Now that is listening to your customers and acting on their suggestions!

Another favorite of mine on Twitter is Guy Kawasaki, whose stats are below:

Guy Kawasaki

108,435 tweets

296,097 following

1,195,766 followers

Kawasaki has done marketing with top brands like Apple. He was one of the Apple employees originally responsible for marketing the Macintosh in 1984.

He tweets on things ranging from "are consumers ready to embrace social commerce?" to "13 ways to use turkey leftovers."

The New York Times, Google, Facebook, Apple, and Whole Foods Market, as of fourth quarter 2012, have the largest number of followers for business, according to Twitter and Twitaholic.com.

The New York Times shares recent headlines with links to their website, where followers can read the full articles.

Google, which now performs over one billion online searches each day, shares their latest products and interests directly to their followers. They promote Google Maps and other products and tweet between one and four times per day.

Facebook, which has over 1 billion users, shares its latest features, applications, upgrades, and links to their latest client reviews. They tweet on average a few times a week.

Apple uses tweets to share news about their latest technology, to perform surveys, and to update Apple users on the latest news. Apple is tweeting at least once per hour—most days, considerably more.

Whole Foods Market offers recipes, healthy eating information, FAQs, surveys, and giveaways. They tweet at least twice per day.

Twitter is great for word-of-mouth advertising, keeping customers up to date on the latest offers, and creating popularity for products and services. Apple and Whole Foods seem to have created a nice balance of marketing and information their clients want to hear. Look to what other people and companies are doing for ideas, and you may find that Twitter turns out to be much more approachable than you thought.

How to Use Twitter: The Basics

Short and sweet, that is what Twitter is all about. Just the basics. It's all about making a big impact with a small number of words. For example, you might want to pull a cool piece of data from a blog post rather than just use the post title in your tweet.

140 characters are allowed, but use 120 instead, which leaves room for people to add "RT @username" for retweets. (Retweeting is when users share someone else's tweets.)

Retweets are a way of sharing the tweets you like. "Add RT @username" before the message for retweets. You can also @reply with your reaction to a tweet.

Mention other users by their Twitter usernames (preceded by the @ sign with no spaces) in your tweets. Mention a celebrity as they often respond to fans. You'll see their response on your Mentions tab. Use this format to talk to others: @McDougallSocial Thanks for the cool Twitter info!

DM stands for direct message and this is how it's done: DM username This is a message.

Follow people: follow username or F <username>

Favorite a tweet: fav username

Hashtags categorize Tweets by keyword

- The hashtag symbol # before a relevant keyword or phrase (with no spaces in between) categorizes those tweets and helps them show up more easily in Twitter Search.

- Clicking on a hashtagged word in any tweet shows you all other tweets marked with that keyword.

- Hashtags can be placed anywhere in a tweet—at the beginning, middle, or end.

- Hashtagged words that become very popular are often trending topics.

21 Tips for Getting Started with Twitter

1. Consider connecting your Twitter account to your blog, Facebook, or website.

2. The best way to gain followers on Twitter is to regularly engage and contribute in a meaningful way.

3. Set aside a specific time each day to use Twitter for business purposes, sharing content, and engaging with others.

4. Stick to the 80/20 rule of marketing. Spend 80% or more of your Twitter time on activities that are not self-promotional, or you will be disliked on Twitter.

5. Reply to questions in a timely manner.

6. Put a "Follow Me" icon on your website and your blog and a link to your Twitter profile in your e-mail signature. Integrate the fact that you are on Twitter into your other marketing efforts and brand your Twitter profile consistently with your other social accounts and marketing.

7. Don't get too personal or too negative. Google indexes tweets, and the Library of Congress archives them, so don't say anything on Twitter you wouldn't say in person to your customers or in public.

8. Don't use corporate rhetoric and jargon—be a human being!

9. Listen first and then respond when you can add value to the conversation.

10. Update your status at least once a day.

11. Complete your profile and biography so that other people can learn more about you.

12. Use a real and clear photo of yourself.

13. Don't immediately follow hundreds of people. They will check out your profile to see whether they might want to follow you back. If you are following hundreds of people who have no or poor content, you're just a spam account.

14. After tweeting regularly, follow more people beyond your friends, based on your interests.

15. Avoid using punctuation in your username.

16. Don't thank everyone publicly for following you, as it's not always necessary.

17. Twitter success is more about engagement than follower count. Don't be tempted to go out and buy followers.

18. Place links 25% of the way through tweets for the best click-through rates.

19. Use action verbs rather than nouns and add "via," "@," "RT," "Please," or "check" to get better click-through rates.

20. Best times to tweet include weekends and later in the day, rather than in the morning.

21. Learn how to include images or videos in your tweets.

Cool Software for Twitter

Bit.ly: A great URL shortener that makes it possible to put long URLs into tweets. A free Bit.ly account will give you access to a dashboard where you can shorten and share links to multiple Twitter accounts. You can also see the stats for any Bit.ly links you share through your dashboard.

Hashdictionary: Keep track of conversations that include hashtags on Twitter.

HootSuite: A well-respected tool for Twitter management that also integrates with HubSpot.

Tweet Adder: Find and engage with like-minded Twitter followers, manage followers/following and posts.

Tweetbeep: Keep track of your brand reputation by getting alerts through email when your brand is mentioned on Twitter.

Twellow: The Twitter Yellow Pages.

Twitter Grader: A site that ranks your influence in the Twitter world based on an algorithm. You can also see where you stand in your town, city, state, or country.

Again, your success on Twitter is based on two things: the quality of the content in your tweets (or what you link to) and who you follow that follows you back.

After you sign up for a Twitter account, your first action is to do simple searches on Twitter for people in your niche who already have a healthy number of followers. The goal is for you to look at who is following those accounts, and to follow those people back.

Why?

Because if those people are following "PingGolfClubs" and you manufacture a Ping-like set of clubs at deep discounts compared to what Ping charges, there is an excellent chance that followers of "PingGolfClubs" will be interested in following you as well.

That really is the key on Twitter...you want to have relevance to the people you start to follow, knowing that a large percentage of them will follow you back if they see great content in your tweets.

In our experience, we typically find that when you first start on Twitter, you need to first load your Twitter account up with some nice tweets, as no one wants to follow back a blank account. So throw in five or six rock-solid tweets before following anyone.

Once that is in place, start to find those Twitter accounts in your niche that could be relevant to you. Then look at all of the people following those accounts. These are the followers you want to follow in the hopes they will turn around and follow you back.

Follow a hundred people as you start out. Do not go overboard, or you will violate Twitter's terms of service (Twitter guidelines and terms of service change often, so stay on top of them). Then three days later, go in and *unfollow* everyone who did not follow you back. That will enable you to go after more new followers.

On and on this will go, with you tweeting super content and eventually getting followers more naturally...and the account will grow.

Twitter is a great way to network yourself and your business to those people who love your business niche. It is a great way to show consumers just how passionate you are about your business by steering them to amazing content every day. (It's called the web for a reason!)

You need to not just have a "Follow Us on Twitter" button on your site...that's soft. You need to work Twitter and be reaching out and contacting people based on hashtags and interests.

By growing a strong following you prove you are an expert. This builds trust and credibility that can close deals and can convince journalists you are just the person they want to interview/link to in their next story. Twitter may not jump right out at you initially as a place you care to be, but it's truly become a serious weapon being used by your competitors to take market share from you. Don't fall too far behind or you may not have what you need to stay in the game.

LinkedIn: Really Simple Steps to Get Started

When it comes to talking to decision makers online, *nothing*—and I mean nothing—compares to the power you command when you fully understand what LinkedIn can really mean for your business.

In a study of over 3,000 HubSpot B2B customers, LinkedIn generated the highest visitor-to-lead conversion rate at 2.60%, four times higher than Twitter (.67%), and seven times better than Facebook (.39%).

While dear old Facebook gets all the press, Facebook does *not* deliver *sales* the way LinkedIn can if you are trying to go business to business. There are more than 175 million business people who are active on this site and they want to know what you know and who you know to make more money.

When it comes down to it, people are on LinkedIn to grow more business. Being active on LinkedIn is like fishing in a barrel, especially if you fish with the right shotgun!

Executives from all the Fortune 500 companies are on LinkedIn. Sixty-six percent of users are decision makers. The household income is the highest among the social media sites at $109,000 per year. Seventy percent of the people on LinkedIn are between the ages of 24–54, and the user base skews male.

It bears repeating here, perhaps more than with regard to any other of the other social sites: you have to be willing to give, ask questions, offer and request recommendations, and spread your cool content to make LinkedIn work best.

Facebook and Twitter are surely a softer approach that may draw people in to content differently, but when you are on LinkedIn, you need to bring your "A+" business game and you need to bring it weekly, if not daily.

Now that is *not* to say that you should focus on LinkedIn only. You should not. I say this simply to emphasize that each and every social marketing outlet does and accomplishes things differently.

LinkedIn Benefits and Possibilities

- Awareness of your products and services, especially for B2B

- Sales research to know your prospects' interests

- Find funding

- Recruiters can find talent

- Drive traffic to your site and content

- Get noticed by journalists

- Promote events

- Get and give free advice

- Make global contacts

- Meet influencers through referrals

- Build trust with recommendations

As with any social media effort, be sure to follow the golden rules:

- Know your audience.

- Know their hopes, dreams, and what keeps them up at night.

- Listen first and then engage by starting conversations.

- Be honest and authentic.

- Give content and advice freely. Deepen relationships by answering and asking questions.

- Only offer your product or service once they know, like, and trust you, and you are in their sphere of influence.

- Build fans first and then customers! Don't expect pushing your ad in front of people's faces to work here.

LinkedIn works best when you have tons of contacts. Make sure you have a strategy to generate a couple thousand contacts or more if you can, if you really want to take full advantage of the system.

Define Your Goals on LinkedIn, Including:

Build a profile that draws people in like a magnet so sales come to you.

Build a huge network so you get contacted by journalists and potential new customers.

Brand yourself as a thought leader.

Close a certain amount of sales per year from LinkedIn.

Land a dream job.

Develop a Strong Personal Profile Page

Add a compelling unique value proposition, who you are, who you help, and how you help them. Also explain how you got to be so good at what you do, and add an inspirational statement about your mission. For ideas, look at competitors who do a great job of making profiles as well as LinkedIn experts like Dan Sherman.

Character Limits for Each Field in the LinkedIn Profile

Company Name: 100

Professional Headline: 120

Summary: 2,000

Specialties: 500

Website Anchor Text: 30

Website URL: 256

Headline: 120 characters

Position Description: 200 minimum and 2,000 maximum

Interests: 1,000

Phone Number: 25-character limit (Viewable only by first-degree connections)

IM (Instant Message): 25-character limit (Viewable only by first-degree connections)

Address: 1000 character limit (Viewable only by first-degree connections)

Skills: 25 skills with 61 characters per skill

Status Update: 700 characters (unless used for Twitter Feed, then it's 140)

Complete Your Profile 100%

Incomplete profiles say that you don't think LinkedIn or its members are worth your time. Update the information at least once every quarter. Refreshed content leads to higher LinkedIn rankings and visibility to everyone in your network.

Add Keywords

Add keywords to your Professional Description, Summary, Headline, Current Position, and Past Position (job titles and company names), Skills, and Recommendations. LinkedIn generally allows 15 keywords in the same field. Use the maximum number of keywords.

Embed a Quality Head Shot Photo

Make sure it is business-oriented and professional-looking—no party snapshots, please!

Make a Compelling, Keyword-Rich Headline

Here's an example of how I'd write mine: SEO and social media marketing expert who loves to share advice | 18 years' experience | Author | Speaker

Website Section

You can list three websites here. Make your own custom benefit-oriented titles that link to your sites/pages. Here are mine:

- **Free Internet Marketing Tips**

- **Interactive Agency Near Boston**

- **Search & Social Seminar**

Summary

This is a critical part of your profile. In 2,000 characters, give people a feeling for who you are, who you help, how you can help, and how to contact you. Make it scan- and skim-friendly and include a call to action.

Skills

LinkedIn gives you one box in which you can add up to 50 keywords. Viewers of your profile can click on a keyword and learn more about that particular skill, including companies in which that skill is common, other professionals with that skill, and LinkedIn groups with that skill.

Work Experience

List as many relevant jobs as possible that help you brand yourself.

Sections

Use sections to further personalize your LinkedIn profile. Enhance your profile by adding information about patents, publications, certifications, charities, and languages. Or choose specific applications to showcase your graphic (artistic, photographic) or written skills. Upload PowerPoint (and other format) slide shows via SlideShare or YouTube videos via Google Docs (or also via SlideShare). Add Amazon reading lists (great for authors promoting books), import your blog, and so on.

Make Your Contact Information Stand Out

The whole point of LinkedIn is to connect, so include a real email address as part of your professional description and repeat it again at the bottom of the profile in the contact information. Add your phone number, as you never know what amazing lead might call you.

LinkedIn Recommendations

Social proof is the key here. Seventy-eight percent of people trust reviews by their peers while only 14% trust advertisements. That puts the power in the hands of the people and lets them choose based on people who come highly recommended. Send unsolicited recommendations regularly as these often prompt people to respond in kind or simply helps you to make friends. Ask for recommendations and offer a first draft you write yourself (including keywords) that really highlights your strengths. Your contact can use your draft "as is" or add to it. Indicate that they can always change it, but generally they will use what you give them. Having more recommendations also helps you rank better in the LinkedIn search engine.

Get at Least 500 Contacts!

One or two hundred contacts is good but over 500 is great. Over 10,000 and you are a networking superstar. You won't connect deeply with all the people but it opens the door for greater connections. Use LinkedIn's Advanced People Search to search by company and job function to find prospective customers and invite them to become contacts. See if you know someone who knows that person and can make a recommendation or introduction.

Connection levels

Level 1 – Message them for free

Level 2 – Get a level one to introduce you to make them a level one

Level 3 – Similar to level two

LinkedIn etiquette is to forward all requests for connections as the person who receives a request doesn't have to say yes. So it is common for people to share your requests with their peers, as they know they can ignore it if they feel like it.

You can contact second- and third-level connections directly in a few ways:

1. Send an InMail. This is a message using the LinkedIn system. Unless you are a paid member of LinkedIn, InMail costs money.

2. Join a LinkedIn Group that person also belongs to. As long as they have not blocked the feature on their end, you can communicate directly (through the LinkedIn system) with anyone you are in a group with.

3. Find their email address in their profile.

Introductions are best, but if your network of connections isn't working, there are some alternatives you can try.

Don't Invite Too Many People You Don't Know

Understand the etiquette. If you don't know someone, be very careful reaching out to them if they are not in an Open Networking Group. When you invite someone, they have a chance to say "I don't know you" (known as an IDK). If five people say that (essentially marking your request as spam), you get put on LinkedIn's blacklist. At that point, you have to put in someone's email address in order to invite them, which can slow your progress to a crawl in many instances.

Web Marketing On All Cylinders - John McDougall

Here's how you fix it:

Send an apology to LinkedIn's customer service at cs@linkedin.com, and they might let you off the hook one time.

Follow Up

Develop a note template that you can customize and send brief notes to all those who have accepted your invitation to connect. Wait two weeks so you don't seem over-eager.

Create Your Company Page

Click on the "Companies" tab on LinkedIn's upper navigation bar and you'll be taken to a page where you can either search for companies or add a company.

Company pages don't have as many features as LinkedIn personal pages—the four sections, or tabs, are "Overview," "Employees," "Product Pages," and "Statistics." They're great ways to push out updates about your business and link to content of interest to your customers and prospects.

Update Your Status at Least Once a Week

LinkedIn personal profiles and company pages are similar to status updates on Facebook. You can use them to post brief company news and links to articles you've read or cool business content you have created.

Each time you post an update, you appear on the home page of all your LinkedIn contacts, so they'll automatically see what you've been up to lately. Share your success stories and thought leadership ideas as marketing opportunities.

How to Do a Status Update on LinkedIn

Hover your mouse over the LinkedIn Home Tab

Select "LinkedIn Home"

A dialogue box will appear with the words "Share and Update"

Update your status

You will also have the option of sharing a link

Click on the "share" button

Limit your updates to roughly two or three times a day (depending on what your audience reacts well to). You can feed LinkedIn updates to Twitter because Twitter can be updated more often. Sending Twitter into LinkedIn is bad if you send everything and you start overdoing your daily updates. Also make sure that information like what you had for lunch doesn't come into this very business-focused network. Better yet, unless you're a professional chef or a restaurant critic, think twice about sharing the lunch news via Twitter too often...

Apps

Use apps to display slideshows and video. Check out Apps from SlideShare, WordPress, Portfoliodisplay, and Google Presentations, etc.

Job Seekers

LinkedIn is a great tool to help you land that dream job. Ensure your profile is complete and up-to-date. Your LinkedIn profile is your chance to showcase your skills and talents and help the right people and opportunities find their way to you. Users with complete profiles are 40 times more likely to receive opportunities through LinkedIn!

Search on LinkedIn Jobs and message key Contacts. Use an "inside connection" to help get you access to a company or job you are interested in. Use the JobsInsider Toolbar to access job listings from your browser.

Daily or Weekly Tasks

Reply to messages

Answer questions through LinkedIn polls, groups, or status updates

Ask questions through LinkedIn polls, groups, or status updates

Start discussions in your groups

Share content in groups and in status updates with a link

Send new invitations for people to join your group

Send recommendation requests

Write unsolicited recommendations

Ask and You Will Receive

Ask for new business/contracts once you get to know someone and have been helpful to them.

Ask for an introduction to someone.

Ask for advice.

Ask for a job.

Ask people to sign up for a seminar or webinar.

Ask for publicity.

Ask for random stuff.

I have used this Wayne Gretsky quote previously, but it's worth repeating: "You miss 100% of the shots you don't take."

Give and You Will Receive

Give helpful advice.

Give unsolicited recommendations.

Share industry news and case studies of how you have been successful.

The more you share, the more friends you will make and the more business you will get eventually.

Analytics: What to Track

Number of connections

Number of groups joined

Number of groups started

Number of people who have joined your group

Engagement on your groups

Number of leads, phone calls, face-to-face meetings, and closed deals

Number of questions asked/answered

Number of recommendations given and received

Amount of traffic to your site from LinkedIn (place link to your site in your profile, event postings, etc. and add your LinkedIn URL in other forms of marketing)

Create, Join, and Participate in LinkedIn Groups

Look for LinkedIn groups where prospective clients might be, then join them.

Sign Up for All 50 Groups LinkedIn Allows

LinkedIn's "Groups" feature is a great way to get connected. Sign up for the maximum 50 groups your are allowed to join as it only helps you and you don't have to do much in them. Ask and answer questions in groups to increase your visibility and make connections.

Join LinkedIn Open Network Groups

People in these groups won't mark you as spam and increase your ability to generate a huge contact list. Toplinked and Invites Welcome are two of the best paid groups that can quickly increase your contact database (around $20 to $50 a year).

Create Your Own Groups

One truly awesome power of LinkedIn lies within the groups. And the Holy Grail within the groups is for you to create your own groups.

By creating and controlling your own group on LinkedIn (you are allowed to create 10), you can then head to other like-minded groups and invite those people into yours!

For example, let's say you are an executive recruiter specializing in information technology (IT). You create a beautiful and powerful LinkedIn profile that is less like your resume and more like a helpful sales page that explains to people what you can do for them.

Then you set up a group on LinkedIn called "Join Now If You Want To Switch IT Positions." Yes, you literally name it that because you want to filter out everyone who is not interested!

Then you head to every IT group that you can and you join them.

And once you are accepted into those groups, something magical happens...you get to email each and every person in that group, asking them to join your group! Wow...talk about leverage!

Try searching the group directory using keywords, region, industry, and job titles.

As a business owner, when you truly understand the possibilities on LinkedIn that allow you full access to the people who you really want to talk to, you'll be floored.

Try This Seven-Day Plan to Get Started

Day 1. Sign up, research competitors' and experts' profiles, create your own profile fully (don't forget to use keywords), and add five connections to people you know who are on LinkedIn already.

Day 2. Give three unsolicited recommendations and ask for three recommendations.

Day 3. Join five groups and make a list of ones you would like to start.

Day 4. Answer a few questions in groups

Day 5. Ask five connections to introduce you to new contacts.

Day 6. Add twenty-five new connections. Use Advanced People Search.

Day 7. Create your company page.

Hey, the phone is ringing. It just might be someone from LinkedIn! Now it's your turn to make more connections than you could have ever imagined.

Pinterest in Four Hours Over Four Days or Less

Welcome to the fastest-growing website in the history of the web. (Sorry, Twitter.) And while you may have heard about Pinterest, it is what lies behind its curtain that has the most crazy potential for your business. Users shifted to visual content in 2012 because a picture is worth a thousand words and Pinterest figured out how to take advantage of this simple fact in an elegant way.

Pinterest is likely to be the hottest social media platform for business marketers in 2013, according to Forbes. Get familiar with what makes it tick as soon as possible. It's time to ride the visual wave.

What Is Pinterest?

Pinterest is a pinboard-style social photo-sharing website that allows users to create and manage theme-based image collections ("pinboards") about events, interests, hobbies, and more. Users can browse other pinboards for inspiration, "re-pin" images to their own collections, or "like" photos. Pinterest's mission is to "connect everyone in the world through the 'things' they find interesting" via a global platform of inspiration and idea-sharing. "Pinners" can create, share, collect, and repost information in picture, image, or video format. Pinterest may not be right for everyone, but it may be easier, more fun, and more beneficial to your business to make visual versions of your content than you think.

Pinterest Is Driven by Photos

We are sitting at a crossroads of content right now and the marketplace is telling us that people are tired of reading all day long and like a visual break. No matter what business you are in, there is a visual aspect to it that you must tap into.

People love sharing images and video more than ever. The bright minds at Pinterest saw this coming. Pinterest users are predominantly women, and 70% have a household income of $100,000 or more. And yes, that is the sweet spot.

With Pinterest, you can create a visual library of your goods and services, and putting a call to action in your "pin" will help you increase people's engagement with you.

On Pinterest, one of the quickest ways to go viral is to "repin" the photos of others. That will bring you some great attention. Some 80% of all pins are repins.

45 Killer Tips on Using Pinterest for Business

1. Create content: Repinning versus creating new content is the most common activity, so if you become a content creator you are in the elite.

2. Mix original content with content created by others that you curate/share.

3. Be sure to craft the story told by your pinboards to appeal to a particular audience. The more focused on a specific audience, the better.

4. Tall images work better.

5. 200-character descriptions get repinned the most.

6. Link descriptions to your site to get potentially more referral traffic than Google+, YouTube, and LinkedIn combined.

7. Include photos, infographics, videos, and text.

8. Include some business and some personal content.

9. Have at least 10 boards with a minimum of 10 pins each.

10. Move your most important Pinterest boards to slots 2, 3, and 4 on your profile as these are the most visible.

11. Besides your profile picture, pinboard cover photos are the first images visitors see, so make them great.

12. Make short and relevant board names.

13. Don't be overtly promotional or you will lose followers.

14. Start a conversation with people interacting with your important boards, repin, or like their pins, etc.

15. Pin content from sites that you know will interest your target audience.

16. Start following users and/or individual boards that you like and engage with them to help build your own fan base.

17. Comment on and "like" the pins of other users and businesses. After all, it is a social medium.

18. Pins should always link to the original site the content came from. Check the source of the pin and don't repin if the source looks fake. (From Pinterest's "Pin Etiquette" Guidelines: Credit Your Sources!)

19. Consider adding your URL on images so it will always be connected to your brand.

20. Pin across a range of boards.

21. If you sell products, add prices to your pins.

22. Pin regularly, not everything all at once. Pinterest is not like Facebook and Twitter, where the visibility of a post in a newsfeed is limited to a short period of time (hours). Pins will remain in view for days or weeks. Pinning for a few minutes a couple of times per day is enough to get you started.

23. The best times to pin are weekends and between 2 pm and 4 pm.

24. Use @tags to notify the user you are engaging with.

25. Use hashtags (#) to highlight keywords.

26. Thank people for repinning your content.

27. Pin new content to your boards regularly.

28. Drive fans from other social platforms to your boards with references to specific content ("Hey, what do you think of the cover design for my next book?"), not just a generic request to "join me on Pinterest."

29. Research what your customers are pinning by searching on the Pinterest dashboard.

30. Take time to set up your account properly. If you own a business, set up an account in your business name, using your logo. Set up the links to your website and social media channels on your profile.

31. Add the "pin it" button on your website, blog, and social media platforms. Add the "follow me" button for websites to your home page, email footer, and email newsletters.

32. Linking Facebook and/or Twitter to your account gives your pins more exposure. Choose which pins are posted out on an individual basis. Facebook links only to your personal profile (not business pages), so Twitter linkage may be better for business posts. Post to Facebook when appropriate.

33. Typing in "www.pinterest.com/source/yoursite.com" displays a long list of your pins and repins made directly from your site.

34. Make your blog images kick butt so you get more pins from the blog.

35. Text reworked in Photoshop-type programs can also make for very cool pics (such as inspirational quotations made to look nice).

36. Cool tools to consider: Instagram, Pixlr, Tweegram, Snagit, Pinstamatic, the Pinterest mobile app, Pinerly, and Pinstamatic.

37. Be a thought leader with how-to information, training videos, infographics, tutorials, and tips.

38. Check out what your competitors are doing for ideas. Whole Foods and Oprah are a couple interesting examples.

39. Run a competition dependent on pinning, repinning, commenting, or liking. Allow users to post on a competition or event board.

40. Describe the pins with keywords so they are more likely to be found on Pinterest's search engine.

41. Build relationships and referral traffic that will be inspired to take an action.

42. For SEO, use keywords in pin descriptions, boards, and titles (which become the URLs such as "pinterest.com/mcdougallsocial/seo"). Use the maximum space in the "about" section and add keywords in it.

43. Pin images from your own website when you can, as it should be the place where you want traffic to go. Use permalinks and not the URL when pinning blog posts.

44. Start telling people to share your pins.

45. Track success. Check out recent followers, likes, comments, and repins from the left-hand side of your Pinterest home page. Look at referral sources using Google Analytics and see how engaged visitors are and what actions they are taking. Make additional/similar content to what has driven engagement and sales when people click from Pinterest to your site.

23 Ideas for Creative Pinboards

Pinboards are a great way to show off how cool or interesting your brand is, engage followers, and generate leads. Here are some ideas to get you started:

1. Create visually charged testimonials to inspire trust.

2. Turn existing, printed collateral material into pinboards.

3. Create visual case studies.

4. Share the latest news, information, and updates in visual format.

5. Create boards that show your staff/team members.

6. Make a virtual tour of your business.

7. Feature your awards.

8. Share inspiration.

9. Archive your advertisements.

10. Highlight videos.

11. Feature products/services.

12. Run contests.

13. Feature charities you work with.

14. Inspire user-generated content.

15. Add highlights from your blog.

16. List data/statistics.

17. Provide details via infographics/flowcharts.

18. Add inspirational industry quotes.

19. Make people aware of events/conferences.

20. Share industry tips.

21. Archive historical information.

22. Feature cartoons.

23. Publish news.

Get Started on Pinterest in Four Hours Over Four Days or Less

Day 1, Hour 1: Create your Pinterest account. Use your email or your Facebook or Twitter account. I started with my email, as you can turn Facebook and Twitter on or off later. You will be asked to follow five people to get started. Look at this as just training wheels. You can delete them later if you decide not to follow them after all. Experiment by deleting all followers and adding more. Make some comments, add some pictures of anything just to get started (and then delete them). Just have fun exploring, searching, and playing around.

Day 2, Hour 2: Strategize about what boards will mean the most to your business. Pick three to five really important subject areas. Share your company's personality as well as content that is based on keywords (such as "Historic Photos of Golf Clubs" or "Fresh Seafood Recipes"). Research what your peers and competitors are doing.

Day 3, Hour 3: Collect images that you have already from your blog and website in a folder and make subfolders by board name. Then have a heart-to-heart with yourself about how you will get more great images made. Do you hire a designer? Do you learn image editing tools enough to make your own? However you choose to do it, make a plan, because you will quickly run out of images and other material that you already have in post-able format. Then post the material you have available to share and add descriptions and links back to your site.

Day 4, Hour 4: Engage with other people on Pinterest by commenting on and liking pins. Ask people you know to share your pins. Later, when your boards are amazing, you can ask influencers to interact with and share your pins. Add the "pin it" button on your website, blog and social media platforms. Add the "follow me" button for websites on your home page. Look at referral sources using Google Analytics to see if anyone has come to your site from Pinterest and what their engagement levels are once they get to your site.

While this is just a start, it will help you build confidence and you can get more advanced from there.

Pinterest is more powerful than you know and is pure genius. Now get pinning!

Social Networking with Google+

Wait, what the heck is going on? Almost all of us have fallen in love with Facebook as the number one way we stay tapped into the lives of those we know and supposedly love. So why would any of us need another seemingly more complex approach to how we "friend" people?

Google+ seems superfluous until you look at it for the smart move that it really is.

On Facebook all of our "friends" (who are not really all "friends," by the way) get to see all of what we're up to, unless we are careful to assign each friend a specific level of access to what they see. If we don't do this, our boss gets to see crazy wedding pictures and old girlfriends get to see that we're no longer "single."

Yikes, that is potentially a mess.

But do I want to abandon my precious way of doing things? And why would anyone really do that?

Here's the answer...because it's Google.

Google was smart enough to understand that these "circles" ("circles" let you organize people into groups for sharing across Google products and services) make perfect sense in that they keep your work life separate from your social life. Some could cross over, but there are things that you are willing to share with one circle that you would never share with another circle.

But does the world really need this? Do you have time for Google+? Isn't it just another thing to do?

No.

Who do you have your free email accounts with?

Who do you turn to for images?

Who do you get your RSS feeds from?

Who runs all of that?

Google. They know exactly what they need to do in the coming 10 years to be the premier social circle provider.

From your photos in one circle to your videos in another, to the fact that no one can peek in if you do not want them to, Google+ is actually ahead of its time.

For this to work, you need to create your circles and you need to be as specific as possible as you can with them.

You need to look at the massive interaction you will get if all of your Google properties are talking to one another in a strategic way.

You need to start establishing yourself on Google+ right now.

Creating and Optimizing a Google+ Account

Google+ and/or Author Rank may be a big part of the future way Google will place sites in the search engine rankings. If you want to future-proof your site for even the possibility of greater social signals being part of the organic algorithm, it's crucial that you at least get started with a Google+ business page and dedicate at least one person to making a Google+

profile for Author Rank. While full optimization is ideal, having the process started shows Google that you are on the right track.

Five Reasons to Use Google+

1. Google+ and/or Author Rank (which requires a Google+ personal profile) may eventually increase search rankings. Getting Google+ shares and "+1s" for your site already has an impact on search rankings for those who are logged in to Google.

2. Google+ is an upcoming social channel owned by Google whose future depends on it working. Therefore they are placing added importance on having Google+ pages and profiles.

3. Google+ can provide excellent branding via your authors' faces appearing in the search engine results pages, increasing branding and click-through-rates. (Greg Boser of Blueglass says he sees an increased click-through rate of 40%!)

4. Google+ and Google Local have merged, making Google+ truly critical for Google local/mobile results.

5. Google+ Communities rank in the search results and are another way to extend your presence there.

To achieve Author Rank you need to have an optimized Google+ profile. After you optimize your profile, you'll need to go to your website and have it optimized for Google+ by including an author bio page which links to your Google+ profile, and by adding the "rel=author" tag on your content. These steps help "connect the dots" with Google and tie your profiles and bios together. Author Rank also plays a big role in blogger outreach—now if you post on other blogs for publicity you can add more authority to them by linking them back to your Google+ profile (see Figure 2).

Additionally, for local searches Google is replacing Google Places with Google+ Local. By optimizing your local page, you can increase the chance of your website being seen in the search results.

Google Local results dominate for many local searches, and Google+ now plays a major role in these local results. Additionally, Google is displaying links to Google+ business pages in these listings, and incorporating Google Reviews, Sitelinks, and even Author Rank-style profile photos within the Google Local results.

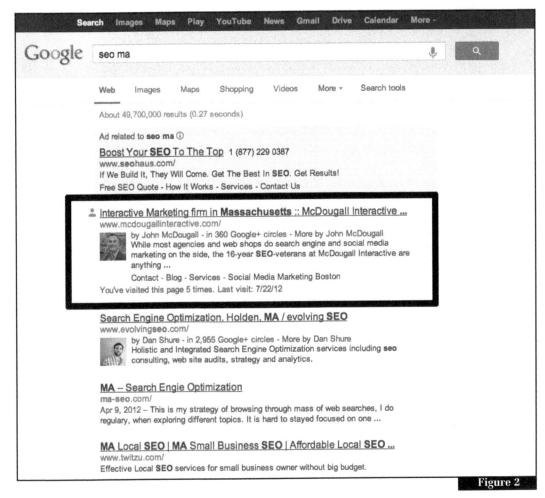

Optimizing Your Google+ Profile Account

Optimizing your Google profile is important if you are going to be the face of your company. This is your personal profile, but you will be connected to your company through links to your business page. Linking your Google+ profile to your Google+ business page is also important for helping your Google+ page to show up strong in the search queries for Google.

The Process

1. Use your company's own email (e.g., "name@your-domain.com") or your own personal Gmail account to sign up for a Google+ account.

2. Write a detailed and factual biography for your introduction. Create hyperlinks to your business or other sites related to you.

3. Link to all your social media profiles, websites you contribute to, and sites you own in your settings.

4. Upload a professional profile picture of yourself. This is the same picture that will be used in the search results for Author Rank.

Optimizing Your Google+ Business Page

Your Google Places page has already been converted to a Google+ page. Google still has additional plans to further merge Google+ Local with Google Places, but it's clear that optimizing the Google+ page for your business is now essential for local search. The steps for optimizing your Google+ page are similar to optimizing your Google+ personal profile.

1. Create a Google+ page from the dashboard of your Google+ profile.

2. Link all your business social media accounts and any other websites you own to the Google+ Page.

3. Write a detailed introduction, including facts about the business. Make sure to hyperlink any other business ventures, relevant details about yourself, or other projects you may have.

4. Upload a professional profile picture. This profile picture will be the face of your company, so business owners often use a version of their logo.

What Is the Difference Between a Google+ Profile and a Google+ Business Page?

A Google+ profile is for a person, whereas a Google+ page is for an entity like a company or other organization. Google+ users are able to create Google+ pages. It's just like being able to make your own Facebook page for your business from your Facebook profile. Google wants you to do all your business branding on Google+ pages, reserving the Google+ profiles for individuals. For example, if we tried to make a McDougall Interactive Google+ profile, it would be deleted and we would be asked to create a Google+ page instead. On a Google+ page you will have a "+1" button, which is similar to the "like" button on Facebook.

Online Video and the Essentials of YouTube Optimization

Online video may create more engagement than the 30-second TV spot.

Online video content works for multiple marketing goals, encourages interactivity, can be targeted to customer profiles and life cycles, and can be used to extend offline campaigns.

Considering that video SEO is easier than traditional SEO, YouTube is the second-largest search engine, and YouTube has a self-serve video ad service that is more flexible and targeted than cable spends, you would be wise to push video. Video. And then some more video.

Again, video content does not have to be overly produced at all; in fact, sometimes low-end content can be very effective as it shows you care more about the quality of the content than the lighting. The point is that you want to create content that will get noticed by the authorities in your world.

After you've created a compelling short video and included a killer keyword in the title, upload it to YouTube (the monster in the video space). Don't stop there—you should also upload it to 10 to 20 of the best video marketing sites out there and especially MetaCafe.

Here is an assortment of video marketing sites, but you will have to experiment to see what works best in your industry.

Vimeo.com	MetaCafe.com	Blip.tv
Veoh.com	Viddler.com	Revver.com
Flickr.com	gofish.com	videobomb.com
dailymotion.com	mojoflix.com	ifilm.com
heavy.com	Kyte.tv	UStream.tv
qik.com		

Be sure to link all of the videos that are not on YouTube *to* your YouTube video, which will explode your rankings for that keyword.

The larger point here is that you need to point one piece of content to other pieces of content on social media to make your lead horses (like YouTube) explode.

Surprise! YouTube Has a New Ranking System

YouTube is getting smarter.

Most often, users venture beyond the original video that brought them to YouTube, thanks to "Related" and "Suggested" content. YouTube plasters their site with recommended videos to ensure that you stay awhile.

How does YouTube determine which videos get recommended? The answer to that question has something to do with a semi-complicated (and semi-secret) algorithm. One of the biggest factors of said algorithm has been the view count. If many people clicked a video, YouTube figured that it must be relevant and worth watching. The problem was that there are countless misleading thumbnails, titles, descriptions, and keywords out there. A popular tactic used by some people was to flash a quick shot of a bikini-clad woman in the middle of their non-bikini-related video. YouTube's latest ranking system has a pretty smart way around this problem: If people click a video but don't actually watch it, the video's views are valued significantly less.

Don't just take my word for it.

"Our algorithms are offering suggested videos (that include both related and recommended videos) that are based on which videos contribute to an overall longer—and more engaging—viewing session, versus the number of viewers who clicked on the video. So if you're making videos that people love and stick around to see, you'll find more of them appearing in our related videos, helping to grow your audience."—YouTube.com

This is good news for everyone, except the black hat marketers. Assuming you aren't into spamming and buying backlinks in bulk, YouTube's new algorithm will benefit you, both as a user and a content creator. As a YouTube user, you can expect higher quality and more relevant content to be recommended. For example, after watching a music video, I clicked a related video of a band I had never heard of. I actually liked the new band and was convinced that YouTube might understand my musical tastes better than most of my friends. Way to go, YouTube!

For the content creators out there, the future is looking brighter than ever. If you make quality content that users enjoy, YouTube's going to try to make sure those users see more and more of your work. How do you know if people are actually sticking around until the end of the video? For YouTube partners, there is a downloadable report under analytics called the Audience Retention Report. Ultimately, the goal is to make quality content to increase user engagement. If you're reading this and already trying to figure out a loophole to boost your rankings...simply making longer videos won't help. I'm guessing it has something to do with a sliding scale or viewing ratio, but regardless, instead of wasting energy trying to trick YouTube's algorithm, focus that attention on creating good videos that people want to watch. Please.

The basics to cover fall into five categories:

1. Title and Description

2. Tags

3. Popularity/Views

4. Inbound Links/Embeds

5. Ratings and Comments

Just like in traditional SEO, having clear and not spammy but keyword-driven titles, descriptions, and tags helps. You also need links to your videos for people to comment on, view and rate as well.

Advertising Is Redefined by Google AdWords for Video

Here's how traditional advertising typically works. You pay to blast your message out to a large audience (e.g., airing a television commercial), and hope that it reaches some people who turn into customers. It works, but it's usually pretty expensive. Let's say you own a local restaurant and want to run a television ad. The first step is making the ad, then figuring out who should see it. Your local cable network would work with you to target a specific demographic, then advise running your ad during a certain time of day or program. All of these variables affect the cost. Prices range wildly, but from our experience if you are planning on running a local campaign on cable TV, expect to start at around $20,000. If you want to run an ad during prime-time television, like an NFL game, you'll need deep pockets.

Again, traditional advertising works, but there might be a cheaper and more effective alternative on the rise. When you run a television commercial, many of the people who see it won't turn into consumers. Heck, many of the people won't even watch it. Basically, you're going to end up spending a lot of money on irrelevant views. Google's found a way around this.

Google AdWords for Video allows businesses to advertise on YouTube. You can opt to only pay for an ad when the viewer actually watches it. The viewer has the option to skip it, so there's a good chance that the actual views will come from engaged individuals. It's also very possible to run a legitimate campaign with just a couple hundred dollars. Seriously!

Google puts the media buying in your hands. If you run a campaign with AdWords, you'll have access to detailed analytics to ensure that every penny is spent in the right place.

I wouldn't say AdWords for video means the death of traditional advertising is imminent, but things are certainly changing. Online video is a vital part of a successful business marketing plan. If you have online video, AdWords should definitely be something you consider. It's low-risk with a potentially huge payoff.

Online Reviews and Recommendations

Google Reviews

In the new online landscape, the line has blurred between the importance of inbound links to your website (even great ones), and reviews from real people on sites that the search engines recognize as real.

Now, in addition to the links that point to your site using your best keywords, you'd better have reviews about your products or services coming in from *real* people in very different locations and they'd better be honest.

Google+ Local now comes up for an amazing number of searches sandwiched between the paid ads and the organic results. Even ranking reports blur the local ranks with organic ranks. This is bad news if you only do SEO and ignore your local listing because it pushes you down in many cases. The solution is to kick butt at optimizing your local listing (learn more about that in the local chapter, Chapter 14). One component of local optimization is getting reviews. They help you rank in Google+ Local and Yelp. Yelp pages rank in Google and you can rank in both Yelp and Google, but beware, as the road is fraught with peril. On the one hand, you need reviews, but on the other hand, I have to mention that Yelp despises people encouraging reviews and Google prefers that you let people naturally give them. If you are getting too many reviews or you try to do the reviews via proxy, they will be removed. This has annoyed many people and rightfully so, at least with Yelp. If I had a dime for every client that said Yelp is screwing them, I would be rich.

One example is a wonderful dentist in Los Angeles. She has tons of reviews online and a great reputation. She was getting huge business through Yelp, and when a couple of negative reviews were posted that she felt were clearly beyond unfair and maybe created by a competitor, Yelp filtered her good reviews and tanked her reputation. Now she is losing loads of business. A search on Google for "Yelp is corrupt" brings you to sites like yelpis-corrupt.org. It claims that the Yelp folks are "extortionists" and that the sales staff has repeatedly advised that if "we only advertise with them, they could 'help us.'" While I have no idea whether Yelp is really corrupt or if it's just a flawed system, the fact remains how reviews are handled will affect businesses that rely on Yelp. Be aware of this and follow the results of the lawsuits filed against Yelp, and find a reasonably natural way to encourage your actual customers to give you reviews.

The reason that Google+ Local puts so much emphasis on reviews is that the search engines have made the determination that reviews (good or bad) from real men and women should be more important than anything you could ever say about yourself (through linking).

That makes total sense here.

So the question is, if you are running a great business, what are you doing to capture *real* reviews?

It's important to go about review solicitation according to Google's guidelines. Definitely read their documentation at support.google.com.

I personally believe it is okay to ask your customers to leave you a review, but it is not okay to ask them to leave you a positive review.

Here are three ways to get reviews:

1. Give customers who come into your physical locations little cards asking them to review you.

2. Send satisfied customers emails asking for a review.

3. Use incentives on QR codes to build them.

Do you have a plan in place to get this new currency online?

Perhaps more than 90% of all online businesses never take the time to do this one thing that is now paramount in the eyes of the search engines. That is losing you more money than you know.

Keep in mind it is safer to get reviews a few at a time, rather than in large batches at the same time. This helps to avoid them being taken down.

Getting lots of great reviews can shoot your most competitive local keywords through the roof.

Google and Yelp both have the ability to severely filter reviews that come in, so it's important to get good reviews in a variety of places on the web.

Product Reviews for SEO

Product review creation and optimization is a powerful opportunity to drive traffic to your site and drive readers to convert into buyers. Regular blog posts using long tail keywords to capture people searching for opinions on products and product specifications can generate tons of traffic and help convert customers. Some of the biggest blogs on the web are tech blogs with reviews. But what is also amazing is content that your customers create. Outsourcing long tail optimization to your own customers via reviews, ratings, and comments has a solid place in e-commerce SEO and is a foundational part of social media as well. Not to mention that reviews placed in product pages can increase conversions in addition to SEO! Just make sure the reviews are being indexed by Google. Many product review software packages such as Bazaarvoice display the reviews right on the product pages in a way Google can see/crawl, but some don't. Google and Bing are getting better at crawling the JavaScript that can block reviews. Having separate review pages, such as on a subdomain for each product, is typically not a benefit. It is usually better to give the benefit to the product page itself. Google a sentence from a review and see if it appears in the search results. If so, you're on your way to having it help your ranks.

Testimonials and Recommendations

Some of the most influential components in all advertising are testimonials and recommendations. From Google reviews to LinkedIn recommendations, you simply can't afford not to make this social connection.

Are you asking your target customers what would have prevented them from buying this product/service?

It is important to get your customers to talk about their objections because it makes them more believable and relatable by someone in the early stages of the buying cycle.

Ask your customers what they liked as a result of buying this product/service.Now customers can talk about why the purchase was worth it, despite their initial objections.

As I mentioned in the LinkedIn review section earlier, you can write intelligently crafted reviews for customers and send them for approval. As long as they agree with what you say, then the review will be more powerful if you have used at least these two questions. For more information on the science of testimonials, check out the ebook *The Secret Life of Testimonials* by Sean D'Souza. In *The Psychology of Persuasion*, Dr. Robert Cialdini discusses the key factors involved in getting people to buy and make decisions. One of his key principles is that of social proof, such as testimonials and reviews.

Still think your IT guy can do your web marketing? As you can see, the world of Internet marketing ranges from studying psychology and technology to copywriting and design!

Sharing Presentations with SlideShare

One of the most beautiful ways to get your entire message across to those who are interested in your niche now comes from a place called SlideShare. SlideShare is the world's largest community for sharing presentations. These presentations can easily be seen on SlideShare itself, on mobile devices, or embedded on other sites through the use of widgets.

SlideShare is among the 200 most-visited websites in the world. Besides presentations, SlideShare also supports documents, PDFs, videos, and webinars.

People are flocking to SlideShare and using it as a search engine to find presentations based on keywords! These could and should be your keywords.

SlideShare and sites like it (that in my opinion happen to pale in comparison to this one) enable you to put a beautiful presentation together and let others experience it for themselves. Rather than asking your audience to sit in on a live or a taped webinar, here, you have the opportunity to show off your chops in a presentation format.

And people are loving it and sharing it (hence the name) like crazy.

The best way to approach SlideShare is to imagine someone watching a presentation about you without you being there.

Be bold and be powerful with your presentation. Be *very* visual. And be willing to let people know that there's more...a lot more...when they deal with you directly.

Imagine creating one gorgeous and *compelling* slide presentation and then having it go "viral" based on the depth of your knowledge. It only takes one influencer in your niche to make that happen if they find your SlideShare presentation.

Our strongest advice here is to create one terrific presentation at first and to take your time with it. Build it up to become something that people must have and make it very visual and factual. Then push it through all your other social outlets like Facebook, Twitter, Pinterest, and Tumblr.

Sharing Documents with Docstoc

As the name might suggest, Docstoc was created as a place to share documents through the business-minded community. That then evolved, naturally, into more of a pseudo-Kindle format where now people are publishing to Docstoc and people are following and downloading from those writers.

No matter what your niche, there are rabid fans waiting to absorb and devour your content.

Why not take your white papers (your descriptions of how you do things the way you do and why) and ebooks and load them up where the world can see them?

White Papers for Docstoc

White papers are authority reports or guides that help your readers understand a specific difficult issue, help them to make better decisions, or help them solve problems.

The idea here is that you have been willing to put down in writing how things really get done and you are more than happy to share that depth of what you know with people who will benefit from it.

Why would you give out so much free information in white papers? Because it builds your reputation as an authority and someone people can trust.

Ebooks for Docstoc

Ebooks can be a great lead generation tool that you can also upload to Docstoc.

Say you have ebooks where you outline the *Top 15 Ways to Generate More Solar Power*, or a document about the *Top 6 Ways to Sell ATVs Every Day*. Put these into a beautiful format and upload them to Docstoc.

Even better, why not Facebook the Docstoc links to your fans and tweet the new arrival to your followers? Why not socially integrate every single thing you do to become the force you know you need to be?

Docstoc is something that must be in your toolbox.

Increasing Traffic with Social Bookmarking

Bookmarking enables users to add, annotate, edit, and share bookmarks to web content.

Let's say you find an incredible article on fly fishing in Alaska and you want to be able to get back to that article and all the gorgeous photographs in it whenever you want.

Social bookmarking enables you to "bookmark" the page and to drop that bookmark into a digital file in your account at that social bookmarking site.

Top social bookmarking sites include the following:

1. Twitter
2. Reddit
3. Pinterest
4. StumbleUpon
5. BuzzFeed
6. Delicious
7. Tweetmeme
8. Digg
9. FARK
10. Slashdot
11. Friendfeed
12. Clipmarks
13. Newsvine
14. Diigo
15. DZone

You can get server-crashing levels of traffic if your story goes viral on a site like Reddit or Digg. If people write about you all over the web and link back to the story that sits on your website or blog, you can generate loads of great backlinks.

Also check out niche social bookmarking sites such as:

1. Ballhyped – Sports

2. Chictini – Fashion

3. AutoSpies – Autos

4. Livestrong.com – Health and Medicine

5. Hacker News – Web Development

By bookmarking your content, people are more likely to share and link to your content. It's not the link from the bookmark itself that aids your rankings. It's the indirect effect.

Bookmarking is great for:

- Increasing social buzz,

- Making your content easier to share, and

- Driving traffic.

There are hundreds of great bookmarking sites. Get on them and flourish but learn the etiquette first, such as where some sites like Digg don't want you to submit your own content, so as to keep it pure and non-marketing oriented. Otherwise you will get banned *very* quickly.

Extending Your Social Reach on StumbleUpon and Tumblr

Minus the nerd talk, StumbleUpon is a great bookmarking site where you have the opportunity to get found by people inside StumbleUpon. As you "stumble upon" new pages that you love (perhaps your own), you will want to tag those bookmarks widely to make sure that you get in front of more people who are using StumbleUpon as a search engine.

StumbleUpon also has a nice advertising platform where you can get pay-per-click ads for a fraction of what it would cost you on Google. Granted, it's more of a social than a purchase-oriented click, but it is certainly traffic that you can get in front of for less.

Same goes for Tumblr... but Tumblr is apparently loved by the search engines.

On Tumblr (which is very similar in scope to Twitter) you have a feed and then people follow that feed so that when you post photos, videos (very popular), or stories, people get to keep track of what you are up to. Tumblr also has, like so many other social sites, an RSS feed which is something that you have to start working with.

By amassing all of your RSS feeds from social bookmarking sites, you get to push those feeds through RSS aggregators.

This can increase the number of links pointing back to your site.

Tumblr is adored by Google and is definitely worth a look.

Taking and Sharing Photos on Instagram

Instagram is a free photo-sharing program launched in October 2010 which enables users to take a photo, apply a digital filter to it, then share it the way we share on Twitter or Tumblr.

Instagram, now owned by Facebook, came out of the gates with such force that Apple named Instagram as app of the year in 2011, saying that the app makes it "near impossible to take a bad shot."

Nice endorsement.

More importantly, how do you tap into this monster of a site and get the traffic and the interest and eventually the sales you need?

How to Market on Instagram

1. **Instagram Cannot Be the Only Tool in Your Toolbox**

   Clearly, Instagram is a great mobile marketing tool, but it is not the only tool. By design, Instagram works best with visual-friendly content sites like Pinterest, Tumblr, and Facebook. Why? Because these are the places where people talk about great photographs.

2. **Start Involving Your Community**

   Start thinking about creating scavenger hunts, contests, and many other ways to have visuals drive action. Use visuals for all the power they really have and let people "play" with your shots as much as possible.

3. **Let Your Employees Be Involved**

   Encourage everyone in your business to take the most realistic pictures they can as often as they can. Unlike Pinterest, photos on Instagram can be more gritty and real and you need to play that out.

4. **Use Hashtags That Get You Noticed**

   Use photo-specific hashtag tag names where possible (as opposed to brand attributes) as a better way to engage the hashtag craze.

   Also try Instagram group hashtags and contest tags to gain greater recognition.

5. **Create Your Own Hashtag and Engage People Who Use It**

   Creating, using, promoting, and monitoring your own hashtags makes some cool things happen, in that your own hashtags let you monitor the dialogue about your products and your brand from the outside. This allows you to jump into the conversational fray when you want to.

   The use of original hashtags (now extremely popular on Twitter) should be a priority for you.

6. **Geo-Tag Instagram Photos**

When in doubt, go geo! In the latest Instagram update, users now have the ability to transfer that location information to Facebook, Flickr, Twitter, and Foursquare all at the same time. They can even convey where the photos were physically taken.

With geo-tagging, restaurants, retailers, and any other brand can promote their location and their products using and promoting geo-tagged Instagram photos.

7. **Find the Perfect Timing**

Very simple. Statistics show that the best time to post to Instagram is between 5 pm and 6 pm locally. Go figure.

While Instagram is a great site, make sure you extend the reach of your images on other places such as Flickr.

Sharing and Getting Found on Flickr

Flickr is considered by many to be the premier online photo management site.

Flickr is driven by two core values:

1. They seek to make photos available to the people who matter to you most, and

2. They strive to enable newer ways to organize your photos every day.

The basic idea behind photo-sharing sites is that you upload your photos, name them, and then tag them. You do this so that they can get found, just like content gets found on Google.

Here's an example. Suppose you own a cupcake business. You take photos of all of your newest cupcakes. Of course you are going to use some of the actual names of the cupcakes in your titles of your photos (like "Cinnamon Caramel Glazed Cupcake") but in your tags you could and should say things like "hard to make cupcakes" or "cupcakes for corporate events" or "dessert ideas for caterers." This enables you to get found more often as people use Flickr as a search engine.

That really is what is happening to social marketing in general. People are using each piece of it like a search engine.

10 Flickr SEO Tips for High Visibility

Photo-sharing is huge in the online community! Standing out from the pack and generating traffic from search engines is important for maximum exposure. Here are our top 10 Flickr SEO tips:

1. **Optimize your photos for maximum effectiveness.** Tag each photo and upload a higher-quality image. This makes your images easier to find and easier to download in the size that the user may want.

2. **Promote your Flickr profile wherever you can.** Integrate your Flickr profile with other social networks—submit a photo to StumbleUpon, automatically post photos to Facebook, and tweet pictures regularly to your Twitter site. If you have a blog, integrate a Flickr slideshow. Add a link to your Flickr profile in your email signature. Promote it as much as possible.

3. **Use your own images in your blog posts.** Bloggers tend to go to Flickr to find high-quality images for their articles. If you are a blogger, try to use your own pictures in your posts. Link the photo to your Flickr profile so that, when someone clicks on the image in your blog post, they will be taken directly to your Flickr profile.

4. **Get involved with Flickr groups.** Being on Flickr is a social activity. Join groups relevant to your interests and your pictures, and share to them. Comment on the other pictures shared to the group. Get involved and engage other users.

5. **Add a Creative Commons License to your photos.** As stated before, bloggers like to use Flickr photos in their posts. By adding a Creative Commons License to your photos, any blogger can use your photos in their posts as long as they give you the credit for the image. This is a great way to generate traffic and allow bloggers to have a high-quality image for their article.

6. **Use your Flickr statistics to analyze sources of traffic.** Flickr's analytics are only available to Pro users (Pro is the paid version), but just as Google Analytics can help you optimize your blog posts for the main sources of your traffic, you can do the same with your images and Flickr's statistics.

7. **Invest in a Pro account.** Not only do you get access to those statistics, but a Pro account also allows you to upload more pictures, remove ads, and have more organization options.

8. **Include keywords in your photo descriptions.** Decide which keywords you want to target and then include these keywords in your description. Wisely-chosen keywords will generate traffic.

9. **Create new titles for your photos.** Uniquely name each photo instead of letting your camera's default file name serve as the photo name. Including the keyword in the title is even better. A photo titled "Stop Sign at the Intersection" will work much better than "DC000105."

10. **Change your file names, too.** In the same vein as changing the titles of the photos, changing the file name will help the indexing of your photo. Search engines also consider file names, so use your keywords in your file names, using a hyphen in between words ("keyword-rich-file-name-here.jpg").

Ranking Your Flickr Profile Quickly and Easily

I know what you're thinking right now after reading that headline...who uses Flickr anymore? Well, aside from bloggers and amateur photographers, anyone who keeps a close eye on what is working well in the search results is using this massive photo-sharing site. Flickr is still being treated extremely well by Google and if you're bringing quality to the table, you can tap into tons of quality traffic.

Why Indexing or Ranking Something Fast Matters

You might be asking yourself, "Why do I care if my content ranks or indexes quickly?" You should care because a common content marketing strategy is writing on current trending topics. Let's say you're a tech writer. You would obviously want to be ranked first for your blog post on the iPhone 5s the night it was released, because that would be the biggest surge of traffic for that topic. If your website isn't getting crawled often enough or fast enough, sometimes it can take weeks for Google to realize you updated your website. Flickr is important and helpful because it can rank high so quickly and easily, making it a great way to funnel traffic to your site for trending topics.

Setting Up a Mini Social Signal Network

Below I outline how you can index your Flickr account quickly with what we could call a "mini social signal network." You will learn what you will need to make a mini social network and how it works.

What You Will Need

You need to create two accounts for this small social signals network, a Pinterest account and a Tumblr account. We use these sites because when you add a picture to a blog post, it allows you to show the source of the image, which means you can link to Flickr.

• **Pinterest** quickly gained notoriety for giving websites huge amounts of referral traffic. Pinterest is often known as the murderer of Flickr, but our research indicates Flickr is currently still treated better by Google in terms of ranking compared to Pinterest. That could change overnight, so don't just do one or the other.

• **Tumblr** has been around longer than Pinterest, but never hit the huge levels of referral traffic that Pinterest is famous for. Don't overlook Tumblr, because many large companies take advantage of Tumblr's impressive referral traffic and how easy it is to set up. Examples include *The New Yorker*, *Rolling Stone*, and Search Engine Land. With Tumblr's built-in content drip system, you can plan months of content ahead of time to post automatically. That's probably my favorite feature of Tumblr.

What to Do

Take the photo, tag, or URL from your Flickr profile and post it to Tumblr and Pinterest's photo section. This creates a social signal to your Flickr photos. You can expand this to all your content marketing and try to find even more sites like Pinterest or Tumblr to post these photos. Another idea: StumbleUpon is a great profile that allows you to source content. Social signals like the one we made from the steps above took the place of "pinging" in the Internet marketing realm, and they will most likely keep getting stronger and stronger in Google's algorithm. While many sites like WordPress still utilize "pinging" in their posts, I do not believe it actually does much to help your content get indexed. For more on pinging, see below.

Why Social Signals Thrive While Pinging Suffers

The same people who are still pinging their backlinks are the same ones who think keyword stuffing meta keywords is a valid SEO practice. Since you're reading this book, you now know better.

"What's pinging?" It used to be a common practice utilized by (most of the time) black hat linkbuilders. Pinging is like saying to Google crawlers "Hey, this is new/updated!" While its purpose was to alert Google of your site's new content, it was soon taken over by black hats pinging their low-quality backlinks. Since this whole system of pinging backlinks or new content on your site was so abused by undesirable sites, it appears that Google has completely stopped paying attention to "pings" or assigns them very little value over other factors. On the other hand, using social signals (retweets on Twitter or shares on Facebook) appears to offer similar results to what pinging used to provide and it's much harder to abuse.

Web Marketing On All Cylinders - John McDougall

Three More Ways to Optimize Flickr

Here are three tips that you can apply easily that will make your Flickr show up more often for search results and bring more traffic to your website.

1. Fill Out That Profile!

    No one wants to look at a boring profile, or worse, one that is not filled out at all. Taking the time to think of good copy and making your Flickr profile entertaining to read can do wonders for how people interact with it. This is also a good chance to optimize your profile for branded keywords that show up for even more search queries. In the description section of my Flickr profile, I also link out to my other social media sites both for branding purposes and to increase their rank along with my Flickr's.

2. Connect Networks

    Linking your profiles or pages from sites like Facebook or Google+ to your Flickr is a wise idea and can help Google by showing it where it can find you or your brand on the web. This is also another quality backlink pointing at your Flickr that can make it show up for more search results.

3. Share

    This ties into what I said above about connecting your social media networks…and it's easy, too. Just make sure to share your Flickr profile as often as possible. Simply tweeting "Hey, check out my Flickr" is often enough to get some great traffic to it and hopefully funnel that to your website.

Taking Advantage of Online Discussion Forums

There seemed to be a time where everyone congregated on forums. Forums are not dead but certainly are not booming as fast as full-featured social media communities.

The leader in the forum space depends on the niche, and the number of communities around a given topic varies widely. You will have to research what the biggest forums are in your area of expertise but there are great rewards to be had if you can connect to other people passionate about sharing their ideas and asking questions online.

Pros and Cons of Having Your Own Forum

Pros

- Grow or engage in a vibrant community

- Establish relationships

- Convert visitors to clients

- Ask users to make suggestions

- Help others

- Huge volumes of SEO-friendly user-generated content will get added to your website

Cons

- Monitoring for spammers

- Monitoring content

- Hosting responsibilities and the bandwidth required

Forums might be a static throwback of the last decade, but they are still a great knowledge resource. Well-run forums come with built-in trust because the users know that the moderator will drive conversations toward constructive topics. Therefore, when you do put in links to your site (only when appropriate after sharing something relevant) and they stick, you are more likely to receive quality, well-targeted traffic. Just don't do this unless it is about building high-quality relationships or you run a substantial risk of penalties post-Google Penguin. If you can build a forum on your own site and create a community, Google will see it and give you credit for being an authority, as long as the content is real and engaging.

User-generated content of various kinds is great for differentiation because it can add engaging content to your site that your competitors don't have. Engagement is essentially an SEO ranking factor, and the influence of engagement metrics will almost certainly grow. So getting users engaged, whether it's through blog comments, forums, or shares, will help you considerably moving forward.

Summary

Let's recap the top things to keep in mind about social media marketing:

1. People do business with people they know, like, and trust.

2. It is trackable all the way through purchases and leads.

3. It requires personable, memorable, and useful content.

4. Listening and sharing are key elements (not broadcasting).

5. People love to be first finders and share, so take advantage of that.

6. Stop worrying about social media hurting your brand through negative comments.

7. Negative comments are an opportunity to share solutions and win over customers.

8. Leverage user-generated content.

9. There are well over a billion active users of social media, and that number is growing fast.

10. Social media is about creating trust and getting customers to believe in you. (Hint: Engage people who will engage others.)

11. Don't get so lost in calculating ROI that the *Risk of Inaction* makes you lose money and brand equity.

12. Social media can help you grow a huge list of potential customers to email and nurture.

13. Social media buttons on your site make it easier to spread and promote your content.

Build Your List—It's Everything

The DailyCandy site was basically a list and sold for $125 million. Groupon is just a list of people who want deals, and it is the fastest-growing company of all time! Not the fastest-growing in the web space, the fastest period. Even Google, one of the other fastest-growth companies, is envious of Facebook and its "list" of customers. The new Internet is not just search but share. Share with your lists and keep them engaged.

Beware the Top Social Media Mistakes

1. **Expecting immediate results:** Patience is a must. It takes work to build a valuable online presence.

2. **Lack of tracking systems:** Tracking systems take assists from social to other channels into account. (Currently, HubSpot does this better than Google Analytics.)

3. **Using the wrong network:** Research which one will work for your niche.

4. **Direct promotion of products:** Avoid pushing your products before building up a trusted network.

5. **Offering no value:** In order to get a lot, you need to give at the very least a little.

6. **No focus on relationships:** The social web is just that, social. Invest in others and value will come your way.

7. **Spamming:** There is a fine line between spamming and tactful self-promotion. Err on the safe side until this line becomes clearer.

8. **Wrong mindset:** Social media is different from any other marketing tool. Take time to *learn these differences* before diving in too far.

9. **Poor or inconsistent branding:** It is a subtle touch, but carrying a consistent brand over multiple online channels allows your efforts to accumulate.

10. **Too professional:** The social web is, by its very nature, very laid-back. Entertainment and engagement hold high value in addition to business content.

11. **Not professional enough:** Yes, it is a double-edged sword. Lean toward casual, but stay clear of crass.

12. **Trying to do too much at once:** Get good at one social networking site at a time and you will have better results. Trying to do 15 social sites at once will likely just result in a mess and lead to frustration.

13. **Not registering your names:** Protect your brand or username from social media identity theft and use Knowem.com to see if your name is still available at over 350 popular social networking websites.

Social media works like dating. You don't just pull out an engagement ring and propose when you first meet someone. You need to take them on a journey through the top, middle, and eventually to the bottom of the marketing funnel with ebooks and blog posts, then comparison charts and case studies. Only then should you try to get them to buy now, sign up, or fill out a lead form.

Tracking Social Media ROI

Tracking social media is a big topic, so I'll cover that in detail in the analytics chapter (Chapter 11). If you do nothing else for tracking, at least track referrers in Google Analytics and check out HubSpot as a deeper level of tracking across time and channels.

Creating and Socially Sharing Content Must Be in Your Marketing Mix

This is the new way of thinking. You create great and powerful content and then tell your circles about it, tell your friends about it, comment on other blogs about it...and it becomes something. It helps you rank in Google and it strengthens your brand by making you a trusted thought leader and even a friend. This chapter is really just an introduction to the many social media tactics and how to share your content and engage customers. My hope is that it will give you a better sense of the landscape so you can start your journey with a clearer vision and sense of direction.

Chapter 8

Engaging Content Is King

Most top websites are popular due to the content, not necessarily the design. There are plenty of popular sites that look bad, but very few cool-looking sites with poor content that ever get recognized.

Great content can make you a thought leader and increase brand recognition, trust, credibility, customer loyalty, and authenticity.

To create great content, start by listening to your customers and asking them questions. You can also use social media listening tools like Radian6 to see what people are saying in your space. A new tool called Bottlenose can help you quickly identify what keywords are buzzing, and Google Trends is helpful for seeing which topics are trending up or down. However you do your research, make sure you write more about the topics your customers lose sleep over than just the topics that are part of your sales process.

When it comes to search engine optimization (SEO), content is and always has been king. Search engine "spiders" need relevant, fresh content to chew on if a website is going to rank highly with the search engines. Social media is just a mirage if it's not based on quality content, and public relations (PR) that doesn't tell a story or share a trending topic is not worth anyone's time to read. So get on board the content marketing train and customers will be pulled to you instead of you always pushing stuff on them.

Clearly, search and social is now a hungry content monster that needs to be fed, and link building is nearly impossible without content.

The emphasis on content means you are, in many ways and no matter what your business, a publisher. If you want to think like a publisher, you need a content marketing plan. The first step is creating a calendar.

Develop a Content Marketing Calendar

Your team's content marketing calendar is like an editorial calendar for a magazine, which sets out what topics will be covered when. Your content marketing calendar should include a month-by-month content schedule and go out as far as one year. Appointing one person to manage the editing and upkeep of the calendar can help avoid confusion about what was supposed to happen when (and who is responsible).

Consider the following when brainstorming your content for the coming year:

- Business Quarters

- Selling Cycles

- Seasons

- Holidays

- Events

- Product Launches

- Deadlines

- Company Goals

- Metrics for Tracking Content Success

Monthly Calendar Creation

If you set your calendar up as a spreadsheet, each content project has its own row, ordered by the publication date. Due date and publication date should be filled in chronologically. The remaining columns should be filled out following these recommendations:

- Title/Description

- Keyword Targeted (Even infographics and videos can rank for keywords)

- Search Volume/Number of searches per month

- Competition Score from HubSpot, SEOMoz, or Google AdWords. It is important to see the difficulty level of each keyword in terms of ranking.

- Status (In process, completed, published)

- Type of Content (Blog post, article, tweet, white paper, etc.)

- Author/Producer/Designer

- Target Audience

- Distribution Channels

- Promotion

- Social Updates if different from promotion

- Metadata Tags

- Success Metrics

- Image Sources

Using an editorial calendar for content marketing will help keep your content organized in a way that makes sense and is easier to track over time.

Make sure when you create content that you include several content styles such as:

1. Original, in-depth content

2. Curated content (reviewing content someone else made)

3. User-generated content

It is ideal to have a balance of these types of content as it makes your job easier. By developing twice as many curated pieces as in-depth original pieces, you can pump out batches of content more quickly. And if you can get users to share lots of user-generated content, your load will get even lighter.

Why Is Fresh Content So Important?

Really good website content needs to be constantly updated. Search engines prefer fresh content, so if your goal is to "set it and forget it" with a few optimized articles on your site, you might as well throw in the towel when it comes to gaining organic search engine ranks. A blog, for example, is a great way to add regular content. User-generated content (such as blog comments, forum posts, user reviews, and testimonials) is a great way to keep things fresh.

Content for Conversion

Content plays a psychological role in converting visitors into customers. Overall website size matters to Google, too. If you search Google for *site:lendingtree.com* you will see a site with about 8,000 pages indexed. Do the same search on any local competitor that offers mortgages and you will likely see no more than 10–100 pages indexed. When vying for top ranks and top traffic, you can't expect Google or customers to treat you with the same respect they give to sites with large amounts of content unless you have lots of great content of your own! That has to become your new mindset if you want to really win this SEO/Internet marketing game.

Marketing Companies Can't Make Pigs Fly!

Your site is only as good as its content, and if the content is poor no amount of magic inbound marketing dust will help you get to the number one spot or become a legend in social circles. Ask yourself: If there was no such thing as the Internet and there were no brochures, what would your pitch be? What is the information that communicates your uniqueness? Try to ensure the things you do off-line and the pitch you give to people in person are replicated in a digital format.

It all starts with who you are and what you represent. Without this, all the geeky SEO tricks in the world won't help you. If you don't have an agency helping you understand your company's positioning, you should work on defining your brand before writing a single tagline. Once you know your positioning—for example, are you a high-cost provider like a Ritz-Carlton hotel or a lower-cost provider like a Best Western—then you can clearly state your company's unique selling proposition and back up the brand with key conversion points, including your content.

Writing for Personas

Knowing the personas of your website audience is critical to writing good content. If you write content with an image of one of your targeted personas in mind, the content is more likely to make an emotional connection with your target audience.

Then There's SEO Writing

Good SEO writers are well-versed not only in adding keywords, but in adding them eloquently and with proper branding in mind. We've all seen pages where it looks like keywords were just haphazardly added to existing text. If your keywords stick out like a sore thumb, experiment with reducing the density or adjusting the writing. Google is now penalizing people for over-optimization, so choose and use specific keywords in your content but don't overdo it.

Breaking out new pages for key topics in an existing page is a great way to add more content with less severe repetition of keywords. If there is one sure way to get yourself noticed in the wrong way, it is to deliberately "keyword stuff" your pages with too many keywords. As long as you can create a *quality* new page for a given extra topic, go for it. Just don't add pages merely to increase your page count. Pages that don't create engagement may be ignored by Google. Some experts say that pages with a high bounce rate should be deleted, as they will drag down the rest of your SEO. So while larger sites are an ideal, don't make your site big by adding "fluffy" pages just for sheer mass. Quality is key and Google is getting better and better at tracking quality. Google can track if users hit the "back" button and return to their search results, so be careful not to drive that hard-earned traffic to pages that deliver a limp user experience.

Google's Panda and Penguin Algorithm Updates

What impact do Google's recent updates to its search algorithm have on your content creation efforts? Plenty.

The **Google Panda** search algorithm update that was first released in early 2011 is designed to penalize sites with weak content while rewarding sites with quality content. As long as you are producing good, quality content, your website should not suffer any negative effects from Panda. If you don't add unique value to the web or if your site has duplicate content, you're toast. Not to mention your users will think you are lame. So the days of weak content are coming to a close and the era of high quality is upon us.

Google Penguin This algorithm update penalizes black hat link-building techniques that rely on heavily sculpted "exact match" anchor text (sites where 60% of anchor text was for "money" keywords) and comment spam, among other tactics, to artificially inflate search rankings. Part of this update is about devaluing links from crummy sites that no one visits. In a way, this update is also about quality.

Google+ Author Rank

In June 2011, Google introduced rel = author, the code and process that allows a web page to announce the author of the page by pointing to a Google+ profile page (which must link back to the site for two-way verification). This is incredibly powerful for Google, as it allows them to verify the author of a web page or blog post. Content is now scrutinized in much greater detail, so Google can trust content and links again. Anyone serious about developing content should get on board and build their Author Rank. You can learn more about this in the social media chapter.

Unfortunately (but perhaps not surprisingly), people are already gaming this system, as demonstrated by the following advertisement for a freelance content writer, seen online in November 2012:

> *We are looking for people with Google+ accounts, with high author ranks, to write and publish articles for us, with our link, on good quality websites, and also share our content, websites, plus 1s using Google+. Giving us good promotion and links from your high ranks Google+ account.*
>
> *This is an ongoing job, which we can negotiate the terms.*
>
> *Most importantly, if you have a high Google+ author rank, please respond, and we can negotiate what you can do for us.*

But why game it by outsourcing your content development in a questionable way when you can develop real Author Rank?

How to Add Keywords to Text the Right Way

Here's an example of keyword-heavy text:

Cheap Golf Clubs and Discount Golf Equipment from Golf Zone

Great buys on discount golf equipment with great service! Brand name, <u>cheap golf clubs</u>, <u>golf bags</u>, <u>golf balls</u>, <u>golf gloves</u>, <u>golf shoes</u>, <u>golf accessories</u>, and <u>golf apparel</u>. In addition to cheap golf clubs, you get our money-back guarantee and free shipping on orders over $99!

This is a very busy chunk of text with a lot of keywords. Since this is text for the client's home page, that is probably all right, as the goal is to express the variety of equipment and accessories for sale on the site. You may have noticed the focus on "cheap golf clubs" and "discount golf clubs," and the fact that we mixed in conversion elements (like "money-back guarantee" and "free shipping") with the more mundane SEO elements.

Now let's look at an example of a product category page for the same website:

Discount Golf Bags

Golf bags are an important accessory for golfers looking to enjoy their round of golf. Whether it is a stand bag, cart bag, or even a custom golf bag, the right bag can make all the difference in the world! Golf Zone is your window into top quality discount golf bags.

In this example, we are being much stricter about what we optimize for, because this page is really about one topic: discount golf bags. Stay focused and use both the exact phrases you are targeting and some variations on those phrases, so the search engines don't see the page as overly optimized.

Engaging Content Is Persuasive

Internet marketing is not just about keywords anymore. Sounding convincing and pointing to action items can dramatically increase your conversion rates. Using trigger/action words and mentioning awards, press stories, or books you have written can make your content more believable. Again, you want to position yourself as an authority in your field... someone people should listen to!

What's essential for engaging content? Always include:

- Catchy titles

- Trigger words (words that the user searched with and action phrases like "buy now")

- Thought leader content that brands you as an expert

- Social proof that you have the best deal (testimonials, reviews, "likes," etc.)

Remember, a good web writer is only as good as the conversions he or she creates. So if you don't test to see what is working by tracking goals in analytics and testing variations of advertisements, you will never know how well your favorite copy is working. Check out Google's Content Experiments tool in Google Analytics, which helps in optimizing variations of content such as headings and graphics. (Note: Chapter 12, which is about increasing conversions, elaborates on both this and analytics in more detail.)

Create a Sense of Urgency

Use phrases like "sale ends January 14" and "register today for 15% off." When you include real offers in your content, you give people a reason to act *now*.

Clearly Express Your Value Proposition

Don't make customers think. Some of the best marketers realize that people online actually like to and very much need to be told what to do. Make it obvious what you're good at and why they should buy from you versus someone else. It's your job to show potential customers why you're the best, and your website should be a natural extension of that.

Make It Scan- and Skim-Friendly

Copy on the web is different from off-line copy. Readers are generally moving from site to site, instead of reading just one book or piece of content. So you need users to see the point, and fast, or you're going to lose them when they navigate away from your website. Internet readers tend to scan copy for keywords and important points, and your content needs to cater to this reading style. To make your writing scan-and-skim-friendly, try the following:

1. Use large fonts for descriptive headlines

2. Use descriptive subheadings

3. Use short sentences and paragraphs

4. Use bullet points

5. Highlight or underline important words and phrases

Latent Semantic Indexing: What It Is, Why It Matters

If you think writing for the search engines is simple, think again. Latent semantic indexing (LSI) allows a search engine to determine what a page is about beyond just simply noting that it contains the keywords the searcher was looking for. A page about Apple will generally also have terms such as iMac or iPod on it. A good writer will keep this in mind when developing content for the web and use a variety of terms that "belong" with the theme of the main keywords. Google prefers sites that appear more natural and that have occurrences of a wider variety of terms than just the main ones you hope to rank for. To find related search terms:

1. Search Google using a ~ for search results with related terms. Googling ~*books* will return pages with terms matching or related to books, and will highlight some of the related words in the search results.

2. Use a lexical database such as the one at http://wordnet.princeton.edu/

Tips for Hiring Writers

The truth is, most small business owners don't have time to generate new content for their websites, often struggle with regularly generating a small amount of weak text, and sadly are often too afraid to give a professional writer a try. One way or another, you will need regular content that changes and increases or you will not be highly regarded by the search engines or your prospects.

While some people look overseas for cheap writers, be careful about outsourcing the work to vendors in places where quality is low. You get what you pay for. Make sure your content is high quality as well as optimized for search engines and that it includes relevant calls to action. If you don't have time to write it yourself, give a writer a try. You might just be relieved and surprised to see projects you have had on the back burner for years completed in days or weeks. Don't let a lack of content keep you from getting that next big deal. When you find a writer, be sure that your contract spells out that you will own the copyright on the content your writer creates for you. Basically, you're hiring a ghostwriter—you can even put your own name on content like ebooks or blog posts. This practice is more common than you may think and can be quite effective if, for example, you are struggling to keep up with your blog and need someone to provide regularly updated content.

How to Do a Competitive Content Analysis

A competitive content analysis is exactly what it sounds like. You will analyze your website content and compare it to your competitor's content.

Step 1: Find your competitors

You probably know who your competitors are, but take a closer look. Make sure you create a list of a few different kinds of competitors. If you're a small, local company, look at some small, local competitors as well as some larger, well-known ones. Include some that rank well for your favorite keywords. This ensures that you are taking a broad look at your industry and getting the best information from your analysis.

Step 2: Begin your analysis using a sitemap tool

We like using AuditMyPC sitemap generator for this step.

To begin, all you need to do is input the web address. (Tip: check the "exclude images" box, as it will save you time in the end.) Hit the green "start" button and wait.

The bottom right-hand corner is where you can watch the crawl. Based on the size of the website, the crawl will last anywhere from 2 minutes to 15 minutes. (Tip: input "site:*we-baddress.com*" into Google and you will have a rough estimate of the number of pages that will be crawled.)

Once the crawl is complete you can move on to the next step.

Step 3: Export site map

Click on the "sitemap" button and you will see a page listing all of your URLs, titles, and other technical information. Yes, it is a little intimidating, but don't panic, it will get cleaned up soon!

There are a few substeps in Step 3 that you must complete in order to successfully export your sitemap to an Excel spreadsheet.

Step 3A: Export delimited file

Click the "Export" button and choose "Delimited file" from the menu. Save this file to your computer.

(This is important if you want the file to open nicely in Excel.)

Step 3B: Open with Excel and separate text into columns

Run Excel and choose "Open" from the "File" menu. Find your file (you may need to choose "All Files" from the Open dialog box in order to see the file on your computer). When you open the CSV file in Excel, it will put all of the text into the first column. Choose "Text to Columns" from the "Data" menu (Excel 2007 or later), and in the dialog box choose "Delimited" by "Semicolon" and click "Finish." That will separate the data into Excel columns. Make sure that you use the semicolon as your delimiter so your list comes out clean.

Once you successfully open your file, you will see a large list of words and numbers that probably don't make a whole lot of sense initially. This is where you will have to use your organizational skills and be a bit creative in order to come out with some good information.

Step 4: Organize your spreadsheet

I recommend that you delete all the columns after "mimetype," which leaves you with only the four most important columns to organize: URL, Title, State, and Mime Type. This step makes your spreadsheet cleaner and easier to understand.

In order to organize this spreadsheet and have a useful sitemap, you will need to have some Excel skills (if you don't, recruit someone who does!). The goal is to have a list of all the different pages on each site so that you can compare your content to your competitors' content. This process can be a bit tedious, requiring patience and time, but it is worth it. There are several different methods for organizing this list, but these are the items to delete:

1. Any failed page (but make a note of these—they sometimes represent bad links on your site).

2. Any images (indicated under "mime type," as sometimes images get crawled even if you check the "exclude images" box).

3. Any duplicate pages (sometimes there is a glitch in the crawl that creates a distinct pattern in the spreadsheet. If this happens, just delete those pages).

4. Any "css" pages (these are files with website code, not content pages).

Sort your spreadsheet alphabetically by the "URL" column (click column "A," click "Sort & Filter," choose "A to Z" and "Expand Selection"). If you have your pages organized with subdirectories, this will sort many of your similar pages together and make it easier to visualize. Once you have organized this spreadsheet, take note of these two pieces of information:

- How many total pages there are on a site.

- Where the bulk of the content is (blogs, services, about us, etc.).

Repeat this entire process—all four steps—for your own website as well as for at least three competitors. The more competitors you analyze, the more valuable your information. Once finished, you will be left with a complete list of all the pages on each website you're analyzing. I like to add these as individual tabs in an Excel document. This list is valuable because it not only tells you *where* all of the content lives, but also *what type* of content it is. Look at your most successful competitor's site. Where does their content live? What are they doing that you aren't doing? Look at your weakest competitor. What are you doing better than them? Get what I'm saying? There is no secret formula once you have your lists complete. You can always go back and add more competitors or revise your lists when you have time. But, for now, this is a great way to start improving your content and engage your customers and viewers.

You should also look at what your competitors are doing in terms of content on:

Facebook	Twitter	LinkedIn	Google+
Pinterest	Instagram	YouTube	SlideShare
iTunes	Reddit and Digg		

Website content needs to be varied to "speak" to different audiences. The many styles of content include:

Funny/Humorous   Informative and Educational

Useful   Curated or Aggregated from Other Sources

Experiment with different content styles to make your site more interesting.

The social media chapter offers greater detail about what to do with your various forms of content, but here are some tips on the types of content to consider creating.

Content Development Categories

1. A page for each individual product and service

2. Curated blog posts—reviews and analysis of other people's posts

3. Deep, original blog posts that showcase your expertise and thought leadership

4. Video blogs (expert interviews, "how to," FAQ videos, etc.) with transcriptions

5. Viral videos (videos that you create with the goal of getting them highly shared)

6. Podcasts with transcribed text

7. Top 10 lists

8. Product reviews

9. White papers

10. "How to" articles

11. Frequently asked questions (FAQs)

12. Case studies

13. Testimonials and video testimonials

14. Email newsletters

15. Widgets (such as an interactive vacation planner or mortgage calculator)

16. Ebooks

17. Infographics

18. SlideShare presentations

19. Ebrochures

20. Slideshows based on statistics in your industry

21. Historical information about your company or your industry

22. Webinars

23. Wikis

24. Online training

25. Press releases

26. Local content such as city/town pages

A great tactic is to take one piece of content that you worked hard to create, such as a white paper, and repurpose it into video, infographics, and slideshow formats. That way you get a lot more mileage out of each chunk of original content (see Figure 3).

While I won't go into detail on every item in the list above, I want to give you an example of what we do with one of our favorite tactics, podcasting.

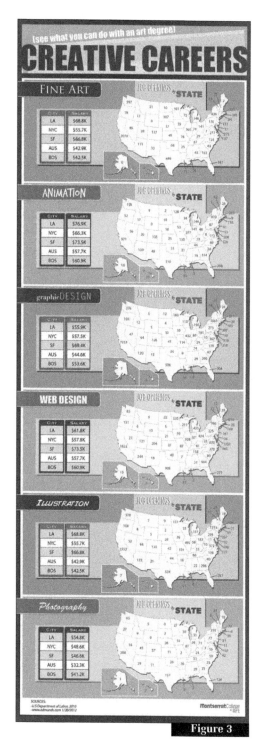

Figure 3

Podcasting for Content

I have always been an advocate of adding extra content to websites, both to benefit the users and to grow the size of the site. In fact, over the years I have been a bit of a broken record on this subject. Even when other SEO techniques were higher up on the hotlist, I pushed and pushed for content. Yes, link building is still as important as (or even more important than) content, but getting good links is a lot easier with quality content or "link bait."

Considering that for almost two decades, we have been advising our clients to give us plenty of content for site updates and SEO, it's nice to see that our focus on content has proven effective. It gives me great pleasure to see such a simple technique become such an amazing solution as our clients' websites continue to dominate search and social results.

So how can you get new articles and information on your website quickly without writing short, weak articles just for the search engines? Try podcasting, which features audio recordings of interviews or dialogues. Talk about what you know, or interview other experts in your field. When you break out of the text rut, you can gain a whole new audience with your streaming audio files and you can use the transcriptions of your podcasts for SEO/social media channels. The following mini case studies demonstrate some possible uses of podcasting and how you can produce juicy information with ease.

Case 1

Online Music Store Owner

> She's obsessed with knowing every detail of every product on her site. When she is on the phone, she nearly completes a full-length review of a half-dozen products and makes cross-comparisons. Yet when she tries to write something for the website, she draws a blank.
>
> **Solution:** Make a list of 15 questions about five models of tenor saxophone. Discuss the metal used in each, the pads, the country in which they were made, etc. Record a 20-minute conversation (interview-style or monologue) using a digital voice recorder. Transcribe the recording and use the resulting text to make a web page. Add images of the store and all the instruments reviewed to make it spicy and give the reader something to look at while listening to the podcast. Then repeat the process with new questions (and/or new musical instruments). Try to develop a theme or angle like product comparisons or features like "Ask Dr. Sax...."

Web Marketing On All Cylinders - John McDougall

Case 2

Art Gallery Owner

The owner has a passion for art. He devours books on artists and the various styles of art. He has long, long conversations about art with clients and anyone else who will listen. In fact, he's an artist himself, but not much of a writer. When it comes to the website, he struggles to write quality content—especially given that the art market has some heavy-hitting authors and doctorate-level dealers.

Solution: Interview the artists that his gallery represents or descendants of featured artists who are no longer living to engage in a more natural and conversational way than a formal article allows. Record and transcribe the interviews, then take photos of the artists' studios and the artists at work, and add them to the text. Consider including images of the sketches and photographs used by the artists, or pictures of what has inspired them. Ask a few offbeat questions to get some anecdotal details that won't usually be found in an artist's statement, book, or biography.

Case 3

Retirement Home

The owner of a retirement home is at a loss to create website content, because her business offers a service that many people don't think about until they must. She blogs regularly, but wants to spice things up and show the world that assisted living doesn't have to be stodgy or depressing.

Solution: Interview employees of the facility as well as the board members, all of whom are passionate about providing an enriching environment for seniors. In the interview questions, use highly searched keyword phrases to prompt searchable answers (for later transcription). Interview residents of the facility for regular features on what makes a great retirement home and interview the staff for podcasts about elder care issues. If guest speakers come to the facility, ask if they would allow you to record their presentation for a podcast.

Make Your Content Easy to Find

Collect your podcasts and other media in a section on your site that is properly mapped on the site's navigation. For example, the easiest way to do this is to create a blog, which you can populate with those juicy transcripts as well as other created content. Take care to optimize the URL of your blog as well.

Here are examples of optimized URLs:

Joesmusic.com/blog
Joesmusic.com/blog/yahama-saxophones-vs-dc-pro

At the very least, put your content in a folder on the server that creates a category that Google can relate to, like:

Modernartgallery.com/artistinterview/jeff-weaver.html

Or as we did in this live podcast example:

www.mcdougallfinearts.com/jeff-weaver-podcast.aspx

A Podcast How-To

For as little as $150 (or less) to get a quality digital voice recorder (or just use your smartphone's voice recorder), 10 minutes to make a list of a dozen or so questions and a half-hour max per session, you can start adding new content that won't get left on the back burner. Once you have the podcast, you would be crazy not to add the text to your site (even if that means editing out parts you don't like), so take the time to transcribe your podcasts as well. (If you don't like transcribing recordings, there are transcription services to do this for you.)

If you want to do an interview with someone not local to you, you can use your telephone as a recording device. There is an easy option for conference call recording at Freeconferencecalling.com, which is a service that allows multiple users to call in and for the conference to be recorded in MP3 format. The quality is reasonable, given that phone calls are low-quality, audio-wise, to start with. The service itself is free and the call-in number is a standard US phone number, so no charges beyond the usual cost of a phone call apply.

As a backup, many people use GoToMeeting for online demos and tech support, and that service has a recording feature as well. The resulting audio is slightly lower in quality than what you get with Freeconferencecalling.com and may have some connectivity issues, but it's something to fall back on in a pinch.

Doesn't that sound easy? Considering that Google checks for fresh content (updated pages, new pages, growing site size, and changes in text and images) and that people love getting something for free, you really have no excuse for not doing at least a monthly podcast and posting the transcription. For some people, it's easier than writing an in-depth article, but it could eventually give you plenty of ideas for articles if you do decide to sit down and do some writing.

Example: McDougall Fine Arts Jeff Weaver Podcast

Some clients look at us like we're nuts when we say everyone with a website should be doing podcasts. But in reality, a podcast is just an audio capture of a conversation. The podcast transcription below will give you an idea of how a simple conversation based on a short list of interview questions can generate a wealth of content in 10–15 minutes. This is content, I should add, that would have been much more painful and expensive to produce through traditional writing methods.

Stevie Black: Hi, this is Stevie Black with McDougall Interactive and I am interviewing local Gloucester artist, Jeff Weaver. So tell me Jeff, which artists would you say have influenced your work the most?

Jeff Weaver: Well, I'm thinking I have been influenced by a lot of different artists over the years. In my early years, I would say I was primarily influenced more by classical-type art which was founded on good drawing, good draftsmanship. I studied quite a bit of that when I was in the museum school—I used to go to the museums quite a bit—everyone from Rembrandt, even to van Gogh. I can't cover the whole spectrum of what I thought was strong drawing and in graphic kind of strong imagery.

Without going through a whole list, which would be quite lengthy, I think that stayed with me in terms of influences. Obviously there are others. Of late, I have been more interested or influenced by a number of 20th century painters, even people that are not so well known, perhaps like Gustav Klimt, whose composition was very strong, Egon Schiele, another Austrian painter, whose drawing was very powerful.

So, of course, people may think of Edward Hopper (when they look at my work). Yes, I do paint buildings and houses, and he also did that subject matter in a very strong way, even in Gloucester. So I think, as a whole I have been influenced by a lot of different artists, but I think primarily ones whose focus or whose strength was good draftsmanship in drawing as mentioned at the beginning.

Stevie: So, as a result of these influences, do you see yourself carrying on any particular tradition of art?

Jeff: I think if there was a tradition I follow, it would probably be American realism. I think saying that means that the subject matter carries a lot of weight in the final product. The subject matter has a lot to do with what I do because perhaps it's unique to this area, especially in this New England area, of a certain vernacular architecture. Things that speak of New England, the way the light is. These kinds of things take a lot of precedence in what I do in my choice of painting.

I think you get the picture, so I'll cut it short. This podcast turned out to generate several pages of text that would have taken the gallery much longer to write.

We featured this on the home page with a link to the full text and photos of the artist and his studio that we took during the day of the shoot.

In another example, we interviewed members of a law firm many times (over the phone) and recorded the audio. We then created a printed book from the material in the podcasts! Just think how proud you will be with your name on a shiny new book that doubles as web content and triples as downloadable content on iTunes!

To summarize, you should remember the following key points:

1. Content drives SEO and social media.

2. Content makes people trust you more as you are seen as an expert.

3. Create an editorial calendar to keep organized.

4. Review the content created by your competitors.

5. Create fresh, original content or be ignored or even penalized by Google.

6. Share your content on social channels.

7. Create a variety of content such as text, video, images, podcasts, and more.

8. Hire writers to help you or use podcasting to ensure you follow through.

Now, let's look at blogging, which is often the heart of a company's content marketing initiative.

Chapter 9

Blogging for Business

Once upon a time, a business could get a huge bang for its buck just by having an online presence—and we mean any online presence at all. One-page websites were the norm for a pretty long time, with content that was nothing more than a virtual brochure.

Today that basic approach to generating buzz online doesn't fly, because content has been re-crowned the supreme king. Since nearly every business has at least a simple website these days, you need to take your online presence to the next level if your goal is to out-perform your competitors on the web. As we've seen, part of that is SEO and part of that is being active in the social media sphere, but blogging and blogging hard is one of the most effective weapons in your online marketing arsenal.

Blogging for business isn't the same thing as keeping an online journal, and your business blog isn't your personal playground for rants, raves, and recreation. Business blogs, while they can be fun and engaging for readers, serve a very specific purpose, which is to develop your brand and give you yet another way to connect with potential customers while also making your business website even more search-engine friendly. When you blog, you add content to your website, demonstrating to the search engines that your site is being continuously updated and expanded, thus earning you credibility. Interestingly, people also see your regularly updated content as a sign of reliability and trustworthiness, so blogging is like hitting a double when it comes to enhancing your online presence. When you leverage the blog for PR and social media as well, it's a home run.

Why should you blog, even though some pundits have said it's passé? While there are hundreds of millions of active blogs out there, most of those are practically invisible. Having an *active* and *engaging* blog can be a huge benefit to a business trying to get noticed on the web. While many businesses have blogs, not nearly as many have blogs that are updated regularly and convey the passion the writer feels for his or her topic.

State of the Blogosphere

Let's look at some observations from one of the largest blog catalogs, Technorati.com. They say the blogosphere is constantly changing and evolving and note that there are five types of bloggers (broken down by percentage of the total).

1) Hobbyist – 60%. Hobbyists spend less than three hours a week blogging and do not generate income from their blogs.

2) and 3) Professional Part- and Full-Timers – 18% They supplement their income, or consider blogging their full-time job, focusing blogs primarily on personal musings and technology.

4) Corporate – 8% They blog full-time for a company or organization. They blog about technology and business, share expertise, gain recognition, and attract new clients. The number of unique visitors and subscribers to their blogs is a key metric of measuring success.

5) Entrepreneurs – 13% Blogging for a company or organization they own, writing primarily about the industry they work in, business, and technology.

Given the percentage of blogs offered by businesses, it may be easier to stand out than you think *if you have strong content and take it seriously.*

In 2011, bloggers updated their blogs more frequently and businesses got more serious about their blogs.

In 2012, blogging escalated in volume, especially in terms of high-quality content and guest blogging after the April Google Penguin algorithm update killed many other forms of link building.

In 2013, there is no question that blogs are at the heart of most content marketing strategies.

Why Should You Be Blogging?

1. Blogging for business adds new content—a big part of search engine optimization—and is a part of social media, so you're killing two (or more!) birds with one stone. By creating the blog on your company URL (e.g., Yoursite.com/blog), each post you create adds a new page of content to the main website structure.

2. Each post can include a video that is both on your business blog page itself and on YouTube. This connects you directly to a top social media site and takes advantage of the ever-so-hot trend of online video.

3. There are millions of blogs, and hence many niche directories in which you can list your business blog. This provides new links to your site and more visibility.

4. Business blogs are PR-friendly! For example, you can announce that you're business blogging with a press release or you can use your blog as a vehicle for press releases.

Web Marketing On All Cylinders - John McDougall

Google thinks highly of websites that appear in the news—don't you?

5. Your business blog can become a source of user-generated content when people add their comments to your posts. More people commenting on your blog means more visitors are engaged in your site, and engagement is a key website value factor (and a key marketing metric to track in general). User engagement is great for improving your Google rankings, too.

   Google supposedly has a patent on a system for evaluating the personas that comment on your blogs and their social profiles. Some who comment might want to hide their real names, sometimes for legitimate reasons like political oppression or other privacy concerns, but others do it to game the system and artificially inflate rankings. This will be a problem and potential ranking factor for a while to come, so keep in mind that it is all being watched in a very sophisticated way. The ideal is to attract fans and influencers who not only read your blog but engage with it through comments, sign-ups, likes, and shares.

6. When people really get into your blog, they can become followers by signing up for your content to be delivered directly to them via RSS feeds or by email. Again, Google may track this and the more of it you have, the better, as this level of engagement is a serious vote of confidence in you that is hard to "fake" or "game."

7. Google picks up on the activity and buzz around your brand (mostly at this time through the corresponding backlinks they help create) and then trusts you more and ranks you better, so you can integrate your business blog with Facebook and other social media to spread your message. Start a LinkedIn group or G+ community around your blog's topic, make sure you're tweeting your blog posts, and keep the conversation going!

8. If your content is really cool or unique, you may be able to leverage sites like Digg or Reddit to drive tens of thousands of visitors to your site within a short period of time. More eyeballs mean potentially more sales, and more visitors and links mean better search engine ranking!

9. Links from other sites to your cool or interesting blog content are worth their weight in SEO gold.

10. Branding via a blog is easier and less expensive than TV ads, radio ads, newspaper ads, and listings in the phone book. You can potentially reach more people with a business blog than you can with traditional forms of advertising *if* you take the time to make your blog amazing.

But I'm Not a Writer!

One of the main reasons my clients give me for not blogging is "I'm not a writer!" Here's a little secret: Most people who have made names for themselves writing online aren't going to be publishing the Great American Novel any time soon. And that's not a problem, because beautifully written, heart-wrenching stories aren't what the audience for blogs is there to read. Long, detailed blog posts can be great (and useful, as we'll see later in this chapter), but most people come to blogs expecting something a lot closer to a news brief. Writing a blog should be fun and simple, not an experience akin to writing a term paper that's due tomorrow.

Keep your copy simple. When your blog takes off, your readers may come from a wide variety of backgrounds and educational levels and you don't want to alienate anyone or exhaust anyone with stuffy, overblown verbiage. Industry terms are okay (if you define them for newbies and non-insiders), but don't load up on four-syllable words just because you think it makes you sound smart. More often than not, it will make you sound pretentious. All this simplicity extends to grammar and structure, too. Keep the parenthetical references, exclamation points, ellipses, compound sentences, and other distractions to a minimum.

Other than that, be confident! Will you make a few grammatical errors or typos here and there? Sure. You may even make the occasional factual error and, if you have great readers, they will call you out on this. When errors crop up, fix them and move on. Don't let them destroy your blogging mojo. Write as if you're an authority, even if you don't feel confident doing so. Confidence will come in time. After a few months of writing your blog, I guarantee you that you'll be a better writer and a more confident one.

Blogging Is All About Content

Blogging is truly all about the content and it's not that hard if you get writers to help you or use podcasting and video to make it easier (see Chapter 8).

As noted above, putting a blog on your business website is a great way to add regular content. And not just the content that you create yourself, either! User-generated content such as blog comments, forum posts, user reviews, and testimonials are all great ways to keep things fresh. Consider how you can relate your expertise and how you can repurpose content from other sources you own with a quick rewrite.

Make sure when you create content that you include several content styles such as:

1. Original in-depth content (May take the most effort to write.)

2. Curated or aggregated content (Reviewing content someone else made) This is fairly easy to write and/or outsource.)

3. User-generated content (UGC) (Easiest since others create it for you, but you must monitor it for spam or inappropriateness.)

It is ideal to have a balance of these three types of content, as it makes your job easier. Some bloggers aim to have twice as much curated/aggregated content as original content, and twice as much UGC as curated content.

The easiest way to get your blog going and develop your own posting momentum is to create an editorial calendar (see Chapter 8 for specifics).

First, decide how often you want to post. Weekly? Mondays, Wednesdays, and Fridays? Your schedule doesn't matter as much as your sticking to it, since readers like to know that there will be new content fairly regularly. If it's not there, they will stop checking in. One post a week is a good place to start if you've never maintained a blog before, but plan to upgrade to twice a week or even daily once you get more comfortable with the blogging process. When you get to the point of making a post a day, that's when the truly amazing results start to happen. When you share and properly promote that much good content, you are *guaranteed* results.

Here's an example. At McDougall Interactive, we had a golf equipment client who we convinced to do their own video camera blog posts and text reviews of golf clubs. They had a warehouse stocking employee who bought into this idea and at times did a couple posts a day. In his first six months of blogging hard, they got 10,000 visits to the blog, whereas before the blog did almost nothing. Another client had one very niche-oriented blog post he wrote on a Saturday that generated dozens of orders in the following week.

Important: Many blogging experts believe that you will need to post at least twice a week to keep the attention of the search engines.

If you're assigning your blog maintenance to someone on your team, don't just hope that someone gets around to making posts. Treat your blog like any other part of your marketing strategy and approach it tactically. Brainstorm content, categories, and topics for a minimum of three to six months ahead. This is your editorial calendar, and it will keep you on track. Plus, you'll never be stuck on a Monday morning, racking your brain for something to blog about.

Kicking Butt on the Long Tail

When McDougall Interactive signed up for HubSpot software and training, they asked us how many leads we wanted. After we told them, they told us that, assuming a two percent conversion rate, we would need x number of website visitors a month. In order to get that many visitors, we'd need to blog five times per week with clear calls to action subtly built in to the right column and posts. HubSpot also told us the blog posts should be largely targeting realistic niche keyphrases to rank for or long tail keywords. The keywords should get about 200 searches a month (based on Google AdWords tool) with a competition score of less than 60 (via SEOMoz's tool).

Striving for higher search volume is okay, but not so much higher that it is unrealistic to rank for. Not that you can't also target top keywords like "golf clubs," but targeting something like "Taylormade golf clubs for tall women" can be very effective. It will get you top-ranked faster and at least get you a small amount of real traffic rather than getting you ranked #62 (on about the sixth page of the Google search results, which few potential visitors will ever look at) or worse for "golf clubs."

Having hundreds or more posts on your blog is like having many fishhooks in the water because it enables you to catch more fish and eventually rank for the short tail search terms because the volumes of content and engagement will start to show Google you deserve more than just long tail ranks.

So start small initially and build your way up as you start to see results. Create a spreadsheet with blog title ideas that use the fully researched long tail keywords you've come up with. Given that the long tail is where most searches are done, always be building volumes of posts and pages that target more and more keywords. Also keep in mind that Google admits 20% or more of the searches done each day are for keywords no one has ever typed in before, so the more content you have, the more likely your site will come up for all kinds of different search terms that nobody could predict would help you.

While the point underlying the strategic comments HubSpot gave us was not really new to us, it was the matter-of-fact way in which they framed it as more of a math problem than some magic fairy dust that gave me an "aha" moment. You simply can't just talk about writing and we at McDougall Interactive simply can't link-build our clients into great rankings anymore. You simply must build a huge base of content that grows weekly (or ideally, daily) if you want your web marketing to be sustainable.

Building Your Business Blog from the Ground Up

Maybe you're still not convinced that you need a blog and you think you don't have the time for one. If blogging is really so hard, how is it that there are hundreds of millions of active blogs—and that's just the English-language blogs. Worldwide, there may be more like a billion active blogs.

You may be tempted to set up your blog the quick and dirty way by signing up for a free Blogger account or opening an account on another blogging platform like WordPress. While that is one way to get a blog going, remember what I said before about blogging working in your favor from an SEO perspective because the content you add to your blog is in effect adding optimized pages to your website. That is only true if your blog is set up as a part of your website. Any content you add to a Blogger blog or a yoursite.wordpress.com blog only serves to increase Blogger's or WordPress.com's SEO/indexed page count, and they certainly don't need your help with content. Then there's the professionalism factor. What looks more professional: *Yourbusiness.blogspot.com* or *Yourbusiness.com/blog*?

The point is, you *always* want to keep control of your content. Posting to a free blogging site like Blogger.com does not ensure that.

To illustrate this point, take a look at this real-life example where one of my team members (John Maher, who has been with me for a decade) instructed a client of ours on this issue. We have removed the client's name from the URLs and replaced it with the fictional "yoursite.edu."

From: John Maher
Subject: Blog redirect

Regarding moving the blog off of blogspot.com and to a yoursite.edu address, there are a couple of options:

1) You can use a subdomain of yoursite.edu, like blog.yoursite.edu, and point that to Google's blogger servers. Then, you set up a "custom domain" on Blogger, which tells Blogger to use blog.yoursite.edu instead. While this is possible, having the blog on a subdomain of yoursite.edu is only marginally better than having it on a separate domain like blogspot.com, because Google considers subdomains to be "separate but related" websites, and content on this subdomain will not have the full effect of boosting the value of the www.yoursite.edu main site that it would if it was in a sub-directory like www.yoursite.edu/blog.

---

2) You can create a WordPress blog and use a plug-in to help with redirects. This is accomplished by creating a WordPress blog on www.yoursite.edu/blog (or a similar sub-directory) and importing your posts from Blogger (there is a built-in tool for this in WordPress). The problem then becomes redirecting the old URLs to the new ones. The correct way is through a "301 redirect," but unfortunately, Blogger does not provide a way to set this up. However, there are some plug-ins that are available which can accomplish much the same thing using a "rel=canonical" tag along with a "meta refresh" directive. The disadvantage of this is that the rel=canonical tag is a suggestion to Google, not a directive, and Meta Refresh is not recommended by Google. But it may be your only option.

Our strong recommendation would be to use option #2, and make this change as soon as possible. I would not wait until a new website is built, for the following reasons:

1) The methods available to us for redirecting blogspot.com blogs to your domain are limited and imperfect at best, and may not work at all. Therefore, it is risky to wait until even more content is on the blogspot.com blog, since proper 301 redirects that would ensure that the value of your posts is not lost, cannot be implemented.

2) Much of the value of any new posts between now and when the new site is built would be lost, because content added to the yoursite.edu domain now would otherwise be able to get indexed, mature (history plays a part in the Google algorithm), generate links, and otherwise influence and increase your Google ranks and traffic now. If you don't move the blog now, while the posts would eventually get moved to yoursite.edu, the main site may not get full credit due to the lack of 301 redirects, and the post pages won't have the same history, link potential, and value of added content that they would have if they were posted to yoursite.edu now.

Even if we could 301 redirect the posts to the new blog on yoursite.edu, the latter reason would still make it worth setting this up now, instead of waiting. It just doesn't make sense to add all of that content to the blog on blogspot.com, where it does no good for the yoursite.edu site, when we could move the blog to WordPress on yoursite.edu now, and start reaping the benefits of added content on the yoursite.edu site now, instead of months (or a year) from now.

I hope that helps to clarify things a bit.

Thanks,

John

Then we had to further instruct the client's website developers, who did not really understand what we were asking them to do. This type of work is not hard but has to be done to very exacting specifications for your blog to perform at its highest level.

From: John Maher
Subject: Blog URL follow-up

I reviewed http://www.yoursite.edu/admissionsblog, and unfortunately, it looks like what your developers have done is to create an "iframe," where they are drawing in the Admissions Blog from blogspot.com into a scrolling window within that admissionsblog page.

Note that if you click on the titles of each blog post, the URL doesn't change from http://www.yoursite.edu/admissionsblog. While this visually sticks the blog content on your website, it doesn't actually move the content there, and it doesn't add to your page count in Google. This would honestly be completely useless for SEO, and it could actually hurt your ranks more than it helps, because all of that content is duplicated on the blogspot.com URL, and Google hates duplicate content.

The real solution is to create a WordPress blog on yoursite.edu/blog (or yoursite.edu.edu/admissionsblog is fine), move all of those posts over to the yoursite.edu blog, and delete the blogspot.com blog (as I said before, we'll need to try to redirect Google from the old URLs to the new ones, which Blogger makes difficult, but we have options). But trying to take the easy way out, like your developers have done here, just won't work and doesn't help our efforts at all. The simple answer—iframes are bad for Google.

We really think that WordPress is the way to go. There are several options for importing posts from a Blogger blog into WordPress, so you shouldn't have to cut and paste each post manually, which would take a long time. If you absolutely can't install WordPress on your site, you could go with option #1 in my email below and use Blogger, but change the URL to a sub-domain like blog.yoursite.edu or admissionsblog.yoursite.edu. As I said, that is not nearly as good as having the content on a sub-directory like yoursite.edu/blog or similar.

Let me know if you have any questions.

John

The moral of the story: Do the slightly more difficult, but much more intelligent thing and have your technical guru set up your business blog on your actual website. In no time, you'll have grown your website into a one-stop resource in your niche that is attractive to both search engines and people because of the sheer amount of high-quality content found there.

Adding a Second Blog on an Additional Domain Name

If you are aware that your website's SEO will be greatly helped by your blog but still want to create your blog or a second blog on a different domain name, here are a few tips.

A second blog on a new URL is a lot of extra work and will require all the same effort on SEO, link building, PR, and social media, but it can brand you as an expert in one niche area. For example, if I start a blog apart from the main McDougall Interactive website that's just about marketing for lawyers and give it a domain name like *InternetMarketingForAttorneys.com*, I can make it really focused. By having my face on the blog and writing only about that topic, I can brand myself (as an expert on Internet marketing for attorneys) in a very focused way. This can work, but you must choose this option knowing what it means to your main site. It is ideal to do this in addition to your main site's blog, if SEO is important to your main site. My actual domain name for my attorney marketing blog is *the-lead-review.com*. This allows me to rank well for very specific law marketing topics that might confuse the theme of mcdougallinteractive.com.

Homesoftherich.net and completely-coastal.com are examples of "small" but popular blogs that get traffic for terms realtors would love. They are not typical real estate blogs, but have content people love that relates to homes and decorating. Owning a blog like this separate from your corporate site can be a great asset to your main site by driving additional traffic to itself. By linking to your main site, it helps you capture traffic that might not have been as interested in your corporate blog. But again, this is a huge amount of effort and often best done in addition to your main site's blog. If you can give your corporate blog an interesting spin, it will be much easier to get started and will immediately impact your site's SEO and social media strategies.

To Do: Set Up a WordPress Blog

WordPress is the most flexible and most-used blogging platform on the Internet today. And Google just loves this platform. Here is a simple guide to getting your WordPress blog up and running. There are many resources online that are a Google search away if you need further assistance.

- Plan out how you want your business blog to be organized. What pages will you have on it? A contact page? An "about" page? Make sure you know what categories you will be using to organize your posts as well.

- Invest a few dollars in purchasing your own domain name. If you put up a free Word-Press blog, your blog will be located at http://yourwebsitename.wordpress.com, which

  is less powerful for SEO results, less memorable, less brand-able, and less secure. Domains are very inexpensive, so purchase one and buy a hosting package for it if you are not already setting up the blog as part of your existing site.

- Your web hosting provider will likely have a "one-click install" option for WordPress. If not, do a search for "WordPress manual install" and find directions, or contact your web hosting provider for further assistance. They may be able to install it on their end. But most major web hosting providers offer you the option to install WordPress with just a few clicks.

- Once WordPress is installed, you need to set it up and add all the details. Under the "Administration" section, start going through each page. Flesh out your profile and your details. Under the "General" page, add a tagline for your site and other general site information. The "Writing" and "Reading" sections will help you customize how your readers navigate and read your content, and how you will be creating it. The "Discussion" page then gives you the options for handling comments, and whether or not you want them at all.

- Under "Posts," you can organize your categories and manage all your posts. Click "Add New" to start adding blog posts. The "Pages" section is similar, but it adds static pages to your blog, not blog posts. This would be where you create and add your contact page, "about" page, etc.

- Once you have a few pages of content created, and posts written and published, go to "Appearance" and play around with different themes for your site. You can also search for and install other ones. If you search for "free WordPress themes" in a search engine (like Google), you can find even more that you may like. It's important to have some content and pages created first so that you can see how your content will be viewed in the theme. Alternatively, have a web designer create a blog "look" that harmonizes with your company branding and existing website. Famous premium themes (meaning you pay to use them) that are great for SEO and are very flexible include Thesis and Genesis.

- Check for plug-ins, which are extensions to your WordPress installation that can offer additional functionality, like built-in contact forms. They install in the same manner as themes do, and you can search the Internet for useful plug-ins. Look for plug-ins that integrate seamlessly with Facebook and Twitter especially, and start moving your content around by simple sharing options. Yoast.com is a great source for SEO plug-ins.

"Social" by MailChimp is an awesome plug-in for allowing comments that encourage retweets and Facebook shares (see Figure 4). Don't just install any plug-in you find, however, as they are often a source of security breaches. WP Plugin Security Check on word-press.org is a good tool that checks plug-ins for bad practices and possible security holes.

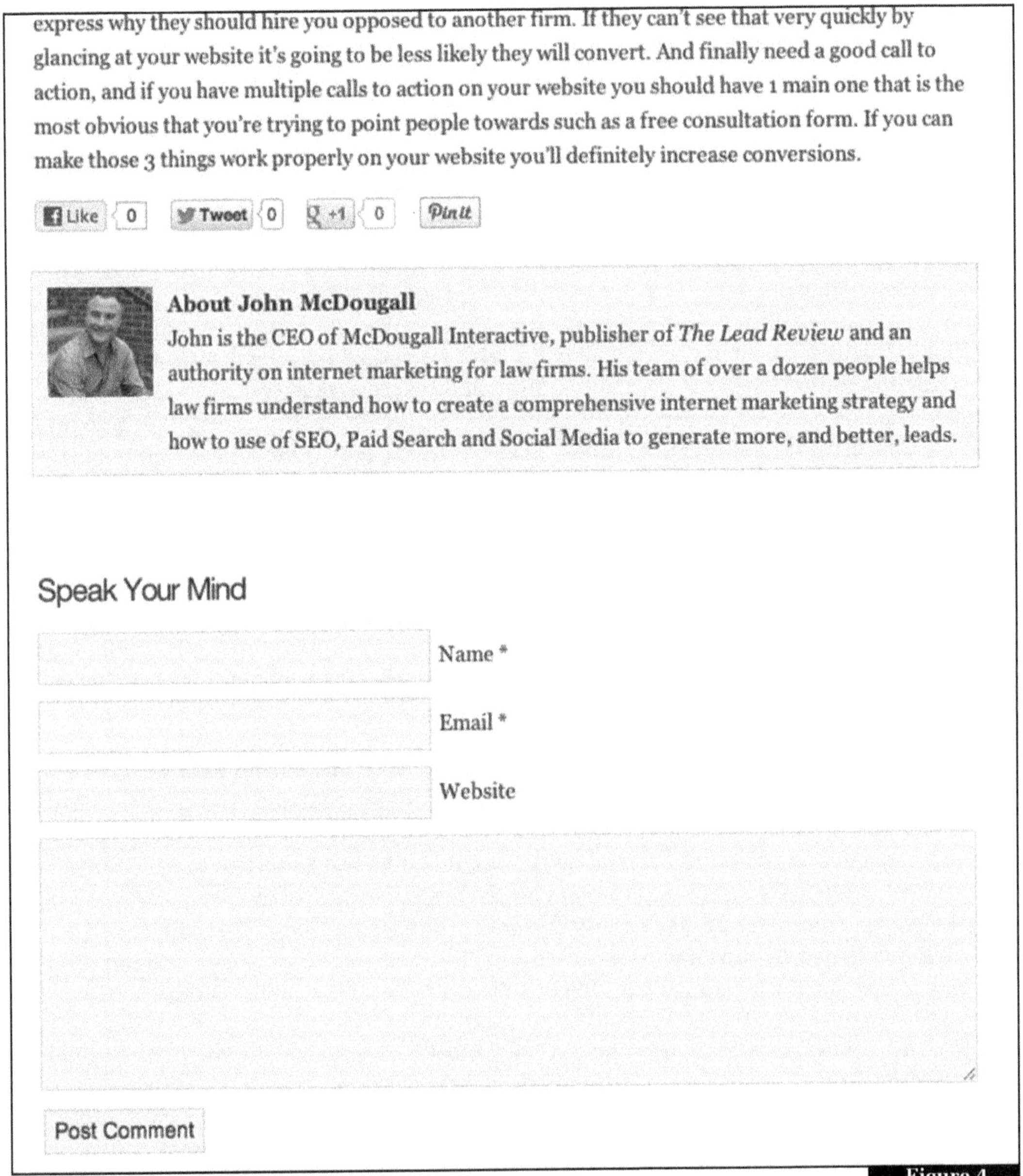

express why they should hire you opposed to another firm. If they can't see that very quickly by glancing at your website it's going to be less likely they will convert. And finally need a good call to action, and if you have multiple calls to action on your website you should have 1 main one that is the most obvious that you're trying to point people towards such as a free consultation form. If you can make those 3 things work properly on your website you'll definitely increase conversions.

f Like ‹ 0 › 🐦 Tweet ‹ 0 › ৪ +1 ‹ 0 › *Pin it*

About John McDougall
John is the CEO of McDougall Interactive, publisher of *The Lead Review* and an authority on internet marketing for law firms. His team of over a dozen people helps law firms understand how to create a comprehensive internet marketing strategy and how to use of SEO, Paid Search and Social Media to generate more, and better, leads.

Speak Your Mind

	Name *
	Email *
	Website

Post Comment

Figure 4

Choose Your Niche and Your Goals

To be an effective marketing tool, a business blog can't jump all over the place from topic to topic. Building a loyal readership that will share your content and inspire others to jump on your bandwagon is, in part, the result of choosing a focus for your blog. Your goal should be to become an authority in your niche, and doing that requires fairly tight consistency of topic. Your readers should know that when they need information about x, you're the go-to source, and they are confident they won't be bombarded with pictures of y and rants about z. Yes, it's okay to bring some of your personal life into your blog if you're a business owner, but your business blog isn't a diary and shouldn't come off like one. Your goal must be to provide content that adds value to the lives of those reading what you are publishing.

Having multiple authors can also be a great benefit. If your blog is about widgets, perhaps you have a group of different writers, each with their own Google+ Author Rank—one who writes about red widgets, one who covers green widgets, and another who's an expert on blue widgets. By having multiple authors around the various subthemes, you will end up with different styles of writing, which makes it more likely that you will satisfy the varied personas who visit your site. If your only writer is an engineer, for example, the content might come off as dry to some readers. Keep in mind that the writing itself can be out-sourced, but the writer personas must be owned by you. That way, someone else or multiple paid authors can "ghostwrite" your content and you get the Author Rank credit.

Depending on your industry, choosing a niche for your blog may be pretty easy or extremely difficult. If the focus of your business is already niche-y, then it's likely that an overarching theme along with micro-topics will present themselves without your having to do any major brainstorming. But if your business' focus is broad, then narrowing down your blog's niche can take some time. The niche you choose may change over time, too, so don't worry about it too much for now.

Why is this so important? People who read blogs like to know what they're getting before they visit your site. That doesn't mean you have to write about the same things all the time, day in and day out, but you should return to the meat of your niche regularly to keep your loyal readers coming back. For example, a credit union might blog about personal finance—specifically personal finance tips related to banking and individual investing. Sometimes a post about frugality in the home or the value of the dollar worldwide might be appropriate, but generally posts stay within the niche.

If you have a broader theme and talk about, for example, both business and personal finance, either create two blogs or at least let people RSS subscribe separately to individual categories. Wells Fargo, for example, has many blogs on various topics.

Whatever your niche, make sure it coordinates with your business goals and has been thought out in terms of matching the keyphrases and keywords for which you want to rank. If one of your products or services makes you far more money than any of the others, then you might consider tightly focusing your blog on that particular topic, so Google sees a lot of content in that area and ranks your site better for those key terms. This is especially important if this part of your business is also highly competitive and you have limited content relating to it on your main site.

Once you do have a niche picked out, it's time to set your goals (keeping in mind that it may take six months or a year to reach them). Your goals will give you benchmarks to hit, which can be important in the early days of blogging when it can feel like you're talking to an empty stadium. What kind of goals do businesses set for blogging? Here are a few examples:

- Write 100 posts and drive traffic

- Sign up 100+ subscribers

- Add a podcast and/or video to your blog

- Attract 10 potential clients with the blog

- Create a post series (e.g., "Questions from Customers")

- Link the blog to your social media profiles

- Run monthly contests

- Get featured regularly on Reddit or collegehumor.com

- Turn a collection of posts into an ebook

- Turn a set of 50 or more posts into a printed book

Accomplishing some blog-related goals takes no time at all, while reaching others can take quite a lot of time and effort. But don't let the work or time involved stop you from exploring even the most ambitious blog goals, like eventually turning your blog into a book. Why not? Aim high with your blog, but expect to put in the necessary work, too. Blogs are not a set-it-and-forget-it marketing tool.

Write About What Excites You

Nothing will turn a blog reader off faster than an author who is obviously not enthusiastic about the topic at hand. The same goes for passion—if you're not passionate about your topic, readers can sense that and will wander away from your site to find a blogger who is. Not every niche has the appeal of, say, celebrity style or auto industry prototypes, but a big part of business blogging is sharing not just information, but passion—because passion helps create engagement. Google is getting really good at detecting engagement, so the days of blogging just to create lots of dumb SEO pages are dead. Really, really dead.

Don't think that the topic that gets you excited will excite others? Business owners who contemplate a blog often avoid blogging specifically because they assume that others will find their niche boring. But the fact is that so much of what makes an interesting and compelling blog is not subject matter, but rather the enthusiasm of the writer. You'll excite your audience—even if your niche is, say, laser hair removal—by sharing your excitement, candidly and sincerely.

In other words: Your job, as a business blogger, is to show your audience *why* they should be excited about the things that excite you! Don't be afraid to tell people online exactly what to do! When you are brainstorming your editorial calendar, keep a few questions in mind:

- What are the questions you hear over and over again from clients and prospects? What are the issues that make your customers lose sleep?

- What knowledge could improve your customer's experience with your product/service?

- What hot trends in your industry are top of mind right now?

- How can your topic be funny or controversial?

- What would customers find most surprising about what you do?

- How can you frame your blog's niche to make it stand out among other industry blogs?

- What gaps in the online information about your business can you fill?

23 Cool Ideas for Blog Content

1. Write posts answering common questions your potential customers have.

2. Interview leaders in your field.

3. Share your perspective on industry statistics and data.

4. Share industry statistics and data that only you have.

5. Use the names of historical figures, TV, cartoon characters, or celebrities in blog post titles like "What Shakespeare Can Teach You About Writing a Blog" or "How Snoop Dogg Would Promote Golf Resorts."

6. Review a book that's relevant to your industry.

7. Make a prediction about the future of your industry.

8. Curate/review content by the best bloggers in your field.

9. Debunk misconceptions about your industry.

10. Write a case study that has a controversial angle.

11. Share news about your company.

12. Create a list of the vital web tools and software in your industry.

13. Review an industry event you've attended and share a valuable insight or perspective about it.

14. Share your success (or a client's success story—with permission).

15. Share your failure or a lesson learned.

16. Recycle your content from other mediums, such as video or white papers, to create a blog version.

17. Create a list (because everyone likes a good list).

18. Take a complex issue and break it down into simple terms.

19. Create a how-to guide, explaining something step by step.

20. Share industry news, including your observations to add value. Use Google Alerts to deliver relevant headlines to your email inbox and write a regular niche news column.

21. Make charts or graphs that explain common uses for your product or service.

22. Use SurveyMonkey to survey your customers and then make a video or write an article summarizing the results.

23. Make a funny video about how *not* to use your product.

Generate Killer Ideas for Your Blog Using Research/Tools

- Use keyword research to discover what people are looking for.

- Study your website analytics to find the content that has resonated with visitors in the past.

- Research trending topics to capitalize on their popularity.

- Follow social sharing statistics in your industry to see what has historically been most popular.

- Check Reddit, Digg, StumbleUpon, Technorati, and Quora to find out what topics are most popular.

- Use Pinterest to see what types of images do well in your niche.

- Search Yahoo Answers for unanswered questions relevant to your industry, and then answer them in your blog.

- Use Google Trends or Trendistic to see what's hot right now.

- Use Google Alerts (free) or Giga Alert (has a small fee but a bit more comprehensive) to monitor Internet activity based on specific topics.

- Check out TheAdFeed.com or AdsOfTheWorld.com to see which TV commercials are doing well and why.

- Use the free version of Majestic SEO to look at what content gets links for your competitors.

Write Content That Inspires Links and Shares

While not every blog post will be a long, deep, highly sharable piece of content, it is important to spice up your content with bullet points, video, and/or images to make it more engaging. Some posts can be fairly basic, but in general, you should at least use an image or two to make them come alive. When you can tweak images to add text to them or make them more original, it sets you apart even further. Having a particular visual style plus an appealing writing style, appropriate tone, evident passion, and the right theme can make your blog go from good to great.

Feeling versus Thinking in Content Creation

Sometimes a post has all the facts and figures it needs to be adequate, but falls short of being inspiring because it doesn't leave the reader with a strong feeling. Keep in mind that while providing details and statistics can be great, tapping into readers' emotions as well can create rabid fans.

What makes a blog more likely to get links and shares? SEOMoz published three blog posts on what makes a link-worthy blog post. They looked at the following elements:

Blog post title

URL

Types of media in the post (videos, images, lists, presentations)

Number of links from root domains (via Linkscape API)

Content of post (no comments or other text on site)

Number of words

Number of "thumbs up"

Number of comments

Category

Author

Many factors go into creating a linkable post, but what stands out is the variety of media you use. Below is a list of the types of media that work well when writing both basic weekly posts and those posts you do once a quarter that are intended to go viral. SEOMoz lists these media types in descending order, from most beneficial to least in terms of creating links. (The same is likely true for social shares.) While this data was based on an SEOMoz's content, it seems to make sense for many sites. However, look at your own analytics to determine the type of posts that drive engagement, links, and shares on your own blog.

Media Most Useful in Creating Links (most useful to least)

All 3 media types—images, video, and lists

Only lists and videos

Only lists and images

Only images and videos

Only lists

Only videos

Only images

None

Web Marketing On All Cylinders - John McDougall

Adding images, videos, and lists makes it easy to get a quick understanding of what the post is about, enticing people to review it, share it, and link to it. When all three types of media are used in a blog post, results are the best. SEOMoz found that posts with videos included will attract almost three times more links than a plain, text-only post, and posts with all three media types (videos, images, and lists) will attract almost six times more links than a plain text post. They also found that long posts seem to attract more links than shorter posts (with 900 words or less for their own site), and posts with between 1,800 and 3,000 words attracted 15 times more links than a post with less than 600 words.

The counterintuitive lesson? Go long when you can, and add all kinds of fun, juicy images, video, and lists! Easy, huh? Well, it is harder to do this than a simple post, but no pain, no gain. Start writing blog posts that are truly engaging, have feeling, and are jazzed up with varied media, and you will get more visitors, links, shares, and sales.

Why Video Blogging (Vlogging) Is Hot

Video blogging (or vlogging) can make the work of maintaining a business blog less daunting for those who aren't natural writers. Instead of waxing poetic in writing about your niche, you create an editorial calendar for video tips, and then shoot as many videos as possible in one or two sessions. Transcribe the text (Castingwords.com can do this for around a dollar a minute), and make sure your *short* videos (about one to two minutes each) are posted in keyword categories on your blog after you upload them to your business' YouTube channel. Each post that includes the transcribed SEO-friendly text helps with SEO by adding content and new page URLs that contain keywords. This gives your site an opportunity to grow on a regular basis, providing instant information to customers and a heads-up to the search engines.

Here's something else to keep in mind: one of the highest forms of ROI can come from having hundreds or thousands of posts ranking for long tail keywords that have high conversion rates. Voila! Sales!

Think you have nothing to talk about on video? Think again! With some creativity, any of the content ideas for blog posts can apply to video. (See the idea lists earlier in this chapter.)

By creating a video blog, you add more engaging pages to your site and will consequently see your search engine rankings go up. When you add the transcribed text of your videos to your site's blog, Google will see your new pages as credible content. By adding video, you can participate on YouTube and will be taking part in two of the main social platforms, blogging and YouTube (both of which allow users to comment).

But the connectivity doesn't stop there. By setting up your blog to feed into Facebook—

for example, announcing on Facebook when you make a really cool video post and then linking back to it—you will inspire quality discussions around topics relevant to your business, not just marketing hype. Social media is most useful when based on themes and quality content, not "me, me, me" brochureware. Add Twitter to the mix (if you can find a valid reason to do so, like announcing mortgage rates, product launches, or mentioning recent posts) and you start to have an even deeper strategy. People will be more likely to link to your blog and amazing content when they see how social *and* authoritative you are.

Get people to share your blog posts on Reddit.com and bookmark you on Delicious, and you will not only have lots of pages that help your SEO, but Google will also see your "citations" all over the web and social sphere. Now write an optimized, mobile-friendly, multimedia news release about your video blog to complete the loop. Video is the wave of the future, as people seek to read less and less.

Podcasting on Your Blog

When I finally convince my clients that content is king and get them adding pages and SEO blog posts to their websites, many of them come back to me to ask how to create a podcast. And why not? Like vlogging, creating a podcast can seem like work for experts, not novices. But here's a secret for you: creating a podcast is pretty easy once you're set up, and gives a double whammy when it comes to website SEO because you have your keyword-tagged audio file *and* your keyword-rich transcript. If you had to take one thing from this book it just might be using podcasts to drive blog content. Podcasting is so easy (if you can talk and answer questions) that you have no excuse not to blog!

Of course, the right equipment is a must-have element of podcasting. You need a digital voice recorder. A quality one can be had for $150 or even less. Then, of course, you need a topic. And you need a list of a dozen or so questions—something that you can whip up in 10 minutes using your industry expertise. Then, all that's left is to decide whether you'll use your questions as prompts for a talk you give or as interview questions for another expert in your field. (For more details on how to record audio, see Chapter 8.)

Guest Blogging for Backlinks

I've covered this in the link building and social chapters, but it's worth re-emphasizing this tactic in the context of your overall blogging strategy. (See Chapter 5 for an example of how this is done.)

Keywords Matter

Keywords matter as much on your blog as they do on your business' website, but when you're posting to your blog—as opposed to writing website content—you also need to think about where keywords need to appear for maximum blog SEO. Here's a blog keyword checklist to keep in mind as you design and post to your blog:

- Keywords in text, especially the first paragraph

- Keywords that interlink the blog to other posts and to your main site

- Keywords in post and page titles

- Keywords in the URL of each page and post on the blog

- Keywords in outbound links

- Keywords in bold tags

- Keywords in heading tags

- Keywords in image alt tags

- Keywords in meta description tags

- Keywords (sparingly) in blog tags

- Vary the keywords so you don't overdo the same ones over and over

If it seems like a lot to remember, consider that many of the blogging platforms you can install in your website have keyword prompts (i.e., the WordPress All In One SEO Pack). Eventually, keyword optimization will become second nature.

At the same time, your business blog will lose credibility among your readers if you load up every post with so many keywords that it reads like spam or gibberish. Finding the best balance between compelling copy and copy that's attractive to search engines isn't always easy, but if you find writing keyword-rich copy difficult, err on the side of great content. The better the content you have, the easier it will be for the search engines to figure out that you're an authority and should rank well.

Basic SEO Tips for Blogs

While your business blog may have lots of strong content, it still needs to be found by the search engines. Fortunately, there are many ways for you or your agency to make blogs more SEO-friendly. Here are a few.

- Change the permalink structure (permalinks are the permanent URLs to your individual weblog posts). By default, WordPress attaches a number to each page on your site and displays that in the URL. Under the WordPress Internet "Settings" section, click "Permalinks" and you can customize the URL structure as desired. Preferably, you want the title of the page in the URL. You can also change the permalink structure of Blogger blogs by editing the code.

- Upload images to your posts and optimize them using image titles and alt tags. Link photos taken by others to the appropriate site (a Flickr photo should be linked to the Flickr profile where it came from, for example), especially if you're using Creative Commons content (royalty-free images that usually require an image credit).

- Send Google an XML sitemap. This will help Google index your site faster and makes it easier to search your site (meaning: it will help your site rank in the search results more effectively). Install a plug-in such as Google XML Sitemaps and let it do the work for you.

- Be consistent in your "slugs." The "slug" of your blog post is the part of the URL that you can customize, right below the title of the post. Have the title match the slug for better rankings—most blogging platforms do this automatically (i.e., yoursite.com/blog/keywords-in-url).

- Make use of internal links, which are links from one page of your site to another page on your site. Doing this increases search engine rankings and also keeps readers on your site for longer periods of time.

- Install a WordPress SEO plug-in like the "All In One SEO Pack."

- Link to related posts using a plug-in that creates a "read more" section below each post. This is great for internal linking, as well as keeping the reader on your site longer.

- Make your post titles "live" links to the post. Most WordPress themes and Blogger designs already do this automatically, but it does help in your rankings.

- Validate the code on your site. The W3C Markup Validation Service will find any errors in your code so that you can clean it up. Having a valid site from a technical standpoint is crucial for those wishing to rank highly on search engines like Google.

- By installing a plug-in such as Sociable, ShareThis, or Social by MailChimp, you can put social media buttons at the end of every blog post. This allows your readers to click the button to share your post on their Facebook or Twitter page if they think it's something interesting and worth sharing.

More On-Page Optimization Ideas

Below is a list of additional on-page optimization tasks that may improve your blog's reach in the search engines.

1) Redirect www. to non-www.

Google views www. and non-www. as two completely different versions of the site, so if no redirection is placed it confuses the Google spiders about which version to show in search result pages.

2) Obtain Google+ Author Rank

Assigning a couple different bloggers with Google+ can increase search engine query click conversions as the authors' faces will show up in the search results. Having Author Rank also potentially gives Google more trust in your content (if it does not right now, I believe it will in the future), which will likely indirectly or directly increase your rankings.

3) Connect your social profiles together with microformats

Webmasters can help Google even more now by adding microdata to their website. One of the most powerful pieces of microdata is the rel="me" snippet, which can be used to claim ownership of social profiles. The most common example of this is in your Twitter profile, where you're allowed to include a URL. Twitter puts rel="me" automatically in that code and your website should link back to your Twitter profile with rel="me" as well, in order to complete that handshake. This is powerful from an online reputation management perspective as well, because Google can now know which profiles are verified as yours to display in search results.

4) "Noindex" date archives

Duplicated/repeated content on websites can be detrimental to Google's trust in a website. If you utilize keyword-optimized categories in WordPress, then having date archives doesn't hold any benefit and just clutters your website with re-used content. For Google to not index those archive pages, you will need to give them some indication that they should not be crawled. This is possible by going into your website's .htaccess file and manually coding it in, or downloading a plug-in that does it for you (Yoast's plug-in can help you with this task).

5) Optimize images with alt tags

Images from a blog can add a lot of traffic through Google images, referral traffic, and even backlinks from people who use your site images on their blog. One of the most beneficial things you can do to optimize your images in the search engines is to use "alt" tags. When you've uploaded an image through WordPress, it's easy for you to add alt tags as they present the "alt tag field" right under your photo.

6) Adding/category-name/ to the URL structure

A good URL structure for an improved silo (batch of content) is "www.url.com/blog/category-name/post-title/". That's because instead of Google determining ranking priority between x number of blog posts from the entire blog, it splits the priority between x number of blog posts in the category (much quicker for the spiders to process and understand).

7) Conditional sidebars for internal linking

Developing what we would call conditional sidebars (unique sidebars for certain areas of the site as opposed to having one global one) to make sure you keep your internal linking in your "silos" can yield big improvements in search engine traffic by having more relevant internal links pointing to related pages. Another benefit: Google will view those conditional sidebars as a change-up in content (in other words, "unique/new content").

8) Add Google Analytics code

Use Analytics to make sure you can track things like referrers, load time, conversions, bounce rates, and exit rates, etc.

9) Reduce load time

Use a tool like Pingdom to track your load time (how long it takes your page to load in a browser) and improve image optimization to decrease the time it takes to load each page. Make sure you have good hosting, as inadequate hosting can be a *huge* drag on your page speed. There are many other ways to speed up a web page, so do your research and really put some effort into this, as it has become higher on Google's radar as they focus on mobile.

Making a Blog Scan- and Skim-Friendly

Short attention spans are the norm among blog readers, and I recommend keeping that in mind when you're composing your blog posts. It's much more common for readers to scan blog posts than it is for them to actually read blog posts, word for word, from start to finish. So what makes a blog scan- and skim-friendly? Let's look at a sample blog post, below:

Clear Headlines Make a Blog Scan- and Skim-Friendly

So do short, to-the-point paragraphs that are no longer than five lines. That's where that straightforward and uncomplicated writing style I recommend comes in handy—it's a lot easier to keep paragraphs short when you're using simple vocabulary. What else makes a blog scan- and skim-friendly?

- Bullet points

- Bullet points

- Bullet points

    1. Numbered lists

    2. Numbered lists

    3. Numbered lists

See what I did in the example above? Basically, you want to make your posts easy for your readers to absorb, making your blog more readable and more memorable. Here are some additional tips:

- Make your headlines descriptive and to the point, so the reader knows what your content is about without having to read the post.

- Make your subheads similarly descriptive, so a reader can jump down to the section in a post that interests him or her most.

- Put your conclusions or main points UP FRONT—this makes your topic and slant clear, while also making your copy more enticing to the reader.

- Condense copy into bulleted lists or itemized lists.

- Underline or highlight important ideas in the text so readers don't have to go looking for them.

Comments, Community, and User-Generated Content

Blogs generally allow users to comment and often have various ways they can share content and become members or subscribers. The more members/subscribers you have, the more value your blog has. The new standard of excellence is the integration of great content and social interaction.

Google tracks the adding of blog posts/pages, which helps your site rank better, and it also likely values blogs that have many subscribers. So, you will really do well if your blog is not just for show or for sales pitches. When you create your business blog, make sure the comment feature is set to ON. This can mean dealing with the occasional bout of spam, but most blogging platforms have spam-blocking that works reasonably well.

Why do comments matter, and why has blogging become a part of the social media sphere? User-generated content is a major factor for success in Internet marketing, and blogs add some of that to your site. Blogging and user-generated content have gone from nice add-ons to being an essential part of the web and online marketing. The search engines are tackling how to best index the "real time" web or the web as people are actively tweeting, blogging, and commenting, so results are more up to date, based on "social proof" and users' votes of confidence (as much as or more than a brand's own content). So taking part in this aspect of social media is more important than ever.

Ideally, blogging is a conversation. You start the conversation by putting information out there, and your readers take the reins by commenting. It can end there, sure, but why let it? You can keep the exchange going by responding to your readers' comments. There are multiple benefits to doing this, even though it means you're spending more time on your blog or paying someone else to handle it. First, when you respond to comments, readers have proof that you're a real person and someone who cares about their concerns. Second, Google looks for levels of engagement, so keeping the conversation going can help you rank better. And third, your blog becomes another venue for customers and potential customers to connect with you when they have questions or concerns. Making yourself available via your blog enhances your image.

As far as the community aspect of blogging goes, you can create and maintain a blog for your business without participating in the larger blogging community. But it sure takes something out of the experience! If you're asking yourself what the point could possibly be of giving yourself yet more work to do in this area of online marketing, the answer is simple. You get the most mileage out of your blog when people find it, and more people are likely to find it if you are part of the big blogging conversation that is happening all over the Internet, 24 hours a day.

Commenting on other blogs, linking to interesting people's posts, writing guest posts, and participating in online communities where bloggers hang out are all great ways to increase your business blog's visibility and network with people who may eventually become customers, partners, or friends.

Promoting Your Blog

Now that you are blogging, get out there and promote it with the following techniques.

Link clearly from your website to your blog and from your blog posts back into relevant pages of your site, so it feels more integrated and to show you are proud of it.

Feed your blog into Facebook, LinkedIn, Twitter, and Google+ to take advantage of automatic sharing or make new summarized versions of posts in these channels.

Add posts to personal and business pages in Facebook and promote through ads.

Vary title text that sends a link to your Twitter following and post 2 to 3 times a day.

Share with Google+ Circles and on Google+.

Share posts on your LinkedIn profile, in groups you belong to, and promote through ads.

Share your posts on Pinterest. You don't need to pin every single blog post on Pinterest. You'll get the best results if you selectively pin your blog posts on subjects that already have a following on Pinterest.

Submitting your own content to places like Reddit and Digg can get you 20,000 visitors in a day, but you have to be an active participant. The general rule is that you should take a real part in such communities, honestly sharing your own content along with content from others if you want to directly be involved. What those sites really want is for people to find your content because it stands out and then submit it for you. Ask a friend or colleague to submit your work to Digg first as Digg penalizes people who submit their own content too often.

Submit your posts to Delicious. Bookmark any article, video, or image that you like, and add tags to it if you want. Adding tags to your bookmarks in Delicious makes it easy to organize and explore.

Create an account at StumbleUpon and start sharing posts.

Tumblr is a microblogging platform and social networking website that allows users to post multimedia and other content to a short-form blog. It's another great place to share your posts.

Technorati is a huge blog database. Improving your Technorati authority should result in increased visibility and traffic. Technorati calculates a blog's authority/reputation based on how many people link to it, including blogroll links from the linking blog's main pages as well as links within the content of their posts. Links older than six months after their very first discovery don't count.

Technorati can't always find all your inbound links, so your blog might be undervalued. Compile a list of blogs that link to you, and that aren't indexed by Technorati. Then ping Technorati with all those pages and your links and authority should rise.

Blog directories – Submit to only the best relevant directories such as Bloglines, BlogCatalog.com, Blogarama, Bloggernity, and blogs.botw.org.

Enable "Email This Post" on your blog, which makes it easy for people to share the post via email.

Send a monthly email newsletter that aggregates your best blog posts of the month.

Allow people to sign up to get your posts via automatic RSS feeds. When people subscribe to your feed via newsreaders or email, they're more likely to read and share your posts.

Put your blog URL in your email signature. Check out wisestamp.com.

Even Google says "Be an active commenter." It is okay to leave comments on other blogs as long as you are not just spamming them with links to your own. People interested in your comments can click back to your profile and check out your blog. If you have something super-relevant to say and your post matches the topic, then share a link.

Join a blogging community and share a relevant link with other bloggers.

Syndicate your blog content to sites like

- IFTTT.com

- blogcatalog.com

- demandstudios.com

- https://kindlepublishing.amazon.com/gp/vendor

- networkedblogs.com

- alltop.com

- outbrain.com

Get seen by the likes of publishers like usatoday.com, CNN, Ehow, and Fast Company by feeding them your content. Pick just two or three to start so you don't go overboard (which can actually hurt your ranks).

Link out to experts. Linking to other experts in your field from your posts can drive traffic to their sites. When they see you showing up as a top referrer in their own website analytics, the etiquette is that they will link back to you!

While it may seem daunting to have so many tasks when blogging, remember that it's best to start by writing about what inspires you and the rest will eventually fall into place as you get more comfortable with each step. If all else fails, get some help from people who really know the ins and outs of the various pieces of the puzzle so you can focus on the elements of the content that matter most to you.

Chapter 10

Highly Profitable Paid Search Marketing

For much of this book, I've been explaining how to get your company's website found using search engine optimization and content-driven marketing techniques. However, purchasing online advertisements plays an essential role in your overall marketing mix that can be highly profitable. Paid search covers a range of tools, from Google AdWords, Facebook, and LinkedIn to YouTube and Twitter advertisements and display advertising. This chapter focuses on paid search, with an emphasis on Google AdWords because that is where most of the money is spent and offers the most advanced features for tracking and managing your ads. Mastering AdWords before you test other paid advertising networks is the best way to learn the ins and outs of managing campaigns and getting results quickly.

What Is Pay per Click?

In building a pay-per-click (PPC) strategy, understanding what PPC is (or isn't) will help you establish the right foundation. PPC or "pay for position" advertising brings targeted traffic to your website in a matter of hours as opposed to waiting weeks or even months for your SEO efforts to product results. Statistics show that using a blended strategy that combines PPC and SEO produces the best return on investment. PPC advertising establishes immediate search ranking, while SEO takes time (meaning you may have to wait months or even years before your website appears at the top of the first page of the search engine results). PPC's key benefits are the fast results and the ability to laser-focus on relevant visitors.

On a search results page, pay-per-click ads appear in segregated areas called sponsored links, at the top and in the right-hand column. If you type in a certain keyword, you'll almost always see a sponsored link on the results page. Advertisers only pay when an ad is clicked on, hence "pay-per-click" ad. Google is the dominant player in PPC advertising, followed by the combined Bing/Yahoo. PPC advertising works because it's targeted, and brings visitors to your website because they've expressed an initial interest in your offerings by searching using very specific keywords. PPC's popularity grew quickly because advertisers liked being able to track where actual sales or leads came from. Google became one of the fastest-growing online advertising channels and has over one million advertisers (see Figure 5).

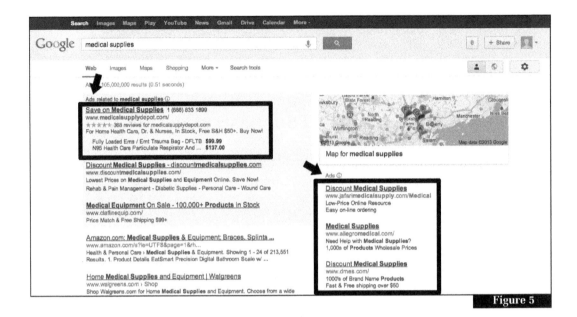

Figure 5

Ads with Google AdWords not only appear on their search engine, but are also syndicated to hundreds of thousands of websites called "content network partners," offering a worldwide audience reach in the billions. These content network partners range from low-traffic niche blogs to popular websites such as WebMD or Huffington Post. Ads can be displayed as small text advertisements or graphical banners, with the website owner deciding on the placement and number of ads to be displayed. When a visitor to these websites clicks on the ad, the click fee is divided (not equally) between Google and the content partner. The money that advertisers are spending on PPC ads represents a majority share of Google's revenue and many content network partners obtain the majority of their funding from this Google relationship, too.

This defines PPC advertising in the simplest of terms. But don't assume that this incredible audience reach means PPC is a classic mass media format of advertising. Instead, PPC advertising has inherent differences in terms of how an advertiser communicates with a potential visitor. The initial interest by the website visitor is generated via a search expression (the search terms someone types into their browser). Encapsulated in this search expression is the seed of a customer's interest. Their quest for a product or service (or their pain points) can be discovered by "reading between the lines" within the search phrase. Even before they have come to your website, they have already, in essence, declared their intention to you.

Google refers to this concept as the "Zero Moment of Truth." Prospects have not even seen your website or contacted you, yet already there is a shopping decision being formed. You'll find it easier to succeed with PPC advertising if you think about this principle for a moment. Making your messaging relevant should be your strategy's leading driver, before

Web Marketing On All Cylinders - John McDougall

you worry about bringing in large numbers of visitors. Your first priority is not building an appeal to reach millions of potential visitors; you should concentrate instead on creating a marketing experience based on relevance. The long-term benefit to this approach is that Google rewards advertisers with lower search costs when they focus on the user experience.

The Hidden Value of PPC

Beyond PPC's utility as a sales or lead channel, it has a hidden value I believe is often over-looked. PPC advertising can help create instant answers to the challenging questions most Internet marketers confront. Using PPC, your business can quickly get answers to questions like the following:

- Is our sales pitch creating interest and curiosity about our offerings?

- Will visitors to our website convert into a sale or lead?

- Are there enough potential prospects to create a sustainable sales or lead funnel to build or maintain a profitable operation?

Ask some or all of these key questions as you build your Internet marketing strategy, since your website must be able to generate enough interest and curiosity among prospects that will lead to business. Define various scenarios that will help you test out your theories. A great PPC strategy should also focus on the how and why of whether you found success (or failure). Using PPC as a testing tool is ideal, because you have total control over the initial interest and the ability to track behavior throughout the entire conversion process.

Smart marketers realize that a high-performing PPC strategy is not just about obtaining the best cost per action (CPA) for a sale or lead, but addresses which marketing and sales efforts will yield a positive ROI. Create a testing environment that continually refines your sales messages to align with customers' interests. The more you understand about how marketing messages need to relate to the online buying process, the more finely-tuned your efforts will be, bringing you better results. Before I discuss what it takes to advance a PPC strategy to this level, let's first review ways to ensure you can obtain the best CPA.

Allocating a PPC Budget

PPC makes it possible to track your marketing return on investment, since PPC can track and measure from a searcher's initial click on your ad all the way to the sale or lead (and even activity in between). A great deal of Google's own business success can be attributed to the fact that advertisers of all sizes found a direct connection between real results and their marketing spend. Establishing the value of a marketing effort is now much easier to do. The old advertising truism that "I know half of my ad spending is working, I just don't know which half," is quickly becoming history. For experienced PPC advertisers, this is now a marketing channel where you don't question whether it will work, but focus instead on how to make it work better.

A sound PPC strategy starts with a reasonable budget. Prices of PPC "clicks" are based on a number of factors, including:

- Your willingness to be placed at the top,

- The number of competing advertisers,

- How many searches are being performed (search volume), and

- Quality Score, a scoring mechanism that Google applies to an ad's performance.

All of these factors combined will define what you spend on PPC. When you have a limited budget, the display times for your PPC ads will randomly be limited by Google in a situation of high click cost and/or search volume. The downside to this is not being able to understand when is the best time to display ads to your prospects.

So, instead of pursuing a broad market strategy with a small budget, it's better to focus on a targeted audience with a limited scope. Select just a few or even one of your products or services to promote, choosing a margin leader or a best-in-class in your industry. You can also pick search terms that are further down in the sales funnel and used by searchers who are ready to take action quickly, in hopes that a buying decision will be more impulse-driven. If you have a limited budget for PPC, you'll have to accept some trade-offs in how you advertise. Instead of focusing on spend targets, establish instead a cost per action (CPA) that works best for your business and create a budget target from that.

Budget by Search Intentions

In PPC advertising, understand that not all search phrases are created equal. Typically, terms aligned to various stages in the buying cycle will have very different costs. For example, in some of the most expensive PPC bidding, lawyers are competing for leads to represent mesothelioma cancer victims. Google estimates the search term cost for "mesothelioma" as $87.17 per click, while "mesothelioma lawyer" is $186.60. Clearly, from this bidding, advertisers have realized that one term is out-performing the other. You may wonder, if a "lawyer"-related term does better than the more general terms, then why not just bid on the high-value terms at the end of the buying cycle?

The answer has to do with what is called attribution or assisted conversions. Through research and website tracking analysis, it's been proven that visitors often make multiple searches during the buying process. They perform many related searches, especially in complex scenarios requiring more research. As in the example of people suffering from mesothelioma cancer, even though these victims are not "buying" a lawyer, they are "shopping" for the right attorney to represent them. Thus, informational search terms such as "mesothelioma" represent the initial starting point in the shopping experience and can assist in the overall conversion process.

Assigning budgets at all stages and understanding their contribution to the process is a critical technique for managing complex PPC spending. If your PPC efforts allocate the whole budget to just certain stages, you risk creating longer-term limitations by not having your ads seen in all of the buying stages. Depending on how complex your sales process is in B2B situations or brand selection in B2C, your overall cost of doing business could be higher. Referring back to the Zero Moment of Truth concept, PPC has the ability to shape your business reputation even before prospects visit your website or engage with you. That's because the more your prospects see your presence in the search results, the more they perceive that your business is a key player in the market.

The ideal PPC budget plan is one that looks at what it will take to dominate a specific keyword group in the search engine results page and one that also complements your organic listings. Define a strategy that ensures your business is seen at all the relevant stages of the buying cycle, along with the appropriate calls to action. Finally, be sure your PPC budget takes into account your target CPA, and use that to measure success instead of a simple budget spend total.

Choose the Right PPC Tactics

Once you have decided to try PPC advertising, Google AdWords is the best starting point. After you've had some success with this, then consider Bing Ad Center, which displays ads at both the Bing and Yahoo websites. There are also many other advertising platforms such as Facebook, LinkedIn, and a range of lesser-known shopping comparison websites, such as Shopzilla or Shopping.com. The CPC costs are much lower, and testing will help you decide very quickly if these second-tier options are worthwhile. Google AdWords offers a wider range of ad formats than many of the other PPC networks, which have only a single option. Many of these other PPC networks provide import tools from Google formats to make campaign creation very simple.

The most basic and commonly used ad format is the search text ad displayed when a person searches at the Google website, but you expand your reach with the content network and all types of interactive screens such as TVs, desktop computers, tablets, and mobile phones. This broad approach means your strategy also needs to address the various devices and locations people will use as part of the shopping process. First, research how people typically would find your products or offerings. Would they be on a mobile phone, while watching TV? Or at work during a lunch break looking to quickly order a replacement coffee supply? A simple technique is to ask your coworkers, sales personnel, and business partners to play the role of a prospect.

Would your prospects go first to a search website to discover more details, or do they prefer to watch a product commercial or demo video instead? Do they search out trusted information sources from bloggers who provide tips or news articles? Is obtaining referral information through social media a strong influencer? It could be a combination of all of these attributes, and you will need to deploy a mix of tactics. The chart below highlights these advertising formats and suggests ways to map them to your own marketing objectives.

Ad Format	Ideal Situation	Drawbacks
Search Text Ads - Search phrases trigger ads at the search websites.	Works across a broad range of market segments and applications. Has good positive ROI & conversion potential.	CPC costs are increasing as competition builds. Requires more management to reduce cost and some search knowledge or experience.
Display Ads - Banner or text ads displayed on content-rich websites such as blogs or information resources, directories, or forums. Ads are triggered by the content of the page via a matching keyword set.	Excellent reach beyond the search websites to hundreds of thousands of websites. Low conversion rate potential and more ideal for building brand.	Generates many curiosity visits (tire-kicking) that don't convert to sales or leads. Pay per individual clicks or by ad impressions. Monitor closely for quality sales or leads.
Video Ads - Promote a video shared on YouTube or your brand message via a video pre-roll ad app.	Ideal for developing a brand message or educating potential customers about a product or service.	Offers low-cost views with only a modest conversion to website visits or sales. Weak calls to action make it difficult to measure positive ROI.

Ad Format	Ideal Situation	Drawbacks
Remarketing - After visitors leave your website and navigate to another website that is part of the content network, a banner or text ad with your message is displayed. The idea is to remarket your message to those visitors even after they have left your website.	Called chasing after the sale, this has great conversion potential because you can track the actual pages visitors have already viewed at your website and tailor a re-offer message based on what they've already seen.	Testing follow-up offers is important for finding the right message that will convert. Requires you to set up some specialized tracking of web pages.
Mobile Ads - Ads formatted for mobile phones that are triggered by a search performed by the user.	Growing number of mobile users shops initially both on the go and at home. Often the first touch point in shopping research process. Set up as a separate campaign to help understand how mobile will influence the buying process.	Prospects may want to call you right away, so provide phone support. Many applications for shopping comparisons are available on smartphones and could create a price-sensitive interest only. Possible low conversion rate from the early stage in the buying cycle.
Shopping Comparison - Product images or specialized selection of mini applications appear in search results to help users select products or services. Often called PLA or product listing ads.	Ideal for common e-commerce products, selecting hotel rooms, and ready-to-buy scenarios. Customers are influenced by price and availability.	Be prepared for price wars. High conversion rate potential. Visitors have limited interest in being "up sold" and just want to buy the desired item/service and leave the site.

PPC Disadvantages

Paid ads will come and go in your marketing mix, based on your willingness and capacity to spend. For some visitors, paid ads lack authority compared to organic search results that have a more lasting presence. Many visitors are not aware of the difference between organic results and sponsored ads, so if you stop paying for PPC or exceed your daily budget, they may assume your business has disappeared if they don't see your ad. By contrast, once you have earned a top ranking position from organic SEO, losing it is a much slower process and your organic ranking can even last for many years. In PPC advertising, your search engine presence will disappear as quickly as it appeared if you stop paying for ads. If you make this a regular action, prepare to deal with rising budgets as there are usually more clicks than you can afford and PPC prices are rising as it gets more competitive.

Finally, PPC advertising is not a "set-it-and-forget-it" type of campaign. Even Google discourages this practice. Optimizing PPC campaigns is a learning process that involves testing, analysis, and research. It takes time to uncover the best terms to target, find ad messages that resonate, develop landing pages that convert, and establish a budget that provides a positive ROI. Experience may be your best teacher for optimizing your PPC campaigns. The less time and knowledge you have about and for managing PPC, the lower your likely results. Here are some key tips and techniques that can help you optimize your PPC results.

How to Optimize PPC Campaigns

Before we dive in, let's look at how Google defines a couple of key terms on support.google.com/adwords:

Campaign: A set of ad groups (ads, keywords, and bids) that share a budget, location targeting, and other settings. Your AdWords account can have one or many ad campaigns running.

Ad group: A set of keywords, ads, and bids that is a key part of how your account is organized. Each ad campaign is made up of one or more ad groups.

Start with Keyword Alignment

One of the most common and basic mistakes in setting up PPC ads is the organization of the campaigns and ad groups that don't focus on an actual advertising intent. Sometimes hundreds and even thousands of keywords are used for the same ad and lack any logical groupings. This is a big mistake, as Google discourages this and will increase your click costs by assigning you a lower Quality Score (more about this later). Aside from the extra cost, when you don't group the keywords by an association, it becomes more difficult to identify the steps of the sales funnel and to bid strategically for the ideal ad position.

Every business has a sales funnel, and it's rare that a majority of your prospects would purchase a product or service without any prior exposure to your selling process. One of the core purposes of marketing is to reduce objections during the early selling stages. Ads that speak directly to their prospects' interests and land on a page that addresses their concerns right from the start can help reduce the length of the sales cycle. Be sure to provide a call to action that is appropriate to the prospect's interest. Here's an example:In doing your keyword research on search terms, you may have noticed that a number of long tail searches are being done. Look for the informational type of searches such as "best widget" or "benefits of using *xyz*." Prospects using these search terms are looking for educational materials, and trying to close the sale too soon will just turn them away. Respond instead with an ad and a landing page that highlights your solution's benefits and has a call to action that focuses on case studies, "how to" guides, or an ebook with tips. The tone throughout should be about providing helpful advice, not trying to sell.

The keyword research you did for the PPC campaigns should have identified some of these associated groups. Google's own keyword tool even helps out by automatically creating the groups for you. This is a great starting point, but no one knows your business better than you, so spend the time to refine these logical groups. A strategic advantage will develop when you continually improve ad groupings that align to searcher intent, as this increases your insights into what prospects are looking for. See the chapter on conversion rate optimization (Chapter 12), for more details.

Maintaining Scent for the Searcher

Another important principle in optimizing your PPC campaigns has to do with maintaining the user scent. Much like a dog tracking the scent of another animal, when prospects start shopping by clicking on your PPC ad, an expectation is established. They anticipate that after clicking on your ad, they will find a web page with wording and images that match their initial search. They expect this "scent" will continue all the way to the "thank you" page for a completed sale or a lead request. When there is a disruption in the scent trail, their attention can be diverted and off they go in another direction, clicking over to a competitor's site and away from yours. Reviewing website performance metrics such as bounce rate and the number of page views will help provide insights into whether (and how much) your website is losing their interest.

Review your entire sales process from the ad to the landing page and to the thank you page so that you ensure you are maintaining scent all the way through. Let's say you are advertising for "puzzles," which is the keyword at the top of the sales funnel, because prospects haven't indicated whether they are looking for a crossword, jigsaw, or online puzzle. Their real intention is still unclear to you at this point, so pre-qualifying your prospect at the ad stage will be beneficial. Your ad copy should contain "jigsaw puzzle" if this is one of your key offerings, because it shapes the expectation for the next step in the sales funnel. If someone searches for the term "puzzles" and your landing page does not highlight this as a central concept, then you create enough user confusion to reduce your conversion potential. Not paying close attention to how you maintain scent reduces your creditability and increases visitor frustration. Even simple mistakes such as bidding on the plural version of "puzzles" over "puzzle," and only showing one puzzle instead of many choices with your graphics, could be creating a negative impression. The more exactly you match the landing page to what the searcher is expecting to see, the better.

Understanding Quality Score

How important is managing scent and associating keywords to specific ad groups? Google believes this is a top priority for optimizing campaigns and has developed a reporting tool called Quality Score to help focus advertiser attention. Google is continually changing its organic search algorithm to create a better search experience by improving search relevancy and extends this same goal to PPC advertising. The more relevant the ads that align to searches in PPC, the higher those ads will rank, even at a lower cost. Quality Score is sometimes a mystery for many advertisers, but Google is providing metrics to help improve the overall ad quality. Here's a quick summary of how Quality Score works and what matters to you.

Google claims there are over 100 factors that go into determining a Quality Score, which is reported on a scale of 1 to 10. An ad's click-through rate and how well your ads performed in the past are two of the main factors, but many other behind-the-scenes factors, such as landing page relevancy, are combined for the scoring. The rating scale they share with advertisers is a summary of how well their ads are doing. Values of 7 to 10 indicate a positive score and you should be enjoying the best cost-per-click (CPC) rate possible. Values of 4 to 5 represent an average rating, an indication that making changes may or may not improve your Quality Score. Finally, values in the range of 1 to 3 mean your ad groups and landing pages will need serious attention. Also, ads with a 1 or 2 rating may not be displayed by Google and could require you to bid up and pay much more to have them displayed.

The most important action to take with Google's Quality Score information is to review it. Google provides this reporting mechanism so advertisers can understand how to make their ads more relevant. You can export quality score reports for analysis via a spreadsheet. Develop an action plan for improving top targeted or top-performing terms to reap the most immediate benefits. An improved quality score should reduce your CPC spending and help increase the number of sales or leads.

Spend Your PPC Dollars Wisely

Paid search advertising is a variable component of your marketing budget. Google will encourage you to increase your spend, even as it provides helpful tips on getting better results. Many of Google's suggestions will be valuable, but others should be taken with a grain of salt. Increase your PPC spending budget only when you have obtained an acceptable ROI, as this will serve as a benchmark for future spending targets.

How can you reduce your PPC spending? Optimizing your PPC management is only half of the picture. Think of paid search advertising much like the computer concept of input and output being handled by a central processor. The input represents the customer interest encapsulated in the search ad to be processed by your website, and the output is a lead or sale that is produced. An important analogy to this basic computer principle also applies, the old saying about "garbage in, garbage out." If you only are concerned about managing the PPC ads, and ignore how the results occurred, you'll find that success with PPC will remain out of reach.

How can you improve ROI with paid search advertising? A critical skill to develop is conversion optimization. As visitors to your website interact with it, pay close attention to the complete experience and make it an ongoing practice to test new methods for converting more leads or sales. The practices described in the chapter on conversion rate optimization should become part of your own expertise (or your PPC manager's expertise). Here are the key starting points for every PPC effort.

- Ensure the conversion tracking process is working.

- Review the quality of the leads.

- Gain insights into how leads are being closed.

Make sure your lead delivery process is working. This may seem very basic, but sometimes the simple things cause problems. Are you receiving all of your leads? Email is often the delivery mechanism for leads, but emails can fail or get trapped by spam filters. When your web developers change any of the call to action forms on your site, keep a vigilant eye on your lead funnel. In fact, test the lead process after any website change. Don't always assume it is working; test it to be sure!

Once you have determined that your conversion tracking is reporting properly, then set up an ongoing dialog with your sales team about the quality of the leads or sales. You or your PPC manager should take an active role in reviewing the selling process to help your sales team understand what characterizes a qualified visit. Ask these questions:

- In lead generation applications, was the call to action the right response for that prospect?

- Does it look like there is serious interest?

- In e-commerce scenarios, was this a single-item purchase, or should there be related products to up sell?

Don't assume a single cost per action (CPA) will apply for all leads or sales types. There are cases when a high CPA is acceptable if it produces better results in the selling process. Take a proactive approach with your sales team and find out how well they are closing the leads that you provide. View search advertising as an integral part of the sales process, since results are easy to track. Using feedback from the sales team will help you develop more insights into what your prospects are searching for.

When to Stop PPC Advertising

A common question in PPC is whether it should be a permanent expense. If PPC advertising is generating sales and leads, but the ROI remains too low, does a continual investment make sense? Tightening marketing budgets may also increase pressure to question this spend. Conversely, obtaining top SEO rankings could lessen your company's sense of urgency to be highly visible in search engines.

If your PPC advertising results are dismal, you may want to invest in a second opinion before pulling the plug. Many consulting firms offer PPC management services and could help you find the right mix based on their experience. This second opinion could help you discover tactical errors that are driving up costs unnecessarily. Search marketing in general is constantly changing, so your in-house management team may lack knowledge of or experience with the latest developments. Likewise, if you are using an outside firm to manage your PPC, you may want to question them on the topics discussed here, such as Quality Score. If they respond with a blank stare, then it could be time to start shopping for a new partnership.

Advertising with Google may also cost more than other PPC advertising options. Not all search advertising should come from Google. There are alternatives that can produce better results that you should test and explore. In the next section, I'll review some of these networks and how they may help you find success in paid advertising.

Beyond Google: Other Ad Networks

Bing Ads Network

Don't overlook advertising on the Yahoo and Bing websites, since they are the second and third most popular search engines on the Internet (after Google/YouTube). The ads you place in Bing Ads will appear both at the Bing and Yahoo websites using the same PPC management interface, or you can use Yahoo's ad center. If you haven't advertised before with Bing or Yahoo, you may want to consider using Bing Ads as it offers a richer feature set for managing your ads.

Trying the Bing/Yahoo network is a logical step after you have established success with Google. Many advertisers have found cheaper clicks and higher ROI using the Bing/Yahoo network, but this is obvious only after testing. In many scenarios, the actual CPC costs are the same and yet the conversion rate is higher or vice versa. This does make the point that search marketing is not always an exact science. Setting up ads for the Bing/Yahoo network follows a process similar to Google AdWords and most of the topics covered in this chapter will apply. There's even an import tool that allows you to transfer Google ads into Bing Ads to get you operational very quickly. If you find success with the Bing/Yahoo network, your only disappointment will be the low search volume. As Google continues to dominate as the number one search engine website, getting modest results from the Bing/Yahoo network will likely continue.

Facebook and LinkedIn Paid Advertising

Facebook and LinkedIn are two other paid advertising networks you should consider. These top social media websites can generate lots of targeted traffic, but do not operate like classic search advertising. Instead of using search terms to generate ads, both of these networks use demographic targeting to trigger the ad display. Don't expect the same results if your strategy and approach have been cut and pasted from Google. A key element missing is that Zero Moment of Truth where the search phrase has disclosed a prospect's initial interest. In ads for Facebook and LinkedIn, it's more critical to create compelling ad copy with text and graphics that will pique a prospect's interest and curiosity. Your approach to LinkedIn and Facebook advertising requires more testing of different customer demographics rather than finding the right search terms. Finally, your business objective with this advertising should not solely focus on creating sales or leads, but on building your brand.

In both Facebook and LinkedIn paid advertising, there are two key points to consider before launching campaigns:

1. Who would be interested in your message?

2. What call to action makes sense?

The obvious answers may not be the most successful. For example, if you sell Harley-Davidson motorcycle accessories, you may think promoting a special sale to a Facebook demographic of 40- to 60-year-old males who love Harleys seems like a logical choice. The call to action is a graphic promoting a one-day sale with an image of a Harley "babe" posed on a bike. You picked the right demographic and created an attractive call to action, but in testing, the sales register did not ring too often. Before you give up, you may want to experiment with other approaches to finding the right audience.

It's important to recognize that people using social media websites are not looking to be sold something; they are spending time at these sites to connect with others. Instead of using a call to action to announce a sale, try instead to land them on your Facebook page and promote a "Like Us" action. Then when you post a new special or deal via your Facebook business page, it will be quickly broadcast to all community members (those who have "liked" your page). Facebook ads can generate sales, but often these are the ones created by testing with a demographic that does not have a direct interest in your product or service. Continuing with our special Harley sale example, you may want to test a market segment of 40- to 60-year-old married females, based on the wives' interests instead of their biker husbands'. Think out of the box here, and try to find an angle that interests this indirect influencer. Targeting "off demographic" has produced great results for many Facebook advertisers, and in this example, there was a higher conversion rate to actual sales. The ad resonated with the "Harley widows" looking for a deal on a gift for their husbands, who love to ride on weekends.

Both Facebook and LinkedIn rely on advertisers to support their businesses, so you can expect to see new programs being developed. A portion of your paid search budget should involve testing various approaches on these sites, since doing so will help you discover the right demographic to target with your messages.

Ten Steps to a Successful Paid Search Campaign

Paid search remains the most effective online strategy in generating instant ROI. Your prospect's interest is clearly stated in the search terms, and when that's aligned with a relevant response, it can often produce predictable results. Paid search contains elements of marketing science, combined with common sense. Based on my company's experience with many clients, here are the top ten steps to take for deploying a successful paid search strategy.

1. Start with the Keyword

Allocate plenty of time to research target keywords and actively refine the results. Your PPC manager should be an expert in using the Google keyword tool, as this is the most important aid for search term research. The Google tool will help identify ads groupings, budgeting issues, and even conversion potential. Investing the time in complete and thorough research will reduce wasted spending at the initial launch of your PPC campaign. It will also help you begin a process of disciplined thinking that will help you identify top-performing search terms. The Google Trends tool is also useful, as it charts the rise or decline of interest in a search term over the past four years as well as new terms. Understanding how people use search is an ongoing learning process.

2. Geo-Target for Specific Markets

Google AdWords gives advertisers the ability to target ads based on specific geographic markets, from country down to state or city. This geo-targeting means you can create ads to be displayed at a prospect's home location. If you are challenged by a tight budget, geo-targeting may help you control costs because you can run ads only in profitable regions, or even ignore entire areas of the target country. Consider implementing geo-targeting as a way to create a more localized business persona that feels easily accessible to your target audience in a particular location. We have seen literally thousands of dollars spent wastefully on clicks outside of a company's target market because the PPC manager did not realize a non-relevant country was targeted inadvertently.

3. Organize Your Campaign

Establishing the right campaign ad structure gives you the foundation for building flexible and adaptable ad groupings. Put some thought into your campaign organization so the ad groupings reflect your business lines or company structure. Avoid creating a single campaign with all of your product lines under it, as it will be harder to adjust budgets or react to seasonal impacts. Over time, you should create or identify the top-performing campaigns that represent your highest-ROI ads and even specific search terms.

4. Think Cost per Action

In measuring the return on investment of PPC, think in terms of cost per action (CPA), not just how much you spend. Before establishing a budget, review your current CPA costs and set new targets. If a budget is too limited, then daily PPC spending limits will occur, and your ads will be randomly stopped by Google. It's always ideal to keep ads running at your target times. Avoid budget planning that only focuses on spending amounts, and take a balanced approach by targeting a lower CPA as another project metric.

5. Link Conversion Optimization to PPC

Integrate conversion optimization with your PPC management. Since you can't avoid CPC fees in paid advertising, maximizing every website visit is the best way to reduce the costs. An ideal conversion rate is one that is constantly going up! Focus your attention on how to turn every visit from paid search into a sale or lead.

6. Ensure Website Analytics Is Working

Running a PPC campaign without any analytics is simply wasting an opportunity to save money. Google Analytics is free to website owners, is easy to install, and provides great insights into how people are interacting with your website. There is even a special Google AdWords-to-Analytics integration that provides detailed information for refining your bidding strategies. The only drawback is that Google also has access to this data, but we have not seen any cases where Google is using this information to the detriment of the advertiser. If you are uncomfortable with Google's access to your business sales information, your alternative is to pay for third-party analytics.

7. Remain Active in PPC Optimization

Avoid the set-it-and-forget-it PPC management mindset. Google AdWords is designed to be a self-service platform that makes ad management easy for advertisers. Don't think that once campaigns are set up they can operate on autopilot. Do you really want to let Google spend your ad money without any of your attention? Schedule daily or weekly tasks related to managing your PPC campaigns. Activities could include: finding new keywords, identifying keywords not to allow automatic bids on (called negative keywords; an example would be "free" jigsaw puzzles), creating new ad groupings, changing bids to test new positions, testing ad rotation, and creating performance reports.

8. Learn Search Insights

PPC offers you the ability to understand search marketing firsthand. Gather insights over time as you refine and optimize your PPC campaigns in terms of how searches are aligning with the products or services you offer. Search engines have become an integral part of the daily lives of individuals looking for products, services, or answers to a range of questions. People rely on search to find information, and the interaction they have with your PPC ads will help you gather insights into consumer trends. You can estimate the popularity of your main competitors' terms or emerging topics by tracking trends in the impression count. From broad searches to very detailed phrases, you can uncover the actual vocabulary people use to find your business and even the type of devices they are using to access your website.

It's also an opportunity to understand if your value proposition is resonating with visitors. Here's a simple but effective campaign that every business should have. Create a brand ad where you use your own company name as the search term to trigger the ads. Rotate a couple of different ads that focus on your key value proposition. Over time, when the sample size is sufficient, this should begin to indicate which message is more popular with your customer base. This is just one example of how PPC can add new business insights.

9. Create a Testing Mentality

Create a testing discipline with your PPC efforts. One of the most effective ways to create a unique competitive advantage is to use PPC as a testing tool for both your marketing messages and conversion optimization efforts. Since you have total control over the search terms used to trigger the ads, it's the ideal input for testing, and setting up fast mini-experiments. Using tools such as Google's website optimizer (now called Content Experiments in Google Analytics) along with Google Analytics, you can create a testing platform to benchmark results. Testing is a missing marketing discipline in too many online marketing programs, and yet can produce highly competitive results.

10. Understand Search Relevancy

Search technology is constantly being advanced to align searches to relevant websites. Always review your efforts as they relate to web visitors and question your relevancy factor in the landing experience. Pay attention to reporting metrics such as Google's Quality Score, remembering that your "bounce" rate and conversion rate are good indicators of your website's relevancy. Google will reward advertisers that take this extra step to improve the total experience with the best CPC rates, while you will also benefit with a higher conversion rate.

The Role of Paid Advertising

If you're doing business online, you should consider at least a minimal investment in paid search as an initial test. You just might find that no matter how high the cost per click for certain keywords, you consistently generate sales with a high ROI. The amount you spend, and for what purposes, must be aligned with your specific business objectives but if the ROI is good, you have the option to confidently scale up your budget. Paid advertising has many ancillary benefits and can quickly identify key converting search terms to target in your SEO efforts, provide an ideal environment for your conversion optimization testing, and uncover insights about how people are using search to find your products or services. Paid advertising is just one of the many powerful tactics in a balanced online strategy, and has the unique advantage of being something you can turn on or off when you need more sales or leads.

Chapter 11

Actionable Analytics and Reporting

Once you have a variety of Internet marketing tactics in place, you'll want to get the most out of each one by understanding how well they are working. Website analytics will help you do just that.

Website analytics is the measurement, collection, analysis, and reporting of website data for the purpose of understanding visitor behavior and for making actionable adjustments. Web analytics provides data on the number of visitors, page views, visit duration, conversion rates, and much more.

Why Use Reporting and Analytics?

Just driving more traffic to your website without tracking and analyzing what those visitors do is like adding water to a leaky bucket! To profit from that traffic, you must analyze visitor activity to see why they don't do more of what you want them to do. You need to define and measure calls to action. You also need to test making changes to increase those desired actions, again and again.

The average conversion rate is around one to two percent, but some top sites have conversion rates at ten, twenty, or thirty percent or more. The Schwan's online grocery site is said to have a conversion rate of around 42 percent. They got there by analyzing data and making adjustments to their site. So never accept the average, not when there are such great analytics tools available that can help you get much better conversion rates. Online advertising generates a huge volume of data that can be measured and analyzed. When you know exactly what marketing efforts produce the best ROI, you can then confidently and successfully pour money into these areas. This is a big part of why Internet marketing has become so successful and dominant.

Here are a few reasons to consider using web analytics:

- You get the statistical and often surprising facts on what customers are *really* doing—not just what you think or hope they are doing. You'll learn about the likes and dislikes of your customers and use this knowledge to revise your site.

- Web analytics can help you understand the conversion rate of your visitors and provide you with solutions to maximize the conversion rate.

- You can determine which traffic sources drive the most traffic and which drive the most conversions for your particular business.

- Preventing users from "bouncing" away from your website may also affect your search engine rankings, so using analytics to improve visitor engagement is critical.

- All this can result in a healthier bottom line for your company and improved ROI on all your marketing efforts, because even traffic from off-line campaigns will make you money if the website works better.

If you don't already have a good analytics program and clearly defined on-page calls to action, stop right now and do this before you invest any more in efforts to drive traffic. Analytics is at the heart of increasing engagement and conversions.

Analytics Programs to Consider

Google Analytics

Some 86% of businesses use Google Analytics for web metrics, which is not surprising, since it's free and powerful. Amazingly, 82% of online retailers are using Google Analytics or analytics in general incorrectly, according to Econsultancy. A lack of skills and resources is the main reason analytics is not done right. Many people think you can just install the Analytics code and have any web person review it, but it takes some training and a strategy to really get up to speed.

Google Analytics excels at giving you great insights into how people are getting to and interacting with your website. It shows you where visitors are coming from, what they are actually clicking on, and how they are interacting with your site.

Google Analytics offers these benefits:

- Stretches your valuable marketing dollars since it is free and powerful.

- Includes enterprise-level features out of the box!

- There are many training videos and blog posts available online about how to use it.

- Its omnipresence means you're never without user support.

Content Experiments

Content Experiments is the replacement for the amazing Google Website Optimizer, and is a tool that lets you do A/B testing to experiment with different versions or combinations of headlines, images, and landing pages in order to increase conversions. Using this program, which is now included as part of Google Analytics, could make you more money than all your traffic-driving activities combined. That's because a low conversion rate can mean you get limited sales across the board, but if you increase your conversion rate, you could double or triple your revenue in a matter of months.

Much of this chapter is about Google Analytics because that is what most small to mid-sized businesses use. Because this book is not intended to be a full guide to Analytics but merely a pointer to get you thinking in the right direction, I will leave the step-by-step instructions for other books specifically about Analytics. See the McDougall Interactive blog's analytics section for more details and how-to guides. Some of my favorite analytics gurus are Avinash Kaushik, whose blog is Occam's Razor at kaushik.net, and Jim Sterne, author of *Social Media Metrics*.

Please review the other analytics options below, because no single tool has all the answers.

HubSpot

HubSpot isn't just a tool, it is an attitude. When you sign up for HubSpot's paid service, they put you through boot camp during their required consulting process. They get you to do things like blog almost daily and create downloadable content (like ebooks and case studies), free consultation forms, landing pages, and calls to action for the top, middle, and bottom of the sales funnel. They get you into the type of low-cost lead nurturing that used to only be available for much larger companies.

Yes, HubSpot is software, but it's more than that. As HubSpot says, "Google Analytics shows you raw numbers of users. HubSpot shows you real people." Analytics software is useless without traffic and leads to track and follow up on, so HubSpot combines driving traffic with analyzing and converting it. The software does this by tracking the actions of visitors, corporations by IP address, and visitors by name after they fill out a form on your site.

HubSpot lets you:

- Track real people, not just data.

- Track hundreds of keywords.

- Manage social media profiles and track social ROI.

- Analyze traffic, leads, and bumps from tradeshows and events.

- Hyper-analyze lead details and conversion rates.

- Nurture leads with email and automated marketing campaigns.

- Compare your search engine rankings, links, and social media to competitors over time.

- Get far more leads than through a standard Internet marketing campaign because it brings many elements together under one roof and encourages best practices and much more.

HubSpot connects the dots between things like social media, email, your customer relationship management (CRM) system, and even off-line efforts over longer stretches of time than Google Analytics. From the minute a visitor comes to your site through the point at which they convert into a sale, even if it's months or years later, HubSpot tracks them and gives credit to the channel that first introduced them to you. This is a game-changer and is truly one of the biggest developments in recent marketing history. Google Analytics Multi-Channel funnel reports, and the attribution modeling tool, both use a 30-day lookback window which is not enough time to give full credit across channels (especially if your sales cycle is longer than 30 days).

HubSpot integrates with your website so that leads go into your CRM system (such as Salesforce). Once a customer takes an action, like filling out a form, you not only see what company they came from but *who* they are, and then you get to see every action they take on your site moving forward. It is so exciting to see a specific person return to your site and visit more pages that are important (those you have defined as being a common path of leads that turn into sales). You can set up emails to go out to users who take steps 1 and 2 out of 3 but miss some important content. By emailing them in a helpful way, seemingly "out of the blue," with that next piece of their learning puzzle, you can generate more actual sales than through traditional analytics, which doesn't take this interactivity into account. You might push visitors along the path to conversion by sending emails that share an important blog post about a product comparison or that offer a free trial.

Google Analytics has great data and even A/B testing ability, but HubSpot is fully integrated with your sales team via tools like Salesforce and lead nurturing programs. It is truly analytics on steroids.

Ideally, use both Google Analytics and HubSpot, as they work really well together.

As of this writing HubSpot has three tiers of monthly pricing, with Basic starting at $200, Professional starting at $600, and Enterprise starting at $1,000.

The pricing is also dependent on variables like the number of your sales contacts, the number of leads you generate per year from your site, and the number of email addresses in your list, so you will need to get a custom quote.

ClickTale

ClickTale is a paid tool that gives you playable videos of user activity on your site and lets you analyze such items as scroll reach, heat maps (visual representation of where people click), conversion funnels, form drop-outs, and more. ClickTale does things Google Analytics simply cannot, by letting you actually see what visitors do in a format that allows replays. Did the boss tell you to add a huge rotating banner and put the call to action at the bottom of the web page? Well, he will thank you when you show him that people never scroll down far enough to see the banner or the call to action. Conversely, if people actually do scroll down, ClickTale can tell you how many clicked on the call to action, which will also make the boss happy. Great websites are made by creatives working in tandem with more analytical types. You need real data to justify every creative change you make on your site, and analytics tools like this can provide that data.

Crazy Egg

Crazy Egg has been referred to as the poor man's ClickTale. It is a highly regarded tool that starts at only $9 per month and has a free 30-day trial. With Crazy Egg, you can see where users click and discover what Google Analytics is not telling you, thanks to heat map, scroll map, and overlay tools.

Adobe (Omniture) SiteCatalyst

Omniture is expensive (around $5,000 per month) and more complicated to install and use than Google Analytics. However, it has powerful testing systems and integrates well with Salesforce and email systems. This lets you connect information gathered by your sales team with your web data. Google Analytics Premium is a flat $150,000 per year and is a competitor to this advanced tool. You really need deep pockets to enter this domain. To put this in perspective, we only come across clients with Adobe (Omniture) SiteCatalyst once every few years, now that Google Analytics is so powerful.

With that said, some people are mad enough about things like the Google "not provided" issue that there could be a small but growing trend of Google Analytics defectors. Picking up the slack would be Piwik, Omniture, and Webtrends at the enterprise level and Clicky, Statcounter, Mint, Mixpanel, KISSMetrics, Hubspot, and others on the small to medium business end.

Set Up Tracking Systems

In order to have a reasonably complete sense of what is generating sales and leads, you must have multiple forms of tracking in place. Until you are truly tracking these key items in the tracking systems list below, you are not really in a position to judge your return on investment.

1. **Tracking a unique phone number on your site.** Mongoose Metrics is a tool that displays a different number to each visitor in order to let you know what keyword made the phone ring. If you are only looking at shopping cart sales or form submissions, be sure to also have a solution for phone tracking.

2. **Form submissions.** By setting up Google Analytics and/or HubSpot to register a lead each time a form is submitted, you can see the rise or fall in your form conversion rate on a monthly basis. The "thank you" page is a key part in this process because visitors see it only after they've hit the "submit" button. So, you can be sure of a conversion when it is tracked as a pageview in your analytics software.

3. **Shopping cart sales.** By setting up a "receipt" page for your transactions and registering it in analytics, you can measure the dollar amount and number of shopping cart sales. You should also add a snippet of code to each step of the checkout process, known as a shopping cart funnel. That way you can see where in the funnel people drop out before the sale is complete and start to correct the issues that prevent conversions.

4. **Live chat.** We have successfully increased the number of conversions on many clients' websites by using live chat. Since some customers don't want to call, fill out a form, or even use a shopping cart, a live chat feature can reach the customers you would have lost otherwise. Ngagelive.com allows you to have a 24/7 answering service that frees you from having to staff the chat window. Ngagelive.com doesn't pretend to know your business; they essentially just record the visitor's contact information and questions and tell them they will have someone get right back to them. LivePerson is another service that lets you do the chatting yourself. For law firms, we often see 30% of the leads coming from tracked live chat sessions. We can also see what keyword and search engine or social site initiated the chat.

5. **Email address clicks.** You can also tag email address clicks to register as a conversion, so those don't go unnoticed when adding up all your sales/leads.

6. **Printable/PDF application downloads.** While it does not guarantee they filled out a form or provided their contact information, tagging links to the PDFs in Analytics will give you a better sense of how many people are downloading printable PDFs or applications.

7. **Printable coupon/specials downloads.** This can help track off-line conversions.

8. **Third-party applications.** Banks and mortgage companies, for example, often don't author the software that allows people to apply online. They commonly have to send users off their own website in order to have them access the secure application form area. Other examples of third-party applications include "booking" applications for hotels and resorts. Unless you add snippets of Google Analytics code to these off-site pages—at least in the "thank you" page of their website forms—you will never get information about how many people signed up. This is not always an easy task, because you must work with their IT people and have a knowledgeable analytics person describe exactly what to do. You should also add a snippet of code on each step of these third-party applications, which will allow you to see where the drop points are in the sales funnel and correct issues that stop conversions.

If you don't have these types of tracking systems in place, you won't get a full ROI picture and will likely never be satisfied with your outcomes.

Attribution Tracking

One thing to be aware of is that Google Analytics is largely a system that uses a last-click methodology. This means that if someone originally found your site through Facebook a year ago, then six months ago found you through an SEO/organic search, but today made a purchase or became a lead after typing your domain name into the address bar on their browser, you would falsely assume that the lead was just from the direct type-in. If that same person came into your site today after seeing a paid search ad and you only gave credit to PPC without realizing that Facebook and SEO had helped make that person aware of your brand over the last year, you would be making a fatal mistake. This mistake would be pouring loads of money into PPC, thinking it was more responsible for leads/sales than it actually was. So, having a solution for attribution tracking is an essential part of a complete ROI tracking program.

Off-line Conversions

When factoring in all the leads that were generated by a website but not tracked (such as people using a search engine to discover you, then going to your brick-and-mortar location or calling to make the purchase), the ROI on search marketing becomes staggering and impossible to ignore. Be honest with yourself and your Internet marketing agency, so that they can see what is working and what is not. If they charge a standard monthly retainer, your fee won't necessarily increase just because you admit you got lots of off-line sales due to web marketing. In fact, they might just work even harder so that you become their best case study!

Tracking Off-line Conversions

You may not realize the impact that your website has on off-line sales. It could be bigger than you think. It is estimated that nearly one quarter of total off-line sales are influenced by the web.

The problem comes in tracking these off-line conversions. While web analytics packages allow you to track online conversions of your website visitors, tracking off-line conversions can be trickier. Here are a few tips for tracking off-line conversions from your website:

- At a minimum, create one new 800 number that you use only on the website, or even a unique 800 number for each online ad campaign. By using a unique 800 number, you can partially track online consumer activity to an off-line sale point. Then go a step further and track the percentage of calls to the unique 800 number that convert into sales.

- Create a coupon download that can be printed for use in stores, or unique offer codes users can redeem at stores or over the phone. This can help you to attribute off-line sales to online leads.

- When a purchase is completed, ask the customer to fill out a post-purchase survey. Offer an incentive, like 5% off their next purchase. Use the survey to ask how the customer discovered your business, as well as what they liked or didn't like about their experience. Pre-purchase surveys, which target the browsing consumer, also work, and are best when accompanied by some form of incentive.

- If you have a brick-and-mortar store or location, ask your sales associates to keep a spreadsheet of people who come in holding printouts from your website.

- After an off-line sale, ask the customer to visit the website to sign up for a rebate or to register for a product warranty. Then you can gather demographic, geographic, and contact information, as well as information on consumer activities—including how the customer discovered your company and the product or service.

Using the above strategies for tracking off-line conversions will give you a much clearer picture of your website's performance. Even a little effort, like using a unique 800 number on the website and offering e-coupons that are redeemable off-line, will go a long way toward helping you track your online advertising efforts.

Tracking Conversions Originating from Off-line Advertising

The following types of campaigns can be integrated into your analytics tracking with some extra effort.

- Radio

- Television

- Print

- Billboards

- Direct mail

Print advertising (including newspapers, magazines, flyers, brochures, banners, and Yellow Pages ads) can all be integrated. For example, you can track these in your analytics program via:

- Separate domains

- Custom URLs

- PURLS (or personalized URLs) that use the customer's name in a mailer and on your website

- Custom phone numbers

Create a spreadsheet of ads to track and keep notes on the URLs associated with each ad. Track the visits to your site, the number of pages visited, and what paths visitors took, then determine how many of these people actually converted online. You can set up goals for each ad campaign and see a dollar amount in Analytics for sales or leads generated.

Bring It All Together

In an earlier chapter, I shared the old saying, "I know half of my advertising works; I just don't know which half." Well, now you are a few steps closer to reaching the holy grail of tracking.

Sales don't always happen on the first visit. They tend to develop over time and through multiple touch points. You can guide visitors on a more persuasive journey, but only if you know how to use the tools that track their actions. In the next section, I outline some of the most important things to know about analytics strategy and using Google Analytics.

Defining Goals and Key Performance Indicators (KPIs)

Without goals, any analytics tool is useless. Measurements that help you see how you are doing against your goals and objectives are called Key Performance Indicators (KPIs).

Depending on your industry and type of business, you will require different KPIs. You'll also need to customize your web analytics tool especially for your site.

What are your top three KPIs? Examples could include:

1. Conversion rate (or conversion rate of the blog or from SEO specifically)

2. Days and visits to purchase

3. Average order value

4. Visitor loyalty and visitor recency

5. Share of search for a particular term against a competitor

Knowing just how much you can track will get you and your team excited. No strategy is complete without being driven by measurable objectives. If you have Google Analytics installed and don't yet use it effectively, you're about to enter a whole new world.

Get Started: Install the Code

Sign up for a Google Analytics account and install the code ASAP! Until you add the snippet of code onto all your web pages, you won't be collecting any data. You can view reports within 24 hours, but it will take some days to get more meaningful data. The real magic happens with month-to-month comparisons over a span of years. For example, how many visitors and conversions did we get from non-branded keywords via SEO last December compared to this December?

Now that you have the code installed and adjusted, it's time to start using analytics to improve your website and user experience.

Acquire, Engage, Convert, and Retain

Nokia has a methodology they call AECR (Acquire, Engage, Convert, and Retain), which is very similar to the REAN model described in Chapter 12. (See the conversion optimization chapter for more on Reach, Engage, Activate, and Nurture.) As you plan your Analytics activities, make notes on what you want to track and how your goals fit into the REAN or AECR model.

A successful website is one that meets the goals *you* define for it. Successful marketers map out how they will acquire customers, engage them, convert them, and retain them.

Analytics is where the rubber meets the road in getting this done. Think about how the various reports and tactics in Analytics map to these four key areas of marketing.

The Google Analytics Interface (Basics)

After your code is installed and working properly, you can log in to Google Analytics and start reviewing various metrics and reports.

You will see the following navigation items:

Home | Standard Reporting | Custom Reporting

The home link is where your main dashboards will be.

The **Standard Reporting** link takes you to all kinds of amazing data using the left-hand navigation.

The main headings of the Standard Reporting navigation are as follows:

Audience

Here you will find reports on what countries people came from, new vs. returning visitors, mobile usage, browsers used, and visitor flow, etc.

Advertising

Information fed from your AdWords campaigns after you link it to Analytics.

Traffic Sources

Information on where users came from, including direct, referral, an ad campaign, and paid or organic search, is displayed here.

Content

Information on all pages, landing pages, exit pages, site speed, site search, AdSense, content experiments, and in-page analytics is found here.

Conversions

Information on goals you are tracking, including goal paths, goal funnel visualization, goal flow, e-commerce, multi-channel funnels, and assisted conversions is found here.

Take your time and click on all of the links to get a feel for what is available and what you might like to add to your dashboard.

Add any item you want to your dashboard by clicking the mini navigation that looks like the list below:

Advanced Segments | Email | Export | **Add to Dashboard** | Shortcut

Click "Add to Dashboard" and a widget that contains the data from the report you like will be sent to your dashboard. You can only have so many widgets on a single dashboard, so if you find yourself running out of space, simply create additional dashboards for different data sets. To check out your various dashboards, use the **Dashboards** menu on the left, when on the **Home** tab.

The Dashboard lets you see a lot of important data at a glance. Set up a dashboard that contains the essential data you need to manage your organization. A typical marketing dashboard contains things like where your visitors are coming from, the keywords they used in the search engines, and a list of referring websites. Your most popular content, essential data about your visitors, and a summary of your goals can also be included. Separate dashboards can be created for different campaigns to report on their effectiveness. Each department can develop its own dashboard to see statistics that relate to department goals.

These four widgets are essential:

- Visits - Timeline (can also include a Metric)

- Goal Completions and/or Transactions - Timeline

- Source/Medium - Table

- Bounce Rate - Timeline

If you want even deeper options with more customization than standard widgets, then click the **Custom Reporting** link from the main top navigation and you can create reports with multiple layers of data. Use the drag-and-drop interface to create reports with the metrics/dimensions that you want.

If you want reports emailed to you and your team, click the email link in the mini navigation bar below.

Advanced Segments | **Email** | Export | Add to Dashboard | Shortcut BETA

You can email each dashboard report separately and schedule them on the days/times you choose.

The things you can do with Google Analytics are practically endless. To keep it simple, I will skip going into more detail on how to navigate around the program. There's plenty of helpful information online if you want assistance using Analytics. Instead, let's shift our focus to a conceptual level and review a list of the top things to consider using or doing with Google Analytics.

What to Set Up Before You Have Full Data

1. Set Up Goals in Analytics

When visitors come to your website, you want them to do something. The activities you set for users to do are called "goals." Make sure you understand how to set up goals in Analytics, because until you track form "thank you" pages, shopping cart "thank you" pages, and conversion rates for ads, you really won't have enough information to determine ROI. Goals give real meaning to your analytics reporting.

Keep in mind that while these reports give you information about conversions from all traffic sources, you can also use "Goal Set" tabs in the other reports to view the goal completions broken down by visitor type or traffic source, and so on.

2. Filter Out Internal Traffic

Configure your analytics to exclude your company's internal visits to your website, and also exclude the visits from your web development team. (They spend a lot of time navigating through your site, and you don't want their "work visits" to distort the numbers you hope to track about visits from prospects and customers.)

3. Integrate AdWords

You can only monitor your AdWords revenue, conversions, and ROI after you link Analytics to AdWords. Use the instructions in support.google.com to complete this task.

4. Integrate AdSense

If you have an AdSense account to monetize your site, you will want to link your AdSense and Google Analytics accounts to gain more insight into your AdSense performance. You will be able to see which pages and referrers generate the most revenue, and optimize your site's performance using AdSense Reports. (See the instructions in support.google.com.)

5. Set Up E-commerce Tracking

Link e-commerce performance to keywords and marketing campaigns to show ROI, etc. Setting up e-commerce tracking is a two-step process that includes enabling e-commerce tracking in an account profile and adding e-commerce tracking code to your site. (See the instructions in support.google.com.)

Key Items to Track with Analytics

Now that you have completed most of the Analytics setup, let's dig into the key items to track.

Traffic Sources

Here is where you learn how users find your website. Every month, look at a breakdown of the amount of traffic from various sources such as direct traffic, organic search, paid search, social, email, and ads. It is also a good idea to compare the bounce rate and the volumes of traffic from each source. In the case of search visits, these reports also show what keywords visitors used when they found your site.

Direct Traffic

This is when users type your domain name into the browser's address bar directly, or come to your site from bookmarks or email links without tracking codes (not when users come from advertising or SEO). Keep in mind, lots of advertising will generate more direct traffic over time as brand awareness increases, so make sure you are using attribution tracking beyond Google Analytics' 30-day window to give some credit to the sources that may have led to an eventual direct type-in.

Referral Traffic

Traffic coming via links from other sites, including from social sites are called referrers. Facebook and YouTube traffic will be listed here. Are you paying for a listing on a directory website in your industry? Look here to see if the traffic you're getting from that listing is worth the cost.

Search Engines

The "Search" reports detail the keyword searches that sent traffic through search engines like Google, Yahoo, and Bing. Make sure you click on the "organic" and "paid" links under the chart to separate your non-paid from your PPC traffic. If you're doing organic SEO, looking at non-paid search engine traffic and goal completions/revenue is a key starting place to determine how well you are doing.

Keywords

Search reports include a list of keywords that visitors typed in when they found and clicked on your site. You can view the "Overview" report, or the individual "Organic" and "Paid" reports to see the keywords for that particular source.

One important statistic to track here is the number of unique, organic keywords that are driving traffic to your site. At the bottom of the keyword list, it will say something like "1–10 of 1,613." Pay attention to the "1,613" part—that's the total number of organic keywords driving traffic to your site. The more different keywords that are driving traffic, the more long tail keywords your site is ranking for in the search engines. You may not be able to track the ranks of all of those keywords, but you can track the growth over time of your long tail search traffic.

You can also use the filter box to only show keyphrases that include a certain keyword or keywords. You can also click on "advanced" to bring up the Advanced Filtering options, where you can include or exclude keyphrases containing certain keywords. If you change "Containing" to "Matching RegExp," the filter accepts "Regular Expressions," the easiest of which to use is the pipe (|) character (this stands for "OR" in a list of keywords). So you might filter the list by "discount | cheap" to show all keyphrases that contain the word "discount" OR the word "cheap." Search Google's online Analytics help for "What are regular expressions" to learn more. This is also useful for filtering out (or including only) variations on your company's brand name.

Also note that on each of the above reports, you can click on the "Goal Set" tabs (if you have Goals set up), and/or the "E-commerce" tab (if you have the e-commerce module set up) to get details on how well each of your traffic sources is converting.

If the keywords report is mostly showing your brand name, then you are not doing a good job at SEO. If you are getting traffic from a keyword on page 2 or 3 of the Google search results, imagine how much more traffic you will get when you improve your rank even further! Go after these "striking distance" keywords aggressively.

If you see "(not provided)" those are the keywords searched on when people are logged into Google. Some people have observed 50% of their keyword information to be lost because of this situation. The SEO world is very annoyed with Google's decision to block keyword information from being tracked in this way, and it is only getting worse. Make use of other tools to complement Google Analytics, like Google Webmaster Tools and Alexa.com. Also see Avinash Kaushik's blog post, "Smarter Data Analysis of Google's https Change: 5 steps" on kaushik.net.

Branded versus Non-Branded Phrases

You can set up a report in your analytics that will show you visitors from the search engines to your website using keyphrases that do not contain your brand or company name. You can use this data to see if your site is getting found in the search engines from SEO efforts, as opposed to merely searching for you by name.

Audience

Click on the "Audience" menu in Google Analytics, and then the "Overview" report. This overview shows some important statistics for your site.

Visits

The first is "Visits," which is the number of visits (separate sessions) to your site. This may be the same person visiting twice in two different browser sessions, or it could be two different people. Either one counts as a visit.

Unique Visitors

"Unique Visitors" eliminates those visits that came from a repeat IP address during the selected time period. Both are valuable to track over time.

Keep in mind, if you're comparing calendar months of data, and you get fairly regular daily traffic, shorter months will get less traffic than longer months. Make sure you are comparing the same number of days, or even better, compare that month to the same month from the previous year in order to view year-over-year changes in traffic. This also eliminates any seasonal changes you might have in your business.

% New Visits

What percentage of visitors were "new" as opposed to "returning" visitors. Technically, a "new" visitor is someone who does not already have the Google Analytics tracking cookie for your website in their browser. Visitor tracking cookies have an expiration of two years, so a "new" visitor should be someone who has not visited your site in at least two years. However, if the user deletes cookies from their browser (as people tend to do every so often), or if they are visiting your site on a different device (work computer, mobile phone, etc.), they would be counted as a "new" visitor again the next time they come to your site. This is a good way to measure new versus returning visitors in general, but take these numbers with a grain of salt.

Bounce Rate

The bounce rate shows you how many people landed on a page and then immediately left without viewing another page on your site. Most of the time a bounce is a bad thing, unless a person came for one very specific purpose on that page only (for example, to a "directions" page to get directions to your location). Over time, you should see the number of unique visitors increasing and the bounce rate decreasing. It's difficult to say what a "normal" bounce rate is—there are simply too many factors involved—but some say a good bounce rate is one that is going down. Certainly over 50% is a very bad bounce rate.

Aim to improve your site, make it more relevant to the search terms people use to find your site, and try to get users to take further action on your site through persuasive architecture. These steps will lower your bounce rate by keeping users engaged. It doesn't make sense to spend lots of effort driving traffic to your site, only to let visitors "bounce" and leave your site without seeing all of your content.

Exit Pages

This report is found in the Content menu, under "Site Content" and then "Exit Pages." It gives you a breakdown of the number of exits, pageviews, and the percentage of exits as a percentage of pageviews. An "exit" page is the final page that a visitor sees before leaving your site. Top exit pages are a great place to start optimizing, because they are likely not doing a good job of pushing users through the site. To decrease exit rates, add calls to action and other conversion enhancements, as well as links to content that you want your visitor to find. Many people confuse bounce rates and exit rates. An exit is the last page a user visited, even if they visited other pages prior to the exit page. A bounce is a single-page visit, when someone hits just one page and exits immediately without viewing another page.

Landing Pages

Also found in the "Content" section of Google Analytics, a "landing page" is the first page that a user hits on your site. Make sure the top landing pages offer relevant information and drive users to view additional content or take further action on the site.

In particular, look for landing pages that have a high number of entrances *and* a high bounce rate. Such pages are costing you a lot of visitors, so you should work to lower the bounce rate on these pages. Do this by giving visitors the information they need right away, then sending them to other relevant pages through obvious and well-marked links.

Pageviews

This is the total number of views of a page on your website (in the Audience Overview report, this includes all of the pages on your website). A user visiting the home page and then two other pages would have viewed three pages total, and each page would have one pageview.

Pages/Visit

Pages per visit is the average number of pages each visitor looks at before they move on to another site. It is calculated as the total number of pageviews divided by the total number of visits. Generally, you want to engage visitors and get them to view more than a few pages on your site because deeper engagement equates to better conversion rates and loyalty.

Average Visit Duration

This is the average length of time spent by each visitor on your site. This can be a good measure of how engaging your website is, and if it offers deep content that keeps people on the site. The longer people stay, the more likely you can entice them with an offer, if your website is properly designed.

Frequency and Recency

This set of reports is found in the "Behavior" section of the Audience menu. Frequency (shown in the "count of visits" report) shows how many people visited only once and how many came two or three times or more. If people are coming back often then they are more loyal. Loyalty is good.

Recency, shown in the "Days Since Last Visit" report, shows the gap between visits. Do people come back as often as you publish new content?

Considering people often don't buy on the first visit, you should be tracking their engagement over multiple visits, as they flow through the stages of the buying cycle while eating up your content designed for each stage.

New Visitors versus Returning Visitors

Also in the "Behavior" section (and shown in the Overview report as well), this is the number of new visitors (first-time) versus returning visitors (people who have been to your site before). The "new visitors" percentage is the same as the "% new visits" data listed in the Overview report. If a cookie is not present on the visitor's computer—or they cleared out cookies or are using a different device—they will be shown as a new visitor each time, so don't take this as a perfect metric. It can be useful to look at over time to see if you are gaining a more loyal audience.

In-Page Analytics

In-page analytics shows you visually how users interact with your web pages. It will show you a percentage for every link on your site and, when you mouse over the percentages, the number of people who click on each link. Are users finding what they're looking for or seeing the content you want them to see? This report will help you find places you could improve. You may be quite surprised when you see the links people click and the ones they don't.

Tracking Conversions with Google Analytics

Google Analytics can help you see how well you're doing at converting visitors to leads or sales. Let's take a look at what you can measure and track.

Conversion Rate Calculation

If you have 100 site visitors and one sale or form submission, then you have a 1% conversion rate. You need various goals set up in order to track the conversion rate for things ranging from shopping cart sales to form submissions to how many people downloaded a PDF. You will also want to track your conversion rates from social media versus paid search versus organic search.

Goal Flow and Funnel Visualization

Goal Flow and Funnel Visualization are two of the reports in the "Goals" section of the Conversions menu. The Goal Flow report shows a visual representation of the goal completions and where those converting visitors came from, either by source, keyword, campaign, or other dimension.

The Funnel Visualization report simplifies reviewing a conversion funnel. You can determine at which page people are abandoning their shopping carts, and then use that information to improve the conversion process and save conversions/sales.

Multi-Channel Funnels

The Multi-Channel Funnels reports provide attribution information. When users view your site several times and come from different sources like Twitter, paid ads, organic, or a direct type-in, a conversion has only historically been tracked based on their last most recent click.

Google Analytics now shows every touch point a visitor had with the site in the 30 days prior to conversion. This allows you to give partial credit to a number of channels and therefore make better decisions on how to direct your ad spend. Unfortunately, these reports give you just 30 days of data, but they can help you to determine if, for example, organic search is "assisting" your paid search campaigns or hurting them.

Reverse Goal Path

This is one of my favorite reports. It shows you which pages users visited along the path to conversion, by showing you the pages leading up to a goal completion.

Once you see which pages are proven pathways to success, you can create additional experiences like this on your site.

Conversion Rate by Keyword

When you know which keywords drive visitors who actually convert, you can increase your focus on intensely optimizing your rankings for those keywords. You can also adjust the landing pages that visitors reach from those keywords. So make sure to look at which keywords are driving conversions or, at the very least, which keywords are generating high engagement.

Micro Conversions

Micro conversions are not as big as an actual sale or lead generation from someone filling out a form, but are small wins that you will want to track.

Event Tracking

Events can now be used as goals, so you can track events like PDF downloads and video views without affecting other metrics.

Tracking Video

You can set up reports on how many people watched and interacted with your video content. Interactive events such as pressing the play, pause, and rewind buttons, as well as the time spent watching, can all be tracked.

A Few Miscellaneous Tracking Options

Demographics

Google Analytics lets you see what countries people are coming from to view your site and what languages they speak. If you have sales offices in different countries, you can filter the results to see how many conversions you get from each region.

It's likely just a matter of time before Google Analytics automatically has gender and age from logged in Google+ users. In the meantime (only if you have a very strong business reason, as it may decrease your conversion rate), you can get this data from web forms (by asking visitors to select Mrs. or Mr. or using ServiceObjects.com's DOTS Name Validation service, which determines gender from the first name of users) and potentially from crawling the Facebook Connect social graph.

Comparisons

Google Analytics provides many ways to compare time periods. By comparing current data to the past, you can see how your website's traffic has increased. By looking at only organic traffic referrals, you can see if your search engine optimization efforts are working. You can also track how conversions are improving over time.

Tracking Site Search

If you have an internal search box on your website, perhaps you'd like to know which keywords your website's visitors are typing into that "site search" box. Well, you can get that information, and it's usually very simple to set up using Google Analytics.

The Google Analytics "Site Search" reports can give you lots of very useful information, for example:

- What products/services users are searching for (you may need additional calls to action for popular products or services)

- Whether or not users found what they were looking for (through engagement metrics like time on site, etc.)

- Searches for products or services that you don't have content for (but should)

- What questions users have (which you could answer on a page or in a blog post)

You can use the information that you gather to help you design appropriate calls to action or develop new content. Using your own visitors to give you input on what topics to write about on your site means you're more likely to rank highly in the search engine results for those keywords.

Campaign Tracking

Links from banners on other websites, pay-per-click advertising, social media updates, or email campaigns can all be tracked by tagging so that you can measure which of these are creating engagement back at your own site.

Real-Time Data

Google Analytics now offers real-time data. You can view activity on the site as it happens, and drill into the top active pages, top referrals, keywords, and geographic locations driving the traffic.

Site Speed

Found in the "Content" menu, the Site Speed reports give you average page load time. A slow site speed hurts you in organic rankings and paid search. Did you know that a one-second delay can result in a 7% decrease in conversions? Monitor your site speed like a hawk, as it has grown in importance, due in part to slow mobile browsing and huge mobile visitor volume.

Webmaster Tools

Some Google Webmaster Tools data is now incorporated into Google Analytics. These reports are found in the "Traffic Sources" menu under "Search Engine Optimization," and require you to link your data with your Webmaster Tools account. You will see three data sets in Google Analytics:

Queries

Here you can see some of the keywords that might be hidden (not provided) in the standard Analytics reports.

Landing Pages

You can see what Google Webmaster Tools sees as your top pages sorted by impressions, along with click-through rates.

Geographical Summary

Looking at specific countries, you can see how it might be worth doing some international SEO.

You can also get a better sense of which Google property (web, image, or local) sent visitors to you. Webmaster Tools provides impressions, average position, and click-through-rate data.

Secondary Dimensions and Table Filters

In each standard table report in Google Analytics, you can add a second dimension to deepen your reporting. Say you are looking at a keywords report (the first dimension); you can see each keyword's landing page by using the second-dimension drop-down menu within the report table. You won't have to leave the report or switch between reports to view this additional information, which is very convenient.

Pivot tables are extremely powerful data summarization tools and are commonly used in spreadsheet programs like Microsoft Excel.

With pivoting, you can add a couple of additional dimensions to view your metrics by, and when you couple pivoting with secondary dimensions you'll get a total of five different data points to look at simultaneously (Percentage, Performance, Comparison, Term Cloud, and Pivot).

You can further enhance your reporting view with the pivoting view, which is the very last view option, available on the top right of each report table.

Advanced Segments

One feature of Google Analytics that beginners often overlook (maybe because Google doesn't make it very obvious) is Advanced Segments. On any of the report screens, including the dashboard, an Advanced Segments link appears directly below the report heading.

By default, Advanced Segments is set to show "All Visits." By selecting from the drop-down menu, however, you can filter the traffic that is used in the selected report to show only traffic from a particular segment—New Visitors, Returning Visitors, Paid Search Traffic, Non-paid Search Traffic, Search Traffic (total), Direct Traffic, Referral Traffic, Visits with Conversions, Visits with Transactions, Mobile Traffic, and Non-bounce Visits.

This feature can be very helpful, because it allows you to quickly and easily narrow down the traffic to just those visits that you want to view statistics for at that time. Want to see your most viewed pages, but only for organic traffic? Go to the "Site Content" report, and select the "Non-paid Search Traffic" segment.

Selecting two or more segments at a time will show you the data from each segment separately, but within the same report (Google Analytics will even graph the data with differently colored lines to help you visualize the data). This is useful for comparisons—for example, if you want to compare New versus Returning Visitors, or Paid versus Non-Paid Search Traffic, or even compare them to only Visits with Conversions.

Social Engagement

Use Google Analytics to track how visitors interact socially with your site. Make sure to check out how much interaction is happening from users on mobile devices as the numbers will likely surprise you and encourage you to better your site's mobile experience.

Google Analytics' new social reports (found under "Traffic Sources") break down how many of a site's visitors are socially engaged with the site, and show you how many of your visitors +1'd site content versus how many "liked" it, as well as the pages that caused these social interactions. Social plug-ins like ShareThis integrate easily with Google Analytics, and pass social interactions back into the program.

At the very least, look at the following (Amount of visits | Pages/Visit | Avg. Time on site | % New Visits | Bounce Rate) for Google +1, Facebook likes/referrals, Tweets, etc.

Since social media is so hot, let's dive a little deeper into what you should be tracking and thinking about regarding social media and ROI.

First of all, be aware that there is more to ROI tracking than just tracking hard sales. Social media has many other benefits you should take into consideration.

Below are the four key social media metrics to track as outlined by Avinash Kaushik on kaushik.net.

1. Conversation Rate
2. Amplification Rate
3. Applause Rate
4. Economic Value

Let's break each of them down.

Conversation Rate

On Google+, Facebook, your blog, etc., how many user comments are your posts generating?

What things spark more conversations?

Track the number of comments per social interaction such as a Tweet, Facebook post, picture on Flickr, video on YouTube, or a pin to Pinterest.

Amplification Rate

How much of a ripple effect do you get from the followers of your followers?

- In Google+ there is a way to track this (right click and view Ripples).

- On Twitter, look at the number of retweets.

- Look for "shares" when posting on Facebook or Google+.

- On YouTube, it is the share of clicks per post or video.

Facebook Insights tracks this through something called virality.

In your blog, it is shares of posts on LinkedIn and retweets, etc.

YouTube Insights community engagement shows how many times viewers rate, favorite, or comment on your videos.

Your job is to figure out which types of content increase the number of times users "forward" your content, and create more of that.

Applause Rate

This is a measure of how relevant and valuable users think your content is. If you do too much "me, me, me" and sharing of your brochures, few people will applaud you. Below is a list of how to track a "thumbs-up" in different channels.

- Twitter: Number of favorites

- Facebook: Number of clicks on "like" button per post and their names

- Google+: Number of +1s per post

- YouTube: Number of likes per video

- Blog: Number of likes, +1s, etc.

Applause helps with SEO, because your brand's content is being shared and then linked to. These may be intangibles in terms of immediate hard cash, but these activities spread good brand energy and result in more traffic through the sharing/backlinks and the new SEO rankings.

Not only will all of this make more people aware of you, but if done right, those people may now trust you more. The old-school brand value of an expensive TV ad is being tested now that social media is proving that interacting with customers can cost less and have a stronger long-term effect.

Economic Value

If you can't show any economic value for your social media efforts, your board members or managers will likely neither fall in love with social media marketing nor increase your social media budget. Make sure that you don't expect the same hard ROI as you get from SEO or paid search, because social tends to produce more early-stage-of-the-buying-cycle traffic.

Actual Sales and Leads

You can track the number of clicks sent to you from each social media site. You can also track things like the pages people read when they get to your site, how long they stay, what they purchase or if they fill out a request form, etc. So by all means track some amount of actual conversions but also track and think about the other softer engagement factors as well.

Costs Avoided

Each click has a value, considering you would have to pay for it some other way, like a paid ad. If users all bail out after clicking from a social media site to your site, then you need to address the value of your current clicks and content.

Even if people don't stay long on your site when coming from a social click, bloggers, journalists, and other site owners may be linking to you and bookmarking you via social interaction. This can help to reduce your PR and ad spends.

If you gain a strong presence in social media, it can build your brand equity—especially if you capture the email addresses of new customers brought in from social channels and continue to engage them and track their lifelong value.

Calculating Social Media ROI

ROI = (Gain from Investment - Cost of Investment) Cost of Investment

Here are the two main types of impact from social media marketing:

1. Revenue

2. Costs avoided

If you can tie anything that leads to either of these to an action, it can be factored into your ROI.

Before calculating your social media ROI, you need to map what your goals are and what value you assign to such items as:

- Sales

- Advertising – visibility/trafficPR – press stories driven from blog content

- Word-of-mouth – referring posts on other medium- to high-profile blogs

- Research – customer insightsRegistrations

- Referrals

- Links

- Votes

- Reduction in costs

- Decrease in customer issues

- Lead generation

- Reduced sales cycles

- Employment applications

- Speaking invitations

- Store visits

- Coupons redeemed

- Email newsletter sign-ups

I highly recommend that you put an actual monetary value on things like capturing an email address or views of a white paper, so that you can feed some financial data from goal completions into Google Analytics.

You also need to track how many of each of the above items you are getting *before* the campaign begins, and how much it will cost to set up your social media campaigns. For example, if you make $4 per year from any given person on your email list, then you have a baseline you can use to judge the value of new email addresses that social media brings in (assuming they convert at the same rate as your main list).

Social Media Costs to Document

- Social media program setup

- Ongoing maintenance and training

- Content production, including employee time

Business Calculations

- What is the lifetime value of a customer?

- What does an average lead cost in any other medium?

- What do you make, on average, per customer?

- What are your calls to action?

It's important to document all interactions with customers from form registrations and white paper downloads to webinar attendance and Facebook/Twitter interactions. Make note of each of the various levels of contact in the path to a completed sale. That is the only way you can really get a full picture of which campaigns are assisting and/or closing sales.

Below are some calculations courtesy of my friend Paul Gillin, who is a highly regarded social media marketing author. This should help you think about how to value different items and the long-term value of each customer. More details are available in *Social Marketing to the Business Customer* by Paul Gillin and Eric Schwartzman (John Wiley & Sons, 2011).

Calculating the Lifetime Value of a Customer

1. Typical customer spends $10,000 a year with you

2. He/she is with you for five years

3. Your profit margin is 10%

4. Lifetime value of a typical customer is:

($10,000 × 5) × .10 = $5,000

Value of a Visitor

Let's assume you have 10,000 visitors per month, converting to customers at the rate of .5%, and the lifetime value of a customer is $5,000 (as established in the previous example). Calculate the total value of business that one month of visits can be expected to generate as follows:

(10,000 × .005 × $5,000) = $250,000

To calculate the value of a visitor: ($250,000 10,000) = $25

Monthly visitors	Conversion rate (.5% or 5/1000ths)	Lifetime value of a customer	Calculate (10,000 x .005 x $5,000). This is the total value of business that one month of visits can be expected to generate.	Divide by total monthly visitors	Calculate value of a visitor ($250,000 10,000)
10,000	.005	$5,000	$250,000	10,000	$25

Value of a Blog

Let's say you want to start a blog with the expectation that it will increase monthly visits by 1,000 over the current level of 3,000. Let's further assume that you budget $6,000 per month to maintain the blog. Here's how you can calculate return:

- Monthly Visits from Search: 3,000

- Estimated Visits with Blog: 4,000

- Value of a Visitor: $25

- Monthly Value of a Blog: $25,000

- Monthly Blog Expense: $6,000

ROI $25,000 - $6000 $6,000 = 316%

Value of a Tweet

- You send 50 tweets a month

- Your tweets generate 1,000 visitors to your website

- 2% become leads

- 5% of those become customers

- The lifetime value of a customer is $5,000

Therefore the value of a tweet is:

$(1,000 \times .02 \times .05 \times \$5,000)\ 50 = \$100$

Conversion Rate and Its Impact on ROI

Driving thousands of people to a terrible website through search and social is useless, because those people aren't going to convert and you won't get the full benefit of your SEO or social media optimization. A site with a 3% conversion rate versus a 1% conversion rate would have seen a greater return of real dollars. So when looking at how effective your campaigns are, don't just look for immediate ROI from social media or, worse, just give up. You must also fix the issues that cause your website to drop the ball after the leads come into the funnel. You must nurture those leads, follow up, and make sure to close deals.

The bottom line is this: to calculate ROI, you need very deep analytics and CRM tools that let you understand what customers are doing over the time that elapses before a sale happens.

Salesforce Integration with Forms and Social Media

Smart new marketers are tying Salesforce into all "touches on the website," such as if someone subscribes to an email newsletter, makes a comment, downloads a white paper, visits Facebook, and then buys. All this can be stored in Salesforce to map the sales process and factors that assisted in sales. Again, HubSpot, which is partially owned by both Salesforce and Google, makes this integration and lead nurturing *much* easier.

Success and Analytics

Analytics tools are simply amazing, but they are only tools. If you really want greater ROI for search and social media marketing, you must increase your efforts in the realm of analytics. By knowing what customers do or don't do, and which pages drive more engaged visitors, you can adjust the site to deepen engagement and put more money into the tactics that generate the most sales.

Chapter 12

Dramatically Increase Sales with Conversion Rate Optimization

Driving traffic to your website is a good start, but it's not enough. Your potential customers are overwhelmed with advertising messages and have endless options at the click of a mouse. If you want to truly get more leads and turn them into sales, you must actively work on increasing your conversion rate (the ratio of leads or sales to the number of visitors). By piquing their interest and then leading them on a journey that lets *them* feel in control, you can guide your website visitors along the path to conversion.

In the old days of advertising and marketing, there was little proof of what tactic worked. It was harder to demonstrate cause and effect, by linking a particular ad campaign to a specific set of sales results. Now, with deep website analytics tracking, we can discover which tactics drove sales and which ones assisted in sales, making it easier for companies to confidently increase their marketing budgets in the right places.

Set Up Tracking Systems

In order to have a reasonably complete sense of what is generating sales and leads, you must have multiple forms of tracking in place. These include:

- Tracking of unique phone number(s) on your website (ones that are not shared with customers anywhere else)

- Form submissions

- Shopping cart sales

- Live chat interactions

- Email address clicks

- Printable/PDF application document downloads

- Printable coupon/specials downloads

- Third-party applications (i.e., mortgage applications submitted through a partner website, not on your main URL)Off-line conversion tracking

- Attribution tracking/conversion assists

See the analytics chapter (Chapter 11) for more details on each of these things to track. Once your tracking is in place, you can focus on increasing your conversion rate.

How to Calculate Conversion Rates

If you have one hundred site visitors and one sale you have a 1% conversion rate.

This is a simple formula:

Total Conversions ÷ Total Views ×100 = Conversion Rate

Here are some examples of how you could compute conversion rates for different scenarios and transaction types:

Landing Page Conversion Rate

Number of Lead Forms Filled Out ÷ Traffic on Landing Page × 100 = Conversion Rate

Website Lead Conversion Rate

Number of Lead Forms Filled Out ÷ Total Traffic on Home Page × 100 = Conversion Rate

Shopping Cart Sales Conversion Rate

Number of Sales ÷ Number of Visitors × 100 = Conversion Rate

Conversion optimization is all about increasing the percentage of visitors that "convert" into buyers. When you look at your conversion rate on a monthly basis and carefully test key elements to make your site more persuasive, you will be amazed by how much more ROI you can achieve from the same amount of traffic.

Conversion Optimization Benefits

If you optimize your conversion rates, here are the potential benefits you can realize:

- Increase sales

- Decrease customer acquisition costs

- Decrease click costs

- Decrease bounce rates

- Recover lost leads and/or reduce shopping cart abandonment (when people click away from your site without purchasing the items they've placed in the online shopping cart)

- Cross-merchandising to increase average order size and units per sale

- Segment and optimize conversion funnels by campaign type, demographic, traffic, and purchasing habits

- Increase repeat purchases, visitor frequency, and customer loyalty

Scientific Intuition (My term for combining art and science)

Listening to your gut is not always the best idea, but it is actually a good place to start. There is nothing worse than launching a new website that you love and your customers hate, so you can't stop there. In order to make the most money online, you need to leverage scientific testing tools like Visual Website Optimizer in combination with the creative process, to find the best solutions for high ROI. You need to fuse the power of the creative team with the rational energy of scientists.

Google has discontinued Google Website Optimizer for multivariate testing, so I recommend using the more feature-rich and very popular Visual Website Optimizer, especially if you want to engage in multivariate testing.

As you complete tests that prove statistically which creative elements (such as headlines, offers, etc.) get more leads/sales, put new tests in place right away for continuous improvement. There should be no damage to creative egos because in the end, the test that won should stay as the "live" creative, not the things the boss or the art director likes.

Planning a Conversion Strategy

To get the most out of your conversion efforts, you need to have an organized strategy that aligns with your company's business goals.

The role of a conversion optimization plan is to identify and prioritize all web page test opportunities and ensure:

- Business goal alignment

- Brand alignment

- Rigorous review of web analytics insights

- All traffic-driving methods in sync with the plan

- Alignment of offers and calls to action with the plan

- Traffic volumes significant enough for recommended tests

- Testing and measurement tools in place

With this strategic process in place, you can manage the campaign and align it with your goals and brand, all while delivering strong ROI.

Here's an example of how a bank might set up goals, key performance indicators (KPI), and a strategy and hypothesis to test.

The Business Goal: Our primary goal is to make the personal banking section more engaging and in line with the *"Bank Local. Bank Smart."* tagline. By doing so, we hope to achieve a greater number of conversions.

Our Main Key Performance Indicator or KPI: Is an increased conversion rate of leads from the various services/sign-ups from the personal banking section.

Strategy/Hypothesis: Initially through a reworking of the existing web page layout and by using more persuasive copy and images, we hope to make the personal banking section convert better quickly.

Long-term: The lack of content supporting the "Bank Smart" theme is a serious conversion issue. Customers are used to websites with better content.

Prioritize and Know What to Test for the Biggest Impact

In order to properly prioritize what to test, at McDougall Interactive we use a system we learned from Bryan Eisenberg, who wrote the book *Always Be Testing*.

Consider the following three factors when determining what to test:

Time

Impact

Resources

Then calculate on a scale of 1 to 5 what level of time, impact, or resources each test would take, with 5 being the best and 1 being the worst.

Here are some examples:

Test redoing the website navigation

> **Time 2** (It will take quite a bit of time)
>
> **Impact 5** (It will have a strong impact)
>
> **Resources 2** (It will require lots of resources)
>
> 2 x 5 is 10 x 2 is a total score of 20

Change the headline from features to benefits

> **Time 5** (It will take a small amount of time)
>
> **Impact 5** (It will have a strong impact)
>
> **Resources 5** (It will require very little resources)
>
> 5 x 5 is 25 x 5 is a total score of 125 or the best possible score

You can see from this example that it is possible to prioritize nicely. You just need to list all the things you want to test in a spreadsheet and then do the math. If you have 100 test options, you can boil it down to a schedule of testing at least several per month (top companies do dozens of tests a month or more) and come up with a six-month testing calendar.

Before digging into specific tactics and how they fit together, it's important to understand some key concepts of conversion science.

Your conversion rate hinges on the following three main factors, or the **Conversion Trinity:**

Relevance: Does your content closely match what the visitor expects to see?

Value: How clear is your unique value proposition and how quickly and consistently is it communicated to visitors?

Call to Action: How obvious is your main call to action?

If we do nothing else, we need to properly address these three critical factors in alignment with your business goals.

Personas

Another important concept for you to understand is that of personas (types of people who may be visiting your site), since they are at the heart of most conversion methodologies.

In 325 BC, Aristotle wrote of the hedonic, proprietary, dialectical, and ethical temperaments, so this concept is not new. Books, movies, and TV shows can often be good examples of showcasing multiple character types to make an interesting story that connects with many types of people.

The four main personas used in many conversion marketing programs and their attributes are below.

Competitive

Attitude: Business-like and power-oriented

Time: Disciplined and fast-paced

Requirements: Your qualifications, records, and values

Weakness: Documented evidence stressing results. As explained in Bryan Eisenberg's book, weakness refers to the things that will make this persona convert, by appealing to their weakness.

How to Present: What you can do for them

Problem Solving: Support ideas and conclusions

Facilitate Decisions: Provide options, probabilities, and challenges

Spontaneous/Amiable

Attitude: Personal and activity-oriented

Time: Undisciplined and fast-paced

Requirements: Evidence that you are trustworthy and friendly

Weakness: Show personal attention and interest

How to Present: Why you are the best solution

Problem Solving: Support their feelings, interests, and excitement

Facilitate Decisions: Provide guarantees and opinions, not options

Humanistic/Expressive

Attitude: Personal and relationship-oriented

Time: Undisciplined and slow-paced

Requirements: Who you are, what you think, and who you know

Weakness: Give recognition and approval

How to Present: WHO you have provided solutions to

Problem Solving: Support their ideas, intuitions, your relationship

Facilitate Decisions: Offer testimony and incentives

Methodical

Attitude: Businesslike and detail-oriented

Time: Disciplined and slow-paced

Requirements: Evidence of your experience and knowledge

Weakness: Documented evidence and preparation

How to Present: How you can provide a solution

Problem Solving: Support their principles and rational approach

Facilitate Decisions: Provide evidence and service

Eye-tracking studies have shown that users can be broken into four groups in terms of web surfing patterns that map to the personas above.

Have "Something for Everyone"

A simple way to grasp this concept is to think of the cast of "Star Trek." It is clear that each of the personas represented by the main characters approaches the world differently. So whether your site is visited by someone like Captain Kirk or someone like Spock, make it rock! Imagine the impulsive Captain Kirk surfing just the top of your site just looking for proof you are in the news, while the methodical and logical Mr. Spock visits every page, and even the bottom of every page, looking for charts and graphs.

If your site is really appealing to methodical engineers but unappealing to spontaneous moms, competitive CEO dads, and humanistic types who require knowing more about who you are and who you have served, you will have received conversions from only 25% of the potential audience. That means you've left 75% of the money you could have generated on the table!

Customer Personas

Below are some personas our agency developed to help us think about what "supermarket aisles" we needed to create on our website and how to write specifically to the needs of different groups.

1. **Business Owner Bob** (Older Type A, alpha, looking for proof, case studies, news, ROI)

2. **Marketing Sally** (Marketing coordinator, intermediate knowledge, good with details)

3. **Enterprise Erin** (Senior marketing director with advanced knowledge in traditional marketing)

4. **Small Biz Tim** (DIY type)

5. **IT Scotty** (Tech guy asked to review our site or looking for referrals, requires geek-level details)

6. **Ad Agency Jim** (Not looking to hire us for himself but for his clients; appreciates or requires creativity, talent)

Another way to categorize potential visitors is by company size:

1. **Small Business** (Looking for how to/DIY info, cheap price, free, extras)

2. **Large Business** (Senior marketing director looking for budget calculator, trends)

You might also categorize them by job type:

1. **I work at an agency**

2. **I am an in-house marketer**

3. **I am a business owner**

General website user personas are:

- **Searcher** (Looking for knowledge about a product or company, etc.)

- **Doubter** (Still forming an opinion)

- **Knower** (Wants to take an action)

- **Customer** (Looking for service/support or to login, etc.)

There are many ways to break visitors into groups. It takes creativity and brainstorming to do it well, but in the end your customers will enjoy your site more if they feel like some of the content is specifically for them. Many studies have shown significantly increased conversion rates when personas are considered when writing content for a website.

Example: Create a Persona

You can use a basic template like this to get the ball rolling when creating personas for your website.

Persona #1

Name: Business Owner Bob

Insert an image here to make it more visual
(this helps writers to write to someone specific)

Age: 40–70

Gender: Male

Job title: President

Daily routines: Numerous meetings, dealing with vendors, putting out fires, reviewing the numbers, travel.

Pain points: Never enough time in the day

Goals: Grow the business, keep customers and employees happy.

What they value: People who work hard and who are honest.

Favorite sources of info: Still may read the paper but more and more online. Traditional nightly news.

What experience are they looking for? Exceptional organization, professional, high ROI.

Site usage: In and out just to verify we are the real deal.

Content: Report on where Internet marketing is headed. News, case studies, testimonials.

Common objections to your product or service: Don't want mindless reports but clear action steps. Need to prove ROI. Too time-consuming to work with us.

Level of technical knowledge: Reasonable but often think they know more than they do about sites. They think all users will like what they like and their pitch.

Brands they identify with: BMW, Mercedes

Persuasion Architecture

The Persuasion Architecture method of creating personas was developed by Bryan and Jeffrey Eisenberg of Market Motive, and is based on the Myers/Briggs behavioral studies adapted by David Keirsey in the 1950s.

The four primary temperaments defined by Keirsey:

Sensing/Judging (SJ)

Sensing/Perceiving (SP)

Intuitive/Feeling (NF)

Intuitive/Thinking (NT)

The temperaments were renamed by Bryan Eisenberg to be more intuitive to use:

Methodical (SJ)

Spontaneous (SP)

Humanistic (NF)

Competitive (NT)

There are numerous sites where you can take a free Keirsey Temperament Sorter test, and the results are often eye-opening.

Design for all four temperaments by adding things that entice each user type (persona) and then use analytics to track which ones are dominant in terms of being the most common visitors to your site.

For example, try using hyperlinks with varied persona-enticing copy:

Methodical: Click here to see a list of the benefits of our diet plan and a <u>timeline of expected weight loss with documented case studies</u>.

Spontaneous: Try our diet plan today and <u>start feeling great right away</u>.

Humanistic: Read <u>testimonials of recent customers</u> who have worked directly with our award-winning founder <u>Joe Trainer</u>.

Competitive: Read our comparison chart that shows <u>how we stack up against the competition</u>.

Some people will be very interested in details, facts, and figures, while others will be influenced by eye-catching pictures that make them spontaneously react. Different personas require different web design elements and types of copy to be persuaded to follow through.

You also need to be aware that there are various stages of the buying cycle.

Stages of the buying cycle:

1. Problem Recognition
2. Informational Search
3. Evaluation of Alternatives
4. Purchase Decision
5. Purchase Completion
6. Problem Solved?

Sellers follow a different process:

1. Prospect for needs/desires

2. Establish rapport

3. Qualify the need/buyers

4. Present to the qualified needs/desires

5. Close on satisfying the needs/desires

Once you understand some of the above ways of mapping out your marketing actions to make them more successful, you can dive into making site adjustments and know your efforts are rooted in strategic thinking.

Ask these questions when mapping out your site conversion architecture:

What is the primary objective of the home page?

What is the most visible call to action on the home page?

Do you have a call to action for the top, middle, and bottom of the marketing funnel?

Is the most visible action on the home page the most important?

How does it create the following?

• Attention (colors, size, font)

• Interest (words and selling points)

• Desire (how it will make them feel)

• Action (verbiage should use trigger words and have credibility/security)

How does your website address each of these stages of the buying cycle in terms of content?

1. Problem Recognition (Can they find you easily?)

2. Informational Search (Do you have general information about your products that helps them become educated?)

3. Evaluation of Alternatives (Do you have comparisons of your products or services and your competitors' so they don't have to leave the site to go find it?)

4. Purchase Decision (Do you make it easy to find the call to action when they have decided to buy?)

5. Purchase Completion (Is it easy to complete the purchase?)

6. Problem Solved? (Will they have buyer's remorse or will they feel satisfied?)

Who is your audience?

What motivates your customers?

Does your home page talk more about you and your features rather than what is in it for the customer and what the benefits are? (If you answer "yes," rewrite your copy to focus more on benefits.)

What actions do you need customers to take?

What information do they need in order to feel confident taking action? Consider using some of the following.

- Your years of experience

- Awards

- Case studies

- Testimonials

- Comparisons to others

- Guarantees

- Privacy policy

- More info about the company

- A photo of your warehouse

- Photos of your team

- Free shipping

- Guaranteed shipping in 24 hours

What are your hot selling points when you close a deal off-line?

What are the top three categories, services, or product pages on your site? (Use this same list of questions on each of these pages.)

Is your price conducive to conversions?

Without the right price, conversions will be low. You have to be sure your price matches your brand and has a unique selling position in relationship to other offers people will find online. Sometimes sites with an incredible amount of traffic get no sales and others have incredible conversions based on the price or simply the perception of value.

Trigger Words

Use trigger words, action words, and/or inspiring words: the right emotional triggers take the same basic message to a new level. The best words to use are the ones that the searcher used to find you. If they searched using a keyword phrase like "buy Taylormade golf clubs," then it should say "Buy Taylormade golf clubs" on your website. The more your headlines and website copy match what the user is looking for *exactly*, the more likely it is they will convert. That is called "matching scent" (keeping the trail of thought that the user was on already). Get into the mindset of looking for what are considered "buyer" keywords, as these are the golden nuggets.

Good choices when you're considering trigger words are phrases that inspire action, like "buy now" and "register today for 50% off." Action words get people thinking about doing something, and when phrased correctly, move them to do it in the short term, i.e., now. Inspiring words are the trigger words that give people confidence that your brand or product is trustworthy and going to deliver on its promises. Inspiring words to include in your web copy might be:

> Acclaimed, Authentic, Award-Winning, Bargain, Bonuses, Boost, Certified, Completely Confidential, Convenience, Copyrighted, Custom, Cutting-Edge, Cut Costs, Desirable, Enticing, Essential, Exceptional, Foolproof, Free, Free Gift, Fully Automated, High Demand, High Quality, Highly Regarded, Hot Product, In Demand, Jam-Packed, Licensed, Lifetime, Limited Time, Luxurious, Most Advanced, Most Trusted, Necessity, New Release, One of a Kind, Only (#) Left, Only (#) Made, Priceless, Quality, Rare Opportunity, Secure Investment, Special Edition, Time-Saving, Top-Rated, Unique, Valuable, Wise Investment

Design Matters

Your site and user experience design matters in terms of conversions and also to the search engines as well.

If your visitors have a hard time finding their way around your site, you will lose them. Having your logo on the top left of the page, along with easy-to-follow navigation and a clear site hierarchy (good organization), is paramount when trying to keep people from leaving your site. During your website redesign, review the pages people visit most and find a way to make it easy to get at that same information in your new design.

Using a wireframe (a simple black and white graphic that can be hand drawn or done with a tool like balsamiq.com and that shows where items will be placed before doing an actual design) is a great way to make sure you have all your conversion items mapped out properly BEFORE the designer gets into creative mode (see Figure 6).

Increasing the rate at which users act on your campaign is simple. You need to *tell* them what to do, by effectively incorporating a clear call to action in your website design! That means first going above

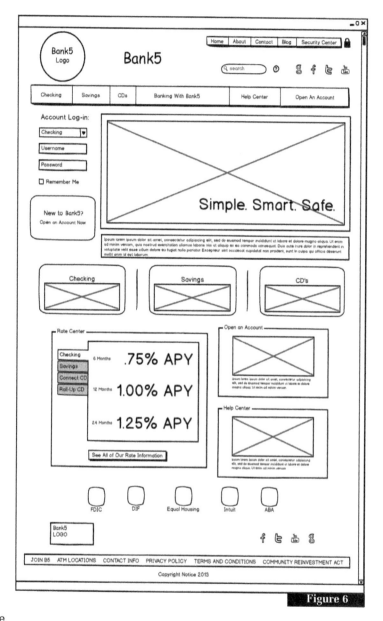

Figure 6

and beyond the usual "Submit" and "Click Here" buttons; instead, using icons and one-liners that really grab visitors' attention will do much more to inspire them to act. Then there's compelling copy that includes those trigger words and calls to action. When appropriate, keep in mind that better product photos are worth a thousand calls to action.

10 Examples of Calls to Action

1. Buy Now

2. Add to cart

3. Download 11 steps to improving your golf game

4. Use our online calculator to see how much you save

5. Register today to change your life in seven days

6. Free Newsletter Signup

7. Call now for a free consultation

8. Watch our video on how to organize your office space

9. Learn how to choose the perfect engagement ring

10. Read our hotels.com case study

11 Examples of Credibility Factors

1. Being in the news

2. Lists of important clients

3. Testimonials

4. A powerful "about us" page

5. Member of local or regional chamber of commerce

6. Photo of your business

7. Photo of your team

8. A photo of your warehouse

9. Awards

10. Case studies

11. Years in business or experience

5 Points of Assurance

1. Guarantees (service or product)

2. Your privacy policy

3. Shipping within a set timeframe

4. Secure shopping cart

5. Website identity validation

Reduce anxiety, hesitation, and friction by keeping a consistent information scent. Don't keep users in the dark on anything, including shipping, taxes, and returns—especially if you led them in with those. Let them know you are there for them and that customer service representatives are standing by via phone and/or chat. Customer service contact information should be featured prominently near shopping cart buttons.

Long-term, you should analyze your site against the 30 main factors that influence conversion. These are listed below and are from the book *Always Be Testing* by Bryan Eisenberg.

1. Addressing the four main personas or people types for greater conversions

2. Unique value proposition

3. Buying decision process

4. Categorization

5. Usability

6. Look and feel

7. Searchability (use of navigation and the ability to find things on the site)

8. Layout, visual clarity, and eye tracking (using tools like Feng-gui.com)

9. Purchasing process

10. Tools that can get in the way and tools (like ClickTale.com and usertesting.com) that can help

11. Error prevention

12. Browser compatibility

13. Product presentation

14. Load time

15. AIDAS or Creating Attention, Interest, Desire, Action, Satisfaction

16. Security/privacy

17. Trust and credibility

18. Product selection/categorization/search results

19. Navigation/use of links

20. Up-sell/cross-sell

21. Calls to action

22. Point-of-action assurances

23. Persuasive copywriting

24. Content

25. Headlines

26. Readability

27. Use of color and images

28. Overuse of industry terminology/jargon

29. Customer-focused language vs. "me me/we we"-focused language

30. Using reviews

Web Marketing On All Cylinders - John McDougall

Website Conversion Optimization Basics

For every $92 spent driving traffic to websites, only $1 is spent converting visitors. This is a huge oversight and as click costs skyrocket and SEO gets harder, people will slowly realize conversion optimization is an essential part of any Internet marketing strategy.

Start with your specific business goals and then apply calls to action to your website that move people toward the goals you have set. Then you can figure out what your conversion rate is and make plans to improve it.

No discussion of conversion optimization would be complete without a shout-out to the amazing Dr. Robert Cialdini, whose principles can be used to influence people in your marketing.

6 Key Principles of Persuasion by Robert Cialdini
(from his book, *Influence: The Psychology of Persuasion*)

- **Reciprocity** - People tend to return a favor, this is why you see so many free samples in marketing.

- **Commitment and Consistency** - If people commit, orally or in writing, to an idea or goal, they are more likely to honor that commitment because of establishing that idea or goal as being congruent with their self-image.

- **Social Proof** - People will do things that they see other people are doing. This is why McDonald's says over "one billion served."

- **Authority** - People tend to obey authority figures, even if they are asked to do bad things.

- **Liking** - People are easily persuaded by other people that they like. They also buy from you more because if you like them, they figure you will treat them well and "have their back."

- **Scarcity** - Perceived scarcity will generate demand. For example, saying specials are available for a "limited time only" encourages sales.

Keep these principles in mind as you decide which tests to perform. Following these principles can greatly increase conversions.

Now that you have some background on conversion rate optimization, let's dig into some practical things that you can test on your website to see if you can increase sales.

16 Key Items to Test to Improve Conversion Rates

1. **Unique value proposition:** If people don't understand immediately why you are better than the other dozen sites they are kicking the tires of, you won't stand a chance. Test adding mini summarizing statements that express your unique value.

2. **Headlines:** Sometimes changing the wording of a heading even a tiny bit can have an incredible impact on conversions, but you won't know unless you test. Test emotional versus logical headlines and use things like free offers, guarantees, and things that express your unique value proposition. Test headlines that express benefits instead of features.

3. **Calls to action:** Try testing different button colors/sizes/text/shapes. Try different call to action copy such as "Free Quote in 1 Hour Guaranteed," instead of "Fill out this form to get a quote."

4. **Trust and credibility:** Make sure to use things like testimonials, "in the news" mentions, company photos and bios, enhanced "about us" pages, company video, awards, affiliations, and certifications.

5. **"About us" pages:** Make them more personal, less "what you do," more "who you are."

6. **Address more than one persona:** Have content for different types of people.

   Do you address each of the four modalities' needs and in this order down the page?

   Competitive (Proof and business power at top, show what we can do)

   Spontaneous (Personal attention and instant gratification, show how we are the best)

   Humanistic (Who will be affected, reviews, testimonials, who we helped, relationships, family)

   Methodical (Cold hard facts, specifications, features, details, documented evidence)

   Snapshot of possible bank website content per persona as an example:

   Competitive: Boston's best bank, according to industry newspaper *XYZ*. (PR "above the fold.")

   Spontaneous: Interactive poll, survey, widgets, video where users are asked to comment/engage.

Humanistic: Video and text testimonials, more personal "about us" page.

Methodical: Steps in the process of choosing a bank/checking account. Comparison chart of competitors' options.

Ask yourself what content you like most but might be missing for people who are different from you!

7. **Maintain scent:** Make sure that whatever you promised the customer (often in showing them exact keywords) is consistently reinforced in text and visually, from the initial ad copy or banner to the landing page and then through the "check out" process.

8. **Layout, visual clarity, and eye tracking:** A high-quality look and feel can be a major contributor to your success online. Use tools like ClickTale, Feng-gui, and usertesting.com to see what people react to, where they click and scroll, and where their eyes are focused when they look at your web pages. Then test making changes that improve the page based on the results and run these tools again.

9. **Use of color and images:** Create images that connect emotionally. Be aware of what colors mean. Red is a warning sign, for example. Be careful what you do with this color and test alternatives to it unless you do want people to be warned or stop. Try making your main call to action button stick out more than others on your site through the use of contrasting colors. Orange is popular for button text because it stands out almost as much as red, but does not indicate a warning.

10. **Point-of-action assurances:** Place things like links to your privacy policy, security icons, and guarantees near calls to action or buy/submit buttons.

11. **Persuasive copywriting:** Test using more emotional copy with active verbs that entice the reader. Focus more on benefits than on features. Make it less about you and more about them. Speak in the customer's language, such as "You are looking for xyz." For more ideas on this, see futurenowinc.com/wewe.htm.

12. **Readability:** Test lowering the grade level of the reading to reach more people. Average web users are said to have less than high school-level reading abilities. Reduce excess industry terminology and jargon.

13. **Use reviews and test where the reviews are placed:** Reviews leverage the power of the social web. Users no longer want to be bombarded with obvious marketing messages but want to engage in a dialogue about products and services.

14. **Rearrange the order of your copy:** Sometimes your best paragraph is your last one and it is "below the fold." Try switching things up to put your most compelling copy first. Test adding your most factual, detailed, feature-oriented, cold hard facts information at the bottom of the page, since methodical people who will appreciate it may be the only people that scroll that far down the page.

15. **Usability:** Try three usertesting.com videos to see what issues people have with your site and test new alternative navigation and layout options.

16. **Load time:** How many times have you impatiently bailed out on a site when it loaded too slowly? A slow-loading site not only impacts your conversion rate, but can also impact your site's AdWords Quality score and ranking in Google search.

10 Conversion Killers

1. No obvious real value or relevance

2. Tiny "call to action" buttons

3. Small or no phone number

4. Lack of trust—no photo of office or indication of address, no VeriSign security logo

5. Too many form fields and poor layout

6. Forced registration on shopping cart

7. Complex checkout process

8. High price not in line with competitors (unless you already have clear positioning as the leader)

9. Lack of reviews and testimonials

10. Too many features, not enough benefits

8 Examples of Top Converting Websites with Quick Observations

While these sites' look and feel will likely change over time, the essentials I'm focusing on won't change. I think it is important for you to see live examples of highly converting sites. I'll describe each of these sites in the text below, and you can also visit the McDougall Interactive blog to see the screenshots from the original blog post this was taken from. Here is the URL: mcdougallinteractive.com/blog/2012/10/8-examples-of-top-converting-websites-with-quick-observations/

A side note: the blog post was fed to Google+, which prompted Bryan Eisenberg (my conversion optimization teacher from Market Motive) to call me on my cell phone. He suggested I could improve it by using images. Then he used it in a webinar that explained how blogs convert better with stronger images, and retweeted it to his 23,000 Twitter followers. That generated numerous retweets through the "social" comment plug-in by MailChimp and brought in more traffic to the McDougall Interactive blog.

Example #1: Big, bold headlines and clear calls to action

www.salesforce.com

- The first thing you see is a big, bold headline with benefit/emotion.

- Calls to action to the right with a nice clean image make for simple top section.

- Calls to action are broken into three stages:

    1. View demos (Early-stage persona – those looking to learn more)

    2. Editions and pricing (Mid-stage persona – those looking to check prices)

    3. Free trial (Final-stage persona – those looking to get started)

- Boxes below the top section have attractive icons to make a visual connection with each category. This makes it easy to engage with the site.

- The "mega" drop-down menus offer simple navigation for good usability.

- Trust: Three million success stories and counting!

Example #2: Point of action assurances in the button

www.constantcontact.com

- Big, bold headline with benefit/emotion.

- Clear "call to action" button (emphasizes "free" and "no credit card required," answers common objections right at the button level).

- The copy is *very* sparse but highly impactful.

- Nice bulleted section of benefits below and essential details that are easy to scan and skim.

- Trust at the bottom: Awards, accreditation, and partners.

Example #3: Bold thought leaders with video testimonials

www.conversion-rate-experts.com

- Has a client list at the top, testimonials, case studies, "as seen in the news," and brands the company as a thought leader. All of these impart trust.

- Video is others speaking about how they were helped, rather than a big sales pitch. This *social proof* is very powerful.

- Downloadable content is the main call to action, rather than only targeting people who are ready to sign up. Shows trust and confidence.

Example #4: Photo of the impressive building at the top imparts trust

www.bhphotovideo.com

- Categories on the home page with visual reinforcement steer people down "aisles," instead of pushing individual items on people that likely don't match their needs.

- Photo of the building at the top imparts a sense that it is a large, reputable company.

- Navigation with visual reinforcement makes for awesome usability.

- Great thought-leader blog is highly engaging and excellent for SEO.

Example #5: Photo of "Steve" skyrockets sales

www.gundogsupply.com

- Uses a real person in the logo! They made $10 million more in one year due to this personalization. The following link shows how they did it: http://webmarketingtoday.com/articles/snell-compelling-content/

- "Steve's pick" badges show what he recommends in each category. Since he is a trusted thought leader, people choose these items effortlessly. He has done the thinking for them.

- Making the site more personal and showing the people behind the company made a massive difference in conversions.

Example #6: 42% conversion rate through strong, consistent unique value proposition (UVP)

www.schwans.com

This is one of the top-converting sites on the web, with a conversion rate of 42 percent!

- Headline says "Check Out ONLINE ONLY Special" (a UVP) and has call to action button.

- Like B&H Photo, Schwan's uses visual categories on the home page instead of pounding people with featured items.

- Good overview video and amazing "about us" section.

- Uses a rotating banner, which many conversion experts don't like. It seems to work here and has a call to action button in each banner, with headline and value proposition.

A strong banner with a headline and bold image is usually where visitors start their journeys. If you barrage them with marketing offers from multiple departments featuring current events, offers, and news, they get frustrated and bounce. What is the solution? Test sending half your traffic to a version with a static banner with a bold headline and a benefit-oriented UVP and maybe a few bullet points. Send the other half to a version with rotating banners and see which converts better.

Example #7: Personalized recommendations put content in context

www.amazon.com

Amazon personalizes the user experience, so recommendations are tailored to you specifically. This doesn't always work, but when it does, it is very helpful.

In the future, sites will need to know more about each customer and provide only calls to action that they haven't seen or acted on yet. At a recent HubSpot conference, the founders said, "If content is king, context is God."

Make sure your marketing pitches are within the context of what your prospects are looking for, not delivered using a shotgun approach. The more you show customers and prospects that you value their needs, the more they will listen to your messages. The more you blindly take generic swings at the masses, the more they will be turned off.

Amazon is famous for doing A/B testing. They are always testing. Are you?

Amazon sometimes gets rid of things that increase cart conversions in favor of promoting sales through partner ads near the cart button! (That's because they make more when they don't have to ship and process things.) Don't necessarily copy them, as their goals may be different than yours, but do evaluate their tendency to *test*.

Example #8: An emotional experience, not a cluttered maze

http://basecamp.com/

Huge headline and big pictures. An emotional experience, not a cluttered maze. Amazing how some sites have to cram in a million details when others, like Apple, do better with big, simple headlines and lush, inspiring images. This is the difference between the annoying sales guy who bores you with details and the effective sales person who subtly hooks you by getting you to imagine yourself happily using their products or services.

Now that you have some good examples and background, ask yourself what you think is the number one thing that increases conversions for *your* business. The call to action mapped to the buying cycle technique as seen below is one of the first places we start when increasing conversions for our customers.

Map Calls to Action to the Buying Cycle

Having a call to action for each of the stages of the marketing funnel/buying cycle is an amazing way to increase conversions. Have a call to action for each of these stages:

- Top of the funnel

- Middle of the funnel

- Bottom of the funnel

In Example #1 above, Salesforce did a nice job with this. Below are the funnel stages and insights.

Top of the funnel

Stage: Roughly 80% of web traffic is in this "research and surfing" stage

Call to action ideas: Guides and ebooks

Question to answer: What do I need?

Middle of the funnel

Stage: Roughly 15% of web traffic is in this "compare and contrast" stage

Call to action ideas: Case studies, webinars, comparison charts/guides

Question to answer: Why do I need it from *you*?

Bottom of the funnel

Stage: Roughly 5% of web traffic is in this "buy it now" stage

Call to action ideas: Consultations, audits

Question to answer: Why should I act/buy *now*?

What Makes a Good "About Us" Page?

Another great tactic to increase conversions is to make your "about us" page better, since so many people will check it out to see who you are and what you're all about. We see this consistently in analytics for many sites.

1. They passionately tell you who they are, not just what they do.

2. Behind every business there are honest and trustworthy people—show them off.

3. Write more fun or interesting copy. Don't be boring here.

4. Don't pretend to be larger than you are in terms of company size, or trying to seem something or someone you're not. Show off your real self.

5. Some cool stuff you can add to your "about us" page:

    *   History timelines—perhaps with animation/historic photos like Schwan's does

    *   The team's social media connections

    *   The company's Twitter, Facebook, LinkedIn, and Google+ links

    *   List of top clients

    *   Show off when you have been featured in the news

- Awards, certifications

- Video interviews with the president and/or team

Sell Using AIDAS

AIDAS is a marketing acronym that describes a common list of stages used when selling a product or service:

- **Attention:** Attract awareness of customers

- **Interest:** Raise interest by demonstrating advantages and benefits (instead of focusing on features)

- **Desire:** Convince customers that they want and desire the product or service and that it will satisfy their needs

- **Action:** Guide customers towards taking action or purchasing

- **Satisfaction:** Satisfy the customer so they buy again and become a product or brand "cheerleader"

The theory is that using AIDAS can help you market effectively. Sometimes it's recommended to split the AIDAS formula into two pairs of promotional steps:

1) Attention + Interest

2) Desire + Action.

Keeping in mind these various stages that users go through can help you decide what types of headlines and images to use to get attention, pique interest, and close deals that make people feel good. Otherwise, you may inadvertently leave out essential parts of the closing process and lose sales.

Set Goals with the REAN Model

Business goals should be defined before attempting any marketing according to the newer REAN model.

REAN (which stands for Reach, Engage, Activate, Nurture) was first coined by Xavier Blanc in 2006. It helps you plan ahead and analyze the complex marketing activities that are needed to build and nurture customer relationships. REAN stands for:

- **Reach:** Marketing activities needed to raise awareness of your brand, product, or service. Off-line and online, from SEO to TV ads.

- **Engage:** The gradual, often multi-channel set of activities needed to engage prospects. In analytics, measures the click depth and time spent interacting with your website.

- **Activate:** The actions your prospects should and do take (i.e., defined and tracked calls to action)

- **Nurture:** The activities needed to nurture relationships, such as the use of CRM, email newsletters, offers to come back to the site, etc.

Map your goals as follows:

Reach: We hope to attain 50% more visitors to our website for keywords relating to *Fuzzy Red Widgets* through SEO and PPC.

Engage: We hope to attain 50% greater click depth and click duration by adding testimonials, case studies, video demonstrations, and a blog.

Activate: We hope to increase our conversion rate on the following:

Goal 1: More sales through the shopping cart for Fuzzy Red Widgets.

Goal 2: More downloads of our Fuzzy Red Widget white paper.

We will do this through testing headlines, and changes in buttons, text, color, images, font, and copy.

Nurture: We hope to receive five more orders for Fuzzy Red Widgets per month and add three new prospect names and addresses into our system each day/month, etc. through the "download the Fuzzy Red Widgets white paper" form. We also hope to attain one more sale per month of Fuzzy Red Widgets through email newsletters offering coupons to people who have indicated interest specifically in this product.

By using an organized set of steps, you can improve your workflow and prospects for long-term success. Here are some of the people who typically work on marketing campaigns and how they can benefit from a system such as REAN:

1. The top people in a company (e.g., a president or small business owner)

2. The marketing person or department

3. The "geeks" or techies (e.g., programmers, app developers)

If the president wants a splash page, you can tell her, "No problem, we can A/B test that with Visual Website Optimizer." If the results are poor, she will be more likely to listen to you when you have statistics proving that *x*, *y*, or *z* doesn't work. You can also state that the splash page is hampering the levels of reach, by hurting SEO rankings and engagement by turning people off, and so on. An organized model feels more "official" and helps you cover the critical steps with consistency.

If the geeks say the form on the site works just fine, you can share the analytics statistics and point out that you are trying to follow certain very detailed steps along a path of conversion. If they can play ball with your systematic steps, they will be helping a greater cause. Geeks like minute details and following a logical plan, rather than vague creative direction. Think like a geek when you're presenting the REAN model.

If there is a battle between you and the marketing director, the geek, or the president over the best option, you can use analytics to ensure you are staying on track to satisfy the various points along the REAN model by selecting the best creative choice. If you can't get funds for Saleforce.com and tie in with the site's forms or shopping cart, you can point to the official marketing plan and note how important it is to follow each step in the system—such as nurturing leads through a CRM system/email newsletter.

Test with Visual Website Optimizer

Testing is the lifeblood of running a successful website. Without experimentation, there is no way to tell whether your online marketing efforts are paying off. Here are the two types of testing you'll see referenced most often:

- A/B Testing

    - Testing variations of a page

    - Especially helpful when comparing overall design or single elements within a design

- Multivariate Testing (MVT)

    - A/B testing, while useful, has its limitations

    - MVT testing involves testing combinations of multiple elements

    - Dramatic results can be obtained by varying the copy, design, images, and other factors online

    - MVT will give you the winning combination you need to stay ahead of the pack

In addition to A/B tests where you send half the traffic to one page and half to a similar one that has specific variations, Visual Website Optimizer lets you track multiple items at one time through multivariate testing. This helps you determine the best collection of offerings that will help you achieve maximum conversion rates.

You can test headlines, images, offers, calls to action, and so on, and after the software has collected enough data, it will give you (after 100 conversions) statistically reliable reports as to what makes the site most effective at closing deals.

To run experiments, you'll need to add the snippets of code on your site that will enable Visual Website Optimizer to vary your traffic to the different versions of your page.

Define and track your goals, and make adjustments on an ongoing basis. By using reporting software tools like Google Analytics and Visual Website Optimizer, you can make informed decisions with regard to adjusting your site and calls to action.

It is critical to understand which elements to test (the ones that will have the most impact) so you don't do too many things at once and get lost in a sea of data. Start small and be certain which elements are making a difference before doing more complicated tests.

Landing Page Optimization

You can increase conversions by creating specific landing pages on your website targeting the specific search terms your prospects are searching on (instead of always directing visitors to come to your home page or various website pages first). By making specific landing pages for each term your prospects searched to find you, you will increase conversion rates, enhance your visitors' experience, and generate greater ROI. Landing pages are great to test in paid search against the alternative of sending them to a page on the main site. By having a more targeted page that removes distracting navigation elements and links, and that has one primary call to action (or very clearly defined action items), you can keep people focused on the desired action rather than surfing your site.

11 Key Features of an Effective Landing Page

1. A compelling and benefit-oriented headline

2. Sub-headline

3. A brief description of what is being offered, usually with benefit-oriented bullet points

4. At least one supporting image or short video

5. Call to action such as a form or an action button. Keep the form very short and offer something of value, like an ebook or white paper, in exchange for the visitor's contact information.

6. Trust and security items, such as testimonials, customer logos, or security badges

7. Remove or limit extra navigation

8. Keep the objective simple and clear, as complexity increases friction and visitor anxiety

9. Ensure the messaging matches the "scent" throughout the entire conversion path. In other words, say the same exact thing in the ad, the headline, and throughout the checkout process (if there is a shopping cart).

10. Create lots of landing pages, because having a page for very specific topics makes users feel the page is exactly what they were looking for.

11. Make your unique value proposition (UVP) very clear

Online Branding and Your UVP: Essential for Conversion Optimization

Your brand is the soul of your company. When you can clearly state your company's benefits and back up your brand's key conversion points, you will close more deals. Online branding requires many headlines and scraplines (mini statements that summarize your UVP) because users scan and skim a webpage very quickly and your key points need to stand out clearly. Keep a notebook of all your ideas, since you may find that each page could have its own mini scrapline defining not only a keyphrase, but also the page's reason for being. The more concise your mini statements are, the more quickly customers will "get" what you do and your unique value proposition.

Use a highly trained interactive designer to help you build a clean-looking site that is easy to use. Work with your designer to:

- Make sure you base the look and feel of the site around your logo and traditional print campaign colors, and use general formatting that is consistent across all mediums.

- Avoid using too many different fonts and font styles.

- Avoid using too many colors or colors that are not part of a defined palette.

- Make sure the design has set places for calls to action or the things you want people to click, see, or do (typically located middle-right)

- Make sure your navigation (Home, About, Services, etc.) breaks out the content into logical keyword groupings, and that you have a way, as the site expands, to add pages that won't make the site harder to use.

If you don't have a place for clear calls to action and initially build your website in a way that will make it easy to add lots of content later, you will likely have to redesign the site later for better search marketing and conversions, as well as a better user experience.

The Top 4 Branding Mistakes

Branding means creating an awareness of your business' unique value and personality. It sounds simple enough, but you'd be surprised how few business owners take the time to do it right. Here are a few of the most common mistakes marketers make:

1. **Not doing detailed research.** A logo and tagline are only an extension of your brand. Before you develop any creative, make sure you have done your homework on what the current perception of your brand is, from the perspective of both customers and employees. Then determine who your target audience is and what they react well to. You must also research where you fit into the overall landscape of competitors so that you fill a void and have a strong offering that sets you apart from others. Do you have the lowest or highest price, or the best customer service with awards to back it up? Having this information can help you determine what your real value is and what your brand positioning should be.

2. **Lack of focus.** Companies often change their identity when the wind blows and make haphazard logo, tagline, and copy changes that don't keep a consistent message. The big brands tend to reinforce the same message for long periods of time. Below are a few examples of long-lasting taglines.

Famous Taglines

Think different - Apple Computer
Think outside the box - Apple Computer
The ultimate driving machine - BMW
Calgon, take me away - Calgon Toiletries
Please don't squeeze the Charmin - Charmin
Like a rock - Chevy Trucks
Have a Coke and a smile - Coca-Cola
A diamond is forever - DeBeers
Nothing sucks like an Electrolux - Electrolux
When it absolutely, positively has to be there overnight - FedEx
It's not just for breakfast anymore - Florida Orange Juice

We bring good things to life - General Electric
Nothing runs like a Deere - John Deere
Every kiss begins with Kay - Kay Jewelers
Finger-lickin' good! - Kentucky Fried Chicken
When banks compete, you win - LendingTree
Good to the last drop - Maxwell House
Just do it - Nike
Pepperidge Farm remembers - Pepperidge Farm
You are now free to move about the country - Southwest Airlines
Yo quiero Taco Bell - Taco Bell
Silly rabbit, Trix are for kids - Trix Cereal
The few, the proud, the Marines - US Marines
It's not just a job. It's an adventure. - US Navy
Can you hear me now?...Good! - Verizon Wireless
Drivers wanted - Volkswagen

Is it clear to your customers why they should buy from you versus a competitor? Is that reason expressed emotionally or logically? People buy because of emotion and justify it logically. If your advertising only appeals to logic, your only customers will be relatives of Mr. Spock. Are any of the memorable taglines above a list of features? They are focused on benefits and/or make an emotional appeal.

3. **Trying to appeal to everyone.** Focusing on a niche market for your product can often be more profitable than trying to please everyone. You are better off having a strong defining factor that resonates with a certain type of customer. Then you can truly get to know that market segment, offer a product or service that is really refined for their needs, and create marketing campaigns that consistently work well for this particular group. The more you understand your audience, the more you can do to connect deeply with them and create a lasting relationship built on truth rather than brief flings with the masses (who will eventually lose interest).

4. **Not having a deep enough presence.** Having a deep presence means being in a variety of online media such as top SEO rankings, paid listings, banner ads, social connections, and press releases. The more your name comes up online in a positive way, the stronger your brand.

Now that you have a sense of some of the top elements that influence conversion, I'd like to give you a homework assignment. Pick the keyword that you most want to rank for in the search engines and the main service or product page on your site for that keyword. Then use the system below to increase both rankings and conversions at the same time. Let's put some of what we learned into action while tying it to SEO.

Deeper Clicks Engagement System

Over the years I have noticed that creating content is often a sticking point for clients. I have also noticed that there are times when one product or service could really use more attention. To help illustrate the concept of developing deeper content to achieve better engagement and sales, I have worked out a system for starting with just one area that is important to you. By biting off a small piece of work, my hope is that site owners will make a concerted effort to experiment and then use that experience to develop similar models for other areas of the business.

My Deeper Clicks Engagement System combines the stages of the buying cycle with new website content to deepen engagement, improve rankings, and encourage conversions.

Bear in mind that people are not always ready to buy or act in a definitive way that reaches a conversion. Sometimes they just want to read a review and start thinking about their next purchase or activity. If you want to reach the largest number of people long-term, you want to connect with visitors who are at all stages of the buying cycle.

Consider the following stages/terms:

- "Flat screen TV": Generic term, may be mix of early stages and late stages

- "Flat screen TV review" or "laser printer compare": Likely not quite ready to buy; however, may be susceptible to marketing messages that concern benefits of a particular unit

- "Cheap laser printer": Probably close to the purchase stage, but price-sensitive

- "Best laser printer": Likely not quite ready to buy; however, may be susceptible to marketing messages that concern benefits of a particular unit

- "HP 1200 laser printer": May be close to purchase due to the specific model number used in the search

- "Laser alignment for jet engines case study": Knows what they want and are likely comparing solutions.

The goal is to develop at least a three-tiered content model for each product or service.

1. Early stage: Articles, blog posts, FAQ videos, and top of the funnel calls to action such as guides or ebooks.

2. Middle stage: Comparison option/case study content and middle of the funnel calls to action such as a webinar sign-up.

3. Late stage/ready to buy: The main service sales or product page with bottom of the funnel calls to action such as a form, cart, or "register" or "download" button.

Here's an example: Let's imagine that widget-manufacturing.com has only one page for their hottest items, Fuzzy Red Widgets. The main page for this product is getting a limited number of clicks per month. It is one of the most visited pages on the site, but traffic is not heavy, engagement is shallow, and conversions are light.

The company develops the following new content:

A. Blog Post on "Benefits of Fuzzy Red Widgets"

The blog post has anchor text links pointing to the main page (this is good for SEO and helps that main sales page rank better). It also links to a case study, making a circle of three connected pages. The links look like this:

Check out our <u>Fuzzy Red Widgets Case Study</u> and <u>buy Fuzzy Red Widgets</u> with free shipping.

URL: benefits-of-fuzzy-red-widgets.php

B. Case Study on Fuzzy Red Widgets

This is developed using keywords to incorporate short and long tail terms such as "Fuzzy Red Widgets" and "really rare Fuzzy Red Widgets in Denver Colorado." In terms of links, the case study points to the main page and the new blog post.
URL: fuzzy-red-widgets-case-study.php

C. Fuzzy Red Widgets Main Page

The company just needed to enhance this page with better calls to action, links, and conversion elements.

When you make enhancements like the above, be sure the text includes links to other pages so users can go on a journey that satisfies the stage of research they may be in and piques their interest. However, make the call to action more prominent than these links by making it stand out more.

The fact that the company built two new pages shows Google a depth of unique URLs and title tags around that keyword, thereby increasing thematic relevance. More pages around that topic means you care more about it, which is good for the user and Google. It is amazing how many people obsess over ranking for a given keyword, even though they have only one page on their site about that topic.

Get links from outside your own site to each of the new pages and make sure your main page has the most backlinks from outside sites and from your internal links, so it is most likely to be the highest-ranking page.

This exercise will provide you with a set of keywords for each stage of the buying process that you will rank for. When a user lands on any of the pages, they are drawn into the conversion architecture where there are calls to action that meet their stage and also links to the other pages that may interest them if they are considering moving along the stages. By connecting conversion optimization, content development, and keyword ranking, you are leveraging the powerful relationships between tactics.

For Extra Credit

Doing a press release about any new developments in this product or service area can also bring in extra links and visitors. If you share those three pages and the press releases on your social channels and add "share" buttons on the content, you can also bring social media into the mix. If you can encourage reviews and comments, it gets even better. Users will be impressed by other people verifying how much of an authority and how popular you are, and that can at the very least indirectly lead to increased search rankings. That is a much better way to market your company than bragging about it in an advertisement.

Considering how hard it is to drive traffic and how much is to be gained through conversion optimization, combining these tactics and adding social elements is an incredibly high-test strategy to bring your marketing to the next level.

Chapter 13

Email Marketing Essentials

Did you know that email marketing has the highest return on investment (ROI) of all forms of interactive marketing? Research by the Direct Marketing Association shows that year after year, the ROI for email marketing is higher than any other channel. Despite reports to the contrary, email marketing is far from dead and is in fact a great way to extend the traffic you are getting from search and social media. Include it in your Internet marketing mix and you will be pleasantly surprised when it starts showing up as a top traffic driver and source of conversions in your analytics reports. In this chapter, we'll look at the basics of email marketing—how to create email that recipients want to read and the best practices for email marketing. People really respond to outreach that's opt-in (meaning they signed up for it), and a regular touch in the form of an email newsletter full of helpful or thought-provoking information (or deals available only through the newsletter) are sometimes just what a potential customer needs in order to convert to a loyal customer.

Visits to your web site are like sales calls. Your opt-in email newsletter campaign should be considered a follow-up to these. At the very least, add an email newsletter sign-up form on your home page and send out one email newsletter a month.

If you spend one hour each month writing and sending a quick email to your customers and prospects and you get just one project or sell a handful of products as a result, your efforts are worth it. Sell a couple more products or close some service deals, and you will be amazed when you calculate the ROI for your email newsletter efforts.

Direct sales aren't the only benefit to making an email newsletter a part of your online marketing campaign, however. When you keep in touch with customers and contacts, you have the opportunity to brand yourself as a thought leader or to make people really happy with special deals. The branding impact alone is worth the effort if you use your newsletter respectfully (in other words, don't send out spam!) and share something useful with your customers. The key is creating a unique value proposition (UVP) for those who sign up to receive email from you. You must make people *want* to receive your email by demonstrating that opening and reading it is worth their precious time.

Create Timely, Relevant Messages

Creating original content that is relevant to and timely for your readers is essential. (A little later on, I'll explain how to use segmenting to make sure your emails are super-relevant.) There are two styles of emails that seem to work really well for different types of customers. One is the email newsletter based on the content of your blog, the second is one that features special deals available only through the newsletter.

The first, the newsletter based on blog post content, is typically good for businesses with non-e-commerce sites. One of the easiest ways to create this type of newsletter is to send a monthly or bimonthly email that simply highlights your most relevant recent blog posts. As long as you are blogging consistently, this approach will save you time, since you won't have to create anything new but an opening sentence or two. Your readers will see the intriguing headlines and blog post summaries in the email, and many will save it as a reminder or click on the links in the newsletter and start reading the content on your blog or website.

The second style of email newsletter, which features exclusive deals, works well for businesses with e-commerce sites. Almost all of our top ecommerce clients have the same thing in common when we study their website analytics and ROI: their email marketing is *by far* the most profitable channel and the one that drives the most website traffic. Many of our customers have email lists, built through over a decade of selling on their own and other websites, that run into the hundreds of thousands of names. These lists include customers but also people who signed up for the newsletter after visiting the website or seeing calls to action in social media.

The number one thing they do is offer deals that you simply cannot get anywhere except the email newsletter. These deals are not on the website, but are strictly deals that you will miss if you are not reading the email newsletter. This value proposition is enough to keep the subscriber retention rate high. In fact, the power of the "email list-only deal club" is so strong that we have seen our clients keep most of their list even when they switched from emailing twice a week to daily! This indicates it is more about the relevancy and uniqueness of the information or deals you are sending than the frequency.

Segmenting Your Email Marketing List

If you want to use email marketing successfully, then you have to use segmentation. Simply put, segmenting your list (database of email addresses) means separating people into categories.

Here are some examples of how you might segment your list:

- People who like a particular product or category (if you sell pet food, segment the list by dog lovers and by cat lovers)

- Job description

- Geographic segmentation

- Based on topics they like, as seen by the type of ebooks they downloaded or web pages they visited

- By engagement metrics (how many pages they visit and how long they stay on the site after clicking from past emails)

- Frequent buyers

- Big spenders

- Social media fans

- Those who share your emails with their networks

- By stage in the buying cycle

Even a small amount of segmentation can significantly increase your email click-through rates, subscriber retention rate, and ROI.

How to Build an Opt-In Email List

One of the most important things you can do to build your list is to *ask* for email addresses at every point of customer contact:

- On your website

- On customer support calls

- On brochures, surveys, and feedback forms

- At tradeshows and events

Get permission

Permission mailing means having people either sign up on your website for your newsletter or provide an email address when they purchase something from your company. By doing this, you can collect email addresses without buying a list that may have been created and/or sold illegally.

While building an email list is crucial for online marketing, be aware of a big potential pitfall, the possibility of being penalized for not creating your list in the proper manner. Due to recent laws designed to protect consumers from unwanted emails, an email list is legal only if it is "opt-in." When the person receiving the email has consented to receive mass emails from you, that's known as opting in. Here are some tips on building that opt-in email list quickly, effectively, and the right way:

1. Make it easy to opt in

The main page of your website should have a sign-up form with a box where visitors can enter an email address and agree to receive emails from you. If you have an e-commerce site where a customer will be paying and checking out, include a checkbox during the checkout process that lets customers sign up to receive emails from you. If you plan to use a third-party email service provider to handle your email list, make sure they provide code or HTML that you can insert in your website's code to create the opt-in box automatically.

2. Privacy is key

Make it clear to your users that their privacy will be respected and that you will not sell or otherwise misuse their contact information. Email privacy is at the heart of most email regulations. Inspire confidence in your email subscribers by letting them know that you will not share their information with anyone, and you will only send them emails as described. If you can, provide email frequency information, so they know how often they should expect to hear from you. Indicate whether you will send a monthly newsletter, weekly specials, or daily updates. Some companies offer their subscribers a choice in how often they hear from them and with what type of communication.

3. Plan a giveaway

Contests are a great way to generate interest and get people to sign up for an email list. Announce that you are giving away a prize to email subscribers in the coming weeks. Advertise it through every channel available to you. This will help bring in new subscribers and give you additional exposure.

4. Offer free content as a teaser

Free content is a contest alternative that doesn't have a time limit. Create a free report or ebook that anyone can download for free if they subscribe to your email list. This is a very successful model, and requires little upkeep. Customers will receive a link to download the

Web Marketing On All Cylinders - John McDougall

report once they confirm their subscription. Again, most email service providers can do this automatically for you.

Four Simple Steps to Create an Opt-in List

Step 1. Get people to sign up who otherwise might just do nothing on your site and may never come back. Use a call to action such as "sign up and get 10% off" or simply "sign up for our email updates." You can try testing different subscribe button colors as well as adding or removing a privacy policy link near the subscribe button. Sometimes simply saying "WE VALUE YOUR PRIVACY" under the button can increase conversions.

Step 2. Thank them (on a "thank you" page you can track with analytics) and tell them an email is on the way with a link that they'll need to click on to confirm their subscription. This is know as a "double opt-in." It should look something like this:

Thank you for submitting your information.

Please Note:

A confirmation email has been sent to you@you.com. In order to complete the sign-up process, please verify your email address by clicking on the link sent to you in that email.

Step 3. Explain your privacy policy and "unsubscribe" process, and offer the link to complete the process:

I will never rent, sell, or otherwise distribute your information to anyone for any reason. You can also unsubscribe easily with no hassle.

Please confirm your email address by clicking the link below:

Click here to complete the signup process.

Thanks for signing up!

[Your name and/or company name goes here]

Step 4. Simply say "thanks" after they click to confirm:

Thank you for signing up!

Use the Best Email Providers and Technology

Just a few years ago, emails were opened at an astounding rate, now that rate has declined. Part of the reason is that Google, for example, has put filters in place in Gmail to make sure that you are not getting "unwanted" emails. Other factors include the fact that too many emails aren't carefully targeted to the right groups of people.

The best way to use email marketing now is to make sure that you are working with the strongest email delivery companies.

Using an email service provider (ESP) (like Constant Contact, MailChimp, and a host of others) to deliver your emails helps increase deliverability rates. The best ESPs maintain their own anti-spam controls. The emails sent from an ESP use their own email "reputation" and not yours. By using an ESP, you will be able to push large mailings through ISP-level spam filters, even if you have a new account. Make sure to compare proof of delivery rates before you choose an ESP because some exaggerate their capabilities.

Here's a quick list of ideas for creating successful email marketing campaigns that you can track and that keep subscriber retention high.

25 Best Practices for Successful Email Marketing

1. Create the most compelling subject lines you can.

2. Use a recognizable company name in the "from" box.

3. Add clear calls to action.

4. Add contact information and/or a unique 800 number

5. Ensure that you will get the best email delivery rates.

6. Create a series of emails that all push (through links) to great content that show off how much you know and love your business niche.

7. Use social sharing links in all your emails (i.e., show a link to your Twitter feed, or social media icon that acts as a live link to your page on Facebook or Pinterest).

8. Track everything, including which emails get opened, which get clicks, and so on.

9. Keep rewriting your subject lines and content copy to improve your effectiveness over time. Test effectiveness by sending Version A to a sample of 10% of your email and sending Version B to another 10% to determine the winner before mailing to your whole list.

10. Minimize the use of images in your email newsletter, since they are unlikely to be displayed in many or even most emails, and spam filters are also wary of them. Instead, use HTML and inline CSS (fonts, text, and background colors and layout) to make the emails attractive

11. Be sure that your email newsletter template isn't more than 600 pixels wide so it displays correctly.

12. Put your value proposition and at least one link into the first 100 pixels of height near the top of the newsletter.

13. Keep your text short and easy to scan.

14. Regularly purge the email list of old contacts and/or those who do not engage.

15. Make sure that everyone on the list has agreed to receive your emails.

16. Make it clear that the customers' contact information won't be shared.

17. Make it easy to opt out of the mailing list.

18. Don't overdo it, but know that unique and relevant content trumps worrying too obsessively about frequency.

19. Provide HTML and text versions to ensure people who don't receive HTML emails can read your emails.

20. Put an image of the look and feel of your email newsletter (or the cover of PDF reports they can download from it) alongside the "subscribe" call to action.

21. Make the email newsletter's value proposition clear near the "subscribe" call to action. If you have thousands of other subscribers, say so, since that kind of social proof is persuasive.

22. Include an assurance near the "subscribe" call to action about how you won't sell their information to spammers.

23. Make sure your emails display well on phones and smartphones! Why? Two reasons. First, if all US mobile time online were represented by one hour, 25 minutes of that hour would be used for email. Second, mobile Internet usage is projected to overtake desktop Internet usage by 2014, according to Return Path. In addition, according to digital marketing agency Knotice, mobile email opens are now at 41% and are on pace to surpass PC's by the end of 2013.

24. Set and maintain a consistent email schedule.

25. Send out a test email to yourself and/or your team before sending it to your main list to be sure the content is displaying correctly and that links are working. That way, if something isn't right, you can fix it before sending the email out to the full list.

Successful email marketing focuses on the customer, and offers something they will benefit from directly, not just information about your company or a boring sales pitch.

Metrics and Tracking

Connecting your email marketing with other channels is the ultimate way to track engagement and the assists that lead to the eventual conversion.

If customers don't buy right away or don't buy online, are you able to track the fact that they initially came in from your email marketing but only later purchased after visiting from other channels, including off-line?

Keep notes about your customers in CRM system like Salesforce, or better yet, integrate your website, email campaigns, Salesforce, and HubSpot. That way you can follow visitors on their journey from your email link to your blog, and then off to your social channels and back again, perhaps through a direct type-in. Only then will you have a clear ROI metric.

Key Email Marketing Metrics to Track

List Size

List size matters, but not if it means your customers are disengaged. A large list with poor engagement levels isn't worth as much as a smaller, more engaged list. A smaller list can be more manageable, making it easier to segment it properly and have only the right people on the list. That said, nothing beats a large list of content-hungry or deal-hungry customers.

Deliverability Rate

This is the number of emails that were actually delivered, but it can include emails that end up in spam or junk folders. Closely examine reported deliverability rates, because they can fail to take into account whether an email service provider actually delivered the email to an inbox.

Open Rate

Getting people to actually open your email is as important as getting the email delivered to them. Monitor and constantly improve upon your open rate.

Click-Through Rate (CTR)

The click-through rate is the total number of clicks from links in your email through to your website or landing page.

Conversion Rate

Nothing beats being able to see the amount of sales you realized from your campaigns. Google Analytics' goal and referring sites tools can help you track the actual sales you get from email marketing.

Unsubscribes

A high number of unsubscribe requests may indicate that your content quality, email marketing list, or unique value proposition is poor and should push you to rethink who you are targeting and with what message. An unsubscribe is better than a spam complaint, so make it easy for people to unsubscribe. Don't bury the unsubscribe instructions in tiny type at the bottom of the page. Make these instructions visible by placing them front and center (at the top of the email in a reasonably large font)

Comparisons to Prior Months/Weeks

Be sure to look at year-over-year and month-over-month data to ensure your campaigns are always improving.

Open-to-Click Ratio

This is the ratio of email opens as a percentage of emails sent.

Growth Rate

This is a measure of how quickly your email list is growing. Take the number of new subscribers, subtract the number of unsubscribes and the number of hard bounces (a hard bounce is an email message that has been returned to the sender and is permanently undeliverable). Divide that sum by the previous complete total number of subscribers.

New Email List Subscribers

The number of people who have signed up since your last mailing. As your popularity grows, so should this number.

Which Links Were Clicked

It is also a good idea to track which links get clicked to get a better sense of how customers are engaging with your content.

Getting Started with Email Marketing

For those new to email marketing and email newsletters, signing up for a free trial with a service like Constant Contact, MailChimp, or VerticalResponse can be the perfect way to get your feet wet. Email marketing software is easy to use, with customization options built in, and ready-made templates so you don't have to be a designer to make it look good.

Note that Constant Contact has an aggressive spam policy, so make sure you have a super "white hat" or "clean" list. VerticalResponse is another popular choice with slightly more reasonable practices on what type of lists you can send to; both are relatively easy programs to use. They may not be the most feature-rich programs, but they likely have all you need to do a great job. Try Blue Sky Factory for a more intensive and expensive program that does a nice job integrating with your social media efforts.

Designing Email Newsletters

Be sure you use a clean design or template that matches the fonts and colors on your website (to maintain your brand but opt for designs that focus on headlines not graphics). Keep in mind the average preview pane size is around 638 x 86 pixels, so most people won't even see beyond the first 100 pixels of your email! Make sure that you have your value proposition and calls to action within the first 100 pixels. Large header graphics can cause real issues, so keep it simple at the top of the email. And make sure to create a text-only version as well.

Web Marketing On All Cylinders - John McDougall

Once your template and your initial list are saved into the software program you've chosen, you'll find that sending weekly or monthly emails is as easy as thinking up ideas!

Email Newsletter Set-Up Tips

You Need an Email Newsletter—Here's How to Do It

After you set up your account with an ESP, you will want to set up and send an email newsletter to your email list. Here's how, in 10 simple steps:

1. Look at the email templates available, and choose one that you like. Most email software provides hundreds of templates to choose from, so that you can easily have a professional-looking email newsletter in HTML format.

2. Create your own newsletter template or edit an existing one if you don't like the pre-designed templates. Designing your own template requires no HTML knowledge, as the programs usually have a drag-and-drop interface for creating email templates.

3. Write an enticing and informative subject line. It needs to be enticing to give readers a reason to open it up and read it. At the same time, you will want to be informative enough so that the recipients know who and where this email is coming from. They decided to opt-in to your newsletter, so the subject line must communicate that this is coming from you or your company.

4. Set up the "from" name on your emails as well. This also will help your readers know where the email is coming from and ensure their comfort in opening it.

5. Add your company logo to the template you've selected, choosing colors and fonts that will match the message you are trying to communicate. The "mood" of your company needs to be conveyed in this design, whether it is formal and professional, or loose and fun.

6. Personalize the email to address the recipient directly using the ESP's tools for doing so. This allows you to make the newsletter feel a bit more personalized instead of having a "mass email" feel. According to HubSpot, their customers see much greater open rates when they use the person's first name in the subject line.

7. Integrate your social networks. Most email software allows you to include icons that will link to your Facebook page, Twitter profile, or LinkedIn page. This can widely expand your exposure to the reader. Social media sharing buttons can make your email marketing go viral. Experiment with taking the icons out as well, to see if they help or hurt conversion rates.

8. Import an existing email list from many different common databases for the software to address. Once this is done, you can group or segment subscribers into different categories to send separate and focused emails to each of them.

9. Once your newsletter is ready, preview it to make sure that everything is formatted and designed correctly. You also have the ability to test-send it to be sure that it is not blocked by spam filters.

10. You can then either send it right away or schedule it to be sent at a later time. Don't obsess over the best time to send it, as you will hear conflicting recommendations. I personally like sending newsletters out on Tuesdays at 11 a.m., but I have heard some super-gurus say they get the best results on weekends when other people are afraid to send email newsletters. Test various times and days to see what actually works best for your customers. If you find more people opening and clicking links in your newsletter when they're sent on Fridays than on Tuesdays, then go with Fridays, since that's what works for *your* market.

Email marketing and lead nurturing are connected at the hip, so be sure to read the chapter on HubSpot (Chapter 15) to get additional ideas about how email can be used to nudge people through the stages of the buying cycle.

Chapter 14

How Mastering Local Search
Could Wildly Increase Your Sales

When people want to buy products and services, they tend to search for answers locally first, and they want those answers to be supported by reviews from real people who have done business with you.

For these reasons, you need to have a presence on local search. It's easier than you think, and doing so puts you at a competitive advantage, since surprisingly few companies have tackled even the basics in this area.

Typical local search queries include such things as a street address, city name, or postal code. Examples of local searches include "LA dentists," "Auckland Hotels," "Danvers MA SEO company," and "Rome Car Rental."

Local search advertising is amazingly effective and it is seriously bumping regular organic listings down in the search engine results. Sometimes that frustrates me because I want my SEO-driven pages to rank ahead of local listings, but I just can't change Google's decision to hyper-focus on mobile- and Google+ Local-optimized listings (see Figure 7).

No matter what you sell, there is a great chance that local listings and/or mobile will affect your business.

This is precisely why Google Places opened up 49.5 million websites to allow us to claim our stake on the local landscape.

Google made it crystal-clear when they created Google Maps (which became Google Places and has now become Google+ Local) that they think the world of local search. That is where the marketing world is headed and lots of advertising dollars are being spent...and Google is all about advertising dollars.

Why Mobile Is More Important Than You Thought

Mobile is not the fad you once thought it was. I heard Stephanie Tilenius from Google speak at a conference back in 2010, and she said then that Google now does all things through the lens of mobile. Their entire strategy is focused on mobile because we live in a world where everyone is tethered to their phones (and increasingly, smartphones).

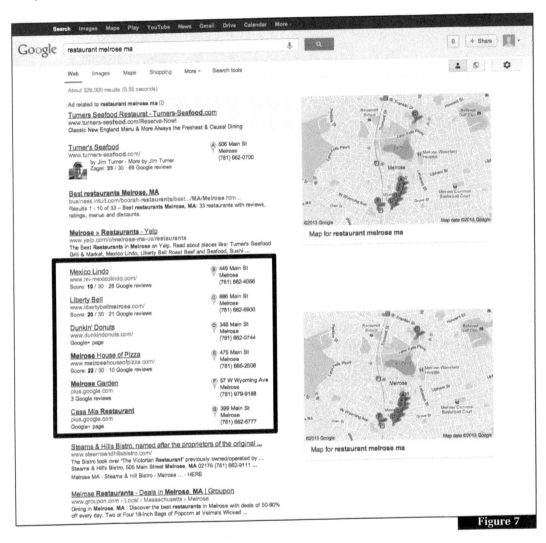

Figure 7

Take a look at these eye-opening statistics:

- According to Comscore, mobile Internet usage is projected to overtake desktop Internet usage by 2014.

- 1.08 billion of the planet's 4 billion mobile phones are smartphones, and 3.05 billion are SMS-enabled, meaning they can send and receive text messages. (Source: Microsoft Tag)

Web Marketing On All Cylinders - John McDougall

- If a mobile site didn't work properly the first time they visited, 46% of visitors are not likely to return. (Source: Gomez)

- We want it now: 71% of mobile browsers expect web pages to load on their mobile devices almost as quickly as or faster than website pages load on their desktop computers. (Source: Gomez)

- We're looking locally: 50% of local searches are done on mobile devices. (Source: Mashable infographic, Mobile by the Numbers http://mashable.com/2011/03/23/MOBILE-BY-THE-NUMBERS-INFOGRPAHIC/)

- Only 19% of US e-commerce sites have an app for mobile commerce, so you have the opportunity to get ahead of the pack.

- We're social: 91% of mobile web usage is for social connectivity, versus only 79% on desktops. (Source: Microsoft Tag)

- If all US mobile time online were represented as one hour, 25 minutes of that hour would be used for email. (Source: Return Path)

The bottom line: Make sure your website is built with options for mobile users and loads super-fast. Responsive web design can help you achieve some consistency across channels and is a good reasonably low-effort option for many companies. Others will want to create unique experiences for mobile users by device type, despite the additional costs to create higher engagement.

Google wants your targeting to be insanely relevant and having a mobile option that solves a local need is what they want from you. They want users to be able to see local listings quickly at the top of the search results and they allow ads to be targeted very precisely by location. Did you know that mentioning a location in mobile advertisements and search results can increase click-through rates up to 200 percent? (Source: ThinkNear)This is what people want and Google is going to give it to them with or without you.

After Google made its sweeping changes in terms of emphasizing Google+ Local, you just have to appear in the local listings.

Old Media vs. New—Rivals or Pals?

Local search is a new version of the waning traditional off-line local advertising, such as newspaper ads, Yellow Pages, local radio, and, to some degree, cable TV spots.

Keep in mind that traditional media venues are actively pushing their own versions of local search. Yellow Pages directory listings, for example, can actually help your Google+ Local ranking position. So while search and traditional media may seem like archrivals, they are in some ways directly connected.

Having a listing in vertical directories such as Lawyers.com, your local chamber of commerce, and such things as your city or regional magazine's business directory can help your overall local search presence. These get indexed by Google and are trust signals to Google of your professional local presence. In addition, reviews of your local business (like a restaurant review in a magazine) with a link to your website can pass positive local ranking signals to the search engine robots. They also can drive business since people click on them when surfing the local magazine sites or see them listed in search results. So any time an offline ad comes with an online component, it increases its value significantly, partly due to the backlink. Magazines used to throw in the online version when you bought a print ad, but now some magazine publishers sometimes have to throw in the print version when advertisers (like realtors) insist on purchasing powerful paid online ads!

There is currently a battle going on amongst local search providers. Local online advertising revenues are expected to reach $144.9 billion in 2014, according to BIA/Kelsey. Facebook, Twitter, Google, Microsoft, Foursquare, Pinterest, Yelp, Ask.com, and Apple all have offerings for local advertising. Pundits estimate that anywhere from 40% to 60% of searches have a local intent. With mobile continuing to boom, local search remains very powerful and critical to many businesses.

While getting listed in a variety of local directories and services is important, I suggest starting with Google+ Local.

Setting Up and Using Google+ Local

Google is a great source for local business information, and local search is beyond hot, given the growing number of people searching for things on the go using a mobile phone. Local listings appear at the top of many Google results, sandwiched between the top paid ads and the main organic search results, even when not searching from a mobile device.

To make a local page for your business, you will need to create a Google+ profile if you don't already have one and then sign in to Google+. You won't show up on the Google maps that come up when you search for local services unless you register with Google+ Local. This is not the same as having your website indexed. For that, you have to register your business with Google+ Local, which is a separate process from having your website appear in the "main" results.

If you really want to be in the top search results, you need to consider at least three of the following:

1. Ranking organically in the "main results"

2. Being listed and ranking well in Google+ Local (local/Maps)

3. Paying per click with Google AdWords and other similar programs

4. You need Citations and Reviews (these are two of the keys to Google+ Local listings)

Google pitches Google+ Local to potential customers as follows:

Claim your business on Google and get these features:

- Manage business listing information

- Post coupons and live updates

- Create and manage Circles, start and join Hangouts, and share content like posts and photos

- See how you're doing with a performance dashboard

Claim your listing at Google+ Local using the following three steps outlined by Google:

1. Submit your information, from basic contact information to photos and video.

2. Verify your listing by phone or postcard.

3. Wait for your listing to appear on Google. In most cases, it shouldn't take more than 12 hours.

Google Is Always Interested in Quality

Google is very interested in the quality level of the sites trying to get ranked. They have very advanced filters to block out unethical people, so while you may not feel this is critical to you, you need to be aware that your ranks will suffer if you are not conscious of how to play the quality game with Google. Essentially, you can't do things like create more listings than you need, over-stuff keywords, or try to fool them in any way. (You can only create one listing per physical location of your company (P.O. boxes don't count), so do *not* in any way try to make an end run around this.)

Sometimes what you think may be legitimate may actually be unethical under Google's guidelines. Just as with organic rankings, Google+ Local has a massive list of items to deal with to get it right. We will cover only the essentials here to get you started.

If you already have a Google Account, sign in with your email and password, and get started on the path to claiming your business listing in Google+ Local.

How to Verify Your Google+ Local listing

After you've created your Page on Google+ Local you'll need to verify it with these steps.

1. Request Your Postcard

    Hover over "Unverified" at the top of your Google+ Page and click "Verify Now."

    Confirm your address and request your postcard for verification.

2. Enter Your PIN from your Google postcard at google.com/local/verify and submit.

Existing information on Google Maps will be merged with your new Google+ Local listing and your business will soon appear on Google Maps. You can now start making posts, hosting Hangouts (Hangouts are places used to facilitate group video chat), and gaining followers.

Once you have claimed and verified your business, go in and edit your listing. This is your chance to make your profile stand out for the search engines. Be as detailed as possible, and be sure to use the keywords and categories you want to be found for.

14 Top Factors Influencing Google+ Local Rankings

1. Your address. Carefully and fully fill in the fields for address, email, and phone numbers, etc.

2. Your business categories. Fill in all the categories that make sense for your business, not just one. Make sure you choose one Google-suggested category before adding customizable categories. You can enter up to five categories.

3. Keywords in the business name are a potential advantage, but many people do not recommend altering your business name to force them in. Certainly if you overdo it, you could get blacklisted. Since it is likely a small factor compared to citations (see #4, below), don't get over-excited about this factor or you will risk penalties.

4. Citation quantity and diversity. Mentions of your business in various directories and local sites are like links in traditional SEO. They pass trust signals to Google that you are legitimate.

General places to get listed:

- Local search engines

- Hyper-local blogs

- Locally focused directories

- Industry-focused directories or blogs

Here are some directories (sites) that may help your Google+ Local listing and/or drive local traffic:

- Citysearch

- InsiderPages

- Yelp

- SuperPages

- Infogroup

- Localeze

- iBegin

- Acxiom

- Best of the Web's Regional Directory

- Yahoo's Regional Directory

- Business.com

- Yellowpages.com

- MerchantCircle

- Foursquare

- Hotfrog

- Kudzu

- DirectoryM

- Dexknows.com

- Local.com

- Mojopages.com

- Manta.com

- MacRAEsBlueBook.com

- Angie's List

- Judy's Book

- Comcast

Some people go crazy with this and get hundreds of listings. Sometimes it works, but if you cross a line you may be seen as a spammer. Start with the best directories and local citations, and test to see if you rank well with them first. Keep in mind that listings that are specific to your niche are also good. For example, lawyers should get listed and reviewed in AVVO.

5. Business data consistency. Watch over the various directories that link to you to ensure that your business name, address, and phone number are consistent across the many sources of local business information.

6. Reviews and ratings. Reviews are a huge help in your local search engine rankings, especially when they are on sites like Yelp, Insider Pages, Citysearch, Yahoo, Super Pages, and Yellow Pages. Get at least one review from Yelp and Citysearch or Insider Pages so you have two non-Google reviews. Google is using what reviewers say about local businesses and showing the sentiment analysis right on Place Pages. Again, it is all about trust and what others are saying in the new social web, not just what you say about your business.

7. Backlinks to your Google+ Local page also help it rank, but post-Penguin (a recent Google search algorithm update) it is best to focus on branded keywords in the anchor text instead of using too many aggressive links from your top keywords.

8. Completing your business profile/Page. Write a good description (up to 200 characters) using the keywords you want to rank for. Add extra information like hours and payment options, etc. Google sends lots of people to these pages and wants the most complete profiles to be at the top.

9. Proximity to location. Don't worry if your business isn't located right near your city's red marker on a Google local map, since, more importantly, it will show up based on search in proximity to the exact location the user specifies in the search terms, such as "restaurants near Boston Common."

10. My Google+ Local and other user content/data. People can make their own maps and this social element, related to the general trend of Google to include user activity, is becoming increasingly important.

11. Traditional SEO factors. Optimize your website for local search so the site itself matches the theme of the Google+ Local listing.

12. Add photos. We recommend adding at least 10, as the more information you have, the more Google "sees" that you care about your listing.

13. Add a link to YouTube videos. Since few companies do this, you really stand out if you make this effort.

14. Mentions of your business on social media sites may grow in importance. So be sure to take part in various social activities online. Google puts much more value on Google+, while Bing relies on Facebook's social information, so don't put all your eggs in one basket.

Beyond Google+ Local, be sure to also get listed in Bing and Yahoo Local, as well as in Yelp. Even though Google is the big dog, there is traffic to be had from a variety of local listings. As always, it is the power of multiple sources that cranks your web marketing engine into high gear.

You'll find more information on Yelp and Google Reviews in the social media chapter (Chapter 7).

Whether you are a realtor, a dentist, a lawyer, a home improvement contractor or a services provider, or operate a golf course, hotel, nightclub, retail store, or local pizza shop, having your brand at the top of the local listing can drive a lot of traffic and increase your sales for a very small amount of effort. Just be aware that others are also trying to master this very specific system, and they will check out your listing for ideas on how to beat you.

Considering Google+ Local is directly tied into social media and mobile and bumps down the organic search results it is absolutely essential that you integrate this tactic into your overall strategy.

Chapter 15

An Introduction to HubSpot

Since HubSpot is such an important and unique tool that I mention numerous times in the book, I want to share an interview that we recently did with them, to give you a deeper sense of what this all-in-one Internet marketing tool is all about.

What are the benefits of using HubSpot?

HubSpot is an all-in-one inbound marketing software platform that includes everything a marketer needs to do his or her job on a day-to-day basis. When you use HubSpot, you don't need to worry about learning how to use five different tools, or figuring out how those tools are integrated, because everything you need is right there in one familiar interface. Because all of our tools talk to one another right out of the box, you can take advantage of synergies between tools that would be impossible when using many different, disconnected systems [from several vendors].

HubSpot is also a leader in inbound marketing, which is a methodology centered around attracting and converting visitors into happy customers through personalized, relevant information and content—not interruptive messages. HubSpot features all the tools you need to do inbound marketing, and expertise from true leaders in the field through an endless stream of content, webinars, and opportunities to interact with our robust base of more than 8,000 customers.

Inbound marketing emphasizes providing free content to website visitors. Why would a company choose to give content away instead of using traditional advertising?

One thing we hear time and time again from businesses is the resistance to providing free content. "Why would the customer buy the cow if the milk is free?" Pamela Vaughn, editor of the HubSpot blog, answered this question. She explained: "Giving away free content to your prospective customers can actually educate prospects about the products and services you offer, and lead to more leads and sales for your business."

Quality content shows prospective customers that your business is a thought leader that knows what it's talking about, which can translate to initial trust in your paid products and services. After all, if the content you're creating is educational and helps your prospects learn something new or solve some problems they have, why wouldn't they think your paid offerings are equally as helpful?

A more tangible benefit is the increase in traffic that free content brings. Pam noted, "Creating content is a fantastic way to get found online and increase various types of traffic to your website. By making sure content is optimized with your best keywords, you'll increase your chances of getting found in search engines and boost organic traffic. By promoting content in social media, you'll increase your referral traffic. By using content offers in paid marketing efforts like pay-per-click or in email promotions, you'll increase traffic from paid search and email marketing, respectively."

Finally, free content results in more educated, qualified leads. Recent research from Google and CEB (http://www.executiveboard.com/exbd-resources/content/digital-evolution/index.html), revealed that leads conduct nearly 60% of the research they're going to do on a product or service before ever engaging a sales rep. That research is happening on and off your site and through a variety of different means. Offering free educational content can help leads navigate their research before they even talk to your team.

Why use HubSpot? Why not just use a collection of separate tools for my marketing?

It is possible to piece together a marketing strategy using a collection of point-solutions, but marketing tools become much more powerful when they are integrated into one seamless system. In HubSpot, your content tools (like the blog, email, content management system, and social media) are all strengthened by shared data and integration into a powerful contact database. This means your marketing can become much more personal, adaptive, and connected to your bottom line. Incidentally, it also saves you from a lot of needless exporting and importing of data.

What are some of HubSpot's key SEO features?

Search engine optimization is central to inbound marketing and a cornerstone of HubSpot marketing software. In 2012, we looked at a sample of more than 150 businesses using closed-loop marketing analytics (two-way messaging with customers), and found that:

- SEO leads (leads from organic search) have a 14.6% close rate, while leads that come from outbound marketing techniques like traditional advertising on TV, radio, and print have a 1.7% close rate.

- SEO leads are also eight times more likely to close into customers than outbound leads.

- In addition, leads from inbound links (referrals) are five times more likely to become customers than outbound leads.

Getting found online starts with creating useful, search-friendly content that will attract visitors and inbound links. HubSpot's Keyword tools helps you do so by enabling you to find the right keywords for your content. The Keyword tools also make it possible to track your performance on those keywords, and the performance of your competitors, over time. The Page Performance tool provides you with an instant diagnostic report for every new website, blog, or landing page you produce. With Page Performance, you're able to check to make sure you have keyword-rich headers, tags, and an appropriate length meta description, among other key metrics.

Finally, within the blogging software, you can get as-you-type advice on optimizing your posts for search.

If you're not a HubSpot customer, you can still get a free diagnostic report on your overall rank and SEO through http://marketing.grader.com and learn from any of our downloadable toolkits how to optimize for search and social media.

What kind of Keyword tools does HubSpot have?

Our Keyword tools make it easy to find the right keywords to create a solid SEO strategy. Users can first find new keywords through our suggestions tool that provides keywords based on a URL or search term. After finding potential keywords, HubSpot analyzes each keyword for potential searches, the user's current rank, and how difficult it is to rank well for those keywords. All this is great data to help you determine which keywords to actually target. Once you've chosen the right keywords, HubSpot keeps you focused by tracking how well your content strategy aligns with your chosen keywords. HubSpot continuously tracks your keywords, monitoring how well they're driving traffic and providing suggestions on keywords to focus on and keywords that could generate more conversions.

How does HubSpot help with link building and monitoring backlinks?

HubSpot tracks all inbound links both on a page and on an aggregate basis. Each link is analyzed based on its authority, the linking domain, and what types of traffic the domain is referring. We break down the traffic type based on visitors, contacts, and customers to inform HubSpot users about how qualified the traffic is. Users can expand on their link-building strategies by researching inbound linking strategies for any domain, including their competitors'. Since HubSpot is an all-in-one application, users can leverage the blogging, landing page, and website software to create content to continuously attract and track more inbound links.

How does HubSpot improve a company's social media management and marketing efforts?

The biggest challenge that marketers seem to face with social media is finding the time to manage it and understanding the ROI. HubSpot's social media tools were designed specifically for marketers. We started with the core needs marketers have and built in the one thing noticeably missing from every other tool available today: an integration with a powerful contact database. Without that, social media interactions are just surface-level. Without that, you have no view into the role social media played in customer conversions. Without that, social media will always be limited. Because HubSpot is a completely integrated platform, social media becomes a serious marketing tool. HubSpot Social Media enables you to:

- Get suggestions for timing your posts and scheduling content at optimal times.

- View engagement data for individual posts.

- Save a list of contacts who clicked on a given message for later lead nurturing.

- See how many leads and customers social media has generated.

- Find and leverage influencers by pulling a list of any contact of yours with more than 1,000 followers.

- Understand your leads' social activity before you call them.

How does HubSpot help with blogging?

HubSpot Blog Software simplifies blogging, but it also makes you a better blogger over time.

- **Coming up with blog ideas:** Because our software is integrated with the Keywords tool, you can get recommendations on topics that will increase your search rankings.

- **Finding time/focus to write:** Finding time to blog is up to you, but HubSpot's full-screen mode helps to reduce distractions. Our analytics show you which posts have been most effective in the past, so you know you're spending your time on a worthwhile topic.

Web Marketing On All Cylinders - John McDougall

- **Getting traffic:** In addition to integration with SEO tools that help your posts get found, the software gives you as-you-type advice on how to improve your posts. Auto-publishing to social media channels helps your content reach a larger audience.

- **Converting blog traffic:** There's no use generating traffic if you can't convert it. That's where an all-in-one platform comes in. With HubSpot you can generate calls to action (CTAs) right in your blog posts and connect directly to landing pages for conversions. In addition, at the professional and enterprise levels, you can use Smart CTAs, which dynamically change based on the interests and experiences of the person looking at them. This helps you to get the right message to the right person.

How does HubSpot compare to WordPress, and is a WordPress blog compatible with HubSpot?

HubSpot has an integration with WordPress that allows you to track traffic from your WordPress site within HubSpot. There's also an importer that will help you transfer your WordPress blog to HubSpot should you choose to move it over. Moving your blog or website to HubSpot brings some additional benefits beyond analytics. You can get built-in, as-you-type advice on how to optimize each blog post, take advantage of the "call to action generator" and dynamically changing Smart CTAs, and trigger emails and other notifications from page views and downloads.

How does HubSpot help with lead nurturing?

HubSpot features a robust yet easy-to-use marketing automation tool called Workflows, which makes it simple to build lead-nurturing campaigns and automate mundane marketing tasks. Campaigns can be triggered based on virtually any criteria, from a list of contacts, or automatically when a lead fills out a form or landing page, or when a lead meets any kind of criteria (a lead score, a value stored on their record, the completion of a certain action, or other criteria). Lead nurturing uses HubSpot's native email marketing tool, so it takes advantage of all the features described below, too.

How does HubSpot help with email marketing?

Email marketing in HubSpot is designed to be a perfect balance between power and ease of use. Setting up an email campaign in HubSpot takes literally minutes. Choose a list, select a template, and build all of the content and settings for your campaign on one easy-to-use screen. A live preview of the message appears on the left side of the tool as you create your message. You can change virtually every aspect of the look and feel of the message with no technical knowledge, including adding text, images, links, formatting, and styling, and more. You can personalize emails with any detail from the lead's record, and even make the emails look like they are coming from the sales rep working with a lead. From a design standpoint, HubSpot comes pre-loaded with over a dozen mobile-optimized, cross-platform-tested email templates, and adding or building a new template is easy.

How does it help with competitive analysis?

HubSpot offers a number of ways to easily track what your competitors are doing and monitor how you stack up. Understanding how you're doing relative to your competition is the first step to determining strategies to crush them.

HubSpot's **Competitors app** allows you to track up to 10 competitors across key metrics such as Marketing Grade, Traffic Rank, Indexed Pages, Linking Domain, mozRank, Facebook Fans, and Twitter Followers. You're able to see a snapshot of your current standings as well as a graph over time so that you can track your progress and standing relative to your competitors. You can drill deeper into each competitor by running a detailed Marketing Grader report for each one. This report provides a detailed analysis of a site's marketing performance on everything from blogging and social media to conversion opportunities and marketing analytics. From the Competitors app, you can also view Head-to-Head reports to easily compare your metrics against any of your competitors' metrics.

HubSpot's **Keywords app** is integrated with the Competitors app to show you where your competitors stand for the keywords you're tracking. When it comes to search, being on the first and second pages of the search results can make a world of difference when it comes to driving qualified traffic to your site. With the Keywords app, you can see which keywords you rank ahead of or behind your competition for. Used with other HubSpot tools, the Keywords app helps you take the next step, writing content that targets that keyword or improving your on-page SEO.

How is HubSpot different in terms of analytics?

HubSpot data is centered around individuals, while platforms like Google Analytics are focused on groups of people. For example, Google Analytics will tell you how many people visited a specific page. HubSpot tells you that John Doe visited this page. This individual information is great for better targeting and personalization of content. While our data is individual-focused, it's also rolled up into easy-to-understand dashboards. Our dashboards alert users as to how each source contributed to a customer conversion and how a prospect moved from being a visitor to a contact to a customer. Finally, our integration with content creation tools makes it easier to do event tracking. HubSpot tracks form submissions, button clicks, and page visits through the click of a button.

Why does HubSpot use cookies?

HubSpot uses cookies for a variety of reasons:

- To provide website analytics that help marketers dissect the origin, actions, and makeup of visitors on their website.

- To track each user's granular individual interactions with your website. (These records are anonymous unless a user decides to disclose his or her information through a form submission.)

- To personalize the content users see on our customers' websites. For example, as a marketer, I could assign an individual contact or group of contacts to a "smart list," and serve targeted messaging and images to members of that list in specific blocks of content on my website.

- To be used by HubSpot's progressive profiling feature, which allows our forms and landing pages to ask new, relevant questions over time, instead of asking leads the same questions they have already answered on prior visits.

HubSpot provides the means for our customers to fully comply with the European Union's "cookies law" (e-Privacy directive) (http://www.ico.gov.uk/for_organisations/privacy_and_electronic_communications/the_guide/cookies.aspx) and other laws governing the use of cookies in their locality. HubSpot does not employ third-party cookies in any way.

Can I create landing pages with HubSpot?

Yes! Landing pages are the center point of a good lead generation strategy, so HubSpot has put a particular focus on making them easy to set up and tightly integrated with the rest of your key marketing channels. HubSpot research (http://www.hubspot.com/state-of-inbound-marketing) shows that companies with 30 or more landing pages generate seven times more leads than those with fewer than 10 landing pages. The concept here is an extension of one of the core tenets of inbound marketing: create good, useful, and keyword-rich content and place it behind a landing page form to enable people to opt in by downloading it for free. Opting in by completing the form enables people to give you a sense of their interests and opens the door for more tailored communications down the line. The core components of HubSpot Landing Pages include:

- **Marketer-Controlled Templates and Design:** Templates have drag-and-drop functionality, and using the editor is just like typing into a Word document, so marketers without technical experience can easily create and publish pages to the web.

- **"Smart" Forms:** One of the most irritating things in online search is having to fill out a form you've already completed a half-dozen times before. HubSpot forms are smarter because they recognize anyone who has previously completed a form on your site and allow you to choose to remove form fields for which you already have good data. This makes forms shorter over time and keeps leads happy. Alternately, as form fields fall away, you can replace them with more advanced questions, allowing you to build a deeper profile of your leads over time. We call this progressive profiling.

- **Contact Database Integration:** HubSpot has a built-in contact database that automatically syncs with customer relationship management systems (CRMs) like Salesforce, which means your days of exporting and importing CSV lists are over. All data from your landing page conversions are stored in the contact database, enabling you to segment leads based on interests, behavior, and form-submission details. This integration also enables lead scoring and other advanced lead management strategies.

- **Social Media Integration:** Social media is a great way to attract people to your landing pages. HubSpot landing pages have built-in social media "share" buttons and tracking for Twitter, LinkedIn, Facebook, Pinterest, and email. There's no extra coding required to track shares through these buttons. HubSpot can show you how many of your visits, leads, and customers have come from social media, and which shares got clicks and interactions.

- **Mobile Optimized with Responsive Design:** Because of the increasing role of mobile in product research and purchase decisions, HubSpot's landing pages templates are built to be mobile-ready out of the box. They were built using responsive design which repackages your page for smartphones, tablets, or whatever device comes next. Think of it as future-proofing your pages.

- **A/B Testing:** At the enterprise level, HubSpot also offers A/B testing, which helps you test any element on your page and make data-driven decisions to increase conversions.

How does HubSpot help with conversion optimization?

One of the best ways to increase conversion is to reduce friction on the way to the point of decision. In 2012, we did some research on the most important design factor on websites, and found that the vast majority of respondents like sites that make it easy to find what they need. HubSpot's landing pages are optimized to be easily readable on any device and enable you to reduce the number of fields in your forms so conversions are quicker. You can test two versions of a landing page and track the conversion rates and leads generated for each one, so you can continually improve your offers and landing page text.

Increasing conversions goes beyond single pages, however. We've found that the best way to increase conversions is to tailor communications and content to match a potential lead's interests and which stage of the decision process they are in. For example, you don't want to force someone to talk to sales the very first time they land on your website. Nurturing leads over time with personalized emails through HubSpot can increase conversions and actually shorten the sales cycle. Plus, it's a better experience overall for your leads.

How many leads did HubSpot customers generate in 2012?

HubSpot has 8,400 customers in over 56 countries, a number that has grown by 42% in the last year. In 2012, 93% of our customers reported an increase in leads, with 38% doubling their lead flow in 12 months. In total, HubSpot's customer base has added 46 million contacts this year with inbound marketing. That's in comparison to 12.4 million the previous year and 4.1 million in 2010.

Here are a couple of my favorite customer success stories:

- Bell Performance gained 600 new online customers in the first year (http://bit.ly/bellhubspot).

- Vivonet increased landing page conversions from 0.9% to 10% and saw a 100% increase in leads from the company website (http://bit.ly/vivonethubspot).

In 2013, an MIT Sloan MBA student completed a research study on the ROI of using HubSpot software. Here are a few highlights of the key findings:

- Overall, users experienced an average of 2.7 times more traffic after 12 months of active use.

- Overall, users experienced lead database growth of 30.4 times after 12 months of active use.

- After three months of use, HubSpot customers generated an average of 33% more leads per month.

You can download the full report at http://hubspot.com/roi.

Tell me about HubSpot's CMS options.

For marketers who need more control of their website or who want to remove bottlenecks in publishing content, HubSpot offers a content management system (CMS). Any business owner or marketing professional can create new pages, update old pages, create landing pages, and build lead collection forms. All pages and blog posts are automatically integrated with Twitter, Facebook, and LinkedIn content-sharing buttons to help you grow your reach with little to no effort. Website Manager is available to all HubSpot customers. Hub-

Spot Pro and Enterprise customers can also integrate HubSpot's marketing platform with external content management systems. It's worth noting that in 2012 and 2013, HubSpot made a significant investment in the next stage of our content system. So you'll be seeing more advances and updates on this soon.

How much does HubSpot cost?

HubSpot's pricing is 100% transparent—you can spec out your own price at hubspot.com/pricing. Generally speaking, pricing starts at $200, $600, or $1,000 per month depending on the product level, and scales up based on the number of contacts you store in our system.

If I'm not ready for HubSpot software but want to improve my marketing, what can I do?

I'd make three suggestions for anyone trying to improve their marketing or get into inbound marketing. Even if you aren't at a place where the software makes sense for you, take advantage of the many resources that HubSpot offers for free.

1) Marketing Grader: It helps to know where to start. Marketing Grader (http://marketing.grader.com/) is a free diagnostic tool that quickly assesses your marketing and suggests a few areas to focus your improvement efforts. You can get a scored assessment of your SEO, social media, blog, email marketing, mobile optimization, analytics, and more. You can also get assessments of your competitors' sites to see how you stack up against them using common metrics.

2) The Inbound Marketing Blog: Located at http://blog.hubspot.com, the inbound marketing blog gets more than 1 million visits each month. It is chock-full of marketing ideas, research, resources, and templates that will make your day-to-day life easier and your marketing more inbound-friendly.3) Resources: We are big believers in quality content (if you haven't picked up on that already!), so each month we release a series of instructive, informative ebooks on common marketing challenges and new ideas. We also offer ongoing webinars on topics like learning SEO, improving your lead generation strategies, landing page optimization, email marketing, and marketing automation. Finally, we offer templates and kits to save marketers time.

What separates HubSpot from other marketing software?

We love our software. But software is just part of the picture. Where HubSpot stands apart from other marketing software tools is in our utter commitment to inbound marketing and helping our customers create marketing that people can actually love. To do that you need more than software. Our approach is three-fold. We offer 1) a proven methodology for attracting and converting leads, 2) the software to execute on that methodology, and 3) the support and services to make you great at it.

Our services go beyond a simple set-up. We've built out a complete inbound marketing academy that customers can tap at any point. They can get free resources and training classes with "Inbound Professors" to brush up on parts of the software or entire marketing strategies. At any point, you can call our support line and talk with one of our staff about the software or any challenges you're having. We also have an entire partner network of marketing agencies that know HubSpot inside and out and can be hired to help you execute your inbound campaigns.

The point is, we see this as a movement and want to make sure that anyone who uses HubSpot for inbound marketing has what they need to succeed at it.

What excites you most in 2013 and beyond about HubSpot in particular and inbound marketing in general?

This is an incredibly exciting time at HubSpot. You can feel it throughout the orange hallways of our building. In 2012, we launched HubSpot 3, the most advanced HubSpot platform to date. We also announced the opening of our first international office in Dublin, Ireland. This year, we aren't slowing down a bit. We continue to improve our software and imagine, plan, and build new tools to make marketing better for both companies and their customers. This year will bring a few new announcements and a stronger-than-ever commitment to being the company that speaks for marketers and the love of good marketing. It's idealistic, but we spend every day backing it up with tools, resources, and support.

As for inbound marketing, I think we'll see a number of trends start to take shape in the coming year, and one underlying theme: Inbound marketing will need to become much more adaptive to the changing ways that people research and buy products or services online.

Today's leads access content from multiple *devices*. They come at it from a number of different *channels*. And, perhaps most importantly, as their experience with your company grows, their *needs and interests* change. I think you'll see inbound marketers begin to do more with personalization across all devices, channels, and lifecycle stages. It will take some time, but I believe the next stage of inbound marketing will enable you as a marketer to pivot around the devices your website visitors use, the interests they've expressed on your site, and the entire history of interactions they've shared with your company.

*   *   *

Now that you have a better understanding of one of our favorite all-in-one tools, let's look in the next chapter at our collection of Internet marketing tools and resources.

Chapter 16

Internet Marketing Tools

Tools are an essential part of Internet marketing and this chapter offers an introduction to the almost endless array of website marketing tools.

All-in-One

HubSpot is a terrific tool that offers a variety of functions ranging from SEO recommendations and social media management to lead nurturing. There are better tools just for SEO like SEOMoz or SEO Book, better tools for social management like Radian6, and better tools just for marketing automation, but as an all-in-one tool, I know of nothing like it.

Eloqua, Marketo, and Pardot, HubSpot's main competitors, essentially have no options for getting leads. Their focus is solely on what happens once a user becomes a lead.

Dharmesh Shah, one of the founders of HubSpot, says that it only "competes" with these other internet marketing systems in the way an iPhone competes with a digital camera. He says, "Sure the iPhone has a camera, but that's not the only reason someone buys an iPhone." See the chapter on HubSpot for more details (Chapter 15).

Auditing/Competitive Analysis Tools

Marketing.grader.com by HubSpot - Plug your URL into marketing.grader.com and it gives you a score—from 1 to 100—reflecting your website's visibility to the search engines, social media presence, blog activity, conversion optimization, and more. The best part is the report, which gives you tips and step-by-step instructions to improve your search-social-friendliness. You can run this tool on any site, so use it to check out your competitors as well.

SEMrush is an SEO keyword research tool that shows you what keywords your competitors are ranking well for and what that traffic might be worth. It also shows you to some degree what your competitors are buying for keywords in AdWords and the cost per click.

Klout is a measure of your influence on social networks like Twitter and Facebook. It's good for finding influencers, but be careful that you don't get over-hyped about it in terms of your actual score because many feel the algorithm it uses is flawed.

Compete.com is one of the most well-known competitive analysis tools for things like comparing unique visitors. The number of visitors it shows won't likely line up exactly with your website analytics, but it is good for getting a ballpark "read" on which sites get lots of traffic.

Search Engine Optimization Tools

SEOMoz PRO is the top SEO software, with dozens of tools and valuable SEO resources. Membership in SEOMoz PRO gives you campaign-based web apps, dozens of SEO tools, webinars, and full access to Open SiteExplorer.

SEOMoz's Open Site Explorer pulls data from over 50 billion web pages and about 10 trillion links. Here at McDougall Interactive, it is our go-to source for exploring links and the links of competitors.

SEO Book offers a great forum and a set of free and paid web-based SEO tools.

SEO Book's SEO for Firefox Plugin is an indispensable quick analysis tool. You get data such as: PageRank, Google's Cache Date, Traffic Value, Site Age, del.icio.us, del.icio.us Page Bookmarks, Diggs, Diggs Popular Stories, StumbleUpon, Twitter, Y! links, Y! edu links, Y! gov links, Y! Page links, Y! edu page links, OSE links to page, OSE links to domain, Blekko domainlinks, Technorati, Alexa, Compete.com rank, Compete.com uniques, Cached, Dmoz, Bloglines, Page blog links, wikipedia, dir.yahoo.com, BOTW, Business, and Majestic SEO linkdomain .

SEO Book's Hub Finder Sites that link out to several competitors are worth getting links from them yourself. You can plug in 2 to 10 of your competitors to see sites that link to as many of them as you specify.

Google Webmaster Tools Essentials is very useful tool that you can use to analyze your website's performance and fix errors.

SEO Browser shows how a search engine looks at your site. It strips away the CSS or any styles, and displays text and links.

Firefox SEO and Social Tool Plug-ins (addons.mozilla.org/en-US/firefox) There are thousands of add-ons for Mozilla and lots of great ones for SEO and social media marketing.

Raven has a tool set including SEO, social media, and advertising tools.

Majestic SEO links intelligence tools for SEO and online public relations and marketing.

Web Marketing On All Cylinders - John McDougall

The link tools are outstanding.

More SEO Tools

- Searchmetrics Suite

- SISTRIX

- UpCity.com

- Web CEO

- Conductor Searchlight

- Ontolo

- Linkdex

- gShift Labs

- FlamingoSoft SEO Administrator

- Trend Matrix SEO Studio

- Apex Pacific SEO Suite

Keyword ToolsGoogle AdWords Keyword Tool (https://adwords.google.com/o/Keyword-Tool): We tend to use this first because it is data coming directly from Google.

The following short list includes tools that are also good for keyword research:

> **KeywordSpy:** http://www.keywordspy.com
>
> **Wordtracker:** http://www.wordtracker.com
>
> **Keyword Discovery:** http://www.keyworddiscovery.com
>
> **Lexical Database:** http://www.wordnetweb.princeton.edu/perl/webwn
>
> **Ubersuggest.org** takes your keyphrase and extracts "Google Suggest" suggestions for it and lets you export results to a text file to give you expanded keyword ideas.

Social Media Marketing Tools

Radian6: A social media monitoring, engaging, and sharing tool that is the industry leader. Starting at $600 per month per domain.

HootSuite: Lets you publish updates, track activity, and analyze results across multiple social networks including Twitter and Facebook. HootSuite also integrates with HubSpot. (HootSuite has a free version.)

Twellow: Twitter Yellow Pages.

TweetBeep: Keep track of your brand reputation by getting alerts through email when your brand is mentioned on Twitter.

Twitter Grader: A site that ranks your influence in the Twitter world based on an algorithm. You can see where you stand in your town, city, state, or country.

Tweet Adder: Helps you manage your Twitter followers.

Twitterfall: It's like an animated RSS reader, but with such nice additional features as location filtering and exclusions. I like Twitterfall as a way to keep up with the very latest in what people are saying about topics you're following, as well as the simplicity of aggregating multiple topics. This monitors the entire Twittersphere, not just the people you follow. It's a good way to impress upon reluctant executives the volume of conversation around a market or brand.

Listorious: Although Listorious has recently been trying to rebrand itself as an expertise locator, its core value is in its collection of Twitter lists curated by members. If you want to find lists of CIOs, or marketers, or people in the construction industry, Listorious is the place to start. I recommend newcomers to Twitter go here to quickly find lists of people to follow, which is the first step in building your own follower base.

Social Mention: Allows for comprehensive social media searching, and indexes blogs, tweets, and message board posts.

More Social Media Tools

- Wildfire APP

- Sprout SocialSeesmic CRM

- Virtue

- Adobe SocialAnalytics

- Buddy Media

- Awareness Social Marketing Hub

- Shoutlet

- Sendible

- Spreadfast Social CRM

- Crowd Factory

- Crimson Hexagon

- Postling

- Engage121

- Syncapse Platform

- Mzinga

Website Analytics Software

Google Analytics: Excels at giving you great insight into how people are getting to and interacting with your website. It shows you where visitors are coming from, what they are actually clicking on, and how they are interacting with your site.

HubSpot: As HubSpot says, "Google Analytics shows you raw numbers of users. HubSpot shows you real people." Analytics software is useless without traffic and leads to track and then follow up on, so HubSpot combines driving traffic with analyzing and converting it.

Google Analytics has great data and even A/B testing ability, but HubSpot is fully integrated with your sales team and lead nurturing program. Ideally, you should use both.

ClickTale: Lets you watch users' click paths and how much they scroll on your website. This tool provides additional essential analytic information that Google Analytics does not.

Crazy Egg: Has been referred to as the "poor man's ClickTale." It is a highly regarded tool that starts at only $9 per month and has a free 30-day trial. You can see where users click and discover what Google Analytics is not telling you, thanks to heatmap, scrollmap, and overlay tools.

Adobe SiteCatalyst powered by Omniture: Adobe Site Catalyst is expensive, more complicated to install and use than Google Analytics, but has powerful testing systems and integration with Salesforce and email systems. This allows you to connect the information your sales team gathers with your web data. Google Analytics Premium is a flat $150,000 per year and is a competitor to this advanced tool.

Mongoose Metrics: The authority for exposing what happens before, during, and after phone calls generated by your website down to the keyword level.

Facebook Analytics/Facebook Insights: Click the gear wheel in your Facebook Fan Page and choose "View Insights" to find the main Insights dashboard for the total number of likes, number of friends of fans available (potential reach), how many people are actively talking about your page, and your total weekly reach.

YouTube Insight (youtube.com/t/advertising_insight): Offers analytics that show what your viewers like and don't like so you can improve your video marketing. You can filter reports by content, geography and date, and there is an interactive geographic distribution map that comes with most reports. You can track most views and subscriptions as well as how long viewers spent watching your videos.

Twitter Analytics (analytics.twitter.com): See how much of your content got shared across the Twittersphere, the volume of traffic Twitter sends to your website, and the effectiveness of your Tweet button integration. You can also see the number of favorites and retweets.

Followerwonk.com: A Twitter analytics tool that provides follower segmentation, social graph tracking, and more.

More Web Analytics Software

- IBM Coremetrics (now part of IBM Enterprise Marketing Management)

- AWStats

- Clicky

- KISSMetrics

- Crazy Egg

- Piwik

- Webtrends Analytics

- VisiStat

- Woopra

- HitsLink

- GoStats

- OneStat

- Deep Log Analyzer

Conversion Rate Optimization Tools

Usertesting.com tests go for about $39 each. You get a 15-minute video of people speaking into a microphone as they try to do assigned tasks on your website. The text summaries and videos show you what is wrong with your site in terms of usability, and/or what people like. Usability testing used to be just for big companies, but now smaller firms can do it for short money.

Google Website Optimizer is a free website testing and optimization tool which is now integrated into Google Analytics as a tool called Content Experiments. Testing alternate versions of headlines, images, and various other elements is the only scientific way to know you are using content that converts.

Visualwebsiteoptimizer.com is an easy to use A/B testing tool that uses a point-and-click editor (no HTML knowledge needed!).

nGagelive.com can help you increase conversions and lets your website users chat with a representative 24/7. By letting the nGage representatives ask for customer contact information and what they are looking for, you don't have to worry about being available to chat. The nGage reps won't answer questions about your business; they just collect information and then you follow up.

Liveperson.com allows you to run your own live chat.

The WeWe Monitor is a customer focus calculator from futurenowinc.com/wewe.htm that can help you to avoid talking about yourself too much!

Feng-gui.com lets you see where visitors' eyes are looking. This is a robotic approximation versus very expensive eye tracking, but it provides great insights and is loved by many conversion experts.

Unbounce.com lets you publish and test landing pages online without developers or software.

Content and Blogging ToolsWordPress is a free, open-source blogging tool and a content management system (CMS). It is simply the best. So many people use it that the add-ons and plug-ins, like Yoast's SEO plug-in, make it a must-have.

Copyscape checks for plagiarism and is partnered with Google. The free search is limited to 10 results. The premium service costs a few cents per search.

Social by MailChimp is a great tool for managing blog comments (http://mailchimp.com/social-plugin-for-wordpress). It integrates WordPress with Twitter and Facebook, so you can collect blog comments in one place. It encourages people to retweet your content, which is often more likely than people sharing your content on Facebook. The tool makes retweeting and sharing easy to do and the retweets help your SEO and social buzz. Having more social activity and interaction makes your blog look alive and helps you be seen as a thought leader. This is one of the keys to increasing conversions. There is nothing more persuasive than social proof, hence the revolution in social media.

Disqus is a another well-respected tool for managing blog comments. (Disqus.com)

The All in One SEO Pack plug-in from Yoast is great for SEO-optimizing your blog.

The Genesis and Thesis themes for WordPress come with loads of SEO and social benefits built right into them.

More Content and Blogging Software

- Blog.com

- Blogger.com

- Typepad

- Posterous Spaces

- Weebly

- Joomla

- Drupal

- SquareSpace

- Acquia

- Sitefinity

- Alfresco

- Textpattern

- Kapost

- Compendium

- Extron

- Movable Type

- CrownPeak

- Ceros

Paid Search Marketing Tools

Acquisio is a worthwhile paid search management tool that has very useful reports.

More Paid Search Marketing Software

- WordStream

- ClickEquations

- Marin Software

- BoostCTR

- Clickable

- Apex Pacific BidMax

- Digital River Keyword Max

- ClickSweeper

- Kenshoo

- AdWords Editor

- BidRank

- WordWatch

Email Marketing

Constant Contact, Vertical Response, and MailChimp are all high-quality, low-cost email options.

BlueSky Factory (now rebranded as **WhatCounts**) is a higher-end email marketing program and has advanced integration with social media.

More Email Marketing Software

- AWeber

- iContact

- CheetahMail

- ExactTarget

- Bronto

- MadMimi

- Campaign Monitor

- Lyris

- SendBlaster

- NetProspex

- Responsys

- PinPointe On-Demand

- MailGen

- Arial Software

Video Hosting and Management Tools

OneLoad (www.oneload.com): A video distribution tool that makes uploading your video content to several sites easy to manage.

More Video Marketing Tools

- Vimeo

- Brightcove

- Viddler

- Brainshark

- Wistia

- Kaltura

- Ooyala

- Vzaar

- Pixability

- thePlatform

- VisibleGains

Marketing Automation Software

Marketo, Pardot, and **Eloqua** are among the very expensive marketing automation tools, but have high-end functionality if you have hundreds of thousands or millions of leads. Try HubSpot if you want to start automating things like lead nurturing but want a less expensive integrated web marketing solution that is easier to set up and use.

More Marketing Automation Tools

- HubSpot

- Pardot

- NetSuite CRM

- Silverpop Engage

- Vocus

- IBM Unica

- Optify

- Sitecore

- Aprimo

- LoopFuse

- Genius.com

- SalesFusion 360

- Alterian

- Net-Results

- eTrigue DemandCenter

- Neolane Leads

- PlanPlus CRM

- Genoo Marketing Automation

Public Relations Submission Sites

Top PR Sites/Tools

Marketwire.com (Starting around $300)
Businesswire.com (Starting around $300)
PRnewswire.com (Starting around $300)
PRweb.com (Starting around $150)

Examples of Free Press Release Submission Sites

PRLog.com

PressExposure.com

Information-Online.com

Free-news-release.com

Miscellaneous

Salesforce.com: Best known for its customer relationship management (CRM) software. You can manage your sales contacts and keep detailed information about their likes and interactions with your company. It is extremely powerful when integrated with your website through contact forms and/or through HubSpot.

AdSense (google.com/adsense): Google AdSense allows publishers to place ads on their websites and share in the profits with Google.

AdWords (adwords.google.com): Google AdWords is an advertising program that uses text ads and display ads where the advertisers only pay when an ad actually gets clicked and sends someone to your website.

Affiliate Marketing Tools: Affiliate marketing allows merchants to expand their reach by paying a commission to publishers (such as blogs) willing to place advertisements on their website that link to a merchant. Get thousands of people linking (with nofollow links) to you and get great visibility that only has a cost if you make money!

Commission Junction (cj.com) and LinkShare (linkshare.com): Two outstanding affiliate marketing tools.

Bitly.com: Offers URL shortening/redirection service with real-time link tracking. Essential for Twitter, etc.

Basecamp (37signals.com): Project management software used by millions of companies to increase productivity and collaboration. It is also a great way to make sure all your marketing information gets backed up off your team's computers.

Qualaroo (Qualaroo.com): Consider offering a one- to three-question survey on your site (using Qualaroo) to see what customers are feeling and to get feedback. This type of market research for pennies on the dollar is well worth trying.

WiseStamp.com: Put your blog URL in your email signature.

Google Trends (http://www.google.com/trends)

Google Insights (http://www.google.com/insights/search)

Evernote (evernote.com): Simple note-taking software to keep you organized. Works well with paper scanners to get all your piles of loose papers into a searchable database.

DoneDone (getdonedone.com): Very simple and highly effective for tracking projects.

Balsamiq (balsamiq): Great for mocking up ideas/wire framing and highly intuitive for non-developers or non-designers. Lots of cool drag-and-drop elements.

Google Reader: Great RSS reader.

"Google Operators": Try using site:yoursite.com as a search in Google, which will show only pages Google has indexed for your site.

Basic operators are here: google.com/help/operators.html

Advanced operators are here: (googleguide.com/advanced_operators.html)

VeCapture (veinteractive.com/vecapture.php): Captures abandoned online transactions and registrations. Shopping cart abandonment software isn't for everyone, but it does work. Our friends at VeInteractive are one of the clear leaders in this space and work on a commission-only basis. You only pay them a percentage when a customer you otherwise would have lost comes back and buys. If you have very little traffic, it likely won't give you a big boost.

Sitemap and page URL/title generator (auditmypc.com/free-sitemap-generator.asp)

Whois.net: Allows you to check a website's age.

ADA compliance check (The Americans with Disabilities Act) (https://addons.mozilla. org/en-US/firefox/addon/accessibility-evaluation-toolb/): Making a site work well for the visually impaired also helps it for SEO because robots and spiders don't "see" but crawl through links and tags.

Clean IP check with mxtoolbox: Check your server's IP block for other websites that may cause your site to be blacklisted. Free: MX Lookup (www.mxtoolbox.com). Paid: DNSstuff (www.dnsstuff.com) Pingdom: Lets you conduct a site speed test, and monitor website uptime and downtime.

Web Marketing On All Cylinders - John McDougall

W3 Total Cache (wordpress.org/extend/plugins/w3-total-cache): Makes your WordPress site load faster.

Xenu Link Sleuth broken link tool (http://home.snafu.de/tilman/xenulink.html): Under "File | Check URL…" enter the URL of the link list/resources page. Also, add the first part of the URL (just through the root domain) to the "Do not check any URLs beginning with this" box, to eliminate internal links. Look for links that come back with a status of "not found" (a 404 error).

The "Wayback Machine" (www.archive.org): An Internet archive that has a huge record of websites and their multiple versions dating back to the early 1990s.

Google Alerts (google.com/alerts): Set up Google Alerts for name, company name, and topics of interest to you. This is invaluable for finding bloggers that have linked to your posts, so you can go to their blogs and thank them in the comments.

Flickr Creative Commons Search–Royalty-free Images (flickr.com/creativecommons and photopin.com): Using Flickr's advanced search, you can find Creative Commons licensed images that you can use with attribution in blog posts, etc.

Camtasia (camtasiasoftware.com): Allows you to make screencasts of your products, demonstrations, etc.

Standard Domain Name Registration Sites

- Register.com

- Network Solutions

- eNom.com

- Namecheap.com

Aftermarket Domain Sites

- Buydomains.com

- Afternic.com

- Sedo.com

- Flippa.com (where you can buy whole sites and domains with content)

Internet Marketing Conferences

Search Engine Strategies – SES (sesconference.com)

Search Marketing Expo – SMX (searchmarketingexpo.com)

HubSpot Inbound Marketing Summit (inboundconference.com)

Social Media Success Summit (socialmediaexaminer.com/upcoming-events)

Social Media Marketing World (socialmediaexaminer.com/smmworld)

Conversion Conference (conversionconference.com)

Pubcon (pubcon.com)

SXSW Interactive (sxsw.com)

eMetrics Summit (emetrics.org)

ad:tech (ad-tech.com)

Affiliate Summit (affiliatesummit.com)

BlueGlass (blueglass.com/conferences)

BlogHer (blogher.com)

Content Marketing World (contentmarketingworld.com)

Internet Marketing Blogs and Sites

SEOBook.com	SEOMoz.com
SearchEngineWatch.com	SearchEngineLand.com
SocialMediaExaminer.com	MarketingLand.com
MarketMotive.com	Mashable.com
Copyblogger.com	ProBlogger.com
Lynda.com	Influenceatwork.com

PR Marketing Websites

HelpAReporter.com: Peter Shankman's HARO Report

ReporterConnection.com: Bill & Steve Harrison's Reporter Connection

InstituteforPR.org: Institute for Public Relations

Web Marketing On All Cylinders - John McDougall

PRSA.org: Public Relations Society of America

IABC.com: International Association of Business Communicators

PRNewswire.com: PR Newswire

PRNewswire.com/mediainsider: Media Insider

ODwyerPR.com: O'Dwyer's PR Market Place

Infocomgroup.com: InfoCom Group - Bulldog Reporter

PRweek.com: PRWeek

Top Paid Directories to Consider

- Yahoo Directory: $299 per year (dir.yahoo.com)

- Better Business Bureau (bbb.org/us/bbb-accreditation-application/)

- Joeant (Joeant.com)

- Best of the Web (botw.com)

- Business.com

Blog Directories - Submit to only the best relevant directories such as:

1. Technorati.com/blogs/directory   2. Bloggeries.com

3. BlogHints.com   4. Portal.EatonWeb.com

5. Ontoplist.com   6. Bloglines

7. BlogCatalog.com   8. Blogarama

9. Bloggernity   10. Blogs.botw.org

Syndicate Your Blog Content to sites like usatoday.com, CNN, ehow, and Fast Company by feeding them your content from the following places:

1. IFTTT.com   2. BlogCatalog.com

3. DemandStudios.com   4. https://kindlepublishing.amazon.com/gp/vendor

5. NetworkedBlogs.com   6. Alltop.com

5 Podcast Directories

1. PodCast411.com
2. RIMpodcast.quickplay.ca/rimpodcasting
3. Social.Zune.net/podcasts
4. Stitcher.com/contentProviders.php
5. Blogdigger.com/add.jsp

5 Video Directories

1. PureVideo.com
2. Searchvideo.com
3. Search.SingingFish.com
4. SearchForVideo.com
5. Blinkx.com

5 Photo Directories

1. Pinterest.com
2. Flickr.com
3. Fotoblur.com
4. Shutterfly.com
5. Photobucket.com

Top Social Bookmarking Sites

1. Twitter
2. Reddit
3. Pinterest
4. StumbleUpon
5. BuzzFeed
6. Delicious
7. Tweetmeme
8. Digg
9. Fark
10. Slashdot
11. FriendFeed
12. Clipmarks
13. Newsvine
14. Diigo
15. DZone

Niche Social Bookmarking Sites

1. Ballhyped: Sports

2. Chictini: Fashion

3. AutoSpies: Autos

4. Livestrong.com: Health and Medicine

5. Hacker News: Web Development

Directories/Sites That May Help Your Google+ Local Listing or Drive Local Traffic

1. Citysearch

2. InsiderPages

3. Yelp

4. SuperPages

5. Infogroup

6. Localeze

7. Begin

8. Acxiom

9. Best of the Web's Regional Directory

10. Yahoo's Regional Directory

11. Business.com

12. Yellowpages.com

13. Merchant Circle

14. Foursquare

15. Hotfrog

16. Kudzu

17. DirectoryM

18. Dexknows.com

19. Local.com

20. Mojopages.com

21. Manta.com

22. MacRAEsBlueBook.com

23. Angie's List

24. Judy's Book

25. Comcast

Top 16 Tactics for Social Media

1. Blogging

2. Facebook

3. Twitter

4. Google+

5. YouTube/Video	6. LinkedIn
7. Pinterest	8. Instagram
9. SlideShare/Presentations	10. Docstoc/White papers
11. Flickr/Images	12. iTunes/Podcasting
13. Social Bookmarking	14. StumbleUpon and Tumblr
15. Forums	16. Reviews and Recommendations

Marketing Books

"Inbound" Marketing Books

Inbound Marketing: Get Found Using Google, Social Media, and Blogs by Dharmesh Shah (New Rules Social Media Series)

The New Rules of Marketing and PR: How to Use Social Media, Blogs, News Releases, Online Video, and Viral Marketing to Reach Buyers Directly by David Meerman Scott

Optimize: How to Attract and Engage More Customers by Integrating SEO, Social Media, and Content Marketing by Lee Odden

Marketing Lessons from the Grateful Dead: What Every Business Can Learn from the Most Iconic Band in History by David Meerman Scott and Brian Halligan

Content Marketing and Copywriting Books

Content Marketing: Think Like a Publisher—How to Use Content to Market Online and in Social Media by Rebecca Lieb (Que Biz-Tech)

Content Rules: How to Create Killer Blogs, Podcasts, Videos, Ebooks, Webinars (and More) That Engage Customers and Ignite Your Business by C.C. Chapman (New Rules Social Media)

How to Write a Good Advertisement: A Short Course in Copywriting by Victor O. Schwab

Content Is Currency: Developing Powder Content for Web and Mobile by Jon Wuebben (Nicholas Brealey Publishing)

The Adweek Copywriting Handbook: The Ultimate Guide to Writing Powerful Advertising and Marketing Copy from One of America's Top Copywriters by Joseph Sugarman

Social Media Marketing Books

Trust Agents: Using the Web to Build Influence, Improve Reputation, and Earn Trust by Chris Brogan

The Impact Equation: Are You Making Things Happen or Just Making Noise? by Chris Brogan

Social Marketing to the Business Customer: Listen to Your B2B Market, Generate Major Account Leads, and Build Client Relationships by Paul Gillin and Eric Schwartzman

Secrets of Social Media Marketing: How to Use Online Conversations and Customer Communities to Turbo-Charge Your Business! by Paul Gillin

The New Influencers: A Marketer's Guide to the New Social Media by Paul Gillin and Geoffrey A. Moore (Books to Build Your Career By)

Social Media Metrics: How to Measure and Optimize Your Marketing Investment by Jim Sterne

Social Media ROI: Managing and Measuring Social Media Efforts in Your Organization by Olivier Blanchard (Que Biz-Tech)

Twitter Power: How to Dominate Your Market One Tweet at a Time by Joel Comm

Google+ for Business: How Google's Social Network Changes Everything by Chris Brogan

Maximum Success with LinkedIn: Dominate Your Market, Build a Worldwide Brand, and Create the Career of Your Dreams by Dan Sherman

Search Engine Optimization Books

The Art of SEO by Eric Enge, Stephan Spencer, Jessie Stricchiola, and Rand Fishkin

Search Engine Optimization (SEO) Secrets by Danny Dover and Erik Dafforn

Conversion Optimization Books

Conversion Optimization: The Art and Science of Converting Prospects to Customers by Khalid Saleh and Ayat Shukairy

Always Be Testing: The Complete Guide to Google Website Optimizer by Bryan Eisenberg

Waiting for Your Cat to Bark? Persuading Customers When They Ignore Marketing by Bryan Eisenberg, Jeffrey Eisenberg, and Lisa T. Davis

Call to Action: Secret Formulas to Improve Online Results by Bryan Eisenberg, Jeffrey Eisenberg, and Lisa T. Davis

Landing Page Optimization: The Definitive Guide to Testing and Tuning for Conversions by Tim Ash, Maura Ginty, and Rich Page

Paid Search and Pay-per-Click Books

Pay-per-Click Search Engine Marketing: An Hour a Day by David Szetela

Advanced Google AdWords by Brad Geddes

Killer Facebook Ads: Master Cutting-Edge Facebook Advertising Techniques by Marty Weintraub

Marketing and Branding Books

Influence: The Psychology of Persuasion by Robert B. Cialdini

The 22 Immutable Laws of Branding by Al Ries and Laura Ries

Enchantment: The Art of Changing Hearts, Minds, and Actions by Guy Kawasaki

Killing Giants: 10 Strategies to Topple the Goliath in Your Industry by Stephen Denny

Winning the Zero Moment of Truth—ZMOT by Jim Lecinski

Blue Ocean Strategy by W. Chan Kim

Me 2.0: 4 Steps to Building Your Future by Dan Schawbel

The End Of Marketing as We Know It by Sergio Zyman

Website Analytics Books

Web Analytics: An Hour a Day by Avinash Kaushik

Miscellaneous Books

Don't Make Me Think: A Common Sense Approach to Web Usability by Steve Krug

Learning Web Design: A Beginner's Guide to (X)HTML, StyleSheets, and Web Graphics by Jennifer Niederst Robbins

Viral Explosions! Proven Techniques to Expand, Explode, or Ignite Your Business or Brand Online by Peggy McColl and Michael Gerber

Don't forget ebooks! HubSpot has a pile of great ebooks that are essential for keeping up to date, since things change so fast.

There is no question that Internet marketing has grown up and become highly sophisticated, given all the tools and resources that have developed around it. It is much harder for just one person to do now, because it requires expertise on many levels, from producing high-quality content and optimizing it for search and social, to spreading the word to influencers and journalists. So buckle up and assemble a team of people good at each of the moving parts, and you will be part of the growing number of inbound marketing success stories.

Internet Marketing Glossary

To make reading this book more enjoyable, I suggest taking a few minutes to review this glossary to get familiar with key terms and acronyms. (Just think how informed you will sound at the next meeting with your team!)

301 Redirect

A 301 redirect tells Google that a web page has permanently moved. When you build a new website, it is important to 301 redirect all of the individual pages to the new page names, so that people looking for your website don't get confused by "broken links" (links that don't work) in the search results.

404 Error

A 404 error is when the server is unable to locate a website address (URL). Correct any pages on your website that produce a 404 error. If people link to pages that you have deleted, this will generate a 404 error and the link energy will be wasted.

A/B Testing

The act of testing two different options of creative (such as a headline in an ad or a call to action) to see which one performs best.

Above the Fold

"Above the fold" generally means the portion of the web page that is viewable before you have to scroll down to see the rest of the page.

AdSense

Google AdSense allows publishers to place ads on their websites and share in the profits with Google.

AdWords

Google AdWords is an advertising program using text ads and display ads where the advertiser only pays when someone actually "clicks" on the ad and sends that person to the advertiser's website.

Affiliate Marketing

Affiliate marketing allows merchants to expand their reach by paying a commission to publishers (such as blogs) willing to place advertisements on their websites that link to the merchant. It is not uncommon in affiliate programs to have over 10,000 publishers displaying your ads/banner ads that cost you nothing unless the clicks convert into sales within a few days.

AJAX

Asynchronous JavaScript and XML (AJAX) allows a web page to request additional data from a server without requiring a new page to load.

Algorithm

A set of parameters a search engine uses to match the keywords in a query with the content of each web page, so that the web pages found can be ordered suitably in the query results.

Alt Tags

The "alt" attribute in HTML is code that displays alternative text when a user "mouses" over an image on a web page. It is especially helpful to visually impaired people. It also helps search engines understand what an image is about.

Anchor Text

The text that a user clicks on to follow a link to another web page.

API

An Application Program Interface (API) allows developers to access software functions. Most major search and social software products have an API program.

ASP/ASP.net

Active Server Pages is a dynamic Microsoft programming language.

Black Hat SEO

Black hat search engine optimization is the practice of doing just about anything—including things that are illegal—to achieve top rankings on the search engine results pages.

Bookmarking

Bookmarking allows you to make note of something you found online and save the URL so you can return to it later.

Cache

A copy of a web page that is stored by a search engine. Search engines store website data for analysis at a later date, as opposed to analyzing it on the fly. You can enter the entire query (including the word "cache") "cache:www.yourdomain.com" in a search engine or browser address bar to see when your site was last stored by Google.

Call to Action

A graphic or text block that directs visitors to act in some specific manner, such as requesting a brochure, filling out a form, or making a purchase.

Canonical URL

The canonical version of a URL (website address) is the most authoritative version indexed by major search engines.

Cascading Style Sheets (CSS)

Cascading Style Sheets is a programming method for adding visual styles such as fonts, colors, and formatting to web documents.

Click-through Rate (CTR)

The click-through rate is the percentage of people who view an advertisement online and click on an embedded link in the ad to be taken to a particular web page.

Cloaking

Cloaking is when you display different content to search engines and searchers on the same web page to fool the search engines.

Content Management System (CMS)

Content management systems like WordPress allow website owners to easily edit the content of their pages without needing help from a web developer.

Conversion

A conversion is achieved when a goal is completed, such as when you turn a lead or prospect into a customer.

Conversion Enhancement

A group of tactics designed to increase sales.

Conversion Rate

The ratio of visitors that turn into a sale after taking an action on a website.

Cookie

A small data file written to a user's local machine to track their activity.

Cost per Action (CPA)

Cost per action is the amount it costs to get one lead or sale.

Cost per Click (CPC)

Cost per click is the amount the advertiser pays each time a user clicks on a paid ad and is pulled to the advertiser's website.

CPM

Cost per thousand ad impressions is what it costs an advertiser to show 1,000 people an ad.

Dayparting

Turning ad campaigns on or off (starting or stopping ad campaigns), changing an ad bid price, or changing other budget constraints based on the time of day you think your prospects will be most likely to buy.

Deep Link

A link that points to a page other than the home page within a website.

Directory

A categorized listing of websites. Most directories are compiled or built by having website owners submit listings.

Dofollow

A "dofollow" link is one that search engines follow and that passes link value.

Domain Name Servers (DNS)

Domain Name Servers are naming schemes used to "point" a domain name/host name to a specific TCP/IP address on the Internet.

Duplicate Content

Material on a web page that is the same (or almost the same) as material on another page. The search engines do not like copies of information.

Dynamic Content

Database-driven content (.asp, .cfm, .cgi, or .shtml, etc.), such as in an online shopping cart online where products are "stored" or a site that draws on a database when building its pages.

Favicon or Favorites Icon

This is a small graphic or illustration that appears next to URLs in a web browser address bar.

File Transfer Protocol (FTP)

File Transfer Protocol allows you to transfer data between computers using FTP software, such as when uploading pages to your website/server from your desktop computer.

Google Bombing

Making a page rank well for a specific search query by pointing hundreds or thousands of links at it with the keywords in the anchor text.

Google Dance

In the past, Google updated their index of web pages roughly once a month. Those updates were called Google Dances. Since Google shifted to a constantly updating index, Google no longer does this. Major search indexes are constantly updating. Google refers to this continuous refresh as "everflux."

Hashtag

A hashtag symbol (#) used on Twitter as a way to group messages ("tweets") by a theme.

.htaccess

Apache directory-level configuration file which can be used to password protect or redirect files. This is one place you can set up 301 redirects.

Inbound Marketing

The practice of marketing by sharing helpful content instead of pushing ads on people. SEO, social media, blogging, lead nurturing, conversion optimization, online PR, and analytic tracking are examples of inbound marketing tactics.

Internet Service Provider (ISP)

A company that sells end users access to the web. Some of these companies also sell usage data to web analytics companies.

JavaScript

A website scripting language that can be embedded into HTML documents to add dynamic features such as drop down menus or rotating images.

Keyword Stuffing

The practice of writing web page text that uses the core keyword an excessive number of times per page.

Klout

Klout is an online tool that allows you to measure your influence in social media.

Landing Page

The web page on which a visitor arrives (or "lands") after clicking on a link or advertisement.

Latent Semantic Indexing (LSI)

Latent Semantic Indexing is a way for search engines to mathematically understand and represent language based on the similarity of web pages and keyword co-occurrence. A relevant search result may not even contain the search term, but may come up based solely on the fact that it contains many words that are similar to those appearing on relevant pages containing the search words.

Link

Underlined text that the user can click on to move from one web page to another or to another position on the same web page. Most major search engines consider links from other sites pointing to you as a vote of trust.

Link Authority

The amount of authority your site has based on how many quality sites link to it.

Link Baiting

The art of targeting, creating, and formatting information that provokes your target audience to point high-quality links to your site. Many link baiting techniques are targeted at social media users and bloggers.

Link Building

The process of building high-quality linkage data that search engines will evaluate to determine whether your website is authoritative, relevant, and trustworthy.

Link Equity

A domain builds link equity over a period of time after it has had other sites linking to it.

Link Juice

Link juice is the amount of energy passed from one link to another.

Long Tail Keywords

Long tail keywords are longer, more precise, and more specific, and thus they are easier to rank for and tend to convert better. For example, a long tail keyword would be something like "Italian leather running shoes" as opposed to the head term "running shoes."

Lurker

Online, a lurker is a person who reads discussions on a message board, newsgroup, or social network but rarely or never participates by adding comments of his/her own.

Manual Review

All major search engines combine a manual review process involving actual humans with their automated relevancy algorithms to help catch search spam and train the relevancy algorithms. Abnormal usage data or link growth patterns may also flag a website for manual review.

Meta Data

Meta data is information in the code that is not visible to the user, such as meta tags.

Meta Description

The meta description tag is typically a sentence or two of content that describes the content of the web page. This tag often dictates the description users see in the search results, so definitely use it. Make sure each page has only descriptions that relate to the concepts on that specific page.

Meta Keyword

The meta keyword is a tag which can be used to highlight the keywords and keyword phrases that the page is about and hoping to rank for. This tag is no longer used by Google for ranking.

Meta Refresh

A meta tag used to make a browser "refresh" and take the user to another URL.

Meta Tags

Code placed in the HTML header of a web page, providing information that is not visible to browsers. The most common meta tags (and those most used in SEO) are meta title, keywords, and description.

Meta Title Tag

The line of code that dictates the text that is at the very top of the browser window. Title tags are one of the top quick fixes for SEO.

Mindshare

A measure of the number of people who think of you or your product when thinking of products in your category.

Mirror Site

A website that duplicates the contents of another website.

Multivariate Testing (MVT)

The act of testing multiple creative elements simultaneously to see which combination of elements will perform the best.

News Feed

On Facebook, the News Feed is the page where users can see all the latest updates from their Facebook "friends."

Nofollow

A piece of code used to prevent a link from passing "link authority." Commonly used on sites with user-generated content, such as in blog comments.

Open Source

Software that is written and distributed in such a way that any software developer can modify it as they see fit.

Organic Search Results

Most major search engines have results that consist of paid ads and unpaid listings. The unpaid listings are called the organic search results and are organized by relevancy (which is largely determined based on linkage data, page content, usage data, domain history, and trust-related data). Some studies have shown that 60% to 80% of clicks are on the organic search results.

PageRank

A logarithmic scale based on link equity which estimates the importance of web documents. Google's relevancy algorithms have moved away from heavily relying on PageRank and place more emphasis on trusted links via algorithms such as TrustRank.

Pay per Click (PPC)

Pay per click is the pricing model through which most search ads and many contextual ad programs are sold. PPC ads only charge advertisers if a potential customer clicks on the advertiser's ad.

Permalink

A permalink is the address (URL) of a specific post within a blog or site.

Personalization

Altering the search results based on a person's location, search history, content they recently viewed, or other factors relevant to them on a personal level.

PHP

PHP Hypertext Preprocessor is an open source server-side scripting language used to render web pages or add interactivity to them.

Podcast

A podcast is a pre-recorded audio or video file, often released episodically and downloaded via an RSS feed.

Proximity

A measure of how close words are to one another in text on a web page.

Quality Score

A measure used by Google to help filter bad ads out of their AdWords program.

Real-time Search

When the search engines index content as it comes out from a site (like Twitter, for example) with no time delay.

Reciprocal Links

Nepotistic link exchanges where websites try to build false authority by trading links, using three-way link trades, or other low-quality link schemes. When sites link naturally, there is some amount of cross-linking within a community, but if most or all of your links are reciprocal in nature, it may be a sign of ranking manipulation. Sites that trade links that are off-topic or on links pages that are stashed away deep within their sites probably do not pass much link authority, and may add more risk than reward in terms of SEO strategy.

Referrer

The source that drove a visitor to your website.

Reinclusion

If a website has been penalized by a search engine for spamming, the website owner may fix the infraction and ask for reinclusion in the search engine indexes. Depending on the severity of the infraction and the brand strength of the website, it may or may not be added back to the search index.

Relevancy

A measure of how useful/relevant searchers find the search engine results they get. Many search engines may bias organic search results to informational resources, since commercial ads also show up in the search results.

Robot

Any automated browser program that follows hypertext links and accesses web pages. Such robots include search engine spiders.

Robots.txt

A file that sits in the root directory of a site and tells search engines which files not to crawl to ignore. Some search engines will still list your URLs as URL-only listings even if you block them using a robots.txt file.

RSS Feed

Setting up an RSS (Really Simple Syndication) feed allows users to subscribe to online content and read it when they please.

RSS Reader

An RSS reader allows users to group articles from various sites into one place using RSS feeds. Google Reader, for example, allows you to quickly and easily view large volumes of content without having to jump from site to site.

Scan and Skim

A web page is considered scan-and-skim-friendly when it is set up with more bullet points and smaller chunks of information, instead of many long, dense paragraphs.

Scraplines

A scrapline is a short phrase used to express benefits or a value proposition. It is like a tagline but not used near the logo.

Search Engine Marketing (SEM)

Also known as Search Marketing. Can mean paid search marketing or search marketing in general, whether paid or organic/SEO.

Search Engine Optimization (SEO)

The art and science of publishing information online and marketing it in a manner that helps search engines understand that your information is relevant to particular search queries.

Search Engine Results Page (SERP)
The web page on which the search engines show the results for a search query.

Sentiment
A person's attitude as indicated by their online comments about a brand.

Server
A computer that hosts files and "serve" (supply) them to the web.

Site Map
A web page that can be used to help give search engines (and human visitors) a secondary route to navigate through your site.

Social Media
Social media refers to the methods people use to interact online and how they create, share, and exchange information and ideas in online communities and networks. Examples of social media sites include Facebook, Twitter, Google+, and LinkedIn.

Spam
Unsolicited email messages that the recipient does not want. Search engine spam refers to people doing deceptive tactics to game the search results.

Spider
A search engine robot that searches or "crawls" the web for pages to include in the index and/or search results.

Splash Page
A feature-rich or elegantly designed, beautiful web page that typically offers poor usability and does not offer much content for the search engines to index.

Static Content
Content that does not change frequently. May also refer to content that does not have any social elements to it and does not use dynamic programming languages.

Supplemental Results
When a search engine thinks your pages are not of high quality, they trust them less and they will be buried in a lower tier of search results that don't often appear to users.

Taxonomy

A classification system of controlled vocabulary used to organize topical subjects, usually hierarchical in nature.

TrustRank

Search relevancy algorithm that places additional weighting on links from trusted websites that are controlled by major corporations, educational institutions, or governmental institutions.

Uniform Resource Locator (URL)

The unique address of any web document

Unique Visitor

A real visitor to a website, not merely an amount of pages one visitor views.

Update

Search engines frequently revise their algorithms and data sets to help keep their search results fresh and make their relevancy algorithms hard to reverse-engineer. Most major search engines are continuously revising both their relevancy algorithms and search index.

URL Rewrite

A technique used to help make URLs more unique and descriptive in an effort to facilitate better site-wide indexing by major search engines.

Usability

How easy or difficult it is for website visitors to perform the desired actions. The proper structure and formatting of text and hyperlink-based calls to action can drastically increase your website's usability, and thus your conversion rates.

Viral Marketing

Self-propagating promotion techniques commonly transmitted through email, blogging, and word-of-mouth marketing channels.

Virtual Server

A server that allows multiple top-level domains to be hosted from a single computer.

White Hat SEO

The SEO practices used by the "good guys." Search engines set up guidelines that help them extract billions of dollars of ad revenue from the work of publishers and the attention of searchers. Within that highly profitable framework, search engines consider certain marketing techniques deceptive in nature, and label them as "black hat SEO." Practices considered within the guidelines are called "white hat SEO." Since search guidelines are not a static set of rules, SEO practices considered legitimate one day may be considered deceptive the next.

Wiki

Software that allows information to be published online using collaborative editing.

Wikipedia

A free, online collaborative encyclopedia that is built using wiki software.

WordPress

Popular open-source blogging software platform that offers both a downloadable blogging program and a hosted solution.

The text for some of the glossary definitions comes from http://www.seobook.com/glossary/, used under a Creative Commons license, as follows: "You can modify [this page], distribute it, sell it, and keep the rights to whatever you make. It is up to you however you want to use any of the content from this page. This work is licensed under a Creative Commons Attribution 2.5 License." Glossary definitions used under this license include: Manual Review, Meta Description, Meta Keywords, Meta Refresh, Mindshare, Nofollow, Organic Search Results, PageRank, Personalization, PHP, Reciprocal Links, Reinclusion, Relevancy, Robots.txt, SEM, SEO, SERP, Site Map, Static Content, Taxonomy, TrustRank, Update, Usability, White Hat SEO, Wikipedia, and WordPress.

Internet Marketing Strategy Planning with PlanSprout

If you're doing web marketing correctly, there are a lot of moving parts. Before building a website or approaching individual tactics, it's vital that you have a documented strategic plan.

Rather than just dabbling in Internet marketing tactics, you'll need to have a robust strategy. As a companion to **Web Marketing On All Cylinders**, our PlanSprout software helps you solidify your plans. The worksheets in plansprout.com can help you organize your strategy and serve as a road map for your team. While using the worksheets in the software, you will learn how the tactics all go together, to kick your strategy into high gear!

Check out **www.plansprout.com** to get started today!